Autonomy and Community

SUNY Series in Social and Political Thought
Kenneth Baynes, editor

Autonomy and Community

Readings in Contemporary Kantian Social Philosophy

EDITED BY

JANE KNELLER
SIDNEY AXINN

STATE UNIVERISTY OF NEW YORK PRESS

Published by
State University of New York Press, Albany

For information, address the State University of New York Press,
State University Plaza, Albany, NY 12246

Production by David Ford and M. R. Mulholland
Marketing by Fran Keneston

Library of Congress Cataloging-In-Publication Data

Autonomy and community : readings in contemporary Kantian social
    philosophy / edited by Jane Kneller, Sidney Axinn.
        p.   cm. — (SUNY series in social and political thought)
    ISBN 0-7914-3743-4 (hc : alk. paper). — ISBN 0-7914-3744-2 (pbk.
    : alk. paper)
        1. Social conflict. 2. Social problems. 3. Kant, Immanuel,
    1724-1804—Ethics. 4. Kant, Immanuel, 1724–1804—Political and
    social views. 5. Kant, Immanuel, 1724–1804—Influence.
    I. Kneller, Jane. II. Axinn, Sidney. III. Series.
    HM136.A85   1998
    301'.01—dc21   97-35898
                                                                CIP

10 9 8 7 6 5 4 3 2 1

CONTENTS

PREFACE

The last decade has a seen a renewed interest in the broadly political and social aspects of Kant's ethical theory. This interest has resulted in extremely influential and important work in the area of political theory by writers such as John Rawls, Onora O'Neill, Ronald Beiner, Howard Williams, and Susan Shell, among others. While some of these philosophers have used Kantian ethics as a springboard for their own philosophical ethics and political theories, a growing number of philosophers in the history of modern philosophy have begun looking more closely at Kant's own work in these areas. The result has been an increased interest in works of Kant that have hitherto received relatively little attention in the English-speaking tradition. The flurry of recent scholarly attention to Kant's less well-known works on politics and social ethics has given rise to a demand for translations of these texts into English, and as these translations appear, there is every reason to expect increased attention to Kant's work. The editors intend the present volume to display some recent results of this growing concern for Kantian approaches to social and political issues, and to extend the scope of recent literature to include contemporary issues.

Of course, in many corners the view still persists that Kant's ethical position is too abstract and arid to have any serious use in thinking about contemporary moral issues. To cite one example, Richard Rorty in a recent book mentions what he takes to be "the basic Kantian assumption that moral deliberation must necessarily take the form of deduction from general, preferably 'non-empirical,' principles" (*Contingency, Irony, and Solidarity* [Cambridge University Press, 1991], 193). This is a much too simplified dismissal of Kant's view of moral reflection and choice, but it is also indicative of how well entrenched is the view that Kant's philosophy may be found wanting in this regard. Even if some of Kant's own comments on the nature of social questions suggest that he was unwilling or unable to accommodate discussion of them within his ethical theory, it is well to recall his view that "it is by no means unusual . . . to find that we understand [an author] better than he has understood himself . . . he has sometimes spoken, or even thought, in opposition to his own intention" (*Critique of Pure Reason*, A 314/B 370).

The present collection is accordingly "Kantian" in a broad sense. That is to say, it represents interpretations and developments of various aspects of Kant's thought that may very well go beyond the letter of the text, and in many cases, beyond what Kant himself might have ever thought about or advocated. The authors do not restrict themselves to quoting Kant on social matters, nor do they for the most part concern themselves with whether conclusions they reach based on Kant's philosophical principles are actually to be found in Kant's texts. The reader should keep in mind that what the authors are here calling "Kantian" social theory may not be identical with Kant's own doctrine in every detail, and may even diverge rather widely therefrom in the end. Yet each contributor shows in his or her own way that a Kantian orientation is a powerful tool in the analysis of contemporary social matters. Taken together, the contributions are ample evidence that Kant's philosophy provides conceptual resources for a social theory far removed from the arid formalism so often attributed to his ethics.

Further, these essays represent contributions to the clarification and resolution of various problems whose significance extends well beyond the realm of academic philosophy. It is the intention of the editors and contributors to develop Kantian responses to the problems that engage society today rather than to argue the finer points of text interpretation. For this reason, the essays are for the most part written with a minimum of technical language and are addressed to generally educated readers and students of introductory ethical, social, and political theory as well as to Kant scholars.

ABOUT THE ESSAYS

The selections, all but one of which appear for the first time in this volume, apply Kant's moral and political views to contemporary social concerns both general and specific: Under the first heading are papers presenting readings of Kant's social theory and theory of human history, the relationship of moral practice to the social contract, Kant's theory of civic duty, and the relevance of Kantian philosophy to contemporary feminist theory. More specific issues of contemporary interest are then taken up in subsequent essays: international relations, race and ethnicity relations, abortion, capital punishment, environmental ethics, labor relations, and the nature of the institution of marriage.

In "Kant's Historical Materialism," Allen W. Wood "recovers" the historical self-consciousness and awareness of the material conditions of the progress of enlightenment in Kant's philosophy. Wood concentrates on Kant's theory of the development of human nature and deals with Kant's conceptions of private property and of conflict. He concludes that far from presenting a timeless and ahistorical account of these conceptions, Kant's views prefigure Marx's inasmuch as they are premised on a theory of history as a scene of not only conflict and strife, but also of deepening inequality and oppression.

If Kant is profoundly concerned with history and the progress of humanity toward civic union, Robert Paul Wolff's essay suggests an intriguing motivation for this concern: Kant's best solution to the seemingly intractable problem of why the moral law is commanded categorically is the unconditional obligation to enter into a social contract. Wolff argues that in the Doctrine of Right Kant finally tries to solve the problem of the *categorical* nature of the moral law by arguing that rationality requires that human beings will the means to the ends they will, and as phenomenal beings, this entails the ability to justifiably appropriate the natural world, or, in other words, it presupposes the right to private property. This in turn is only possible on the condition of each individual's having entered into a social contract that will guarantee such a right. Thus, contrary to standard opinion among Kant scholars, Wolff argues that Kant's moral theory rests on his contractarian account of the state, and for Kant, morality can only first arise within the confines of the social contract.

Once ensconced in civil society, the question of the rights and responsibilities of its citizens arises. Philip Rossi shows how Kant's notion of an "ethical commonwealth" corrects the notion of society as a mere group of clashing competing interests in favor of a notion of mutual responsibility. In "Public Argument and Social Responsibility: The Moral Dimensions of Citizenship in Kant's Ethical Commonwealth" he argues further that this view has ramifications for contemporary citizens in representative democracies because it obliges them to ensure that conditions for reasoned argument prevail and may even override self-interested considerations.

Robin May Schott's essay focuses on the importance of critical rereading of Kant's work in light of contemporary feminist theory. She considers the value of Kantian theory for feminist philosophers, explaining the approaches that feminists have taken in reconstructing Kant, and argues that this critical engagement has contributed to the dynamism of contemporary social philosophy.

The next part of the anthology applies Kantian approaches to contemporary social issues. The first two essays deal with the obligations of civil societies toward each other and toward the individuals of other societies. In her "Crimes against Humanity: A Kantian Perspective on International Law," Sharon Anderson-Gold argues that although Kant maintained an explicit noninterventionist position, his views are based on the fact that a right to self-determination is the presupposition of any political obligations whatsoever. States that violate these rights against their citizens forfeit their claim to being members of the commonwealth and violations of basic human rights may therefore morally require preventive action on the part of an international community. In this context, she connects Kant's view of the international community with the question of outside intervention when nations are involved in "ethnic cleansing" and other crimes against humanity. In his "World Community and Its Government" Sidney Axinn turns to both Kant and Hobbes. He takes up the theme of world government, arguing that the time is now right for giving up nationalism and heeding Kant's arguments for a federation of states.

Charles W. Mills views Kant's social philosophy from two perspectives: the familiar but "idealized" ethic of respect for humanity and persons as ends on the one hand, and the "natural" or "*Herrenvolk*" Kantianism that views some groups of persons as subhuman, the more so the "darker" they are. This latter "dark ontology" was embraced and given force by Kant in his own work and must be seen as the backdrop to Kant's more noble, enlightened views. The ideal may be a liberal polis formed by social contract guaranteeing the freedom of each of its members, but the reality is a "racial polity" in which not all are equally persons. Mills then uses this notion to explain differences in the ways blacks and Jews have experienced and reacted to subordination in the racial polity.

"The Principle of Punishment Is a Categorical Imperative" by Nelson Thomas Potter Jr. develops Kant's views in connection with the careful analysis of a wide variety of capital punishment and general punishment arguments. He shows how Kant's explicit support of the death penalty for murder is based on his moral theory, and then goes on to argue that there are nevertheless good Kantian reasons for rejecting capital punishment on moral grounds. Thomas Auxter suggests further reasons for this last view, arguing that Kant's moral theory does not stand or fall with his theory of retribution, and that moreover, what Kant meant by "retribution" in the context of the late eighteenth century was different from what is now meant by that term. He concludes that contemporary advocates of retribution are far from doing justice to Kant's views on punishment.

The next two essays provide examples of how Kant's ethics can be used to analyze problems that may never have crossed Kant's mind.

Harry van der Linden in "A Kantian Defense of Enterprise Democracy" uses Kant's notion of a "realm of ends" of autonomous and mutually respectful individuals as a model for all social institutions, and offers a concrete exploration of workers' self-management in accordance with Kantian ethics. In "Respect for Persons and Environmental Values," Gerald F. Gaus reformulates Kantian liberalism to make it deal with the matter of respect for animals and nonsentient nature. After an analysis of personhood and autonomy, he frames a notion of "Kantian liberalism" that satisfies the demands of some but not all who have worked on environmental ethics.

The last two essays deal with issues that have concerned feminists, and are of broad social concern in contemporary debates on gender and family issues. Susan Feldman, in "From Occupied Bodies to Pregnant Persons: How Kantian Ethics Should Treat Pregnancy and Abortion," considers a Kantian approach to abortion that takes into account his notions of autonomy, sex, and respect. She explores the question of whether or not the fetus should be granted personhood on Kant's account, answering on the basis of his distinction between actualized and unactualized potential in human beings, and his notion of the "epigenesis" of knowledge in the *Critique of Pure Reason*. In "Kant's Evolutionary Theory of Marriage," Holly L. Wilson explores the remote territory of Kant's views on marriage, and interprets them in light of his concept of "unsociable sociability." She applies Kant's discussion of the stages in the evolution of social institutions to that of marriage, examining in detail Kant's account of the bourgeois marriage of his time. She argues that far from an endorsement of these arrangements, Kant's account should be viewed as an account of one stage in the development of a dynamic institution that may therefore be expected to develop and change for the better.

The authors of these essays vary widely in their readings of Kant and in their own social and political orientation, and provide only a sampling of the variety of approaches inspired by Kant's philosophy. The editors hope that these essays will generate further interest and stimulate additional work on pressing social issues among Kant scholars and students, and also suggest new approaches to those concerned with finding fresh theoretical bases for solutions to problems of contemporary society.

I

Kant and Social Theory

1

Jane Kneller

Introducing Kantian Social Theory

Although there are certainly many philosophers working on contemporary issues from what may be construed broadly as a Kantian
perspective, it is less certain that one may refer to the work of these
philosophers under the rubric of "social philosophy." Indeed, it is not
altogether clear to many philosophers just what the term designates
nowadays, let alone what it might mean to say that Kant had a social
philosophy.[1] Kant maintained definite views on the nature of the state
and its origin and functions so that it is unproblematic to attribute to
him a political philosophy.[2] By contrast, his views on "society" as such
are not so easily isolated. Here I will argue that although Kant's theory
of the state provides a focal point and is of central importance for his
broader account of society, his contractarian theory of the state is itself
only part of a larger story. For Kant, the establishment of the state is a
stage in his account of the social progress of humanity, that is, of the
morally perfected society as the final destination of humanity. In the
final analysis, Kant's notion of the state must be understood as that of
an enabling institution—one that makes possible the prospect of a
human community that is not captured in the notion of social contract.
His social philosophy, I will argue, encompasses but also extends far
beyond his political philosophy.

1

SOCIAL VERSUS POLITICAL THEORY

What does it mean to say that Kant, or anyone for that matter, has a social philosophy? The term is an indefinite one among philosophers today. Contemporary introductory texts in philosophy run the gamut from comfortable conflation of social with political philosophy to conscious separation of them with complete and independent chapters devoted to each. Perhaps most common is the tendency to treat social philosophy under the heading of political philosophy, with a nod in the direction of the distinction: the two areas may be viewed as a matter of focus, with political philosophy highlighting the state and its justi-fication, including questions of its organization, scope, and functions. Social philosophy looks at more intimate spheres of personal inter-action and social relationships, and questions of what constitutes the good society.[3]

In collecting these essays, the editors have construed "social philosophy" very broadly, much the way Anthony Giddens defines social theory:

> It is a body of theory shared in common by all the disciplines concerned with the behaviour of human beings. It concerns not only sociology, therefore, but anthropology, economics, politics, human geography, psychology—the whole range of the social sciences.[4]

The reason for adopting this rather sweeping view of social philosophy is not expedience, but has to do with Kant's own approach to the subject. The three basic questions that, according to Kant, drive rational inquiry (What can I know? What ought I to do? What may I hope?)[5] provided the subject matter of Kant's three Critiques. But throughout his entire career, Kant was deeply concerned with a further problem: "What is man (der Mensch)?"[6] Although Kant does not answer this question explicitly, observations about the nature of humanity and its ends are to be found interwoven in the fabric of his three Critiques, as well as in his treatises and lectures on a great range of subjects, including anthropology, politics, history, religion, and education.

For Kant "der Mensch" is, by nature, many things: rational and free on the one hand, but also natural—a "being of needs"—on the other; a creator, finite but of infinite value, and a subject, ultimately, unknowable "in-itself."[7] In addition, and arguably basic to all of these, is our social nature. For Kant, human beings are not isolated individual atoms of consciousness (even if, for the purposes of analysis, he studies them as if they were). What might be called Kant's "conditional" rationalism guides his account of humanity: *If* we are to make sense of ourselves and our place in the universe, we must assume the "fundamental principle" of the teleological organization of nature, namely, that no organ is without a use, nor is any organization without a purpose.[8] In the "Idea for a Universal History with a Cosmopolitan Intent" he claims that "All of a creature's natural capacities are destined to develop completely and in conformity with their end." Insofar as human beings are characteristically rational beings, the complete development of their nature must occur "only in the species, not in the individual." Answers to existential questions about an individual human being's final purpose, if any are to be found at all, must be sought in his or her social nature. For Kant, even what might appear the most solitary of human accomplishments, learning to "think for oneself," requires that social conditions exist in which such autonomy first becomes possible:

> For any *single* individual to work himself out of the life under tutelage which has become almost his nature is very difficult. He has come to be fond of this state, and he is for the present *really incapable* of making use of his reason, for no one has ever let him try it out. . . . Therefore, there are few who have succeeded by their own exercise of mind in freeing themselves from immaturity (*Unmündigkeit*) and at the same time in achieving a sure and steady pace. . . . But that the public should enlighten itself is more possible; indeed, if only freedom is granted, enlightenment is almost sure to follow. (Emphasis added)[9]

A "freedom to make public use of one's reason at every point" is a condition of enlightenment, and one that only the social order can fulfill.

In his essay for this volume, Robert Paul Wolff argues that Kant wanted to base the categorical demands of morality itself on the necessity of the social contract. Thus the study of social conditions, for Kant, is also the study of the conditions of Enlightenment, and if Wolff is right, of morality.[10] It would be truly surprising if a philosopher so profoundly concerned with human morality and Enlightenment autonomy had no theory of the social conditions of these! Still, the suggestion that Kant had a social theory not identical to his political theory is complicated by the fact that, as a proponent of social contract theory, Kant upheld the view that *genuine* society and culture, as opposed to disorganized or merely provisional groupings of individuals, depends for its very constitution upon a particular form of political organization. Like other classical social contract theorists, Kant held that individuals first become genuinely social creatures, dependent for their very being upon harmonious, or at least non-destructive interaction with others, only on the condition of the institution of a social contract. So for instance, Rousseau says that

> Before examining that act whereby a people chooses a king, it would be well to examine the act whereby people become *a* people. For since this act [of "public deliberation"] is necessarily prior to the other, it is the true foundation of society.[11]

There are, of course, important differences among different contract theorists, but most contract theorists, including Kant, share some version of the position that genuine sociability and culture is possible only on the condition of the creation of a civil state.[12] For Kant,

> The highest purpose of Nature, which is the development of all the capacities which can be achieved by mankind, is attainable only in society, and more specifically in the society with the greatest freedom. Such a society is one in which there is mutual opposition among the members, together with the most exact definition of freedom and fixing of its limits so that it may be consistent with the freedom of others. Nature demands that humankind should itself achieve this goal like all its other destined goals.[13]

This aspect of Kant's contractarian account may be elucidated by contrast with conservative, organic theories of the state in which previously existing social conditions—traditions and traditional authority—are viewed as the legitimate conditions of the existence of the state. Thus Burke wrote in *Reflections on the Revolution in France* that "Each contract of each particular state is but a clause in the great primeval contract of eternal society."[14] For liberal contractarianism, on the other hand, social relationships are likely to be viewed as relationships among individuals who are citizens of a state. Liberal social philosophy then focuses attention on an account of citizens' rights vis-à-vis each other, or of the ranking of their various individual preferences with respect to those of other citizens. The bedrock of social relations is taken to be the political, that is, contractual, context in which individuals have, if only tacitly, placed themselves. If the political context constitutes the social in this way, then a philosophy of social relations, including an account of the social nature of human beings, will always lead back to and ultimately rest upon political conditions and principles. The social, on the traditional liberal contractarian account, must, in this important respect, be subsumed under the political.[15]

The point of the polity is to guarantee the rights of each individual to all freedoms that do not interfere with the freedoms of others. The society that results is a "free society"—one defined in terms of the liberty-protecting function of the state. But as Stanley Benn has pointed out, defining society in terms of the liberal state gives rise to a tension within liberal political theory.[16] Because liberalism is committed to maximizing the individual freedom and pluralism that the social contract is designed to protect, there is a strong (libertarian) tendency in liberalism to severely restrict the state's proper functions, and to give as much latitude as possible to all sorts of "special interests." Given this tendency, the liberal society that is brought into existence by social contract may well be extremely diverse, not to say amorphous. As a result "the society" is exceedingly difficult to identify and to define, containing, as Kant put it "a thoroughgoing antagonism among its members." This raises the question, In what sense do these mutually antagonistic citizens all belong to the same "society"? It is certainly extremely misleading to say that they form a single "community." In a recent essay on Kant's practical philosophy, William Galston finds the same problem already in Kant's political philosophy: "There is, in short, a tension, prefigured in Kant's political thought, between the moral underpinnings of liberalism and the tolerance of diversity that stands at the core of liberal society."[17] The liberal state just by virtue of its protective nature breeds pluralism of social visions among its citizens. Beyond the somewhat vacuous claim that they are all "citizens" subject to the rights, protections, and laws of the state, liberal contract theory as it is traditionally construed does not seem to be able, by itself, to say anything of theoretical substance about the nature and value of the diverse communities and cultures that exist under its protection.

While liberal political philosophy has continued to define society in terms of political freedom, the last half of this century has seen a growing sympathy among liberal theorists toward the view that "the social" may involve other fundamental values that deserve more profound theoretical discussion. Especially in areas of race, ethnicity, and gender, many liberals have argued for the recognition and valuing of cultural and other social differences and even, on occasion, have argued for special protection for various social groups from dominant cultural forces.[18] However, this special valuing could not occur on the theory that "our" society is no more than the system of citizens under the liberal contract. After all, under that system everyone is essentially the same. So in trying to theorize the social, contemporary liberal theorists have obviously gone beyond traditional contract theories in their own approaches. Is there precedent for this in Kant?

Put in Kant's language, the problem is that the contractarian account of society permits no substantive vision of the final purpose of society. In itself this may be a virtue, since it gives the appearance at least of leaving each individual member free to choose his or her own social vision so long as that does not entail actions that hinder the same freedom in others. Kant himself subscribed to some such minimalist account of the state in several places.[19] However, it is also clear that he saw the need for an account of society that went beyond the contractual association in order adequately to theorize the myriad social relationships and characteristic social needs of its individual citizens. Thus there is good reason for contemporary liberals to return to Kant's social theory in their attempts to address the need for a positive liberal vision of society.

The essays that follow in this collection are the attempts of several contemporary philosophers to address social problems from a perspective that draws on Kantian theory. Taken as a whole they present a strong argument for the claim that Kant had a social vision that encompassed and went beyond his contractarian theory. In the remainder of this introductory essay I want to begin the task of fleshing out Kant's social vision. The essays that follow by Allen W. Wood and Robert Paul Wolff also suggest ways of refocusing our Kantian lenses in order to bring into view the picture of human social nature and the social good contained in Kant's philosophy.

KANT'S SOCIAL THEORY

Of course, in addition to his political theory, Kant had a theory of personal morality—an ethics that was intended to answer questions of right in the private social arena, an area left more or less untouched by contractarian politics. Moreover, scholars have been arguing for some time now that Kant did not rest content with the allegedly individualistic, formalist ethics of the *Foundations of the Metaphysics of Morals* and the second Critique.[20] Others have supplemented this approach by arguing that Kant attempted in the third Critique to enrich his account of moral experience with an account of the importance of aesthetic experience in the development of moral feeling and autonomy.[21] Yirmiahu Yovel and Harry van der Linden have both given accounts of Kantian ethics that argue for its essentially social nature, emphasizing Kant's claim that individuals have a duty to promote the highest good and arguing that such a duty, for Kant, is social.[22]

These and other works in recent Kant scholarship make it increasingly more credible to read "through" Kant's ethical theory to a larger vision encompassing history, society, and the emotional life. Insofar as Kant's ethical theory is independent of his contractarianism, such enriched accounts point out a path for elucidating a systematic and substantive account of what constitutes the good society in Kant's work.

But in spite of recent attempts to read the social into Kantian ethics, it might still seem objectionable to some to argue that this constitutes a social theory. That is, it might still be objected that for the liberal political theorist, theoretical accounts of society must be tied to political theory and to the social contract. And Kant's political philosophy *is* undeniably liberal. He clearly believes that genuine society is possible only under the "civilized" conditions created by the social contract and the institution of civil society. In the "Idea for a Universal History with a Cosmopolitan Purpose" he argues that the development of all natural human capacities can be fulfilled only in civil society, where a maximum degree of freedom for every individual is guaranteed by "the most precise specification and preservation of the limits of this freedom in order that it can co-exist with the freedom of others."[23] Under the social contract, human antisocial tendencies are not immediately transformed into harmonious social ones, but, at least, Kant says, when "enclosed within a precinct like that of civil union," antisocial tendencies are forced to express themselves in a way that gradually cultivates social morality.

Be it ever so slow, however, this process does occur, or at least, the philosopher must assume that it does. Just as, if we are to theorize about nature at all, we must assume a principle of purposiveness as a regulative guide to its system, so if we are to write our own history we must assume there exists a natural purposiveness in human efforts, even if human beings are not from the start guided by the thought of this purpose.[24] In fact, it is only long after human beings enter into a civil state that they even begin to be guided by the thought of themselves as purposive as a species.

This gradual awakening of an integrated sense of the social is what constitutes the progress of human history, for Kant, so that the moral cultivation of individuals in civil society becomes an important theme for him. Kant describes the beginning of this process in the "Idea for a Universal History" with the following interesting metaphor:

> In the same way, trees in the forest, by seeking to deprive each other of air and sunlight, compel each other to find these by upward growth, so that they grow beautiful and straight—whereas those which put out branches at will, in freedom and in isolation from others grow stunted, bent and twisted. (46, KGS 8:22)

This metaphor is worth considering in detail. First, it is noteworthy because it represents a kind of compromise between the contractual model of the state, in which metaphors of artifice set the tone (the state is "constructed," "built," "erected" upon the foundation of the contract), and the organic models preferred by conservatives like Burke, for whom the state should naturally "grow" out of an already well-ordered (God-given) social hierarchy. For Kant, human society is natural, like a forest, but composed of individuals who are forced by competition and crowding to train themselves in a direction that, left on their own, they would not take. There is a certain artifice that is forced upon human beings by nature because they are at once social and antisocial creatures.

Thus the metaphor of a natural grouping perfected by the growth forced upon it by its very situation in a group suits Kant's view of civil society very well. But this is only the beginning of an ongoing process. It is true that for Kant the materials of human society are the products of nature—but these materials are, as he puts it in a famous passage, a very "crooked wood"—they must be continually cultivated, pruned and clipped if they are to achieve perfection.[25] The unsociable sociability that forces human beings together and then forces them to stay together under the social contract continues to cultivate and refine them in the civil state. The civic uprightness forced on individuals by the state leads to further civilization. The forest ceases to be simply a result of nature as it becomes more and more cultivated. As it progresses, the human forest becomes more and more like a carefully tended arboretum or garden.

The latter metaphor is apt: Precisely what constituted the well-kept garden was a matter of considerable debate in eighteenth-century aesthetics, and the garden is one of Kant's paradigm cases in illustrating taste in the fine arts. "Landscape gardening," Kant tells us, "arranges nature's products beautifully" (i.e., tastefully). And in a footnote he describes it in the following way:

> Landscape gardening . . . actually take[s] its forms from nature (at least at the very outset: the trees, shrubs, grasses, and flowers from forest and field), and to this extent it is not art . . . and the arrangement it makes has as its condition no concept of the object and its purpose. (KGS 5:323)

One should not try to press the analogy too far, perhaps, but it is worth comparing his account of landscape gardening to the process of human cultivation in the civil state: The "unsocial sociability" that forces human beings together partially against their nature finally produces the civil state, bringing human beings from the wild, so to speak, into the garden. But they do not change their wild ways immediately in this context, anymore than do transplanted shrubs and flowers. Human beings continue to be unsociable, but under the constraints of civil society this aspect of their nature is forced to flower:

> All the culture and art which adorn mankind and the finest social order man creates are fruits of his unsociability. (KGS 8:22)

Unsociable sociability is the unconscious path that humans are forced to follow out of the state of nature and into the civil state. Crucial to this process is the development of taste, which Kant defines as "the power of judgment" that

> consists in disciplining (or training) genius. It severely clips its wings, and makes it civilized, or polished; but at the same time it gives it guidance as to how far and over what it may spread while still remaining purposive. It introduces clarity and order into a wealth of thought, and hence makes the ideas durable, fit for approval that is both lasting and universal and hence fit to being followed by others and *fit for an ever advancing culture.* (KGS 5:320, emphasis added)

As this disciplinarian account of taste suggests, Kant does not paint an entirely rosy picture of the development of culture and the process of civilization. The force of legal discipline in civil society "straightens out" the bent wood of its citizens, only to produce more subtle kinks that in themselves Kant does not find particularly admirable. Civil society can lead eventually to a further phase in the development of human nature that Kant calls "the hardest of evils under the guise of outward prosperity":

> To a high degree we are, through art and science, *cultured.* We are *civilized*—perhaps too much for our own good—in all sorts of social grace and decorum. But to consider ourselves as having reached *morality*—for that, much is lacking. The ideal of morality belongs to culture; its use for some simulacrum of morality in the love of honor and outward decorum constitutes mere civilization [*Civilisirung*]. So long as states waste their forces in vain and violent self-expansion, and thereby constantly thwart the slow efforts to improve the minds of their citizens by even withdrawing all support from them, nothing in the way of a moral order is to be expected. For such an end, a long internal working of each political body toward the education of its citizens is required. Everything good that is not based on a morally

good disposition is nothing but pretense and glittering misery. (KGS 8:26)

Although Kant here agrees with Rousseau that civil society ("*Civilisirung*") is, morally speaking, in itself hardly preferable to no society at all, he argues that it is to be valued more highly because it is (or can be) a crucial step toward moral development, which he equates here with culture ("*Cultur*"). Later, in the *Critique of Judgment*, he admits that refined taste indisputably leads to a great deal of evil by producing in us many "insatiable inclinations." Nevertheless, he continues, the fine arts and the sciences

> involve a universally communicable pleasure as well as elegance and refinement, and through these they make man, not indeed morally better for [life in] society, but still civilized for it: they make great headway against the tyranny of man's propensity to the senses, and so prepare him for a sovereignty in which reason alone is to dominate. (KGS 5:433)

Thus it is fair to say that for Kant, the state first makes possible the conditions under which taste, the fine arts, and "high" culture in general can develop. These lead eventually to genuine, moral sociability, which in turn makes us fit to become truly rational, moral beings suited for a more perfect society. But it is also important to bear in mind that for Kant the mere existence of the individual political state is not enough to guarantee the emergence of culture, since hostilities and preparation for war with other states may very well keep individual states in a condition of a state of nature ("*barbarische Freiheit*") with respect to each other (IUH 49, KGS 8:25–26). Thus civil states are forced towards cosmopolitanism, a federation of states that is a precondition for genuine social progress and a "matrix within which all original capacities of the human race may develop." (IUH 51, KGS 8:28).

At this point Kant's account of the development of the good society begins to separate theoretically from civil politics and to go beyond it. But even cosmopolitanism cannot in itself be said to *constitute* the good society. Such a society—the "highest good" (= Endzweck) of which humanity is capable and toward which it must be viewed as striving as a species, is a society that is not constituted as an amalgam of various different special interest groups under the umbrella of the social contract. It is not a well-kept garden, or set of such gardens. The pruning and disciplining of humanity's social nature is itself only a step toward the development of a society that approximates a unified "common being" (*ein gemeines Wesen*)—a "commonwealth" whose members are determined as rational beings to try to bring about the highest moral good on earth. This duty, as Kant insists that it is, is not a duty to better oneself morally, because mere individual moral self-improvement will not bring about the highest moral good on earth. Rather it is a "determination" or "vocation" of all human beings as members of a rational species. This vocation calls on individual persons to unite with others as members of a "system of *wohlgesinnter* (well- disposed) *Menschen*" to form a community whose purpose is to attempt to bring about the highest good (KGS 6:97–98). That is, it is the vocation or purpose of all human beings as social beings to try to bring about a world in which virtue is systematically combined with happiness, and in which each individual respects and is respected by every other individual. Kant's original metaphor might be pressed home in contemporary terminology as follows: the highest form of society is like a freely formed, interdependent ecosystem in which the flourishing of the whole depends upon the flourishing of each of its members.

Allen Wood has recently argued for a similar point, I believe, when he argues that Kant's ethics is at bottom a communitarian, not an individualistic ethic. "Kant's ethical theory," he says, "is an attempt to articulate the common rational plan through which humanity will find rational concord. Its final aim is a human society free from antagonism, where every rational being is treated as an end and (in the words of a later document with similar aims) the free development of each has become the condition for the free development of all."[26] For Kant, Wood argues, the final purpose of humanity is determined not by a political goal, but by a social morality. For Kant morality itself requires that human beings seek to bring about the highest good possible on earth,[27] and this Kant tells us in the *Religion*, is necessarily a social task. As such it presupposes the civil state, and Kant insists, going well beyond his contractarian precursors, it presupposes a "system held together by cosmopolitan bonds" (KGS 7:333). But as we saw, even a cosmopolitan system is properly speaking only the outer framework for "a progressive organization of citizens of the earth into and towards the species" (KGS 7:333).

Thus, Kant's account of society goes far beyond an account of relations between citizens of a state while at the same time maintaining the historical necessity of the state. Although his account of society's progress *begins* with the social contract, it goes on to encompass a developmental history of society that ultimately detaches from the political to become a theory of social ethics. In the final analysis, genuine human society is characterized as a community of individuals united for the purposes of constituting a moral commonwealth.

On this account any doubts about whether Kant does indeed have a social theory that is distinguishable from his political philosophy may be put to rest. Moreover, precisely because his social theory is not identical to his politics, it is possible to see how Kantian social theory is sufficiently independent of Kantian politics to be an instrument for criticizing various questionable political positions that Kant himself held. Indeed, as some of the following essays suggest, taking Kant's social philosophy seriously may *force* certain questions about the validity of some of these views.

NOTES

All references to Kant's works in this essay are to the Akademieausgabe (Prussian Academy Edition) of Kant's collected works (*Kants Gesammelte Schriften*, hereafter KGS), except the *Critique of Pure Reason*, where references are to the A/B editions of that work. Translations of the works cited usually indicate Academy pagination in the margins.

1. Onora O'Neill and Christine Korsgaard both raised these questions in conversation, and I am grateful to them for pressing these issues.

2. Key texts for Kant's political philosophy are easy to find, and they include: "Idea for a Universal History with a Cosmopolitan Intent" (1784); "On the Proverb: That May Be True in Theory but Is of No Practical Use" (1795); "Towards Perpetual Peace: A Philosophical Sketch" (1795); *The Metaphysics of Morals* (Part II: "The Doctrine of Right" and Introduction to the Doctrine of Right); with the exception of the latter, Hans Reiss has collected these and others in his (second) edition, *Kant: Political Writings* (Cambridge: Cambridge University Press, 1991). Kant scholars have also studied other texts as implicit sources of Kant's political theory. One fine example is Hannah Arendt's reading of Kant's third Critique, focusing on certain passages from the *Critique of Aesthetic Judgment*: cf. *Lectures on Kant's Political Philosophy*, ed. Ronald Beiner (Chicago: University of Chicago Press, 1982).

3. The texts I selected as fairly representative of current accepted views include: *Philosophy: The Basic Issues*, ed. Klemke et al. (New York, St Martin's Press, 1990), R. P. Wolff, *About Philosophy* (Englewood Cliffs, N.J.: Prentice Hall, 1989), B. N. Moore and K. Bruder, *Philosophy: The Power of Ideas*, (Mountain View, Calif.: Mayfield, 1993). In a recent text, William McBride addresses the issue directly: "[to separate social and political philosophy] seems unnecessarily artificial. This is because of the actual interconnection of the two domains at the deep level with which philosophy is concerned and because most of the best-known philosophers in the Western tradition . . . have in fact written about broader social issues as well as political institutions." *Social and Political Philosophy* (New York: Paragon House, 1994), 2.

4. Anthony Giddens, *Profiles and Critiques in Social Theory* (Berkeley: University of California Press, 1982), 5.

**Introducing Kantian Social Theory   13

5. *Critique of Pure Reason*, A 804–5/B 833.

6. Kant posed the fourth question in his lectures on logic, claiming there that the first three questions all relate to the last, so that in a sense all philosophy is ultimately "anthropology." Here, if the student lecture notes may be trusted, Kant's use of "anthropology" is more or less the same as our use of "social theory" in this text. It is "cosmopolitan" or "worldly" philosophy, "the science of the relations of all cognition and of all use of reason to the ultimate end of human reason." KGS Vol. IX, 25, trans. M. Young in *Lectures on Logic* (Cambridge: Cambridge University Press, 1994), 538.

7. Lewis White Beck lists these in his introduction to his edition of *Kant: Selections* (New York: Macmillan, 1988), 20–23. Curiously, he does not mention the social nature of human beings that Kant insists upon, although it may be implied by the "creator" item, since for Kant, no culture is possible without sociability. I believe this omission is typical of a long-standing view of Kant's work on questions of "the social" as not, in Beck's words, "programmatic." The work represented in this anthology undermines this interpretation.

8. "Idea for a Universal History with a Cosmopolitan Intent," KGS 8:13–31. For treatment of the teleological aspect of Kant's theory as essentially practical, cf.. Richard Velkley's *Freedom and the End of Reason: On the Moral Foundation of Kant's Critical. Philosophy* (Chicago: University of Chicago Press, 1989).

9. "An Answer to the Question: 'What is Enlightenment?'" KGS 8:36.

10. In his famous essay "What Is Enlightenment?" Kant identifies Enlightenment with thinking for oneself, and outlines some of the social conditions that help and hinder the development of the autonomy of reason.

11. *The Social Contract*, ed. Donald Cress, (Indianapolis, Ind.: Hackett, 1988), Book I, Ch. V, p. 23.

12. Locke's view is problematic, however, since it maintains the preexistence to the social contract of natural rights to property and punishment. Contemporary contractarianism, as exemplified best by Rawls, has become hard to pin down on this issue. Rawls has recently argued that his version of the contract does not make assumptions about the "metaphysical" nature of persons.

13. "Idea for a Universal History" in *Kant on History*, ed. Lewis White Beck (New York: Macmillan, 1985), KGS 8:22.

14. *Reflections on the Revolution in France* (*The Works of Edmund Burke* [Boston, 1884], 3:359). Contemporary echoes of this general critique may be heard in communitarian attacks on Rawls's version of Kantian politics. Cf.. Michael Sandel, *Liberalism and the Limits of Justice* (Cambridge: Cambridge University Press, 1982).

15. This, of course, does not mean that the liberal can have no social theory. A contractarian can very well give an account of society within the polis, and of how the liberal society ought to conduct itself. Cf.. William Galston in "What Is Living and What Is Dead in Kant's Practical Philosophy"

for a discussion of what he calls the "substantive" justification of the liberal state, which amounts to a social ideal (in *Kant and Political Philosophy*, ed. R. Beiner and H. W. Booth [New Haven, Conn.: Yale University Press, 1993]).

16. Stanley Benn, "Society" in *Encyclopedia of Philosophy* (New York: Macmillan, 1972), 7:473.

17. "What Is Living and What Is Dead," 222. Galston believes that this tension is inevitable and also to a large extent capable of resolution through liberal education. Very much in line with the argument of this and other essays in the present volume, he claims that "Kant's teleological doctrine of human perfection thus exerts an irresistible pressure on the limits of the neutral state" (220).

18. Susan Moller Okin is a good example of a liberal theorist who has argued the need to recognize difference. Cf. *Justice, Gender and the Family* (New York: Basic Books, 1989.

19. Cf., e.g., "Doctrine of Right" KGS 6:312ff., and "On the Proverb: That May Be True in Theory, But Is of No Practical Use," KGS 8:289–90ff.

20. Cf., e.g., Barbara Herman, *The Practice of Moral Judgment* (Cambridge, Mass.: Harvard University Press, 1993); Onora O'Neill, *Constructions of Reason: Explorations of Kant's Practical Philosophy* (Cambridge: Cambridge University Press, 1989).

21. Cf., e.g., Paul Guyer, *Kant and the Experience of Freedom* (Cambridge: Cambridge University Press, 1993), esp. chap. 1: "Feeling and Freedom: Kant on Aesthetics and Morality." Also Jane Kneller, "The Aesthetic Dimension of Autonomy," in Robin Schott, ed., *Feminist Interpretations of Kant* (University Park: Pennsylvania State University Press, 1997).

22. Yirmiahu Yovel, *Kant and the Philosophy of History* (Princeton, N.J.: Princeton University Press, 1980), and Harry van der Linden, *Kantian Ethics and Socialism* (Indianapolis, Ind.: Hackett, 1988).

23. Quotations from "Idea for a Universal History" (IUH) hereafter are taken from Reiss, *Kant: Political Writings*.

24. IUH, pp. 41–42 (KGS 8:17–18) .

25. IUH, p. 46 (KGS 8:23).

26. Allen Wood, "Unsocial Sociability: The Anthropological Basis of Kantian Ethics," *Philosophical Topics* 19.1 (1991).

27. *Critique of Practical Reason*, KGS 5:113–14. I have argued this point in "Imagination and Aesthetic Freedom in the German Enlightenment," *Journal of the History of Ideas* 51.2 (1990).

2

Allen W. Wood

Kant's Historical Materialism

"The common opinion that the eighteenth century was an 'unhistorical' century, is not and cannot be historically justified."[1] Though Ernst Cassirer's statement was written, and cogently argued for, over half a century ago, its truth is still not widely acknowledged. Even more recently, Michel Foucault has observed that it is clear that the Enlightenment was the first historically self-conscious age, simply from the fact that it is the first age we call by the same name it called itself.[2]

Why are we so blind to the fact of the Enlightenment's historical consciousness, its historical view of itself, and its concept of a history as a whole? At least part of the explanation surely lies in another fact also observed by Cassirer: that the conceptual tools forged by the Enlightenment were almost from the start turned against it by critics such as Herder, and the application of these tools by several successive generations in the nineteenth century have made the Enlightenment's historical vision difficult for us to recover. Then too, as the first historical age, the Enlightenment could not use the familiar forms through which every later age could call attention to itself, distinguishing itself from other equally self-conscious ages. In the case of the Enlightenment, the very vehicles of its historical self-awareness—its reflection on biblical narratives, for example, or its resurrection of the conception of natural teleology in opposition to the mechanism of early

15

modern science—appear to us something antiquated and hence rather as evidences of its unawareness of even the possibility of historical novelty.

Yet there is very little in the historical consciousness of later modernity (and virtually nothing in that of so-called postmodernity) that was not already present in some form in the Enlightenment. Even its contemporary detractors indirectly acknowledge this in their very zeal to confront the Enlightenment, to "go beyond" it, to have done with it and put it once and for all behind them. The endlessness of this struggle, as well as its self-destructiveness, which seems to constitute the whole positive content of this kind of philosophy, betrays the fact that the struggle against Enlightenment is only a struggle against themselves, and that its only conceivable positive resolution would be the recovery of the very standpoint they are struggling, in both futility and perpetuity, to reject. My aim here is to contribute to that positive resolution by working toward the recovery of the greatest Enlightenment thinker's philosophy of history and the establishment of a recognizable connection to the best-known later conception of history for which it provided the foundation.

CRITICAL PHILOSOPHY AS HISTORICAL CONSCIOUSNESS

Kant illustrates the way in which the Enlightenment's historical self-consciousness conceals itself from us. Kant is ostensibly concerned with a timeless architectonic of the sciences founded on *a priori* principles and an immutable moral law legislated by a timeless noumenal self. He seldom makes history his theme in his major writings, but deals with it explicitly only in a brief, sketchy appendix (KrV A 852–56/B 880–84) or in occasional journalistic essays and popular lectures (IAG 8:17–31, WA 8:35–42, RH 8:44–66, MA 8:109–23, TP 8:307–13, SF 7:79–94, VA 7:327–33).[3] Some of his deepest explorations into the historical foundations of human reason are presented as part of an ironical, irreverent interpretation of the Book of Genesis (MA 8:118–20).

Yet Kant's philosophy shows itself to be historically self-aware even in its fundamental conception of itself as *critique*. This awareness is expressed quite explicitly right at the beginning of the *Critique of Pure Reason*, in the prefaces to both editions, though somewhat differently in each. In the second edition, criticism is conceived as the transformation of metaphysics from a "groping about" into a science, as happened much earlier to mathematics and logic, and more recently to physics. This conception is grounded in a general account of the coming to be of science, that is, of the sudden historical event through which a domain of human inquiry attains to the "secure course of a science" (KrV B vii–xvii).

According to this account, a science originates when human reason defines and limits a subject matter by legislating in regard to it. Logic was in this regard a relatively easy subject to turn into a science, since in logic reason "has to do only with itself" (KrV B x). Even earlier, however, Kant says, mathematics had become a science through a sudden "revolution," probably the work of a single Greek thinker ("Thales or someone else") who recognized that mathematical cognition is grounded not on what one *discovers* in a figure or its mere concept, but rather on what one has *put into* the figure through its construction (KrV B xi–xii). Kant extends the same account to the more recent revolution in the physical sciences:

> When Galileo rolled balls of a weight chosen by himself down an inclined plane, or when Torricelli made the air bear a weight which he had already calculated to be equal to that of a known column of water, or when in a later time Stahl changed metals into calx and then changed the latter back [B xiii] into metals by first removing something and then putting it back again, a light dawned on all those who study nature. They comprehended that reason has insight only into what it itself produces according to its own design; that it must give itself principles for its judgments according to constant laws and compel nature to answer its questions, rather than letting nature guide its movements by keeping reason, as it were, in leading-strings. (KrV B xii–xiii)

The *experimental* method of modern science, Kant insists, is grounded on this revolution, since experiments cannot be conducted on the basis of "accidental observations, made according to no previously designed plan," but depend instead on a fundamental transformation of the inquirer's relation to nature:

> Reason, in order to be taught by nature, must go to her with its principles . . . in one hand and experiments thought out in accordance with these principles in the other—yet not like a pupil, who hears whatever the teacher wants to recite, but like an appointed judge who compels witnesses to answer the questions he puts to them. (KrV B xiii)

Science originates, in other words, only when human inquirers cease to adopt a trustful attitude toward nature, letting their reason follow what it teaches them through haphazard observation. The beginning of science is the emergence of scientific thought from this tutelage to nature, which is achieved when human thinkers assume responsibility for the questions they ask, determining these questions by a plan of inquiry which they themselves have devised according to the laws of their own reason. The achievement of this state of adulthood is the process which Kant was, a few years later, to give the name "Enlightenment" (WA 8:35). In the second edition preface, the critique of pure reason is conceived as the application of this same revolution in thinking to *metaphysics*, the highest science and the foundation of all the others.

The first edition had represented the critique as a revolution of an even more direct kind. It employs an elaborate metaphor that portrays metaphysics as a sovereign ruling over the sciences (since *Metaphysik* is a feminine noun, the sovereign is a queen rather than a king). Her form of government up to now has been an absolute monarchy, administered by dogmatic philosophers, whose factional squabbles, unregulated by any law, have often threatened the stability of the state, making it vulnerable to skeptics, "a kind of nomad, who abhors all permanent settlement," whose assaults "shattered civil unity from time to time" (KrV A ix), without establishing any other order in place of arbitrary despotism.

Kant's metaphor here not only connects rationalist metaphysics with the political *ancien régime* (initiating an association that was to play an important role in discrediting this philosophy in the years to come) but also portrays empiricism (that of Locke) as politically subversive, prying into the legitimacy of the queen's title by falsely ascribing her origins to "the rabble of common experience" (KrV A ix). The current state of the sciences is presented as one in which the queen, though still asserting her claims, is generally despised, and the prevailing attitude toward her rule is one of "indifference"—a political climate of alienation that leaves the queen on her throne but refuses her any honor or respect.

Kant views this discontented state of things as threatening political chaos, but also as hopeful, offering the possibility of a fundamental and progressive political reform. Kant proposes to summon the monarch before a court of justice, presided over by reason, that will legitimate her rule by upholding her legitimate claims, while limiting her powers by dismissing those claims that do not conform to reason's laws. "This court is nothing other than the *critique of pure reason* itself" (KrV A xii).

It is not difficult to regard Kant's metaphor as expressing also the literal hopes which Frederick the Great's promises of political reform might have awakened in an enlightened and forward-looking man of science. And once, in a footnote, Kant's political metaphor does transcend itself toward political reality in precisely this way. After expressing his dissatisfaction with the age's mood of skepticism and indifference, he turns around and defends this mood as a sign of increasing maturity, which refuses any longer to be put off by pretenses and mystifications. Ours, he says, is the "age of critique," to which everything must submit if it is to retain any honor or authority.

> *Religion* through its *holiness* and *legislation* through its *majesty* commonly seek to exempt themselves from it. But in this way they only excite a just suspicion against themselves, and cannot lay claim to that unfeigned respect which reason grants only to that which has been able to withstand its free and public examination. (KrV A xi note)

It is not only in the metaphorical monarchy of the sciences, then, but also in the real world of the church and the state, that a critique of reason is needed.

The "critique of pure reason," in both editions of the first Critique, thus refers to reason in the role of κριτεζ or judge, as an authoritative decider, under its own laws, of doubtful or competing claims. Reason must cross-examine nature (regarded as a reluctant, untrustworthy, and prevaricating witness) and it is called upon to settle the disputed claims of metaphysics (regarded as a queen whose regime over the sciences is to be transformed from an absolute despotism into a legitimate constitutional monarchy). Reason's assumption of this judicial function is viewed as a critical historical event that is required by the conditions of the time, whether to secure the limited constitutional rule of metaphysics over the realm of the sciences or to put metaphysics itself on the secure course of a science.

The critique of reason is thus made both possible and necessary by the historical fact of *enlightenment*—the emergence of the human mind, and of an educated public, from the condition of tutelage or minority imposed on it by dogmatic learning, ecclesiastical authority, and political despotism. The task of critique is the task of those who would lead this process of enlightenment, bringing the republic of the intellect, as well as the political commonwealth, into a condition befitting the adulthood of its rational citizens, turning each into a community of free beings who take responsibility for their own judgments and follow their own self-given laws.

Kant's philosophy, therefore, is historically conscious and addressed to the specific needs and historical vocation of its time. In its theoretical expression, this vocation is "critique" or authoritative judgment, in its practical expression it is "autonomy," the assumption of a dignity that entitles it to legislate for itself. But a consciousness of

one's own age, its needs and its tasks, always presupposes a consciousness of its relation to earlier and later ages, in other words, a
larger historical narrative providing one's owns time with its historical
horizons. What philosophy of history grounds the critical philosophy's
historical consciousness?

HUMAN NATURE AND HISTORY

The common reputation of Kant's conception of human nature is
based largely on inferences from Kant's dualism of the phenomenal
and noumenal. It is identified, in other words, with the thesis that
what is most distinctively human about us—our rationality, freedom,
historicality—cannot be integrated into a naturalistic picture of ourselves. If we turn away from these narrowly based prejudices and look
at what Kant actually has to say about human nature, however, we get
an altogether different picture. What is most striking about Kant's
actual writings about history and anthropology is their systematic
attempt to comprehend the distinctively human in terms of a conception of the human race as a natural species, using the same biological principles that govern the study of other organisms.

The starting point of Kant's philosophy of history is a heuristic
principle that is to govern our investigation into the natural teleology
of living organisms: "All the natural capacities of a creature are
destined sooner or later to be developed completely and in conformity
with their end" (IAG 8:18). The idea behind this principle is that in
attempting to frame teleological principles to explain the normal life
processes of an organism, we should attempt to account for all its
normal life activities in terms of a coherent set of species capacities,
whose full development can be regarded as an end of nature.
Conversely, it is bad teleological theorizing to consider something to be
among a creature's specific capacities unless the internal organization
of the creature allows, under normal conditions, for its complete
development and exercise.

There is something striking and unique, however, about the species
capacities of human beings: our species exhibits what Rousseau called
perfectibility: the faculty of developing its capacities, varying their
employment, and progressively altering and expanding its own nature
over time.[4] This unique feature of human nature not only enables
different human beings to adopt widely differing ways of life, hence to
adapt to extremely different climates and habitats, populating nearly
every part of the earth, but it also makes possible a systematic alter-
ation of human capacities and activities through long intervals of time,

enabling the human species, or parts of it, to have a coherent history. Kant traces the faculty of perfectibility to reason, since it is this faculty that enables us both to extend our judgments through principles in search of the absolutely unconditioned (KrV A 298–305/B 355–61) as well as to make comparative judgments of value (R 6:27). A being with this as its fundamental faculty will be ever restless, devising new modes of life, and engaged in selecting one such mode over other alternatives, including those presently available. This capacity, therefore, releases the human race from the servitude to instinct (MA 8:111–12) and constitutes its *freedom*, in a properly Kantian sense that is nevertheless an object of a systematic and equally Kantian project of empirical investigation (IAG 8:17–19). The rational perfectibility of the human species has a far-reaching consequence for any teleological account of its capacities. It entails that these capacities cannot be exhibited entirely within the life-cycle of any normal specimen—as can be done in the case of other animals—but can be fully developed only in the species as a whole (IAG 8:119).

For Kant this means, to begin with, that it is fundamentally contrary to the nature of the subject matter to attempt to base a science of society on what some people now call "microfoundations." That is, we must not try to derive laws for it from regularities governing the conscious behavior of individual subjects, using these to construct laws of social behavior. Rather, since the essential capacities of the human race exist only in the species as a whole, distributed among its members and exercised only through their concerted action usually taking place beyond the will or consciousness of any individual, we must seek for natural laws in human life in *collective* regularities, such as those governing the annual statistics of marriages, births, and deaths in a nation (IAG 8:117). The regularities we should look for, in other words, are natural purposes directing human affairs on a large scale, directing the wills of individual human beings who are hardly ever aware of them:

> Individual human beings and entire nations little imagine that while they are pursuing their own ends, each in his own way and often in opposition to others, they are unwittingly guided in advance along a course aimed at by nature, unconsciously promoting an end which, even if they knew what it was, would scarcely arouse their interest. (IAG 8:17)

Yet another corollary of the heuristic biological principle, when applied to the peculiar case of the human species, is that because human species-capacities develop over time, are handed down from each generation to the next, and are progressively augmented, they are indeterminate in character and their complete development is forever deferred into an open-ended historical future. Human reason, regarded as the capacity of perfectibility, produces a multiformity of human lives, human natures, societies, and historical possibilities. For Kant, therefore, as we shall see presently, human history is epochal—a series of determinate periods, grounded on the practical forms taken by reason under differing material and social conditions. The study of humanity as a natural species cannot be a science of unchanging laws governing human behavior, but must instead be the historical study of successive epochs unified teleologically through the concept of a plan of nature leading from each one to the next as an arrangement for the further development of human species-capacities.

From the same considerations Kant infers also that no determinate definition of human nature, no specification of the character of the human species, can ever be given. The traditional formula *animal rationale* can be accepted by Kant only if it is interpreted not as a definition but as a rejection of every attempt to indicate a specific character defining the human race.

> The problem of indicating the character of the human species is quite insoluble . . . [The human being] has a character which he himself creates, insofar as he is capable of perfecting himself according to the ends that he himself adopts. Because of this, the human being as an animal possessed of the *capacity for reason* (*animal rationabilis*) can make himself into a *rational animal* (*animal rationale*), as such he first preserves himself and his species. (VA 7:321–22)

Here Kant accepts the traditional definition of human nature as *animal rationale* only in the qualified sense that human beings preserve themselves and their species only through the variety of specific ways in which they, as *animales rationabiles, become* rational by developing their natural predispositions (VA 7:322–25).

This means that when we set out to study human beings, our object of study must be collective in yet another sense: it must be *historical*, encompassing the process by which people acquire new capacities, assimilate them into their life-activities, and transmit them to their descendants. Thus not only is the human race, as a biological species, essentially historical, but the study of this species must be fundamentally historical. When we follow the heuristic principle with which we began in regard to human nature, our object of study must be the natural arrangements through which the human species continues to develop its collective capacities over time. The full development of these capacities, moreover, regarded as an end of nature, can be conceived only as a historical process comprehending the past but also pointing into the future. Because human nature has reason (or freedom, that is, Rousseauean perfectibility), this process can never be conceived as having an "end" in the sense of a final state in which the process would be completed and therefore cease, but we must represent it to ourselves teleologically as following an unconscious "plan of nature" that arranges for the endless development of human species capacities (IAG 8:27–28).

The theoretical study of the human species, therefore, can consist only in a "universal history from a cosmopolitan standpoint" (IAG 8:29)—that is, a narrative structure encompassing the entire human race and the plan of nature through which its species capacities have developed in the past and will continue to unfold themselves indefinitely in the future. The "grand narrative," which in our time has been declared impossible by Lyotard and his followers, is for the critical philosophy a condition for the possibility of any empirical study of the human species as a natural phenomenon.[5]

HISTORICAL CONJECTURES

In 1785, Kant reviewed the first two volumes of *Ideas for a Philosophy of History of Humanity* by his sometime student, now also his philosophical critic, Johann Gottfried Herder. In the review of the second volume, Kant replies to Herder's criticism of his own philosophy of history, and especially to Herder's objections (which we would now call "methodological individualist") to the Kantian doctrine that the development of human capacities and human destiny is to be found only in the species as a whole, not in individuals (RH 8:64–66).

He also refers briefly to book 10 of the *Ideas*, in which Herder attempts a conjectural history of the beginnings of the human race, founded on a creative interpretation of the Book of Genesis. On this speculative biblical history, Kant comments: "In a trackless desert, a thinker, like a traveler, must be free to choose his own route at his discretion. But . . . the same freedom cannot be denied [someone else] to prescribe a [different] path for himself" (RH 8:64). Early in 1786, Kant made good on this cryptic promise by publishing a short, satirical essay entitled "Conjectural Beginning of Human History," which provides a playful—at times irreverent—alternative interpretation of the same Genesis story of paradise, the fall, and its historical aftermath. It is to the later, properly historical, phase of Kant's conjectures, that I now want to direct attention.

Kant divides the early history of the human race into three main epochs, which he characterizes, respectively, as

1. An age "of comfort and peace"
2. An age "of labor and strife"; and
3. The "unification of society" (MA 8:118)

What is fundamental to each of these historical epochs is the powers and activities through which human beings live, and the resulting differences and conflicts between groups of people.

The earliest human beings, Kant supposes, lived by hunting wild animals and by haphazard fruit-gathering or digging for roots. After the taming of wild animals, the pastoral way of life sprang up next to that of the hunter-gatherer, but without coming into conflict with it, so that despite these differences people continued to live peacefully side by side (MA 8:118). This is the way it was during the first epoch.

Gradually, however, human beings acquired the ability to sow seeds and plant crops. Though more productive, and able to support a larger population, the nascent agricultural way of life is less leisurely, more strenuous, and more subject to the vagaries of climate (MA 8:118). Still more ominously, in contrast to the ways of life characterizing the first historical epoch, agriculture requires a settled mode of life, a permanent habitation, and stable rights of property in land, along with the power to protect them. To farmers, therefore, herders were a nuisance, since their stock would trample or graze off the crops and then move on (MA 8:119). Kant suggests that it was the resulting conflicts between people that made it impossible for them to share the land in peace and hence served to disperse human beings widely over the surface of the earth, thus occasioning even greater variety in their modes of life and further promoting their perfectibility (MA 8:118).

This fundamental antagonism is rooted in economic relations and the ownership of means of production. It ushers in the second historical epoch, characterized by discontent and conflict. This primitive economic antagonism, in fact, provides Kant with his interpretation of the biblical story of Abel, the "keeper of sheep" and his brother Cain, the "tiller of the ground" (Gen. 4:2). Since the pastoral way of life was simpler and more contented, the farmer comes to envy the shepherd as more favored by heaven (Gen. 4:4-5); but when the conflict erupts into violence, what moves the farmer is not envy but rather his right to landed property, which is essential to the agricultural way of life (Gen. 4:8).

We should not miss the irreverent irony in Kant's biblical allusion here. On the Kantian exegesis, Cain's murder appears justified both as a blow for economic progress and as a defense of that right that, on

Kant's own theory, is fundamental to all civil society. When Cain "goes out from the presence of the Lord, to dwell in the land of Nod, east of Eden" (Gen. 4:16), Kant regards this not as a punishment of exile upon blood guilt but as the first founding of a distinct community based on agriculture, to be protected systematically from the incursions of nomadic hunters and herders. It brings an end to the second historical epoch, and inaugurates the beginnings of civilization proper (MA 8:119).

As Kant sees it, the organized coercion necessary to protect property was achieved only after the founding of villages, the development of technical arts—especially, as Kant elsewhere suggests, of mining and metallurgy (EF 8: 363–64)—and the beginnings of market exchange (MA 8:119). These factors made both possible and necessary the creation of "civil order and public administration of justice," as well as the might required to resist the occasional assaults of nomadic peoples (the skeptics of Kant's metaphor in the first Critique) who refuse to recognize the authority and property rights of the civil society founded on agriculture (MA 8:119–20). It is only in such a society that the systematic and well-rounded cultivation of human faculties can first begin. But this was also a society constantly prepared for war, ruled by military despotism, and founded on increasing inequality and oppression, in which luxury and "soulless self-indulgence" is combined with the "abominable state of slavery" (MA 8:120).

KANT AND MARX

Kant's historical conjectures are inspired less by Scripture than by the model of Rousseau's *Discourse on the Origin of Inequality*. But Kant's philosophy of history also goes beyond Rousseau in many ways, especially in its wholehearted acceptance of the civilized condition, with all its miseries, as our condition, and the further development of civilization as the only conceivable source of any remedy for the evils civilization has brought upon us. As should be quite evident by now, Kant's theory of the human race's historical development bears more than a casual resemblance to the materialist conception of history later worked out by Karl Marx. Kant's vision of humanity's historical future as well as its past has more in common with its greatest nineteenth-century descendant than has usually been appreciated.

Kant's *Idea for a Universal History* proposes to view history as the process through which human beings develop their species-capacities. As we have seen, for Kant the decisive trait of the human species—the original empirical meaning of its rationality and freedom—is its ability to devise its own way of life. Thus along with Marx, Kant understands the basis of history as the development of people's socially productive powers, their collective capacities to produce their means of subsistence. In history, these capacities change and grow, and the historical process follows upon this growth. As becomes clear in the *Conjectural Beginning*, history for Kant has passed through several different stages, each of which corresponds to the then dominant modes of productive activity. If the key to historical development is the growth of human species powers, the fundamental or determining powers are productive ones. What fundamentally characterizes each historical epoch is not only the mode of material production characteristic of it, but also the social conflicts this mode of production involves.

Marx's materialist conception, in one of its most succinct formulations, states these ideas as follows.[6]

> In the social production of their life, human beings enter into determinate relations of production which correspond to a definite stage of the development of their material productive powers. . . . At a certain stage of their development, the material productive powers come into conflict with the existing mode of production, or—what is but a juridical expression of the same thing—with the property relations within which they have previously been at work. . . . Then an epoch of social revolution begins.

This closely parallels Kant's account in the *Conjectural Beginning*, especially the transition between the second and third epochs in early human history. The existing modes of production, those of the hunter-gatherer and herder, are challenged by the newer agricultural mode, which represents a higher stage in the development of human productive powers. The resulting conflict is resolved when the victorious agricultural mode establishes itself, or—in juridical terms—its characteristic property relations. The second epoch in Kant's history, the unstable "epoch of discord" is a transitional (or "revolutionary") period, leading to the more stable third epoch, which establishes a civilization grounded on the agricultural mode of production.

Like Marx, Kant regards history as a scene not only of conflict and strife, but also of deepening inequality and oppression—though this trait shows itself mainly in his account of historical developments subsequent to the founding of civil society, to which we will turn in the next section. As in Marx's theory of history, the root of social antagonism is a struggle between groups of people with opposed economic interests, where the different groups represent different stages in humanity's economic development. And in both theories the victory in this struggle tends to belong to the group whose mode of production more fully develops the productive powers of humanity.

Marx's theory of history is "materialist" in more than one sense. First, it treats "the mode of production in material life" as the key to humanity's historical development. Second, and perhaps more significantly, it understands the *social* "form" of human society as grounded on its *economic* "matter."[7] Kant's theory of history is materialistic in both these senses. It treats humanity's activities in producing their means of subsistence as the historical basis for the development of all their capacities—including their moral rationality. And Kant regards the employment of these capacities as conditioning the social relations—in particular, the property relations and political forms—that characterize a given historical epoch. Kant's theory of history, therefore, is correctly described as a form of "historical materialism."

Kant's historical materialism, however, lacks certain features that are very prominent in Marx's theory of history, and Kant applies his historical materialism in a different way from Marx, and to very different epochs of history. For this reason, we should call Kant's materialist theory of history not "Marxist" but rather "proto-Marxist." We are already in a position to see three significant differences between the two theories.

First, Kant views the conflict between modes of production as a simple conflict between those who carry on different forms of productive activity; he does not view it as a struggle between *classes* whose antagonism is built into a single mode of production. Thus in one way Kant goes beyond Rousseau and in the direction of Marx—seeing historical epochs as representing distinct stages of economic organization, and the dynamic of history as a conflict between the representatives of different stages—while in another ignoring a prominent Rousseauean theme that Marx was later to develop: namely, the social dynamic generated by internal social inequalities.[8]

Second, Kant regards the agricultural mode of production as establishing the principle of private property, which then becomes the basis of all civil society based on right, and thus for all further developments of civilization. Kant's theory of right provides for more legal and political regulation of the economic sphere, and for more redistribution of property in the interests of justice, than has usually been appreciated. But in Kant there is no suggestion that any social struggle subsequent to the agricultural revolution will ever call the principle of private property itself into question.

Third, another major difference between Kant and Marx is already hinted at in Kant's description of the epoch of "labor and discord" as a "prelude to uniting in society." This becomes even more apparent if we look at Kant's account of human history subsequent to the establishment of an agricultural mode of production. Kant views the early development of civilization as a prelude to the establishment of a social union under coercive laws, or "civil society" (in the sense of the political state). Kant lacks the *Hegelian* concept of civil society, as a social system of economic activity distinct from the state. Still less does he anticipate the Marxian position that civil society in this sense is the "real foundation" of the political state, a mode of collective human activity that might someday evolve in such a way as to render the political state superfluous. For this reason, there is also no room in Kant's theory of history for the prospect of abolishing the state at some point in the historical future.

PRIVATE PROPERTY AND THE ORIGIN OF THE STATE

Kant sees the founding of political states as *the* pivotal event in human history. Only with the formation of towns do people enter, properly speaking, into a *civilized* condition. Urban life meant the beginnings of a division of labor within society and an economy based on exchange. This gave a new impetus to the development not only of practical crafts, but also to art and culture. This is Kant's interpretation of the Bible's mention of the varied trades practiced by Cain's children (Gen. 4:17–23). The most beneficial fruits of civilized life were "sociability and civil security"; they enabled agricultural societies with urban centers to colonize new territories, increasing the geographical area dominated by the new and more civilized way of life (MA 8:119).

A plurality of different ways of life existing in close proximity also enabled the seeds of human conflict to germinate. Civilization gave rise to new and subtler forms of competition, rivalry and domination, involving vanity, envy, malice, and deceit (R 6:27–33). It is in the civilized condition that we really begin to see the close connection between the development of reason, including the beginnings of morality, and the increase of human vice and unhappiness.[9] "With this epoch there also began the *inequality* among human beings, that rich source of so much evil, but also of all good; and henceforth this inequality was only to increase" (MA 8:119). Civilized life thus provides the proper medium for developing the fundamental human trait of "unsociable sociability"—the simultaneous interdependence between people and their mutual antagonism and hostility. This trait is the key to Kant's conception of human nature and hence to the anthropological basis for his ethical theory.[10]

Kant explains the creation of political states through increasing conflicts between people when they enter into civilized life. In the earliest stages, these conflicts took two main forms: private violence and revenge, requiring a system of public justice, and war, at first chiefly a perpetuation of the conflict with pastoral peoples (MA 8:119–20). At a later stage, he thinks, civilization tends eventually to be victorious over pre-agricultural peoples, who are "drawn into the glittering misery of the towns" (MA 8:120, 231). (Kant understands the "sons of God" in Genesis 6 as a reference to these nomads, and their marriage with "the daughters of men" as their absorption into civil life.) He then portrays a cyclical dynamic in early civil society: The threat of external conflict requires preparation for war, and hence a strong economic base, which can be maintained only if the ruler allows a measure of civil freedom. The absorption of civil society's enemies, however, makes for a time of peace and luxury, but permits civil rulers to become tyrants and destroys the freedom of citizens. The resulting corruption of civil society, which thus "becomes unworthy of its very existence" (MA 8:120), is Kant's way of interpreting the biblical story of the flood (Gen. 6:5-7). Elsewhere he indicates that this state of corruption is usually prevented by the ever-present threat of war between states, and that the hostility between states itself serves the end of progress toward rightful political constitutions (EF 8:367; TP 8:310–11; IAG 8:26).

Kant's friends are in the habit of praising his noble insistence on the evils of war and the need to overcome hostility between nations through a federation of states; they are also in the habit of contrasting Kant's views on war favorably with Hegel's nasty idea that occasional wars are necessary to preserve the ethical health of peoples.[11] But when they do so they mislead us. For Kant too maintains that until civil society has been firmly established on the basis of republican principles of right, the threat of war serves as nature's principal means for protecting individual liberty and keeping social progress alive within the state (MA 8:119–20). Moreover, he regards this point in history as still to be reached, and to be reachable only through nature's expedient of war and the constant threat of war.

Natural purposiveness is seen by Kant to be at work not only in war, but more fundamentally in all forms of social conflict. Social antagonism is nature's way of preventing human beings from falling prey to their desire for contentment, and inciting the human species to develop its natural capacities (IAG 8:20–22). From the point of view of nature's end, the most favorable condition for the human species is the civilized one. But in this condition, social antagonism comes to threaten nature's end, as violence and war disrupt civil life and undermine the freedom individuals need in order to develop their capacities to the full. Therefore, beyond this point nature's own end of developing the powers of the human species requires that people hold their natural antagonism in check, guarding individual freedom and civil peace by establishing their social relations according to principles of right. In this way, violence and war are themselves part of nature's purposiveness. They are nature's way of compelling people to establish their social relations in accordance with principles of reason (IAG 8:22–24; cf. TP 8:310).

Of course, it should be emphasized that for Kant war serves its historical purpose chiefly by making it intolerable for states to retain a pre-republican form and to exist outside a universal federation that will maintain peace between them (IAG 8:24–25). In other words, war is historically necessary as a means to peace. This paradox is characteristic of Kant's philosophy of history, which in general treats the evils of human life purposively as means to the goods opposed to them. The paradox is that it looks as though nature has adopted a counter-purposive means to its end. But this impression can perhaps be removed if we keep in mind the precise nature of the end in question. Peace, like any other human good, is not to be simply provided us through nature's bounty, but it is rather nature's purpose that it should be an achievement of human beings themselves: It is as if nature "had willed that the human being, having finally worked his way up from the greatest barbarism to the greatest skill, the greatest perfection in his way of thinking and thus to happiness (as far as it is possible on earth), should take sole credit for this and have only himself to thank for it" (IAG 8:20). If this is nature's goal, then it is not unsuitable to give human beings a tantalizing conception of their good while putting them in a situation in which that good is so far from being possessed by them that they have no choice but to develop and exercise their capacities in order to acquire it. It is not paradoxical, then, but an inevitable feature of nature's purposiveness in human history, that we must attain peace only through war.

THE HISTORICAL PRESUPPOSITIONS OF RIGHT

One corollary of historical materialism often emphasized by the founders of Marxism is the materially conditioned and historically alterable character of all standards of right and morality. Engels, for example, insists that historical materialism utterly discredits the notion that there are any "eternal truths" in these areas.[12] Kant, however, appears utterly to reject this alleged corollary of the doctrine. In the *Metaphysics of*

Morals, Kant proposes to found his theory of right on "immutable principles" deriving *a priori* from pure reason alone (MS 6:229–30). More generally, he regards the foundation of all morality and right as a "metaphysics of morals," that is, a theory based on *a priori* principles valid for all rational beings, irrespective of time or place. He frequently insists that neither the content nor the validity of this principle is dependent on any empirical facts about human nature or the circumstances of human life.

From such statements, however, we should not infer that Kant's ethical theory has no historical presuppositions. Once we see how Kant's conception of morality and right as metaphysical can be reconciled with a materialist conception of history, we will gain a better understanding of both points of Kantian doctrine. Here we will restrict ourselves to right—to rational principles governing justice, external law, and the political state—both for the sake of simplicity and because Kant's most explicit statements of the historical conditioned character of practical principles are about principles of right.

Cognitions are *a priori* in Kant's view if they arise from the use of our faculties rather than from the course of the experience in which those faculties are employed. But of course Kant holds, quite consistently with this, that every use of our faculties is occasioned by experience, and hence that even the most *a priori* of our cognitions has experience as a necessary condition (KrV B 1). Further, Kant recognizes that human faculties themselves pass through a developmental process, both in the individual and in the species. The fact that our faculties are acquired through an empirical process does not, in his view, compromise the apriority of the cognitions that depend solely on their use. In this way, it is perfectly consistent to hold of certain principles that they are *a priori* and that our knowledge of them is conditioned by a historical process that has conditioned the acquisition of the faculties that enable us to cognize them *a priori*.

Kant holds that the principles of right are *a priori*, dependent solely on the exercise of our rational faculties. He also holds that the development and exercise of the faculties by which we recognize such principles is historically occasioned and conditioned. Kant maintains that it is only within certain social forms that people can actually become aware of pure principles of right, and can begin to apply these principles to their social relationships. It could be said that even in a less developed form of society, these principles are already valid in the sense that they are the only principles that a fully developed reason will eventually arrive at. But until a suitable form of society has been achieved, the historical conditions for formulating and applying these principles have yet to be realized.

In Kant's theory of the state, as in the theories of Locke and Rousseau, private property in land plays the fundamental role. For Kant, the acquisition of property in land is the foundation of all forms of acquisition (MS 6:261–62), and the necessity of the state is deduced as the condition for any adequately grounded right to property (MS 6:264–67). Prior to entry into a state, Kant holds, the right to property can be only "provisional"; "peremptory" acquisition is possible only when people leave the state of nature and enter into the civil condition (MS 6:257). "Therefore something external can be *originally* acquired only in conformity with the idea of a civil condition, that is, with a view to it and to its being brought about, but prior to its realization" (MS 6:264).

Kant's theory of property and its relation to the civil condition is of course intended to apply directly to the present. The thesis that acquisition prior to the civil condition is only provisional entails that we acquire genuine and enforceable property rights only by means of a state and under the conditions specified by public laws given through a general will (MS 6:256). This means that Kant rejects Locke's idea that in a state of nature we may have full-fledged property rights (acquired by means of our labor) that we may rightfully enforce against others. Instead, he holds that it is the function of public law to determine the conditions under which people may acquire a genuine and enforceable right of ownership over things.

At the same time, however, Kant's theory of acquisition, and of property as the basis of the state, refers quite literally to the history through which he thinks the institutions of landed property and the civil condition first originated. We have seen that Kant thinks private property in land originated as a necessary condition for the agricultural mode of production, but that it was established conclusively only after the emergence of an urban way of life led to the founding of political states with the power to enforce this institution by holding the hordes of pastoral nomads at bay and submitting private quarrels to a system of legal justice.

> [Property in land] proceeds only from a will in the civil condition (*lex ius distributivae*), which alone determines what is *right*, what is *rightful*, and what is *laid down as right*. But in the [state of nature], that is, before the establishment of the civil condition but with a view to it, that is, *provisionally*, it is a *duty* to proceed in accordance with the principle of external acquisition. (MS 6:267)

Kant opposes the state of nature not to a *social* condition but to a *civil* condition, saying explicitly that there can be society (though not *civil* society) in a state of nature (MS 6:242). The most natural way to understand the distinction between provisional and peremptory acquisition, and that between the state of nature and the civil condition is historically. This distinction refers, namely, to the early stages of the agricultural mode of production, when farmers began to lay claim to private property in land, but there was as yet no organized civil society in terms of which their property rights could be adjudicated and publicly enforced. It is this historical period that Kant calls "the state of nature" when he contrasts this with the "civil condition" (MS 6:242).

Thus when Kant speaks of leaving the state of nature and entering into a civil condition, he is referring quite literally to a kind of past historical event, namely, the establishment of law-governed states, centered in cities, that protected the property rights of farmers against herders and other nomadic peoples and provided the earliest system of public justice within a culture with an urban center founded on the agricultural mode of production. Kant's entire theory of right thus presupposes a post-agricultural form of society.

It is true that Kant insists that some features of his theory of right—such as the original common ownership of the earth and the social contract—are misunderstood if they are taken as historical facts. Both, he says, are instead "ideas" (or even "fictions") in terms of which we should conceive presently existing institutions (MS 6:251–52, TP 8:297; cf. MS 6:315, EF 8:349–51). It would be a mistake, however, to infer that he means the same to apply to the transition from provisional to peremptory acquisition or between the state of nature and the civil condition (which are never described as mere ideas or denied historical reference). It is rather that Kant's theory of history has no place for events and conditions such as the social contract and original common ownership of land. According to this theory, states were first founded not through contract but through violence and rightful ownership of land began only under the agricultural mode of production (though at first only provisionally, from the standpoint of legal right).[13]

Kant's theory of right must be understood as historically conditioned in the sense that it is only after people achieve a civilization based on agriculture that they are capable of making the transition to a civil condition from a state of nature—that is, from a society, based on a hunter-gatherer or a pastoral economy, which does not have the institution of private property in land and therefore does not need to be organized as a law-governed state, to a civil society grounded on right, the rule of law under a general will. In other words, it is not until people reach a certain stage in their history that they require a condition of legal right and a capacity to regulate their interactions through a collective will and principles based on their common rationality. Until that point, in Kant's view, they live lives typically more contented than those of civilized human beings, but they do not grasp the immutable rational principles of right on which the status of an individual as an externally free rational person depends. On Kant's theory, the development of an agricultural economy and an organized civil society is part of nature's purposiveness in human history, a device employed by nature to bring people into a condition in which they *must* develop their rational powers and view their relations to one another and to their conditions of life in terms of a system of right and property (VA 7:327–28).

CONCLUDING REMARKS

Engels thinks that the material basis of right and morality is not only historically conditioned, but also that it is always destined to undergo historical changes, perhaps that it will never reach any determinate and definitive form. Thus he maintains that each mode of production will have its own distinctive conceptions and principles of right and morality, which are functionally suited to it. Kant's assertion that there are "immutable" principles of right is clearly at odds with Engels's view at this point. But the difference between the two is misunderstood if it is represented as a difference between an "ahistorical" (Enlightenment) conception of right and a (post-Enlightenment) view that is sensitive to the historical conditioned character of moral truth. The difference here, on the contrary, is one between two contrasting applications of a materialist conception of history, consequently two distinct ways of recognizing the historically conditioned character of practical principles.

Kant does not deny that our human species capacities will develop further. Nor does he hold that social and political institutions will remain immutable. On the contrary, his position is that the education of the human race, that is, the development of its capacities—technical, pragmatic, and moral—has perhaps not even properly begun, much less been completed (MA 8:117). The fundamental idea of Kant's philosophy of history, in fact, that the further development of human capacities, which is nature's purpose for the human race, depends on our solving the most difficult of all the problems nature has set us: that of devising a political form that administers true justice among human beings (IAG 8:22–23). Further, Kant contends that in order to solve this problem we must also solve an even larger one: how to bring about just and peaceful external relations among political states (IAG 8:24–26). He is far from thinking that these problems are close to a solution at the present time, and does not pretend to know in detail how they should be solved, though he is persuaded that the universal adoption of a republican form of government and the establishment of a peaceful federation of states are necessary steps on the way to solving them (EF 8:348–57).

Nevertheless, Kant holds that as far as right is concerned, the important material achievement is that of an urban-based civil society founded on an agricultural mode of production. Whatever further changes human society may undergo, Kant does not expect them to alter people's conceptions and principles of right in a fundamental way, but only to alter their application of these principles as they are applied to new conditions. Kant also expects institutions and practices to be brought into progressively better conformity with these principles, as the ongoing process of enlightened reflection on their import makes their content better understood and gives this understanding a wider dissemination. Kant even regards these historical processes themselves as materially conditioned, insofar as he sees the existence of an enlightened public as an inevitable concomitant of varied and expanded economic activity (IAG 8:27–28; TP 8:310–12; EF 8:368).

Engels's views on these matters may be right, and Kant's may be wrong. But if so, then they are wrong because Kant has a mistaken interpretation of the material conditions of right and the historical basis of its principles, and not because he either denies or ignores the fact that right is materially and historically conditioned. Nor should our recognition that Kant's philosophy is bound up with a version of historical materialism automatically be taken as a defense of either Kant or a materialist conception of history. It is rather a challenge to both Kant's sympathizers and his critics to rethink the kinds of issues raised by his philosophy—not only by his philosophy of political right and ethics but even his conception of a critique of metaphysical cognition—and to recognize the historical dimension these issues inevitably involve.

NOTES

1. Ernst Cassirer, *The Philosophy of the Enlightenment*, 1932 (Boston: Beacon Press, 1951), 197.

2. Michel Foucault, "Un cours inédit," *Magazine litteraire* (Paris), May 1984, p. 36.

3. All translations from Kant's works are my own, and citations are to volume and page number in *Kants Gesammelte Schriften*. Berlin: Ausgabe der königlich preussischen Akademie der Wissenschaften, 1910–. Standard English translations are also listed below. The following abbreviations will be used:

EF   Zum ewigen Frieden (1795)
            "Perpetual Peace," in Kant, *Writings on Practical Philosophy*, ed.
            and trans. Mary J. Gregor. New York: Cambridge University Press,
            1996.

G   Grundlegung zur Metaphysik der Sitten (1785)
            "Groundwork of the Metaphysics of Morals," in *Kant's
            Writings on Practical Philosophy*, ed. and trans. Mary J. Gregor. New
            York: Cambridge University Press, 1996.

IAG   Idee zu einer allgemeinen Geschichte in weltbürgerlicher Absicht
            (1784)
            "Idea for a Universal History with a Cosmopolitan Purpose,"
            trans. H. B. Nisbet, in *Kant's Political Writings*, ed. Reiss. Second
            enlarged edition. Cambridge: Cambridge University Press, 1991.

KpV   Kritik der praktischen Vernunft (1788)
            "Critique of Practical Reason," in *Writings on Practical Philosophy*.

KrV A/B   Kritik der reinen Vernunft (1781/1787), ed. Raymund Schmidt.
            Hamburg: Meiner, 1956
            Immanuel Kant's Critique of Pure Reason, trans. by Norman
            Kemp Smith. New York: St. Martin's, 1963. Cited by first edition (A)
            and second edition (B) page numbers.

KU   Kritik der Urteilskraft (1790)
            Critique of Judgment, trans. Werner Pluhar. Indianapolis:
            Hackett, 1987.

MA   Muthmasslicher Anfang der Menschengeschichte (1786)
            "Conjectures on the Beginning of Human History," in *Kant's
            Political Writings*.

R   Religion innerhalb der Grenzen der blossen Vernunft (1793–94)
            "Religion within the Boundaries of Mere Reason," trans.
            George di Giovanni in Immanuel Kant's *Writings on Religion and
            Rational Theology*, ed. Allen Wood and George di Giovanni. New
            York: Cambridge University Press, 1996.

RH   Rezensionen von Johann Gottfried Herders *Ideen zur Philosophie der
            Geschichte der Menschheit* (1784–85)
            Reviews of Herder's *Ideas on the Philosophy of the History of
            Mankind*, in Kant's *Political Writings*.

MS   Metaphysik der Sitten (1797)
            "Metaphysics of Morals," in *Writings on Practical Philosophy*.

O   Was heisst: Sich im Denken orientieren? (1786)
            "What does it mean to orient oneself in thinking?" trans. Allen
            W. Wood, in *Writings on Religion and Rational Theology*.

SF   Streit der Fakultäten (1797)
            "Conflict of the Faculties," trans. Mary J. Gregor, in *Writings on
            Religion and Rational Theology*.

TP   Über den Gemeinspruch: Das mag in der Theorie richtig sein, taugt aber nicht für die Praxis (1793)
          "On the Common Saying: That May Be True in Theory, But It Does Not Work in Practice," in *Writings on Practical Philosophy.*

VA   Anthropologie in pragmatischer Hinsicht (1798)
          Anthropology from a Pragmatic Standpoint, trans. Mary J. Gregor. Dordrecht: Nijhoff, 1974.

WA   Beantwortung der Frage: Was ist Aufklärung? (1784)
          "What is Enlightenment?" in *Writings on Practical Philosophy.*

4. Jean-Jacques Rousseau, *Discourse on the Origin of Inequality, The Social Contract and Discourses* (New York: Dutton, 1950), 208–9.

5. See Jean-François Lyotard, *The Postmodern Condition,* trans. G. Bennington and Brian Massouri (Minneapolis: University of Minnesota Press, 1984).

6. *Marx Engels Werke* (Berlin: Dietz, 1956) 19:8; cf. *Selected Works* (Moscow: Progress, 1968), 182.

7. As is stressed by G. A. Cohen, *Karl Marx's Theory of History: A Defence* (Princeton, N.J.: Princeton University Press, 1978), chap. 4, expecially 88–105.

8. Compare Rousseau, *Discourse on the Origin of Inequality, Social Contract and Discourses,* trans. G. D. H. Cole (New York: Dutton, 1950), 253–55.

9. Compare Rousseau, *Discourse on the Origin of Inequality,* 247–53.

10. Allen W. Wood, "Unsociable Sociability: The Anthropological Basis of Kantian Ethics," *Philosophical Topics* 19.1 (1991).

11. Hegel, *Elements of the Philosophy of Right,* ed. A. W. Wood, trans. H. B. Nisbet (Cambridge: Cambridge University Press, 1992), § 322.

12. Engels, *Anti-Dühring: Herr Eugen Dühring's Revolution in Science* (Moscow: Progress, 192), chap. 9, pp. 118–32.

13. Kant does hold that common ownership of land was characteristic of pre-agricultural societies, but such societies also lie outside a condition of right, since they were prior to the founding of states. Kant does recognize the existence of present-day nonagricultural societies where land is owned in common by the whole people; but in order to regard this as rightful he thinks we need to interpret it as the result of an agreement between the citizens to alienate their private holdings (MS 6:251; cf. 6:265–66). We must do this because we have attained to the standpoint of agricultural society, hence of the immutable principles of right, in terms of which alone the institutions of pre-agricultural peoples can be understood as rightful.

3

Robert Paul Wolff

The Completion of Kant's Moral Theory in the Tenets of the Rechtslehre

THE UNRESOLVED PROBLEM OF THE GRUNDLEGUNG

The announced aim of Kant's moral philosophy, as stated most clearly and unambiguously in the *Foundations of the Metaphysics of Morals,* is to discover unconditionally valid principles of practical reason. Kant conceives his task as falling into three parts, exactly corresponding to the three sections of the *Foundations.* First, he must identify and state the Moral Law, the highest principle of practical reason, by which all rational agents, merely in virtue of being rational agents, are bound. Kant calls that Highest Moral Law, in the form in which it is experienced by imperfectly rational creatures such as ourselves, the Categorical Imperative. In the first section of the *Foundations,* Kant extracts the formula for the Categorical Imperative from a number of commonplace moral judgments that he shares—or so he believes—with his readers. In this way, he hopes to persuade his readers that they already embrace the Categorical Imperative, though not perhaps in the rigorous formulation he presents.

Secondly, Kant must demonstrate that the Highest Moral Principle can be derived, entirely *a priori,* from a conceptual analysis of Practical Reason. In other words, he must show that the bindingness of the Highest Moral Principle follows analytically and necessarily from the mere fact of being a rational agent. To put the same point slightly differently, he must show that someone capable of action, capable of being an agent, will necessarily act in accordance with the Highest Moral Principle, indeed will act out of respect for the Highest Moral Principle, merely in virtue of being an agent, just as a person capable of theoretical reason will, in virtue of that capacity, reason in accordance with the highest principle of theoretical reason—the law of contradiction. Kant's demonstration of this powerful proposition is contained in an extremely compressed and difficult passage of twenty paragraphs in the second section of the *Foundations*.

Finally, in light of the teaching of the first Critique, Kant must connect up his conclusions concerning the principles guiding the choices of rational agents with our experience of ourselves as causally determined beings in the realm of appearance. The conclusions of the first Critique rule out any possibility of demonstrating that we are rational moral agents, for that would constitute knowledge of ourselves as noumenal beings, or things-in-themselves. But Kant *does* claim to be able to demonstrate two subordinate propositions that, taken together, come as close as he believes epistemologically possible to the knowledge that we are moral agents: First, that it is logically possible that we be moral agents (the resolution of the conflict between free will and determinism, so-called); and second, that insofar as we undertake to deliberate and choose, we must act as though we know that we are free, which is to say, as though we know that we are rational moral agents.

In sum, then, the *Foundations* attempts to *identify* and *state* the principle governing the actions of rational agents; to *derive* that principle from an *a priori* analysis of rational agency, thereby proving that all rational agents, simply in virtue of their rational agency, necessarily act out of respect for that principle; and to *demonstrate* that we, as conditioned beings in the realm of appearance, must act as though we know ourselves to be rational agents, even though such knowledge is, strictly speaking, unavailable to us.

It is, of course, a matter of considerable controversy whether Kant succeeds in achieving all three, or indeed any, of these goals. The first is the least controversial, for it merely involves showing that Kant and his audience of north Prussian Pietists share a belief in a particularly rigoristic formalism. It is always open to modern readers to excuse themselves from the conclusions of the first section of the *Foundations* by denying that they share the presystematic moral convictions out of which Kant extracts the Categorical Imperative.[1] The achievement of the third goal, involving as it does the entire complex metaphysical and epistemological theoretical structure of the first Critique, is best left to one side in an essay such as this. But the second of Kant's undertakings warrants our closest attention, for it is here that we find the greatest controversy arising among students of Kant's moral philosophy.

Kant claims to show that certain very general principles of consistency in willing follow from a purely conceptual analysis of rational willing as such. To summarize his text briefly, but not too misleadingly, Kant argues that when an agent gives reasons to itself,[2] it implicitly commits itself, as a matter of logic, to the proposition that such reasons are equally good reasons for any other agent similarly circumstanced. This requirement of consistency in willing can be expressed quite generally in the form of a command, which reason gives to itself, to adopt only those rules of action ("maxims" in Kant's terminology) the reasons for the adoption of which are equally compelling reasons for any rational agent as such. Or, in the more familiar language of the first formulation of the Categorical Imperative: "Act only according to that maxim by which you can at the same time will that it should become a universal law."[3]

The controversy surrounding Kant's derivation of the Categorical Imperative concerns *not* the validity of the derivation but its significance. Many students of Kant's philosophy, and more broadly many students of moral and political philosophy, will readily grant that some principle of formal consistency of willing can be derived *a priori* from an analysis of agency and rationality as such. Much the same sort of analysis of theoretical reason yields the formal principle of noncontradiction.

But logicians unanimously insist that the law of contradiction serves merely as a negative or necessary condition of theoretical truth. A proposition that violates the law of contradiction (such as, for example, the assertion that triangles have four angles) must, as a matter of logic, be false. But neither the law of contradiction nor any other logical law can tell us which of a set of mutually inconsistent, but internally consistent, propositions is true. "Some bachelors are married" may be ruled out by logic, but as between "All bachelors are happy" and "Some bachelors are unhappy" logic cannot decide. Something else—experience, or perhaps the conditions of a possible experience in general, in short Kant's "third thing"—must be introduced to distinguish the true consistent propositions from the false consistent propositions.

What makes Kant's moral theory so controversial, especially in regard to his second undertaking, is the extraordinary claim that the purely *a priori* formal principle of consistency in willing is sufficient to identify, from among the host of possible moral rules, just those that reason commands, and that therefore constitute the substance of morality.

On the face of it, this claim is completely incompatible with the thrust of Kant's philosophy. The central thesis of the *Critique of Pure Reason* is that unconditionally universal knowledge of the independently real is impossible. Kant came to this conclusion at least as early as 1772, when, in a famous letter to his close friend Marcus Herz, he rejected the doctrine he had recently set forth in his *Inaugural Dissertation* of 1770 on the grounds that there was no way the mind could possibly acquire *a priori* knowledge of the independently real. Eventually, of course, he worked his way around to the mature critical thesis that our a priori knowledge is all conditioned, not unconditioned—that it is knowledge only under the condition that its scope is restricted to things as they appear to us rather than as they are in themselves.

So Kant knows, better than anyone else in the entire history of philosophy, that it is fruitless to attempt to establish substantive, nontrivial propositions entirely *a priori*. And yet, here he is in the *Foundations* claiming to do precisely that! It is scant wonder that the attempt has been so controversial.

Kant actually tries three times in the *Foundations* to establish the universal validity of unconditional moral principles. It is instructive for our purposes to review these attempts briefly and remind ourselves why they fail.

The first attempt appears in the second section of the *Foundations* immediately after the derivation of the formula of the Categorical Imperative.[4] "We shall now enumerate some duties," Kant says rather abruptly, and then we are presented with the famous four examples of maxims or subjective policies to be tested for validity by the Categorical Imperative: suicide, false promising, self-indulgent laziness, and lack of generosity. In each case, Kant posits an individual who has formulated a maxim, or subjective rule for action (such as "When life offers a prospect of more pain than pleasure, to end my life by suicide," or "when in need of money that I have no realistic hope of being able to repay, to borrow the money and falsely promise to repay it," and so forth). This individual is, rather charmingly, imagined by Kant still to have a sufficiently vigorous conscience to ask himself (it is always a man, of course) whether such a policy could consistently be willed as a universal law, which is, for Kant, a rather technical way of asking whether the reasons I give to myself are equally good reasons for any agent similarly circumstanced, merely in virtue of being a moral agent.

In all four cases, of course, Kant concludes that the answer is no. Neither suicide, nor false promising, nor slothful failure to develop one's talents, nor systematic ungenerosity is a rational policy. In each case, he claims, it involves some sort of inconsistency of willing.

Kant's arguments in the first and third cases are hopelessly inadequate. Both make explicit and utterly unjustified appeal to the supposed objective natural purpose of some human capacity or psychological tendency. Since Kant himself has offered the most profound criticism of such teleological arguments in the *Critique of Judgment*, it is rather incomprehensible that he would invoke them here. The less said about them the better.

The argument concerning ungenerosity is rather interesting, but it is ultimately inadequate. For a variety of reasons, most scholarly and philosophical attention has focused on the second argument, concerning false promising. The argument Kant actually gives is, as countless readers have recognized, quite worthless. "For the universality of a law which says that anyone who believes himself to be in need could promise what he pleased with the intention of not fulfilling it would make the promise itself and the end to be accomplished by it impossible; no one would believe what has been promised to him but would only laugh at any such assertion as vain pretense."

This won't do, for several different independently sufficient reasons. First of all, it is factually false, as many skilled and persistent liars have discovered. Try telling a modern corporation that it will never again be extended bank credit should it ever file for Chapter 11 bankruptcy! But quite apart from the sheer falsity of Kant's claim, he himself has ruled out such "heteronymous" appeals to consequences. If the maxim of false promising is to be condemned, then it must be shown to involve some sort of internal inconsistency of willing.

The standard reconstruction of the false promising example, with which I entirely agree, is to construe promising as a social practice defined by a system of implicit, but clearly understood, rules, among which rather prominently featured is a rule against false promising. On this view, when I utter the words "I promise" in the appropriate social context, I am implicitly endorsing, or committing myself to, or willing, in Kant's language, the entire system of rules that constitute the practice of promising. To say "I promise" while also adopting the maxim of falsely promising is thus to will a rule and its contradictory, and thereby to be involved in inconsistent willing. Since the Highest Moral Principle, derived *a priori* from an analysis of rational agency as such, proscribes contradictory willing (just as the Law of Contradiction proscribes contradictory judging), the maxim of false promising is shown to be incompatible with the Categorical Imperative. According to Kant, a perfectly rational agent (such as an angel) would never engage in false promising, any more than a perfectly rational cognitive subject would ever assert a self-contradictory proposition. A being like ourselves, who is capable of rational agency but is not perfectly rational, will experience the inconsistency of the maxim of false promising as a categorical command never to make false promises.

The example of false promising is the closest Kant ever comes to establishing a substantive moral principle purely *a priori*. But it takes only a little reflection to recognize that the injunction against false promising is not actually a categorical substantive moral command. Rather, it is hypothetical in form. What Kant's argument, suitably reconstructed, demonstrates is that false promising is incompatible with the practice of promise-making, from which it follows that we must, in all consistency, choose either not to endorse, participate in, and commit ourselves to the practice of promising or else not to make false promises. But there is nothing in Kant's argument to dissuade us from forswearing the institution of promising altogether. Indeed, there is even nothing in Kant's argument that counts against refraining from participating in the practice of promising but deliberately misleading others into mistakenly believing that one *is* participating, and, in the context of that deliberate deception, uttering the words "I promise" when having no intention of doing what one is pretending to commit oneself to doing.[5]

The crucial point, as we shall see presently, is that Kant has no plausible *a priori* argument in support of the claim that a rational agent will necessarily enter into the practice of promising, or more generally into whatever overarching practice is implicit in the truthful use of language, from which the obligation in particular to participate in the practice of promise-making might be derived. In effect, Kant is at this point in his exposition unwittingly assuming that the agents of whom he is speaking have some minimal commitment to honorable social interaction with which, as he quite rightly argues, false promising is logically incompatible. To the thorough reprobate who simply rejects such a commitment, however, Kant has no valid objection.

Kant himself appears to recognize the inadequacy of the four examples as a demonstration of the substantive import of the Categorical Imperative, for several pages later he makes a second more systematic attempt. Speaking generally, Kant always distinguishes between the form and the content of a judgment, usually attributing the form to the pre-existing structure of the mind itself, and the content or matter to experience. Thus, in the first Critique, Kant attributes the spatiotemporal form of perception to the mind, and the sensory content to experience; and, at a higher level of analysis, he attributes the categorial structure of our cognitive judgments—their causal or substantial structure—to the mind, and the perceptual content of those judgments to experience.

In analogous fashion, Kant distinguishes between the form and content of practical judgments. The form is the universality or particularity, the unconditionality or conditionality with which the practical judgment is asserted. The content, or matter, is, in the case of practical judgments, the end or goal at which the judgment aims. For example, in the practical judgment, "Seeking as you do to safeguard your principal in your investments, put your money in government bonds," the form of the judgment is that of a hypothetical or conditioned imperative. It commands, but only on condition that the agent to whom the command is directed fits the statement of the condition under which the command is valid (i.e., on the condition that the agent does in fact seek to safeguard the principal of its investment). The matter or content of the practical judgment is then the goal at which the judgment aims, namely safeguarding the principal of an investment.

Hypothetical imperatives do not command absolutely or universally or unconditionally because there is no necessity that every agent meet their limiting conditions. *If* I seek to safeguard my principal, then, to be sure, the judgment commands me to put my money in government bonds. But if, let us say, I seek instead to maximize my yield, even at the risk of some diminution of principal, then this practical judgment does not speak to me.

In order for a practical judgment to command absolutely, it is not enough that it specify a condition to which, as a matter of fact, all actual agents conform. There are such imperatives, according to Kant— namely those whose condition is, "Seeking as you do your own happiness . . ." Kant believes it to be a law of nature that all human beings seek their own happiness, but seeking one's happiness does not follow from the nature of rational agency as such. Hence it is logically possible for there to be rational agents who do not seek their own happiness, and for whom, therefore, hypothetical imperatives with such a condition would not be relevant.

At this point in his discussion, Kant recognizes, as indeed he should, that only a practical judgment with both form and content can provide substantive moral guidance. There *is* a form that necessarily commands the universal assent of rational agents, namely consistency. If there were also a content—an aim or end or goal—that all rational agents necessarily take as their own, then Kant would be in a position to claim that he could produce universally binding, unconditional practical principles. But is there such an end or goal, such a content? If even happiness will not do, despite the fact that, as Kant himself insists, all human beings do seek it, what can possibly be advanced as a candidate for a universal end?

As the example of happiness shows, any candidate for the role of universal end must, in some sense, be an end independently of the desires, wishes, aims, or goals of individual agents. It must, we might say, adapting Kant's language from the first Critique, be an *end in itself*, by which I mean something that is an end by virtue of its own nature, and that must therefore, in all consistency and rationality, be recognized as an end by any agent.

In perhaps the most famous passage in any of his ethical writings, Kant claims to find just such a universal end or end-in-itself:

> But suppose that there were something the existence of which in itself had absolute worth, something which, as an end in itself, could be a ground of definite laws. In it and only in it could lie the ground of a possible categorical imperative, i.e., of a practical law.
>
> Now, I say, man and, in general, every rational being exists as an end in himself and not merely as a means to be arbitrarily used by this or that will. In all his actions, whether they are directed to himself or to other rational beings, he must always be regarded at the same time as an end. All objects of inclinations have only a conditional worth, for if the inclinations and needs founded on them did not exist, their object would be without worth. The inclinations themselves as the sources of needs, however, are so lacking in absolute worth that the universal wish of every rational being must be indeed to free himself completely from them. Therefore, the worth of any objects to be obtained by our actions is at all times conditional. Beings whose existence does not depend upon our will but on nature, if they are not rational beings, have only a relative worth as means and are therefore called "things"; on the other hand, rational beings are designated "persons" because their nature indicates that they are ends in themselves, i.e., things that may not be used merely as means. Such a being is thus an object of respect and, so far, restricts all choice. Such beings are not merely subjective ends whose existence as a result of our action has a worth for us, but are objective ends, i.e., beings whose existence in itself is an end.[6]

This is clearly the right move on Kant's part. He has demonstrated that universality is the formal precondition of rationality in willing; if he can now show that all agents, insofar as they are rational, take certain ends as *their* ends, then, applying the analytic rule that the agent who wills the end wills the means (a rule that follows directly from an analysis of what it is to will an end), Kant will be able to derive a system of substantive, universal moral principles that are unconditionally valid.

Unfortunately, the claim that humanity is an end in itself, although uplifting, is, when we examine it more closely, incoherent. To say that something is an agent's end is to say that the agent seeks to bring about that something, or perhaps that the agent seeks to bring that something into existence. Thus, to say that my end is the downfall of the American government is to say that I seek to bring about the downfall of the American government. To say that an architect's end is an office building is to say that the architect seeks to bring the office building into existence. What, then, can it mean to say that *humanity* is some agent's end?

Surely it cannot mean that the agent seeks to bring humanity into existence—leaving to one side the particular set of willings involved in procreation or cloning. We might suppose that it means treating humanity (i.e., the capacity for rational agency), whether in myself or in others, *with respect*. But attractive as such an injunction is, it cannot serve the logical function of providing the matter for a purely rational form of willing, unless we already know what it means to respect humanity.

A standard interpretation of Kant's formula has it that "respecting humanity" in another agent means "taking that agent's ends as my own ends," which is to say, according it (we are still speaking of noumenal agents) the respect of giving its independent ends weight in our own deliberations, independently of our own ends. On this reading, when I treat a slave as a means only, and not also as an end-in-him (or her) self, I am using the slave as a means to my ends, while taking no account of, making no allowance for, failing to respect, the slave's independent purposes or ends as a rational agent in its own right.

But this cannot be what Kant has in mind, for, as it stands, it makes no distinction between the morally acceptable or permissible ends of agents (myself and others) and the morally unacceptable or impermissible ends. Surely Kant does not mean to suggest that I show respect for humanity in a sadist when I respect—that is to say, allow for, make room for, accommodate myself to—his or her plans to inflict wanton pain on a victim! Obviously, this most plausible interpretation of Kant's formula of humanity as an end-in-itself makes sense only so long as some way can be found to distinguish proper from improper ends.

But that was supposed to be the task that the formula would perform! It was designed to identify an end, or a group of ends, that any rational agent as such would take as its ends, thereby fleshing out the hollow formula of consistency in willing. Now, it appears that the formula of humanity as an end-in-itself requires some prior criterion of the rational acceptability of ends before it can even be put forward hypothetically as a candidate for the solution to Kant's problem.

Thus, Kant's first two attempts to extract substantive moral principles from his purely formal analysis of rational willing fail because of two fundamental problems: First, his failure to demonstrate that rational agents have a standing, unconditional obligation to enter into, or participate in, rule-governed social practices in the context of which the notion of contradictory willing can be fleshed out and given substance; and second, his failure to identify obligatory ends, adoption of which follows necessarily from the mere fact of being a rational agent, and the existence of which would, in a different but equivalent way, provide substantial content for the purely formal principle of consistency in willing. Kant's *third* attempt in the *Foundations* is directed precisely at compensating for both of these failures—namely, his invocation of the social contract tradition of political theory under the guise of what he calls a "Realm of Ends."

> By *realm* I understand the systematic union of different rational beings through common laws. Because laws determine ends with regard to their universal validity, if we abstract from the personal difference of rational beings and thus from all content of their private ends, we can think of a whole of all ends in systematic connection, a whole of rational beings as ends in themselves as well as of the particular ends that each may set for himself. This is a realm of ends, which is possible on the aforesaid principles. For all rational beings stand under the law that each of them should treat himself and all others never merely as means but in every case also as an end in himself. Thus there arises a systematic union of rational beings through common objective laws. This is a realm that may be called a realm of ends (certainly only an ideal), because what these laws have in view is just the relation of these beings to each other as ends and means.
>
> A rational being belongs to the realm of ends as a member when he gives universal laws in it while also himself subject to these laws. He belongs to it as sovereign when he, as legislating, is subject to the will of no other. The rational being must regard himself always as legislative in a realm of ends possible through the freedom of the will, whether he belongs to it as member or as sovereign. He cannot maintain the latter position merely through the maxims of his will but only when he is a completely independent being without need and with power adequate to his will.
>
> Morality, therefore, consists in the relation of every action to that legislation through which alone a realm of ends is possible. This legislation must be found in every rational being. It must be able to arise from his will, whose principle then is to take no action according to any maxim which would be inconsistent with its being a universal

law and thus to act only so that the will through its maxims could regard itself at the same time as universally lawgiving.[7]

This language is, of course, a direct echo of Rousseau's characterization of the republic brought into existence by the social contract.[8] It specifies the procedure by which a collection of self-interested individuals can transform themselves into a republic by entering into the mutual agreement referred to as a social contract.

Even after they have done so, there remains the problem of determining what substantive laws this body politic will enact. Rousseau begins boldly enough, arguing that a true social contract, *contra* Locke or Hobbes, involves the giving up of private interests and the universal adoption of a new goal or purpose or interest, the General Good. Only a group of individuals unambiguously aiming at the general good can be said to have a general will, says Rousseau, and only such a group has the moral right to require that its members abide by collective decisions.

The positing of the general good as the aim or end or goal of the general will is, on Rousseau's part, an attempt to solve the same problem that Kant would later address through the identification of humanity as an end in itself. The general good is to provide content for the otherwise purely formal requirement that the general will express itself through universal laws rather than particular commands. But Rousseau, unfortunately, is no more successful than Kant was later to be in providing content for the laws of the ideal republic.

Furthermore, what is explicit in Rousseau's doctrine remains implicit in Kant's, namely that the theory of the social contract is thoroughly hypothetical in form. *If* individuals enter into a social contract, *then* they will be bound, collectively, by their general will, provided some content can be found for that will. But should an individual decline to join the social contract, preferring instead to continue in a state of nature vis-à-vis his or her neighbors, there is, or so it would appear, no argument that either Rousseau or Kant can put forward to persuade that individual that reason requires participation in a collective agreement to establish the framework of a legitimate state.

At the close of the *Foundations*, despite Kant's introduction of the evocative notion of humanity as an end in itself, and his invocation of a Rousseauean conception of a republic regulated by a social contract, we are left with the two problems outlined earlier: First, how to demonstrate that rational agents as such must, in all consistency, enter into collective agreements that establish structures of social practices in the context of which substantial meaning can be given to the notion of contradictory willing; and second, how to demonstrate that rational agents who have thus constituted themselves as a realm of ends or republic will, *qua* rational, arrive at a single universal, necessary, and therefore objective set of substantive laws as the content of their collective rational willing.[9]

Kant's most successful attempt to solve these two problems appears not in the *Foundations* but in the *Metaphysics of Morals* for which the earlier work is intended *as* a foundation or groundwork. Before turning to that text, however, it might be worth pausing for a moment to observe the relationship between the unresolved problems just stated and the work of the most prominent contemporary political theorist, John Rawls. In his widely read work, *A Theory of Justice*, Rawls undertakes to demonstrate that rationally self-interested individuals, placed in a situation designed to mimic that of noumenal agents, will necessarily choose to commit themselves to a set of general principles regulating the basic structure of any society of which they may be members. By virtue of the conditions of deliberation—characterized fancifully by Rawls as consisting in a "veil of ignorance"—the choices made by these individuals will be universal and necessary, hence objective, and will at the same time be sufficiently specific to yield substantive social imperatives.[10]

Rawls's treatment differs fundamentally from that of Kant, of course, inasmuch as Rawls posits rationally *self*-interested, which is to say in Kant's language *heteronymous*, individuals. Nevertheless, as Rawls has refined and revised his theory, he has moved more and more in the direction of a Kantian reinterpretation of his central ideas. Rawls's theory is a good deal more technically sophisticated than Kant's, involving as it does notions drawn from modern neoclassical economic theory and the branch of mathematics known as Game Theory. But, not surprisingly, Kant's theory is a great deal more profound than Rawls's, for whereas Rawls posits a society of rationally self-interested agents, thereby giving up entirely any attempt to identify unconditional principles of morality, Kant holds firm to the idea of rational agents as such, abstracting even from their self-interest, and appealing only to what can be derived from their character as agents, which is to say from the fact that they possess practical reason.

THE RESOLUTION OF THE PROBLEM
IN THE *RECHTSLEHRE*

It is in part I of the *Metaphysics of Morals*, the "Theory of Right" or "Theory of Justice" (*Rechtslehre*) that Kant finally mounts a full-scale frontal assault on the problems left unresolved at the end of the *Foundations*. This fact—assuming for a moment that my reading of the situation is correct—has a very interesting significance. Contrary to Kant's own conception of the relationship between his moral and political theory, it would appear that they are not separate and co-equal branches of the Metaphysics of Morals. Rather, they are a single integrated theory, in which the central thesis of the political theory is required to complete the argument of the moral theory. In this regard, it is suggestive to compare Kant both with Rousseau, who influenced him, and with Rawls, whom he in turn influenced.

Kant begins the *Rechtslehre* by introducing the concept of justice. In a section entitled "What is Justice?" he writes:

> The concept of justice, insofar as it relates to an obligation corre-sponding to it (that is, the moral concept of justice), applies [only under the following conditions]. First, it applies only to the external and—what is more—practical relationship of one person to another in which their actions can exert an influence on each other (directly or indirectly). Second, the concept applies only to the relationship of a will to another person's will, not to his wishes or desires (or even just his needs), which are the concern of acts of benevolence and charity. Third, the concept of justice does not take into consideration the matter of the will, that is, the end that a person intends to accomplish by means of the object that he wills; for example, we do not ask whether someone who buys wares from me for his own business will profit from the transaction. Instead, in applying the concept of justice we take into consideration only the form of the relationship between the wills insofar as they are regarded as free, and whether the action of one of them can be conjoined with the freedom of the other in accordance with a universal law.
>
> Justice is therefore the aggregate of those conditions under which the will of one person can be conjoined with the will of another in accordance with a universal law of freedom.[11]

Thus, as Kant states two paragraphs later, "the universal law of justice is: act externally in such a way that the free use of your will is compatible with the freedom of everyone according to a universal law."[12]

Kant glosses this, almost immediately, as follows:

> [T]he concept of justice can be held to consist immediately of the possibility of the conjunction of universal reciprocal coercion with the freedom of everyone. Just as justice in general has as its object only

what is external in actions, so strict justice, inasmuch as it contains no ethical elements, requires no determining grounds of the will besides those that are purely external, for only then is it pure and not confused with any prescriptions of virtue.[13]

There are a number of problems in Kant's doctrine here, arising principally from his insistence on speaking as though the distinction between the noumenal and the phenomenal (or the internal and the external, as he puts it here) can actually be drawn *within* experience. All such claims, implicit or otherwise, are, of course, strictly incompatible with the teaching of the first Critique, but since that particular problem does not play a central role in my discussion, I shall simply ignore it, and refer the reader to other places where I have explored it at length.[14] The real difficulty for my present purposes is the fact that this conception of justice as justified universal reciprocal coercion does not provide the unconditional *a priori* substantive content for moral principles for which we are searching.

The problem, very simply, is that despite the appearance of Kant's formulation, which is cast in categorical language, the injunction is still hypothetical. IF you choose to coerce others, THEN you yourself must submit to a like coercion. Note, by the way, that it is as yet unclear how narrowly this injunction constrains us, even should we choose to coerce. It would appear that there is a very wide range of reciprocal coercions compatible with the injunction, including some that Kant would presumably not find attractive. For example, would his principle be compatible with a system of laws that authorizes blood feuds and duels?

But even if Kant can demonstrate that a group of individuals, by committing themselves to the fundamental principle of justice, thereby so severely constrain their subsequent legislative choices that only a single system of laws is compatible with that principle, that system will still have a merely hypothetical status, for it will command only those who have chosen to enter into the social contract. What Kant needs— what he has needed from the very start—is an argument designed to show that failure to enter a social contract can only issue from an internal contradiction in willing. In short, Kant must show that a rational agent *as such* necessarily seeks to enter into a social contract, and does so as soon as possible.

To return for a moment to the failed example of false promising from the *Foundations*, if Kant could show that the institution of promising is required by the fundamental principle of justice (not, one would imagine, too difficult a task), and if Kant could also show that a rational agent as such necessarily enters a social contract, then he could conclude that rational agents as such are not only, in all consistency, required by mere reason alone to keep such promises as they make, but that they are also required, by the dictates of *a priori* reason, to adopt the practice of promise-making. He then really could conclude, as he wishes to, that false promising is an example of contradictory willing all the way down.

I do not believe that Kant accomplishes these extraordinary tasks. If I did, I would, in all consistency, forthwith embrace his ethical theory. But I think I can show that he makes an extremely imaginative stab at the second of them in the *Rechtslehre*, where, as I shall suggest, he advances an argument designed to show that we have an uncond-itional obligation to enter a social contract.

The key to his argument is the concept of property:

> An object is mine *de jure* (*meum juris*) if I am so bound to it that anyone else who uses it without my consent thereby injures me. The subjective condition of the possibility of the use of an object is *possession*.
>
> An external thing is mine, however, only if I can assume that it is still possible for me to be injured by someone else's use of the thing even when it is not in my possession. Consequently, there would be a self-contradiction in the concept of possession if it did not have two meanings, namely *sensible* possession and *intelligible* possession. Sensible possession means the physical possession of an object, whereas intelligible possession means the purely de jure possession of the same object.[15]

Kant goes on to discuss the distinction between sensible and intelligible possession in ways that are thoroughly problematic, involving as they seem to the legitimacy of a distinction between the phenomenal and the noumenal *within* experience. We can leave that difficulty aside for our purposes, for which it is of course the concept of intelligible possession, or possession *de jure*, that is relevant. Almost immediately, Kant states what he calls the Juridical Postulate of Practical Reason, which asserts that "it must be possible to have any and every external object of my will as my property" (*Rechtslehre*, p. 52, KGS 246). In other words, as Kant explains, "a maxim according to which, if it were made into a law, an object of will would have to be in itself (objectively) ownerless (*res nullius*) conflicts with Law and justice."

Before analyzing how Kant justifies this postulate, and uses it to accomplish his fundamental aim in his moral theory, it is worth pausing to remind ourselves just what is being claimed here, for a great deal of contemporary importance is at stake. It is not too much to say

that Kant is here laying the groundwork for the refutation of all manner
of environmentalist and ecological doctrines, as well as a number of
nationalist doctrines based upon a conception of the objectively
privileged territory, homeland, or place of a people. Kant himself, of
course, is looking backward, not forward. His intention is to destroy
the last vestiges of feudalism, and lay the groundwork for a thoroughly
rational commodification of natural objects.

What the principle says is that anything can, in principle, be
someone's possession. There is nothing unownable. It does not follow,
needless to say, that everything is actually owned; only that there is
nothing—no tree, no river, no plot of land, no species of animal or
plant, no planet, no solar system—that by its nature resists ownership,
that is such that it cannot be the rightful possession of some individual
or group of individuals. And possession here implies rightful use of the
possessed thing, by the owner, in pursuit of the owner's purposes, and
also alienation or legal transfer of the possession of the possessed thing
to another rational agent.

Needless to say, this conception flies in the face of the precapitalist
traditions against which Kant is arguing. To suggest that the Earl of
Northumberland *owns* Northumberland, and can sell it to the King of
France, should he choose, is fundamentally to undermine the notion of
hereditary family possession implied in the familiar allusion to the earl
as simply "Northumberland," as in one of Shakespeare's plays. Donald
Trump, on the other hand, can perfectly well sell the Trump Shuttle to
Delta, should he find himself a bit short of cash.

In a more modern vein, any suggestion that the human race stands
in a symbiotic, or fiduciary, or other moral relationship to nature is
completely incompatible with Kant's postulate. Equally incompatible,
of course, is any form of religious or quasi-religious privileging of
species or things other than the human species or other species of
rational agents, should they exist. In the coin of Kant's Realm of Ends,
the principle "Treat humanity always as an end, and never simply as a
means" is inscribed on the obverse. On the reverse, however, is found
the correlative principle, "Anything else may be treated as a means
only."

Kant now offers an extremely strong interpretation of the concept
of intelligible possession. "A thing is externally mine," he says, "if it is
such that any prevention of my use of it would constitute an injury to
me even if it is not in my possession (that is, I am not the holder of the
object)." What Kant is speaking of here, as he indicates immediately, is
intelligible possession, or *de jure* possession. The language might lead
us to conclude that Kant is deliberately trying to construct a justification for the most thoroughgoingly unregulated period of capitalist

expansion, but that would be a trifle hasty, I think. Kant's postulate is perfectly compatible with positive legislation to constrain the ways in which property owners deal with their property—zoning laws, and so forth. What the postulate says is that all such laws must be acts of a legislature constituted by a social contract. They cannot be deduced, independently of legitimate legislation, from the nature of the objects themselves. It is not that an owner must be allowed to do with his or her property whatever he or she wills, but that such freedom must at least be possible, in order for there to be *de jure* possession.

Having defined the concept of *de jure* possession, Kant immediately makes what is for him, by this late stage in the unfolding of his system, an entirely predictable move. He asks for a deduction of the concept of purely *de jure* possession of an external object (what he calls, parenthetically, *possessio noumenon*). That is to say, he seeks to show that the concept finds legitimate employment, indeed must find legitimate employment, within the realm of experience.

Put as simply and clearly as I am able, Kant's argument for the possibility of *de jure* possession is this: Since I am a phenomenal being— since I am, in other words, a rational agent that manifests its agency in the realm of appearance—my will at least potentially requires the cooperation of nature for the fulfillment of its purposes, whatever they may turn out to be. Even if I adopt the extreme stoicism of an Epictetus, seeking only virtue and not the powers or pleasures of the world, nevertheless I shall find myself compelled to employ some portions of nature as means to my ends.

But the laws of nature are such that I can use a portion of nature as a means to my ends only by appropriating it, and thereby excluding others from a like appropriation of those same portions. In short, for the accomplishment of what I will, for the enactment of my maxims, I require *property*.

Were I an incorporeal being, not manifesting my agency in space and time, I might have neither the need for, nor indeed the possibility of, property. Imagine, for example, that I were merely a noumenal rational agent whose acts consisted in the contemplation of pure ideas or the endless elaboration of the relationships among abstract logical constructs.[16] In that case, my appropriation of *modus ponens* or the law of the excluded middle would in no way exclude others, for the contemplation of a timeless truth of logic does not require that others be denied its use or enjoyment. But because we *are* phenomenal beings whose agency is manifested in space and time, *my* appropriation at least potentially excludes *you*.

Kant's argument thus far can be summarized in a series of conditionals, preceded by a declarative assertion that comes as close as he thinks possible to the flat claim that I am a rational agent. The argument looks like this:

1. Insofar as I act, I must assume, though I cannot know it, that I am a rational agent, which is to say, that I am free. (This is the conclusion of the third section of the *Foundations*.)
2. If I am a rational agent, then willing an end, I necessarily will the means. (This, Kant has persuasively argued in the second section of the *Foundations*, is analytic.)
3. If I will the means to the fulfillment of my ends, then, as a phenomenal being—one whose agency is manifested in the realm of appearance—I must legitimately appropriate, which is to say take *de jure* possession of, portions of the spatiotemporal realm as means.
4. If I must take *de jure* possession of some portion of the spatio-temporal realm as means, then it must be *possible* for me to do so. What is more, there must be, in principle, no portion of the natural world that it is not possible for me to possess, inasmuch as there is nothing in the nature of willing as such that places limits on what might, according to the laws of nature, serve as means to my ends.

From all of which it follows that *de jure* possession must be possible.

The question remains, however: *How* is *de jure* possession possible? What is required for such legitimate possession to be actual? Locke, of course, had begged this question in the *Second Treatise of Government* by simply asserting the right of property as a truth revealed by the natural light of reason. But Kant, correctly in my view, recognizes that this is a radically unsatisfactory grounding for the right of property. Instead, like both Hobbes and Rousseau before him, Kant grounds the right to property in a prior mutual agreement, or social contract, among all those who, in the pursuit of their ends, may come into conflict with one another in the appropriation of portions of nature.

Legitimate ownership involves the exclusion of others from the use and enjoyment of a portion of nature, an exclusion that may be instituted by force if necessary. Such a use of force, Kant argues, if in all consistency universalized, entails mutual constraints among all the members of a society—where society here can be understood quite simply as the totality of persons who, in the pursuit of their ends, are likely to interfere with one another. So Kant concludes that the possibility of property entails the existence of a social contract.

And now Kant concludes his argument in a strikingly bold and imaginative fashion. The central text is section 8 of the first chapter of the first part of the *Rechtslehre*. Here it is in its entirety:

When I declare (by word or deed), "I will that an external thing shall be mine," I thereby declare it obligatory for everyone else to refrain from the object of my will. This is an obligation that no one would have apart from this juridical act of mine. Included in this claim, however, is an acknowledgment of being reciprocally bound to everyone else to a similar and equal restraint with respect to what is theirs. The obligation involved here comes from a universal rule of the external juridical relationship [that is, says the translator, the civil society]. Consequently, I am not bound to leave what is another's untouched if everyone else does not in turn guarantee to me with regard to what is mine that he will act in accordance with exactly the same principle. This guarantee does not require a special juridical act, but is already contained in the concept of being externally bound to a duty on account of the universality, and hence also the reciprocity, of an obligation coming from a universal rule.

Now, with respect to an external and contingent possession, a unilateral Will cannot serve as a coercive law for everyone, since that would be a violation of freedom in accordance with universal laws. Therefore, only a Will binding everyone else—that is, a collective, universal (common), and powerful Will—is the kind of Will that can provide the guarantee required. The condition of being subject to general external (that is, public) legislation that is backed by power is the civil society. Accordingly, a thing can be externally yours or mine only in a civil society.

[And now, Kant concludes with a dramatic flourish:]

Conclusion: If it must be *de jure* possible to have an external object as one's own, then the subject must also be allowed to compel everyone else with whom he comes into conflict over the question of whether such an object is his to enter, together with him, a society under a civil constitution.[17]

The conclusion of the argument prior to this point, you will recall, was that *de jure* possession must be possible, or, as Kant puts it in the text before us, "it must be *de jure* possible to have an external object as one's own." Combining this with the conclusion of the argument just quoted, we can now conclude that it must be allowed to compel others to enter with one into a society under a civil constitution. Since this necessity is universal, it of course follows that others have an equal right to compel me to enter civil society.

We can now see that in the text of the *Rechtslehre*, Kant finally provides what was missing from the argument of the *Foundations*, namely a demonstration that such obligations as faithful promising are not hypothetically, but are rather categorically, imperative.

Kant's argument is open to criticism at every stage, of course, though it is nonetheless, in my estimation, extremely interesting. Before sketching some of those criticisms, let me call attention once again to an implication of the argument that goes directly counter to the most common impression concerning Kant's ethical theory. Kant is generally viewed as a rigorist, an objectivist, a universalist, a theorist who claims to be able to demonstrate *a priori* the universal validity of very power-ful moral principles that are binding on all agents regardless of their nature or circumstances. And this impression is quite correct. But readers of Kant almost always draw the natural conclusion that he believes these moral principles to be binding on us even in the absence of a legitimately established state. In the familiar language of liberal political theory, Kant is seen as siding with Locke on the question whether the moral law is binding on agents in a state of nature. But it should now be clear that Kant's argument actually entails the opposite conclusion. The procedural obligation to enter into a social contract is certainly binding upon agents in a state of nature, but the moral principles enacted into law by the legislature of a state thus established are binding only after, and on the condition of, the establishment of the legitimate state.

Kant clearly does not intend this consequence of his moral theory. Quite to the contrary. But his failure to provide a satisfactory theory of obligatory ends forces anyone wishing to embrace his moral theory to rely upon the legislation of the legitimate state as the only source of morally binding substantive principles of practical reason.

And this leads us ineluctably to the question sketched above, whether a legitimately established state, based upon a unanimous social contract and committed to embodying the fundamental principle of justice in its laws, is thereby constrained to a *single* structure of justice that thus constitutes the objective, universal, unconditionally binding system of principles of practical reason? This, I take it, is essentially the question originally posed by John Rawls in the earlier versions of his theory, before he drained it of its force and interest by an endless series of ad hoc adjustments, concessions, baroque elabora-tions, and qualifications.

If the answer to the question is yes—if, let us say, a legitimately established republic of rational agents in search of principles com-patible with the fundamental postulate of justice must necessarily come upon and agree to Rawls's Two Principles of Justice—then by com-bining Kant's argument and Rawls's, we would have a very powerful defense indeed of a universal system of moral principles. The argument, in a nutshell, would go like this:

- Rationality as such entails consistent willing.
- Consistent willing, for a phenomenally appearing agent, entails the possibility of property.
- The possibility of property entails the necessity of establishing a state through a social contract.
- A legitimate state composed of rational agents will necessarily enact one and only one set of fundamental principles of justice, namely the Two Principles of Justice.
- Therefore, we are all, as phenomenally appearing rational agents, obligated universally and unconditionally to form legitimately grounded political communities with those with whom we come into contact, and in those communities to enact the Two Principles of Justice as the fundamental laws governing our interactions.

There are three stages in this argument: the derivation of the requirement of consistent willing from an analysis of what it is to be an agent; the deduction of the necessity of entering a social contract from an analysis of preconditions of property; and the demonstration that reason dictates one and only one system of principles as the content of a legitimate state.

My own view is that the first stage in the argument, which as I have indicated we find in the pivotal portion of the second section of the *Foundations*, is essentially sound. To be an agent is to be moved by reasons, and the logic of reasons requires consistency of willing. What counts as a good reason for me necessarily counts as a good reason for any agent in relevantly similar circumstances.

The third stage of the argument, I am convinced, is mistaken. Neither Rawls nor anyone else has, to my knowledge, made a convincing case for the claim that free and equal rational agents must, insofar as they are rational, coordinate on a single system of substantive principles regulating their interactions with one another.

It is the second stage that I find especially interesting, in part, I confess, because I have managed to make it clear to myself only recently. Can the material circumstances of human existence—our spatiotemporality, our dependence for the pursuit of our ends on inanimate nature—ground an argument that we have a standing procedural obligation to attempt rational community with those agents with whom we interact? Can we, as Kant claims, *compel* such rational community?

I think we can conclude immediately that we cannot compel others to enter with us in a social contract, for the essence of such an agreement is that it represents mutual willing, and that implies that it is voluntary. But am I required, simply by the constraints of rational consistency, to seek such community with others, or is it consistent with my status as an agent to adopt nothing more than an instrumental stance vis-à-vis those with whom I interact? Is this, after all, the real content of the injunction to treat humanity as an end and not simply as a means?

I honestly don't know. My pre-philosophical inclination is to believe that the answer is yes, that there is something about construing myself as a rational agent that requires me, in all consistency, to attempt to achieve rational community with others whom I consider to be agents as well—though I do not consider myself bound, should they reject that attempt, to treat them as I would have agreed to treat and be treated, had we actually achieved rational community. But at this point, I do not see an argument that can make that conclusion plausible.

NOTES

1. Although it is rather less easy to do this plausibly than one might at first imagine. For an extended discussion of this topic, see Robert Paul Wolff, The Autonomy of Reason (New York: Harper & Row, 1973; rpt. New York: Peter Smith, 1986), 52–92.

2. I deliberately say "itself" rather than "himself" or "herself" because it is as noumenal beings that we are agents, and hence can be said to give reasons to ourselves, and as noumenal beings, we are out of time, out of space, and hence, of course, ungendered.

3. Immanuel Kant, *Foundations of the Metaphysics of Morals*, trans. Lewis White Beck (Indianapolis, Ind.: Bobbs-Merrill, 1959), p. 39 [KGS 4:422].

4. Strictly speaking, the first attempt comes two paragraphs later, after Kant has introduced the *second* formulation of the Categorical Imperative, but this fact, though important for a detailed reading of the *Foundations*, is not sufficiently important for our purposes to justify extended commentary.

5. This point may require a bit more argument, for some people will imagine that when I say the words "I promise" I am entering into the practice of promising whether I mean to or not. It should be obvious that such a claim can only be sustained by appeal to another, more general, thesis to the effect that whenever I use language, I am implicitly commiting myself to certain undertakings, derivable from the nature of language as such, that as it happens involve the injunction not to misuse performative utterances, etc. But there is no better ground for this claim than for the original claim concerning the words "I promise." It may be nasty, underhanded, deceitful, and all-round not nice for me to use language to mislead rather than to inform, but inasmuch as things do not have natural purposes, not axes or hammers, and not language either, there

are no grounds for saying that I am being inconsistent when I use language to mislead or deceive.

6. Kant, *Foundations*, 46 [KGS 4:428] (translation slightly amended—AU).

7. Kant, *Foundations*, 51–52 [KGS 4:433–34].

8. "Immediately, in place of the individual person of each contracting party, this act of association creates an artificial and collective body composed of as many members as there are voters in the assembly, and by this same act that body acquires its unity, its common *ego*, its life and its will. The public person thus formed by the union of all other persons was once called the *city*, and is now known as the *republic* or the *body politic*. In its passive role it is called the *state*, when it plays an active role it is the *sovereign*; and when it is compared to others of its own kind, it is a *power*. Those who are associated in it take collectively the name of *a people*, and call themselves individually *citizens*, in so far as they put themselves under the laws of the state." J-J Rousseau, *The Social Contract*, trans. and introduced by Maurice Cranston (Harmondsworth, U.K.: Penguin Books, 1968).

9. For the criteria of necessity and universality as marks of objectivity, see *Kritik der reinen Vernunft*, B 3.

10. For a fuller discussion of Rawls's work, see my *Understanding Rawls* (Princeton, N.J.: Princeton University Press, 1977; rpt. Peter Smith, 1990).

11. Kant, *The Metaphysical Elements of Justice*, trans. with an introduction by John Ladd (Indianapolis, Ind.: Bobbs-Merrill, 1965), 34 [KGS 6:230].

12. Ibid., 35 [KGS 6:231].

13. Ibid., 36 [KGS 6:232].

14. See R. P. Wolff, "Remarks on the Relation of the *Critique of Pure Reason* to Kant's Ethical Theory," in *New Essays on Kant*, ed. Bernard den Ouden and Marcia Moen (New York: Peter Lang, 1987).

15. Kant, *Metaphysical Elements of Justice* (*Rechtslehre*), op. cit., 51 [KGS 6:245].

16. Note that for modern philosophers, but not for Kant, such contemplation might take as its objects mathematical forms. For Kant, of course, a purely rational agent not possessed of a sensible intuition would have no acquaintance with mathematical forms.

17. Kant, *Rechtslehre*, op. cit., KGS 6:255–56.

Philip J. Rossi, S.J.

Public Argument and Social Responsibility

The Moral Dimensions of Citizenship in Kant's Ethical Commonwealth

Immanuel Kant lived, taught, and wrote two centuries ago as a citizen-subject of the Prussian monarchy. The political, social, and cultural circumstances of the eighteenth century in which he lived were considerably different from the ones in which we live in the United States at the close of the twentieth century.[1] Legislation and the shaping of public policy was in the hands of a small group of aristocrats and civil servants answerable only to a monarch who held power on which neither constitution nor statute placed restraint. There were few institutions or practices that provided the "ordinary citizen" with a voice in matters of state governance. Even those who considered themselves advocates of "republican" principles for the governance of the state, including Kant, did not thereby argue for legislative bodies elected by all members of the general populace under what we, in the late twentieth century, would recognize as democratic procedures. Kant, for instance, considered economic "independence" to be an essential qualification for the right either to vote on legislation or to choose representatives to serve as legislators (TP 294–94/75–77; MdS 314–15/125–26).[2] In Kant's Prussia, as well as in the rest of eighteenth-century Western Europe, this qualification effectively meant that the exercise of active citizenship was solely the province of male property-holders, since they alone enjoyed the requisite economic independence.

63

From later democratic perspectives, this view of citizenship seems, at best, an early "way station" on the track to universal political participation and, at worst, an expression of class and gender biases to which Kant, for all his rhetoric of freedom and enlightenment, seemed no more immune than most of his contemporaries.

Differences of this kind suggest that Kant's writings on political and social matters could provide us with few, if any, useful ideas or reference points for a contemporary understanding of the rights and the responsibilities that devolve upon citizens of a representative democracy such as our own. In this essay I will argue that this is not so: despite the differences between Kant's world and ours, and despite the ways in which Kant's thinking stands in both apparent and real tension with features of the institutions and practices of our contemporary democratic polity, there is much of importance that we can learn from him about our role as citizens as our political culture moves into the twenty-first century. In particular, I will single out for our attention the concept of an "ethical commonwealth," which Kant developed in his later writings to characterize the social relationship we bear to one another as free moral agents. I will argue that there are elements of this concept that may help us address a serious problem in our contemporary public life of which the shrill, angry, and divisive rhetoric of electoral and legislative debate over matters of public policy has become a telling symptom: the erosion of the presumption that genuine and general consensus on societal goals is possible—let alone worth seeking—in a polity that is pluralist, multicultural, and multi-ethnic. This presumption views issues of public policy as matters that bear upon the good of all in a particular society. It thus takes debate on these matters to be, at least in part, an effort to identify, as a basis for decision, the relevant common interests in which all citizens have a stake. In place of this presumption there now often stands a quite different one; this latter presumption views issues of public policy as simply matters in which particular interests compete for ascendancy. It thus takes debate on them to be just one more element of strategy in a "zero-sum" game—or even less: if we win, you lose; but if we can't win, we'll do our best to make sure that you don't win either.

Commentators from a range of political and disciplinary perspectives have noticed this problem looming ever larger in the workings of our current electoral and legislative processes.[3] These seem to have become arenas in which little or no room can be made or given for appeal to relevant common interests that are large enough to allow particular clashing interests to make themselves subordinate in the making of decisions and the shaping of policy. The absence of a place for such an appeal was succinctly put in an observation by Senator

Robert Dole about a piece of legislation under congressional consideration: "Republicans figure out what is best for them, and Democrats figure out what is best for them, and nobody figures out what is best, period."[4] Although Kant's concept of an ethical commonwealth does not provide us with a "quick fix" for this problem, it can, I believe, help us see how a crucial form of moral responsibility to one another is at stake within this ostensibly political impasse; this responsibility, moreover, is so fundamental to the dynamics of civil order in a polity of free citizens, that we need first to attend carefully to it and its implications in order to deal effectively with the political problem in which it has become entangled. I will thus argue that Kant's notion of an ethical commonwealth provides a way to bring the moral dimension of this responsibility into clear focus: our public relationship to one another as agents and citizens in a free society is, at root, one of mutual responsibility to sustain the social conditions for the exercise of one another's freedom. In particular, the notion of an ethical commonwealth will enable us to delimit the following three elements as constitutive of the moral dimension that is essential to our public relationship to one another as citizens:

1. The notion of an ethical commonwealth enables us to understand that the context and function of public debate and disagreement in a free society is as much a moral one—that is, one that bears upon the (social) conditions for the mutual exercise of freedom—as it is a political one—that is, one that bears upon public external regulation of the pursuit of all our various particular interests;
2. It enables us to focus our attention on the shared character of the responsibility that devolves on us all to sustain the moral and social conditions that make that debate possible; and,
3. It enables us to construe the possibility of agreement on societal goals and a commitment to seek such agreement as essential components of the conditions that make public debate in a free society possible.

My case for these elements will develop in two steps.

I shall argue in section 1 that Kant's notion of an ethical commonwealth can be construed to provide us with a moral framework upon which we can construct a proper understanding of our relation to one another as citizens. This framework is constituted in terms of a mutual responsibility to one another that requires us to work together to sustain, as a fundamental social condition for the mutual exercise of freedom, the conditions for reasoned argument and agreement about social goals that are of most fundamental common concern: the terms of our living with each other in one society, including the constitutive (social) ends for human society as well as for the particular polity of which we are citizens.

In section 2, I shall then show how this framework of conditions for reasoned argument and agreement (in Kant's terms, the "public use of reason") provides a place from which to gain useful leverage on the possibility of consensus on societal goals in a polity where cultural, economic, and ideological fissures run increasingly wide and deep. I shall argue that the leverage this framework provides is fundamentally a moral one: when we engage in "the public use of reason" we thereby acknowledge, in the measure that we work toward achieving agreement about social goals in public argumentative exchange, that the appropriate basis for determining policy and practice is the "interest of reason" (KprV 73–82/77–86) to which we ought to make our own particular interests subordinate. The circumstances that, in Kant's view, necessarily surround the exercise of our human freedom morally require us to take such an interest. Our circumstances as free rational beings who have no option but to live together in society are such that we can do so in the manner that befits our freedom only to the extent that we come to uncoerced agreement, through the public use of reason, about the terms of our living with each other. We thus concretely exhibit this "interest of reason"—an inclusive and universal interest in the freedom that constitutes each and all of us as human moral agents—by persevering in our efforts to achieve agreement about social goals in public argumentative exchange. Our perseverance thereby exhibits a "social respect" for one another's freedom—that is, for the potentiality we have as free fellow citizens for constructing a truly common world for all of us to share—that is appropriate to the interest of reason.

1. THE ETHICAL COMMONWEALTH AS A MORAL FRAMEWORK FOR CITIZENSHIP

My goal in this first section is to show how Kant's notion of an ethical commonwealth enables us to understand that, in a free society, the context and function of public debate and disagreement is fundamentally moral as well as political. I will do so by arguing that Kant's notion of an ethical commonwealth can be construed to provide a moral framework upon which we can construct a proper under-standing of our relation to one another as citizens. This framework is a moral one in that it is constituted in terms of a mutual responsibility that free agents make incumbent upon themselves in their dealing with one another in civil society. In particular, the notion of an ethical commonwealth enables us to specify the fundamental mutual (moral) responsibility that free agents take upon themselves in their function as fellow citizens: the requirement to work with one another to sustain conditions for reasoned argument and agreement about matters of common concern inasmuch as these form a fundamental social condition for the exercise of our freedom.

The work in which Kant introduces the notion of an ethical commonwealth, *Religion within the Limits of Reason Alone*, may not immediately seem to have much bearing upon a concept such as citizenship, let alone larger issues of political theory and practice. The principal questions with which Kant wrestles in *Religion* concern the deepest levels of individual human moral agency, most notably the extent to which all human agents must take full responsibility for fixing the moral course of their lives for good or for evil. Yet even as Kant treats of matters that focus upon the moral destiny for which each individual is alone responsible, his discussions also have an important bearing upon an issue which is as fundamental for his political and social philosophy as it is for his moral philosophy: the authority of reason to govern human conduct.[5] With respect to this issue, *Religion* makes a significant contribution to Kant's critical project of establishing the authority of reason; it shows how the authority of reason extends over even the most intractable feature of our human existence and conduct: our propensity to evil. In *Religion*, Kant does more than simply delimit the proper manner by which reason exercises this authority within the deepest levels of individual moral agency in bringing about the moral conversion which overcomes "radical evil"—or, as Kant puts it in his technical language, in establishing "the *purity* of this [moral] law as the supreme ground of all our maxims" (R 46/42). In the notion of an ethical commonwealth he also sketches—though in far from complete form—the way in which this same authority of reason to overcome radical evil can be articulated in social terms. To the extent that the notion of an ethical commonwealth exhibits the possibility of reason achieving a social "victory" over radical evil, it thereby adumbrates an important moral dimension of the fundamental social and public relationship we bear to one another as agents in society. This dimension is constituted in virtue of the fact that Kant takes our citizenship as members of a particular polity, first, to be ordered toward the moral citizenship we share with one another as members of a community of rational free agents ("a kingdom of ends") and, second, to reach its completion in our undertaking to establish an "ethical commonwealth" as the concrete expression of our moral community with one another.

Kant thus introduces the notion of an "ethical commonwealth" as the social locus in which humanity's definitive overcoming of "radical evil" takes place within the particular sociocultural dynamics and arrangements of human life and within the course of human history (R 93–95/85–86). He employs this notion to represent "the establishment and spread of a society in accordance with, and for the sake of, the laws of virtue, a society whose task and duty is rationally to impress those laws in all their scope upon the entire human race" (R 94/86). He designates the concrete locus for this social process of overcoming radical evil as "the church," distinguished into two forms: the variously organized and "visible" historical churches, which embody historical or "ecclesiastical" faith, and the "true" Church, in which "pure" religious (i.e. moral) faith is manifest (R 101–3/92–94; 115–16/105–6). Of particular importance for purposes of our present discussion is the fact that the church, in both its forms, has a public and social character, and that it is through the latter, "true," church that the "ethical commonwealth" finally and fully extends its domain over human activity (R 121–24/112–4).[6] As we shall see below, even though Kant presents the ethical commonwealth in terms of an ostensibly theological model, and thus seemingly restricts its presence to the inner realm of human moral disposition, its full import bears upon the widest range of human conduct in society: it articulates the fundamental moral significance and purpose of our need and willingness to live with one another in a society.

The extent to which Kant's notion of an ethical commonwealth bears upon our relationship to one another as citizens of a political as well as a moral community has received relatively little attention in discussions of Kant's political philosophy.[7] The reasons for this neglect are many and some of the more important ones can be discerned even from the brief sketch that I have just given. First and most obvious is the fact that he introduces and extensively discusses this notion in a work concerned not with politics and public order but with the relation between morality and religion. In addition, Kant casts this discussion of the ethical commonwealth in the language of human moral dispositions—which seems to make its nature and function lie totally within the inner workings of human moral agency. Such language suggests that the ethical commonwealth attains its full expression not as an external realm of human social organization and practice such as a supranational polity but rather as the "true" but nonetheless "invisible" church constituted within the inner realm of human freedom through the practice of "moral religion" by conscientious agents who each strive individually to have an abiding disposition to make the purity of the moral law the supreme ground of all their maxims.[8]

A more fundamental reason, however, for the neglect of the social and political import of the ethical commonwealth is the interpretation into which Kant's political philosophy has generally been placed as representative of Enlightenment thought and as seminal for the development of liberal political theory. This interpretation has generally provided little, if any, conceptual space in the public and political order for the end-in-common that the ethical commonwealth envisions as morally constitutive not just for a particular society or polity but for each and every human society and polity: "a system of well disposed men [sic] in which and through whose unity alone the highest moral good can come to pass . . . a universal republic based on laws of virtue" (R 94/89); "a voluntary, universal, and enduring union of hearts" (R 102/93). There is a complex set of conceptual and historical reasons why this interpretation does not provide such space, many of which have been explored in the recent and still continuing debate about the conceptions of human good that may (or may not) be embedded in various forms of liberal political theory and practice.[9]

We do not have to examine the full set of these reasons, however, in order to recognize the social and political import of Kant's notion of an ethical commonwealth and the moral dimension it imparts to the notion of citizenship. We need to examine just one key element of that set, namely, the elaboration which this interpretation has ordinarily given to a central distinction—between the spheres of the "public" and the "private"—that I believe that Kant himself made only imperfectly. Within this interpretation the public sphere has become identified as the realm of governmental decision, regulation, and legally enforceable rights and obligations, where the state exercises its political authority as a coercive power to regulate external action only; the private sphere, in contrast, is accordingly identified with the realm of individual conduct and personal self-determination, in which individuals exercise the moral authority of their freedom as the power to set ends for themselves and to pursue those ends conscientiously. So construed, this distinction plays a key role in framing this interpretation in that it articulates a fundamental concern of classical liberal theory for the self-determination of the individual and the limits this entails upon the power of the state. This distinction articulates the boundary that limits the coercive power of the state with respect to the moral authority of individuals freely to set moral and personal ends for themselves and to pursue them without hindrance.

From the perspective of this interpretation, Kant is usually read as distinguishing the public and private spheres in an unambiguously "liberal" way; he is thus seen as denying that the "public sphere" has any legitimate authority that it can bring to bear upon the moral authority of individuals freely to set ends for themselves in the "private sphere." According to this interpretation, Kant's account of legitimate political authority, that restricts the scope of its legal (coercive) power to the regulation of external action "so that the free use of your choice can coexist with the freedom of everyone in accordance with a universal law" (MdS 231/56), marks off a clear, and a classical, distinction between the public, political realm of civil legislation and the private, individual realm of moral choice.[10] I take Kant's notion of the ethical commonwealth to suggest, however, that his distinction between the public and the private spheres, his construal of their constitutive elements, and his articulation of their relationship differ in some important respects from the one adumbrated from the inter- pretive framework of (later) liberal political and moral theory. Kant did consider the realm of law and publicly enforceable rights to be constitutive elements of the public sphere; in addition, he placed strict limits upon the state's exercise of coercive political authority with respect to the moral authority of individuals freely to set ends for themselves. In both of these key matters, there is little doubt that Kant can rightly be viewed as a seminal liberal thinker. But these two matters do not provide a complete account of his construal of the public and private spheres.

The authority which Kant denied to the public sphere concerns the actual adoption of ends, be it by individuals or by a society as a whole: he maintains that this cannot be brought about in a legitimate way through the exercise of the state's coercive political power. This limitation on the authority of the public sphere follows, however, not so much from his distinction between the realms of the public and the private as it does from his more fundamental principle that the adoption of ends for action is properly a function of the "inner" order of an agent's freedom: the character of this freedom is such that it cannot be subject to external, coercive constraint, either "public" or "private"—save, perhaps, with respect to the fundamental end of the exercise of freedom itself implicitly contained in "the universal principle of right," which all agree to make constitutive of political society in leaving "the juridical state of nature" (MdS 230–32/56–58; 312–13/123–24).

The authority which Kant denied to the public sphere with respect to the actual adoption of ends, however, pertains to a specific form of authority that may legitimately be exercised in that sphere: the civil and political authority that the state wields in the form of legislation enforceable through coercive power. Kant clearly holds that this authority is fundamental for constituting the public sphere and that it holds broad sway over that sphere. Yet it is not the only form of authority whose exercise in the public sphere is legitimate. Thus, even though Kant denies that civil and political authority, by means of legislative enactments enforceable by the state's coercive power, can legitimately hold sway over individuals' free setting of ends, he does not thereby affirm (as later developments of liberal political theory tend to do) that the public sphere has *no* authority at all with respect to the setting of ends. There would be no such authority, of course, if Kant held that the coercive power of the state constituted the only legitimate form of authority in the public sphere. This is not the case, however, since Kant views the public and the private spheres as *both* fully subject to the authority of reason—and, in particular, to what I shall term the "social authority of reason." He thus considers conduct in each sphere to be subject to principles that can and should be articulated "in public" and that can ultimately elicit, in the course of reasoned argument, a consensus acknowledging their authoritative status (BF 36–38/4–7; EF 368–68/126; SF 19–20/27–29; TP 304–5/82–83). From this perspective, the political and civil power of the state may then be considered just one form of the social authority of reason: it is that authority that has, within a set of conditions defined in terms of the reciprocal (social) exercise of human freedom, legitimate power to use coercion so that the external conduct of citizens stands in conformity with laws of civil order that have been enacted in accordance with "the universal principle of right."

We may therefore understand Kant's notion of an "ethical commonwealth" to be an effort on his part to articulate another form of the "social authority of reason." In particular, Kant envisions the "ethical commonwealth" as the set of social conditions that make it possible for the authority of reason to function through noncoercive means, and noncoercive means alone, to govern human conduct in the public sphere. The notion of an "ethical commonwealth," moreover, is neither Kant's first nor his only effort to articulate this form of the social authority of reason. Two other important and related efforts can be found in his discussions of the articles for perpetual peace (EF 348–60/111–19) and of the "freedom to reason publicly on all matters" or "the public use of reason" (BF 36–38/5–7; cf. TP 304/82–83; SF 19–20/27–29). The discussions of the latter notion are particularly important in that they provide Kant's clearest specification of a central condition for the exercise of the noncoercive social authority of reason: the engagement of all citizens in self-disciplined inquiry and argument as the procedure for reaching reasoned and reasonable settlement of matters of policy and action. These discussions specify the conditions for the exercise of the noncoercive social authority of reason in terms that are considerably more concrete than the presentation, in *Religion*, of these conditions as the four "tokens" that mark the ethical commonwealth as the "true church" (R 101–2/92–93).

Since the notion of "the freedom to reason publicly on all matters" more clearly specifies the moral framework requisite for the non-coercive exercise of the social authority of reason, we can thus use it to articulate the central contention of this section: that the "ethical commonwealth" provides a moral framework upon which to construct a proper understanding of our relation to one another as citizens. In particular, the notion of "the freedom to reason publicly on all matters" enables us to specify the fundamental mutual (moral) responsibility that devolves upon members of an "ethical commonwealth." This responsibility is *to work with one another to sustain conditions for reasoned argument and agreement about matters of fundamental common concern for living together as a society*, that is, about those matters that form constitutive social ends for human society or for the particular polity of which we are citizens. Neglect of this responsibility, as I shall indicate in the next section, has been a key factor in the seeming erosion of public confidence in the presumption that genuine and general consensus on societal goals is possible—let alone worth seeking—in a polity that is pluralist, multicultural, and multi-ethnic.

We may then specify the particular elements of this responsibility by elaborating (more fully than Kant himself did) the social implications of the "three maxims of the *sensus communis*" (KU 294–95/160–62; cf. AP 200/72, 228–29/96–97) that Onora O'Neill sees underlying Kant's notion of "the public use of reason":[11]

1. To think for oneself;
2. To think from the standpoint of everyone else; and
3. Always to think consistently.

While the first and the third of these maxims clearly express Kant's central concern for the autonomy of the individual, the second one immediately and properly places that autonomy within its human social context. This social context is explicitly noted in the *Anthropology*, which adds "when communicating with them" (AP 200/72) and "with whom we are communicating" (AP 228/96) to its formulations of the second maxim. These maxims thus presuppose the possibility that individually and collectively we are capable of both forming and taking a perspective that concretely represents, over against any particular interest that shapes our thinking and enters our communication with others, a larger interest that is (at least potentially) inclusive of "everyone else." As we shall see below, we can understand the possibility of our taking this larger interest as the social expression of the "interest of reason," one of the key concepts in Kant's moral thought. This possibility of forming and taking such a larger, more inclusive and even universal interest—or, put in Senator Dole's language, of "figuring out what is best, period"—provides us with a basis for articulating the moral framework that the ethical commonwealth posits for governing our relation to one another as citizens.

These maxims suggest that the moral framework for citizenship posited by the ethical commonwealth can be construed as *a public, social setting for mutual communication among all citizens for purposes of establishing common bases for decision and action*. Such a social setting makes it then possible for us, in the course of argument, to seek out and identify as a basis for decision, those relevant *common* interests in which we all have a stake; without this social setting, it is far more likely that we will make the course of argument serve simply as an arena for the articulation and adjudication of the particular and settled interests that we each initially bring to the argument. The moral framework for citizenship posited by the ethical commonwealth thus places upon us the requirement to sustain those conditions for reasoned argument and agreement about matters of fundamental common concern for living together as a society, since those conditions provide the context for making decisions on the basis of "what is best, period"—that is, a "common good" acknowledged as normative both in substance and in form.

Kant does not clearly specify what such conditions are. His failure to do so may be one reason why these three maxims can all too easily be taken to have minimal social import: they seem to express principles that pertain to us only individually, as we each make our own efforts to be responsible thinkers. While they certainly do pertain to us in that way, they can also serve as a basis for specifying the conditions that are necessary in any society to make "the public use of reason" effective as the exercise of the noncoercive social authority of reason. These maxims, I believe, provide a basis for formulating what I shall term the "conditions for critical persuasion" that provide the context for us to use our "freedom to reason publicly on all matters" for "figuring out what is best, period" in matters of public policy. These conditions obtain to the extent that all members of a polity, either themselves or through their representatives, consider themselves bound, in virtue of their very engagement in argument over the determination of public policy, to observe the following maxims in their communication and discussion with one another:

a. All parties seek to make their own position *understandable to* all others;

b. All parties seek *to understand* the positions of others;
c. *No position* nor presupposition of a position which is offered to advance inquiry or argument *is considered immune to examination, criticism, or revision;* and
d. The measure of the success of argument and inquiry is the extent to which it yields *a common basis for action,* rather than the victory for any particular position enunciated at the outset of the inquiry or argument.

These conditions provide a public, social setting that embodies a commitment to mutual communication for purposes of establishing common bases for decision and action. They involve elements of all three Kantian "maxims of the *sensus communis.*" They also presuppose— in contrast to Kant's restrictive understanding of active citizenship— that all members of a society are entitled to a voice (either their own or that of a representative accountable to them) on the matters of public practice or policy that constitute the subject matter for the public use of reason.[12]

The first condition presupposes the maxim of "thinking for oneself": one's own communicative efforts rest upon effective self-appropriation of the position one is advancing in argument. The "public use of reason" requires that one make communicable to others whatever one "thinks for oneself." The first and the second conditions jointly make it possible for all parties to the inquiry not only to acknowledge the maxim of "thinking from the standpoint of everyone else" but also to hold one another accountable to it. The public use of reason thus requires that everyone engaged in argument about public matters make a sustained common effort at mutual understanding of the positions advanced in argument as a first step in appropriately engaging and testing them as potential bases for the determination of policy. The third condition seeks to make observance of the maxim of consistent thinking a responsibility that all who are engaged in the argument share by keeping their positions open to (further) public test at each successive stage of argument. The public use of reason thus requires that claims be appropriately qualified or even withdrawn when they fail to satisfy the communicative norms of the first two conditions or the argumentative norms of the third. Such qualification or withdrawal of claims, however, does not thereby entail argumentative disqualification of their proponents from participation in further argument. Put more generally, arguments set within the conditions for the public use of reason are not to be put forth as tactics in a "zero-sum" game: claims that satisfy the norms of the public use of reason do not give "victory" just to those who may have first proposed them. They stand, instead, as an accomplishment of all who have participated in the argumentative process through which they have successfully passed. The fourth condition, finally, articulates the fundamental function of argument conducted in accord with "the public use of reason": to determine a course of action on the basis of mutual achievement and recognition of common interest rather than on the expected satisfaction that the course of action might give to any set of particular interests articulated in the course of argument.

This last condition thus makes explicit how the notion of an ethical commonwealth makes the context and function of public debate and disagreement in a free society a moral one as much as it is a political one. The ethical commonwealth requires adherence to the conditions for "the public use of reason," which will enable us to achieve and recognize, as a basis for action, a common interest that is not simply identifiable with any of the particular interests we might initially bring to the argument. It is appropriate, I believe, to construe the possibility of achieving such a common interest as the social expression of what Kant terms the "interest of reason"—a notion that is both crucial for Kant's validation of the moral use of reason and also fundamental to the moral import of his entire project of critically vindicating the authority of reason. The vindication of the authority of reason has moral import because such authority provides the only adequate basis for a principled social ordering of human existence constructed upon the noncoercive power of reason itself.

On the construal I am proposing here, the "interest of reason" is thereby bound up with the social authority of reason and the means by which such authority is enforced. On Kant's account, over and against the particular interests we bring with us into the public realm and its argument, and in virtue of which we seek for ourselves such things as property, power, and recognition, there is an interest we take—or, more precisely, which reason, in consideration of the circumstances of our human social existence, requires us to take—*in constituting a shared world of action for one another through the exercise of our freedom* (cf. KU 431–34/319–21; AP 328–30/188–90). For Kant, the dynamism of reason is inclusive and its authority is noncoercive; in contrast, the dynamism of our partial and particular interests is exclusive and their authority to sway others is coercive.[13] As a result, a field for common human interaction constructed on the basis of our partial and particular interests can be "inclusive" only to the extent that we can coerce into it others who do not share those interests with us; its inclusivity would rest on the hegemony of power, not the authority of reason. On the other hand, to the extent that recognition of these interests as partial and particular merely restrains us from coercing others onto the field of our interests, we are more likely to construct tribal circles, not a world; the particularity of each field of interaction would set the authority of reason within arbitrary and contingent limits. In contrast, the interest of reason consists in a commitment to engage other human beings in an ever enlarging circle of inquiry and argument to find or to construct an enduring, noncoercive basis for interaction with one another in freedom. Such an enduring, noncoercive basis for interaction with one another and freedom is reason's interest, *an interest that is not simply a particular interest of any one of us, nor merely the aggregate of all of those interests, but an inclusive and universal interest in the freedom of each of us and of all of us*, the freedom that most fundamentally constitutes us as members of the human species.

Kant's claim that there is such an "interest of reason" is also a moral claim: We all can and must take such an interest since it bears upon a basic exercise of our freedom—our constituting a world of action for one another—and upon our readiness to accept the authority of reason for determining the terms for living with one another in the world we have so constituted. Viewed from the context of this "interest of reason," Kant's notion of an ethical commonwealth is an effort to adumbrate the complete social expression of that interest. It is the term toward which the world we construct for one another with our freedom is ordered. Our construction of that world is fundamentally a moral enterprise that takes place in the framework that we, as fellow citizens, have the responsibility to provide and sustain for one another: the conditions for "critical persuasion" that make possible "the public use of reason."

Yet this enterprise—which requires our engagement with one another in reasoned argument about the terms of our living with each other, about the constitutive social ends that make us a polity, and also about whatever ends our common humanity makes incumbent on us—presents a morally and politically daunting task if it envisions the achievement of agreement on even a small range of these matters. The terms of our living with one another, the constitutive social ends that make us a polity, the ends that our common humanity make incumbent upon us—all these are matters on which the studious avoidance of public argument seems to have become the norm. It is by no means an idle question to ask in our current political and cultural circumstances whether agreement on these matters is even possible, let alone desirable, in a polity where cultural, economic, and ideological fissures seem to run so wide and deep that they seem unbridgeable. Yet—and this may be the greatest peril in our current circumstances—the erosion of public confidence in the possibility of agreement on even some of these matters is itself a major step toward the abandonment of reasoned public argument. In the absence of argument conducted under the conditions of the public use of reason, there can only be "games" played in accord with the rules of hegemonic power. If at the very outset we have abandoned hope of reasoned agreement, if we do not believe that *someone's* argument, if not our own, will prove persuasive, then what is the sense or value of our engaging in argument with one another at all? The following section will sketch a response to these issues.

2. The Public Use of Reason and the Possibility of Consensus

My goal in this concluding section is to show how the "public use of reason" provides a place from which to gain useful leverage on the possibility of consensus on societal goals in a polity where cultural, economic, and ideological fissures run increasingly wide and deep. This leverage is fundamentally a moral one: when we engage in "the public use of reason" we thereby acknowledge, in the measure that we work toward achieving agreement about social goals in public argumentative exchange, that the appropriate basis for determining policy and practice is the "interest of reason" to which we make our own particular interests subordinate. The circumstances that, in Kant's view, necessarily surround the exercise of our human freedom require us to take such an interest: free rational beings who, as we do, *have no option but to live together*, can do so *in the manner which befits their freedom* only to the extent that they come to uncoerced agreement, through the public use of reason, about the terms of their living with each other. We thus concretely exhibit this "interest of reason"—an inclusive and universal interest in the freedom that constitutes each and all of us as human moral agents—by persevering in our efforts to achieve agreement about social goals in public argumentative exchange. Our perseverance thereby exhibits a "social respect" for one another's freedom—that is, for the potentiality we have as free fellow citizens for constructing a truly common world for all of us to share—which is appropriate to the interest of reason. In the absence of such respect, any hope to make the public realm an "ethical commonwealth" in which our engagement in reasoned argument yields the terms of our living with each other, rather than just an arena for "zero-sum" games in which the powerful will always prevail, is sure to be illusory.

In sum, the main contentions of this section add up to the claim that the "ethical commonwealth," construed as a moral framework for understanding our relation to one another as citizens, implies a shared civic obligation to sustain the social conditions for reasoned public discourse with the aim of reaching reasoned agreement.

The case for the claim that the "public use of reason" provides a place from which to gain useful leverage on the possibility of consensus on societal goals in our current circumstances of apparently growing social fragmentation can be made in a fairly straightforward manner. This case rests upon the fact that our engagement in "the public use of reason" requires a threefold commitment on the part of those who engage in public argument: first, to the possibility of reaching agreement; second, to persevere in mutual efforts to reach agreement even when none has yet emerged; and third, to let one's own position be fully subject to argumentative analysis, challenge and criticism and thus to possible qualification and revision. The first two parts of this commitment make it clear that, in the current situation of public discourse in the United States, the very possibility of "the public use of reason" is at stake. The two presumptions about the nature and function of that discourse, noted at the beginning of this essay, differ over the possibility of the public use of reason and the (moral) intelligibility of our engaging in it. These conditions are embedded in the first presumption, which views issues of public policy as matters that bear upon the good of all in a particular society. They specify that hope for reasoned agreement is an essential condition for the intelligibility of the public use of reason: it makes no sense to argue with one another about actions and policies that *we* are to undertake as a polity, unless we expect the outcome of our argument to reach reasoned agreement about those policies and the bases for undertaking them. If we do not envision such agreement, we are then left with the second presumption, that issues of public policy are simply matters in which particular interests compete for ascendancy. In this case, argument is no longer "the public use of reason"; it is nothing more than a mask for the interplay of power and any agreement reached in its course simply represents a moment in the current vector of competing and clashing powers.

In the context of the clash between these two presumptions, the third commitment undertaken by engagement in "the public use of reason" takes on a deeper moral "bite," since it denies privileged position to the particular interests anyone brings to the argument. In making this commitment one accepts the possibility that engagement in the "public use of reason" might require rethinking, revising, or even abandoning positions, formed on the basis of particular interests, with which one entered the argument. One has to envision the possibility that agreement—which one is committed to persist in seeking—may emerge from *someone else's* argument, and that one's cherished particular interests stand, at most, on equal footing with those that *others* bring. Conceived in terms of "the public use of reason," the agreement that emerges out of our engagement with one another in argument has a broad moral basis: it arises in function of a mutual recognition of the full moral equality in which we stand with one another, rather than from whatever narrow space we might find where the greatest number of particular interests currently overlap.

This suggests, in my judgment, that skepticism and even despair about the possibility of consensus about social goals has its most fundamental roots neither in just the current circumstances of social and cultural fragmentation nor in the daunting complexity of nego- tiating pragmatic political compromise in a polity that has now come to a clearer recognition of its pluralist, multicultural, and multi-ethnic character. Rather, such skepticism and despair issue far more fundamentally from reluctance—and perhaps even occasionally from willful failure—to acknowledge that we can set the terms of our living together only from a basis of a mutual moral recognition of one another from which we can thereby envision the possibility of our constructing a shared world. This last phrase is crucial, first, for understanding Kant's notions of an "ethical commonwealth," "the public use of reason," and "the interest of reason" and, second, for validating the possibility of our reaching consensus on social goals through argu- mentative exchange that acknowledges the authority of reason.

Like other "social contract" thinkers, Kant clearly sees that mutual moral recognition of one another is fundamental for setting out the limits and boundaries of the terms of our living together: from this recognition issue the "Universal Principle of Right," limitations on the power of the state, and the distinction between the public and the private spheres. Yet unlike many other contract thinkers, Kant also sees that this mutual moral recognition then requires us, in the concrete circumstances of finite human existence, to engage one another in argu- ment and activity to construct a common world. Kant is not so naive as to think that the construction of such a common world will be easy, or that it will ever be fully finished. He nonetheless sees it as a task that we cannot shirk: we cannot extricate ourselves from the social circumstances of our human existence, so we are under the exigency of constructing together terms for our living with one another in a shared world (R 93–100/85–91). Although this interest in having a shared world may be "forced" on us by "nature" (the circumstances of our human existence as finite, needy beings on a planet of finite resources), Kant also sees this construction of a shared world as a matter of a free, noncoerced mutual recognition of a basis for action that has its roots in the "interest of reason," which is universal and inclusive, rather than simply in service of any of our particular interests (cf. KU 431–34/319–21; AP 328–30/188–90). The final term and fulfillment of this task is the "ethical commonwealth," which we more and more closely approximate to the extent that we are able to settle the terms of our living together on the basis of agreement reached through the public use of reason rather than just on the basis of the legitimate exercise of the coercive power of the state.

For Kant, then, the possibility of our reaching agreement on social goals through the public use of reason rests upon the conjunction of two "facts" about our human existence. The first is a "fact of nature": we have no choice but to live as social beings. The second is a "fact of reason": our freedom as rational agents to set ends for ourselves. The conjunction of these two facts means, for Kant, that free rational beings who, as we do, have no option but to live together, can do so in the manner which befits their freedom only to the extent that they come to uncoerced agreement about the terms of their living with each other. While the conjunction of these two "facts" does not provide any guarantee that agreement in any particular case actually will be reached, it does imply that the possibility of agreement must be presupposed or—to use a more properly Kantian term—"postulated" as a condition for reaching agreement. In order to reach agreement, we must think agreement possible; in terms more appropriately Kantian about such a moral matter, we must *hope for* agreement. Kant's notions of the "ethical commonwealth" and "public use of reason," therefore, exhibit his doctrine of hope in its social form. (This may, in part, explain why Kant discusses the former notion in *Religion within the Limits of Reason Alone* rather than in a work on politics.) One element of our "peculiar fate" as free but finite rational beings who must live in society is that, even in the absence of any guarantee that we will reach agreement, we must ever stand in hope of reaching agreement and therefore persevere in engaging one another in argument about the terms of our living with one another. In this case, as in the case of our individual possibility of overcoming "radical evil," Kantian "hope" is not an empty velleity but a disposition to persevere in conduct befitting our moral freedom. Anything else is unworthy of our vocation as free beings.

The implication this has for our own situation should now be fairly clear. The prevalence of skepticism and even despair about the possibility of our reaching agreement on the social goals that set the terms of our living together is a symptom that we have begun to waver in our fundamental moral recognition of one another as free fellow citizens and human beings. In the process of giving long-overdue moral and political acknowledgment to the irreducibly different ways in which persons and cultures exhibit their being human, including the ends they freely set for themselves, we seem to have lost clear sight of the *social and shared* character of our public relationship to one another as citizens. We seem to have forgotten that the two "facts" from which Kant shaped his notions of the "ethical commonwealth" and the "public use of reason" thereby place us into a relationship of mutual moral responsibility: our freedom to set ends for ourselves inevitably takes place within the context of our need to live with one another and thus requires us to engage one another in argument and activity to construct a common "world" for one another. In such a context, respect for one another's freedom consists in more than the ideal set forth by "classical" liberalism, namely, allowing maximum space for all to pursue their own freely set ends with minimal interference from one another and from the state. This context also requires a "social respect" for one another's freedom which Kant's liberalism sketches in the notion of the ethical commonwealth, that is, a respect that enables us to *persevere with one another in public argument* in the hope of reaching agreement about the terms of our living with one another. The absence of such hope is indicative of a diminished understanding of and respect for the potentiality we have as free fellow citizens for constructing a truly common world for all of us to share. The presence of such hope, on the other hand, is manifest when we acknowledge our shared civic obligation to sustain the social conditions for reasoned public discourse, that is, the conditions for "critical persuasion" that enable all of us to engage in "the public use of reason."

Argument, of course, is not action. Providing the conditions for "critical persuasion" does not automatically guarantee that any agreement reached under its auspices will truly be "what is best, period." It may very well be the case that, in our late-twentieth-century circumstances of apparent societal fragmentation, the "interest of reason" requires even more of us than simply sustaining the social conditions for reasoned public discourse. It may require us, as well, to give special attention to the fundamental bases that enable us to establish and sustain what I have termed "social respect" for one another's freedom: the mutual moral recognition of one another from which we can thereby envision the possibility of our constructing, on the basis our freedom, a shared world. The bases for social respect most fundamentally lie, I believe, in the practices and institutions that link us together as a public community in which the exercise of our freedom is ordered to the attainment of justice for all.[14] If this is so, then a further implication of the mutual moral responsibility we have to one another as citizens may very well be that we must make our engagement in "the public use of reason" an effective instrument for securing justice in a free society. Most crucial among the agreements we must persevere in seeking with one another in reasoned public argument are those that bear upon establishing, sustaining, and, when necessary, reforming political, economic, or social institutions and policies so that they most fully secure justice for all. This further claim about the moral dimension of our citizenship is beyond the scope of the present essay. It provides, nonetheless, an appropriate place at which to conclude these Kantian reflections on citizenship because it, too, is a point on which Kant's notions of an "ethical commonwealth," "the interest of reason," and "the public use of reason" may eventually provide us with some useful and challenging guidance. I hope the current discussion has shown that, despite the differences between his world and our own, Kant's work provides a marker against which we can measure our own understanding and practice of the moral dimensions of our citizenship.[15]

NOTES

    1. For an overall picture of political and social institutions in Kant's Prussia, see C. B. A. Behrens, *Society, Government and the Enlightenment: The Experiences of Eighteenth-Century France and Prussia* (London: Thames and Hudson, 1985).

    2. References to Kant's works are given parenthetically in the text using the abbreviations below. References before the slash (/) give the pagination of the appropriate volume of KGS, *Kants Gesammelte Schriften*, Ausgabe der Königlichen Preußischen Akademie der Wissenschaften (Berlin, 1902–); the volume number is listed after each title. References after the slash are to the corresponding English translation.

AP   *Anthropologie in pragmatischer Hinsicht* KGS 7. *Anthropology from a Pragmatic Point of View*, trans. Mary J. Gregor (The Hague: Martinus Nijhoff, 1974).

BF   "Beanwortung der Frage: Was ist Aufklärung?" KGS 8. "What Is Enlightenment?" trans. Lewis White Beck, in *On History* (New York: Bobbs-Merrill, 1963).

EF   *Zum ewigen Frieden* KGS 8. "Perpetual Peace," trans. Ted Humphrey, in *Perpetual Peace and Other Essays* (Indianapolis, Ind.: Hackett, 1983).

KprV   *Kritik der praktischen Vernunft* KGS 5. Critique of Practical Reason, trans. Lewis White Beck, 3rd edition (New York: Macmillan, 1993).

KU   *Kritik der Urteilskraft* KGS 5. *Critique of Judgment*, trans. Werner Pluhar (Indianapolis, Ind.: Hackett, 1987).

MdS   *Die Metaphysik der Sitten* KGS 6 *The Metaphysics of Morals*, trans. Mary J. Gregor (Cambridge: Cambridge University Press, 1991).

R   *Die Religion innerhalb der Grenzen der bloßen Vernunft* KGS 6. *Religion within the Limits of Reason Alone*, trans. Theodore M. Greene and Hoyt H. Hudson (New York: Harper & Row, 1960).

SF   *Der Streit der Facultäten* KGS 7. *The Conflict of the Faculties*, trans. Mary J. Gregor (New York: Abaris Books, 1979).

TP   "Über den Gemeinspruch: Das mag in der Theorie richtig sein, taugt aber nicht für die Praxis" KGS 8. "On the Proverb: That May Be Right in Theory but It Is of No Practical Use," trans. Ted Humphrey, in *Perpetual Peace and Other Essays* (Indianapolis, Ind.: Hackett, 1983).

3. See, for instance, John Gray, "Does Democracy Have a Future?" *The New York Times Book Review*, 22 January 1995; Robin Toner, "Bitter Tone of the '94 Campaign Elicits Worry on Public Debate," *New York Times*, 13 November 1994; Robert Wright, "Hyperdemocracy," *Time*, 13 January 1995, 15–21.

4. Adam Clymer, "Voter Bill Passes in G.O.P. Defeat," *The New York Times*, 11 May 1993.

5. See Onora O'Neill, "Reason and Politics in the Kantian Enterprise," in *Constructions of Reason* (Cambridge: Cambridge University Press, 1989), 3–27.

6. See Philip Rossi, "The Social Authority of Reason: The 'True Church' as the Locus for Moral Progress," *Proceedings of the Eighth International Kant Congress, Volume II, Part 2, Sections 10–8*, ed. Hoke Robinson (Milwaukee, Wis.: Marquette University Press, 1995), 679–85.

7. For example, Howard Williams, *Kant's Political Philosophy* (Oxford: Basil Blackwell, 1983), 260–68, provides a brief account of an important connection, in the realm of international politics, between the "ethical commonwealth" and Kant's proposals for "perpetual peace." Williams, however, does not mention the "ethical commonwealth" in connection with his discussions of citizenship, the public use of reason, or the dynamics of political reform.

8. This is Williams's interpretation in *Kant's Political Philosophy*, 267: "Kant's vision of the true church puts the stress firmly on man's inner ethical dispositions, and hopes for their gradual realization in social and political life. Thus, it is not essential that members of the one true church should mark their unity in outward institutions but, rather, that they should seek always to realize the principles of the church in their everyday lives."

9. See, for instance, R. Bruce Douglas, Gerald M. Mara, and Henry S. Richardson, eds., *Liberalism and the Good* (New York and London: Routledge, 1990); William A. Galston, *Liberal Purposes: Good, Virtues, and Diversity in the Liberal State* (Cambridge: Cambridge University Press, 1991); Alasdair MacIntyre, *After Virtue*, 2nd ed. (Notre Dame, Ind.: University of Notre Dame Press, 1984); idem, *Whose Justice? Which Rationality?* (Notre Dame, Ind.: University of Notre Dame Press, 1988); Michael J. Perry, *Love and Power: The Role of Religion and Morality in American Politics* (Oxford: Oxford University Press, 1991); Terry Pinkard, *Democratic Liberalism and Social Union* (Philadelphia: Temple University Press, 1987); John Rawls, *Political Liberalism* (New York: Columbia University Press, 1993); Michael J. Sandel, *Liberalism and the Limits of Justice* (Cambridge: Cambridge University Press, 1982); William M. Sullivan,

Reconstructing Public Philosophy (Berkeley and Los Angeles: University of California Press: 1982); Michael Walzer, *Spheres of Justice* (New York: Basic Books 1983).

10. E.g., Hans Reiss, "Introduction," in *Kant's Political Writings* (Cambridge: Cambridge University Press, 1971), 20: "The principles of morality would, in one way, go beyond purely legal questions; for they affect private inner decisions by men which can neither be regulated nor enforced publicly. Law deals only with what remains once such inner decisions have been subtracted. It is the outer shell, so to speak, of the moral realm"; Susan Meld Shell, *The Rights of Reason: A Study of Kant's Philosophy and Politics* (Toronto: University of Toronto Press, 1980), 153: "Kant rejects Rousseau's homogeneous and virtuous political community, preferring, along with Hobbes and Locke, cosmopolitan diversity and a clear separation of public and private spheres. Kant conceives the state as an external means to an internal ethical commonwealth; the state remains, however, a purely external means, that is to say a 'means in general' for the pursuit of ends—good, bad and indifferent—which it is up to the individual to choose"; Steven B. Smith, "Defending Hegel from Kant," in *Essays on Kant's Political Philosophy*, ed. Howard Williams (Cardiff: University of Wales Press, 1992), 292: "[Kant] accepts unconditionally the separation of the public from the private, the world of politics from the world of morality." In contrast, see William Galston, *Liberal Purposes* (Cambridge: Cambridge University Press, 1991), 82–89; Patrick Riley, "The 'Place' of Politics in Kant's Practical Philosophy," in *Proceedings of the Sixth International Kant Congress*, vol 2.2, ed. Gerhard Funke and Thomas M. Seebohm (Lanham, Md.: Center for Advanced Research in Phenomenology and University Press of America, 1989), 267–78; Howard Williams, *Kant's Political Philosophy*, pp. 40–49, 125–37.

11. "The Public Use of Reason." in *Constructions of Reason*, pp. 42–49.

12. An argument for this can be constructed by appeal to the "three juridical attributes inseparably bound up with the nature of a citizen as such": namely, freedom, equality, and independence (MdS 314/125; see TP 290–96/72–77); such an argument would require, however, a significant emendation of Kant's notion of independence. For discussions that analyze the difficulties with the scope of Kant's notion of "citizenship," see Wolfgang Kersting," Politics, Freedom and Order: Kant's Political Philosophy," in *The Cambridge Companion to Kant*, ed. Paul Guyer (Cambridge: Cambridge University Press, 1992), 257–58; Susan Mendus, "Kant: 'An Honest but Narrow-Minded Bourgeois?'" in *Essays on Kant's Political Philosophy*, ed. Howard Williams, 166–90; Howard Williams, *Kant's Political Philosophy*, 137–49.

13. Cf. O'Neill. *Constructions of Reason*, 16–17.

14. Cf. Robert B. Pippin, "On the Moral Foundations of Kant's *Rechtslehre*," in *The Philosophy of Immanuel Kant*, ed. Richard Kennington, Studies in Philosophy and the History of Philosophy (Washington, D.C.: Catholic University Press of America, 1985), 12:142: "If what we might loosely call the 'highest good' form of reasoning is inherently involved in why duties of justice are duties at all, then the famous post-Kantian extension of a concern for justice

into social as well as political institutions could be seen as wholly consistent with *Kantian* premises."

15. I wish to thank Paul Eddy, Christine Firer Hinze, and Thomas Hughson for their helpful comments and suggestions. Initial research for this essay was done under the auspices of a research fellowship at the Institute for Advanced Studies in the Humanities, University of Edinburgh.

5

Robin May Schott

Feminism and Kant

Antipathy or Sympathy?

Rereading the Philosophical Canon

The last twenty-five years has witnessed a revolution in contemporary philosophical debates equal to the Copernican revolution introduced by Kant into philosophy.[1] While Kant reversed previous philosophical worldviews by focusing on the human construction of knowledge and morality, feminists have reversed the priority given to claims for sexless, genderless reason by pointing to the sexed and gendered framework of philosophical paradigms.

In this context, feminist philosophers have debated heatedly the questions of whether and how to reread the philosophical canon. On the one hand, some argue for the necessity for feminists to read, write, and teach the history of philosophy. It is argued that feminist work in the history of philosophy is justified for philosophical reasons. Feminists have inherited assumptions from this tradition and need to be self-conscious about them, as Elizabeth Spelman points out so convincingly in *Inessential Women*. In other words, feminists need to acknowledge that our work is formed by a tradition that may incite us to be good daughters or bad, but is nonetheless formative both on a conscious and unconscious level. Arguments for rereading the canon also point to practical necessities (one cannot reinvent the wheel) and institutional grounds (teaching the canon within universities is one of the central ways in which knowledge is socially reproduced).

On the other hand, many feminists (e.g., Linda Singer) have argued that energy is better directed toward creating new beginnings. Rather than interpreting the writings of male philosophers, it may be more fruitful to focus on how women's lives generate radically new ways of thinking and writing that challenge the inherited concepts of philosophical method.

Today, feminists have increasingly come to the recognition that our task is to be both critical and constructive. As Elizabeth Grosz writes, feminists must continue the antisexist project of resisting philosophical assumptions that define "human" by a masculine model, and define the feminine only in relation to the masculine. If feminists do not analyze the ways sexism has functioned in philosophical theories, then feminist theory risks becoming a utopian alternative that leaves untouched existing forms of thought. But if feminist theory is simply critique, it remains on the very ground that it seeks to contest. Thus, feminist theory must be both critique and construct, and Grosz urges feminists to, first, "apprentice" themselves to patriarchal knowledges in order to understand, "how they function, what presumptions they make, what procedures they rely upon, and what effects they produce."[2] Second, she urges feminists to learn how patriarchal theories function in order to use them against themselves. Though it is impossible for feminists to create something that is entirely new, untainted by the very theories they question, they can critically engage with these methods by focusing on their blindspots, contradictions, and silences. Third, Grosz calls for feminists to take traditional discourses as points of departure in order to create new theories, methods, and values. For example, when women's experience rather than men's selects the objects and methods of investigation, feminists not only can develop new theories, but they also demonstrate that philosophical paradigms are not universal.[3]

Feminists readers of Kant have invoked all of these strategies. They have questioned whether Kant's philosophy presupposes a masculine subject, and if so what consequences this presupposition has for his epistemology, ethics, and political theory. They have used Kant's philosophy against itself—for example, to focus on the contradictions between his conception of autonomy and his exclusion of women from equal political rights with men. And they have taken Kant's philosophy as a point of departure for creating new theories—for instance, by analyzing the notion of autonomy in the context of women's experience of friendship or love.

At the present moment, the United States and Europe is witnessing a renaissance of interest in Kant, largely due to the impact of the postmodern criticism of the "philosophy of the subject." Postmodern theorists reject the view of the self that has been embedded in modern philosophy—a view that presupposes a self that is stable, coherent, and capable of rational insight into its own processes and into the laws of nature. For many postmodern theorists, Kant's *Critique of Judgement* provides evidence of a more complex theory of the self than was evident in the either the *Critique of Pure Reason* or the *Critique of Practical Reason*. On the other hand, philosophers who are repulsed by postmodernism's challenge to universal forms of rationality turn to Kant as the most profound bulwark against the onslaughts of skepticism and relativism. In the wake of this revival of Kantianism, it is especially urgent to foreground feminist assessments of Kant.

Feminist readers of Kant nonetheless approach his philosophy from widely divergent points of view. Some view Kant as having contributed significantly to theories of autonomy, subjectivity, and rationality in ways that can further feminist projects.[4] Others argue that Kant is a preeminent exponent of patriarchal views, and that gender hierarchies are inscribed in the very structure of his theories of morality and aesthetic judgment.[5] Still others use the tools of Kant's philosophy to go beyond his own theory. How can one understand the coexistence of such competing interpretations? What are the tensions between the presuppositions of Kantian philosophy and the presuppositions of feminist theory? How in light of these tensions are feminist interpretations of Kant possible? Here I will try to map out the current field of feminist debates of Kant, in order to assess how this work contributes to the creation of new philosophical projects.

FEMINIST INTERPRETATIONS: DEBATED THEMES

Given Kant's explicit endorsement of the subordination of wives to their husbands, and the exclusion of women from intellectual or political rights, it is no surprise that many feminists consider Kant to be an exemplar of philosophical sexism.[6] Here the tensions between Kantian philosophy and feminist theory are mutual. Kant would consider feminists to be concerned with questions of empirical import, of interest perhaps to a particular group but not relevant to universal questions about ethics or aesthetics. Thus, he would exclude feminist questions from the proper domain of philosophy.

Other feminists, inspired by the tradition of German social and critical theory, would argue that Kant's philosophical revolution is a precondition for feminist theory. Kant argued that knowledge is possible because of the activity of the knowing subject, and thus the critique of reason is possible as a form of self-knowledge.[7] The emphasis on human activity as the enabling condition of critique has had enormous impact on post-Kantian social theory. For Marx, it is because the human activity of labor constitutes material life that critical consciousness and ultimately radical social change is possible. For feminist social theorists, it is because social identity is historically constructed that critiques of gender and sexuality are possible.

But there are certain common threads that are present in the views of critics as well as sympathizers (whether cautious or enthusiastic ones). Both groups challenge the accepted topography of Kantian philosophy by which central philosophical concerns are defined as those that are abstract, universal, and transcendental, whereas issues relating to bodily existence, to emotion, or to empirical identity are defined as marginal. Instead, feminists begin with questions founded in everyday life to resituate Kantian questions (e.g., about the role of universals, the construction of the rational self, the nature of moral autonomy, the role of imagination) in the context of relations between the sexes, races, nations, and between humans and the natural environment.

Four thematic areas emerge in feminist debates of Kant (though these areas are by no means inclusive of all current feminist debates):

1.   Debates about Enlightenment rationality and the status of universals;
2.   Debates about autonomy and an "ethics of care";
3.   Debates about women's nature;
4.   Debates about the nature of subjectivity. Here I will briefly summarize the key issues in these debates.

Enlightenment/rationality debates

The Enlightenment claim that progress is possible through the use of reason and the advancement of knowledge is summed up in Kant's dictum, "Have courage to use your own reason!" The claims of the Enlightenment have been one of the most contested themes of contemporary debate. Participants in this debate often respond either positively or negatively to Horkheimer's and Adorno's critique of Enlightenment in *The Dialectic of Enlightenment*. In that work, first published in 1947, Horkheimer and Adorno argue that Kant's definition of Enlightenment, of man's stepping out of self-induced tutelage, marked the beginning of the reign of terror of instrumental reason.[8] They argue that Kant, like the Marquis de Sade, displays the dialectic of Enlightenment in which reason's control over nature and human sensuous nature leads to the instrumentalization of reason and ultimately to the destruction of civilization itself (as evidenced in Nazism and the Holocaust). Contemporary scholars are often either inspired by Horkheimer's and Adorno's identification of Enlightenment rationality with power, or are provoked to contradict them, for example by distinguishing between a "true" and a "false" or reductivist Enlightenment.[9]

Feminist theorists have had a particularly embattled relation to the question of Enlightenment in general, and thus to Kant in particular. Some feminists argue that the Enlightenment tradition of individual reason, progress, and freedom, is a precondition for the discourse of women's liberation and for the political gains that women have won.[10] Even feminists who have a qualified relation to the Enlightenment argue for the need for women to have their turn to fulfill Enlightenment goals. On this view, although women have been viewed by Enlightenment thinkers as not fully rational, and although women have been severely restricted in their educational opportunities, which form a prerequisite for achieving the free use of reason, nonetheless one should demand that the Enlightenment be completed by incorporating previously excluded groups. It is appealing for many to use the Enlightenment tools of rationality and objectivity to argue the case for women's emancipation.

Other feminists, however, argue that the fundamental commitments of the Enlightenment are antithetical to feminist politics and theory, and that feminists must throw their caps in the ring with postmodern critics. On this view, not only have Enlightenment thinkers excluded women from the province of autonomy, but feminist notions of self, knowledge, and truth are seen as contradictory to fundamental Enlightenment commitments.[11] Writers like Jane Flax argue that feminists share with postmodernists a skepticism of transcendental, transhistorical claims for truth, and consider "universality" as itself a reflection of the experience of the dominant social group. On this view, feminists are committed to showing that reason is not divorced from "merely contingent" existence, that the self is embedded in social relations, that the self is embodied, and is thus historically specific and partial. Jane Flax writes, "What Kant's self calls its "own" reason and the methods by which reason's contents become present or self-evident, are no freer from empirical contingency than is the so-called phenomenal self."[12] This desire to detach the self from contingency and embodiment may itself be an effect of particular gender relations, an expression of the flight of masculinity from the temporal, embodied, uncertain realm of phenomenal existence.[13]

Thus, Kant becomes a central figure in feminist debates about Enlightenment epistemology. Some feminists would argue that understanding the formal conditions of universal rational claims is a precondition for coherent claims about knowledge, and for the healthy functioning of a society built on reciprocal recognition of persons. On this view, the formalism of rationality need not imply rigidity, but can elucidate the conditions for an ability to rationally respond to and learn from new experiences, and can therefore provide tools for countering xenophobic fears.[14]

Other feminists, however, point out that Kantian claims for "universal" conditions of reason reflect the experience of the dominant group in society, and thus cannot fulfill the claims of being transcendentally and transhistorically true. Kantian objectivity may be viewed as an articulation of Western culture's commitment to a form of asceticism that requires not only the social subordination of women, but the existential and cognitive suppression of human qualities of emotion and sensuousness that historically have been identified with women.[15] Finally Kantian rationalism can be viewed as an example of impartiality that demands a God-like perspective outside any particular viewpoint, and thus undermines individuals' ability to adjudicate the specific interests or feelings in any individual perspective.[16]

Ethics of Care/Autonomy

Just as feminists have been divided on how to evaluate Kant's epistemological commitments, so they have also given opposing interpretations of his ethical theory. The largest body of feminist work on Kant pivots around the "ethics of care" debates. Carol Gilligan's book, In a Different Voice: Psychological Theory and Women's Development, published in 1982, launched a wave of discussion about the conjunction between sexual difference and moral thinking. In her book she argues that psychological theories of moral development display a distinctly masculine bias by taking boys' moral development as the standard by which girls are measured. In assessing the work of Lawrence Kohlberg, she argues that his theory only accounts for one aspect of moral orientation—that which focuses on justice and rights—and does not account for the ethical orientation of care and responsibility so pronounced in women's moral development. She argues that women's moral judgment is typically more contextual than men's, more immersed in the details of relationships, and more able to reveal feelings of sympathy or empathy. These cognitive characteristics should not be seen as deficiencies, but as essential components for a conception of adult moral maturity that views the self as immersed in a network of relationships with others. In the case of decisions, for example, about whether to have an abortion, or whether to leave their parents or partners, Gilligan finds women to be sensitive to the particular context in which their decisions must be made, to be occupied with questions about who will be hurt and who will be helped.

For many feminist theorists, Gilligan's work has served as a watershed moment in theorizing questions of autonomy, intersubjectivity, and community. It has served as a vehicle to criticize prevailing conceptions of the individual in Western philosophy, which views the autonomous self as disembedded and disembodied. Seyla Benhabib argues that the conception of the individual that has prevailed in thinkers such as Freud, Piaget, Kohlberg, and Rawls is based on a state-of-nature metaphor that provides a vision of the autonomous self as a narcissist who sees the world in his own image. She writes, "Yet this is a strange world; it is one in which individuals are grown up before they have been born; in which boys are men before they have been children; a world where neither mother, nor sister, nor wife exists."[17]

Kant has been an obvious figure for debate in the midst of this contemporary feminist interest in ethics. In Kant's view, for an action to be moral it must be wholly motivated by duty, and must exclude the influence of inclination. His account of the moral law is encapsulated in the categorical imperative: "I should never act in such a way that I could not also will that my maxim should be a universal law."[18] Kant prefigures Kohlberg's understanding of moral development in formalistic terms, and thus his theory becomes embroiled in contemporary debates about justice and care perspectives in morality. Some feminists argue that the moral universalism of Kantian philosophy does not contradict the concerns of care ethics. For example, Herta Nagl-Docekal argues that the formal rule of morality should be understood as both universalist and radically individualizing, and that this formal rule is a precondition for the practicing of an ethics of care.[19] On the other hand, Sally Sedgwick argues that Kant's formalist conception of the moral law is based on a false dichotomy between reason and nature, and cannot be adequate to understanding the complexities of human life that care ethicists seek to incorporate in their accounts of morality.[20]

Other feminists are critical of the turn to a feminist ethics of care. Claudia Card argues that the values exalted by an ethics of care can cover a reality of abuse, in which women are either abused or themselves abusers, and that this ethical view may itself merely articulate the moral damage done to women through the history of their disempowerment.[21] From such a perspective, feminist ethicists would be interested in understanding moral luck, individual separateness, or concepts of autonomy. Marcia Baron argues that Kant's moral commitment to impartiality should be distinguished from treating people impersonally. Impartiality, in this sense, is a commitment to tempering love with respect, which is vital to defend against the threats of possessiveness and paternalism in intimate relations.[22]

Thus, some feminist ethicists argue that patriarchal social structures historically have deprived women of autonomy, and they may look to Kant for providing insights into developing self-determination and responsibility. Alternatively, many care ethicists point out that Kant's conception of autonomy is premised on the notion of a disembodied and disembedded individual, and argue that autonomy needs to be revisioned in order to account for the concrete features of a self situated in particular relations with others.[23] But writers on both sides of this debate seek to revise the concept of autonomy in order to attend to the ways in which individuals are situated in communities of families or friends or of larger groups that bear collective responsibility for political decision making.

Theories of Women's Nature

Many feminist readers of Kant focus specifically on his views of women's nature, inspired by the conception that philosophy is situated amidst social relations. These critics are motivated by the question, how is one to read Kant, or indeed any of the male philosophers in the Western tradition, as a woman.[24] Kant's comments on women's nature are one of the most obvious targets of feminist criticism. For example, Kant asserts woman's character, in contrast to man's, to be wholly defined by natural needs. Women's empirical nature shows their lack of self-determination, in contrast to the rational potential that inheres in their humanity. In the *Anthropology from a Pragmatic Point of View* he writes, "Nature was concerned about the preservation of the embryo and implanted fear into the woman's character, a fear of physical injury and a timidity towards similar dangers. On the basis of this weakness, the woman legitimately asks for masculine protection."[25] Because of their natural fear and timidity, Kant views women as unsuited for scholarly work. He mockingly describes the scholarly women who, "use their books somewhat like a watch, that is, they wear the watch so it can be noticed that they have one, although it is usually broken or does not show the correct time."[26] Kant's remarks on women in the *Anthropology* echo his sentiments in *Observations on the Feeling of the Beautiful and the Sublime*. In that early work, Kant notes, "A woman who has a head full of Greek, like Mme. Dacier, or carries on fundamental controversies about mechanics, like the Marquise de Chatelet, might as well even have a beard, for perhaps that would express more obviously the mien of profundity for which she strives."[27]

In Kant's view, women's philosophy is "not to reason, but to sense." And, "I hardly believe that the fair sex is capable of principles."[28] No wonder, Kant writes, that under these conditions the woman "makes no secret in wishing that she might rather be a man, so that she could give larger and freer latitude to her inclinations; no man, however, would want to be a woman."[29] Are such passages irrelevant to the philosophical significance of Kant's work, or do Kant's views of sexual relations have philosophical import?

Although Kant's later development of the concept of rational autonomy is increasingly at odds with his earlier depiction of women's subjective character, it would be difficult to defend Kant's views of women. Nor can his misogynist views be dismissed as merely reflections of an earlier epoch. For example, the lawyer Theodor von Hippel, mayor of Kant's city of Königsberg, contemporary and friend of Kant, was a spokesperson for equal human and civil rights for women. Thus Kant's views on women must be viewed as reactionary for his times. Hannelore Schroder argues that in the *Rechtslehre*, the first part of the *Metaphysics of Morals*, Kant's justification of the power held by the male head of the household and his views of men's natural superiority over women implies that women cannot consistently be viewed as persons in Kant's account. Thus, in her view, his treatment of women makes a mockery of Kant's universal principle of respect for persons.[30] More sympathetically, Barbara Herman interprets Kant as trying to establish through the political institution of marriage a moral framework for a sexual relationship that in itself is objectifying.[31]

In the context of this debate, many feminists may read Kant as not only devaluing women, but as devaluing human qualities typically associated with women's nature: for example, emotion, desire, and corporeality. Here Kant's views of women can be used as a lever to pry open his philosophical system, to show how the structure of reason is imbued with hierarchical gender values. Feminist social theorists work with the tools of ideology-critique to argue that Kantian philosophy provides justification for existing social hierarchies—not only sexual hierarchies, but also those based on class, race, and colonial relations.[32]

Theories of Subjectivity

Postmodernism's challenge to the "philosophy of the subject" has also had an impact on contemporary feminist debates about Kant's theory of the self. Postmodern philosophers reject the notion of a stable, coherent self, capable of privileged insight into its own processes and into the laws of nature. They reject the view that reason has transcendental and universal qualities that exist independently of the self's particular bodily, historical experiences, or that freedom consists in obeying the laws of a transhistorical form of reason. Many feminists have been similarly skeptical about the universalizing tendencies of the rational self of modern philosophy. They argue that this notion of the self masks the historical specificity of the self, its embeddedness and dependence upon social relations, and see in transcendental claims of the self a reflection of the experience of white Western males.[33]

From this perspective, Kant's theory of the self seems to epitomize a theory of subjectivity shown to be bankrupt by postmodern or feminist critics. Although in Kant's philosophy the activity of subjectivity plays a crucial role in constituting knowledge, these features of subjectivity are understood in formal and universal terms. The "I think" of Kantian philosophy, the transcendental unity of apperception, represents the general and universal features of consciousness, that is, what all representations have in common in order to be united by one self-consciousness, as well as what all self-consciousnesses have in common as a condition for knowledge. Thus, the constituting activity of the self is confined to the formal, universal feature of consciousness, without any trace of the empirical subject.[34]

Post-Kantian thought offers significant alternatives to Kant's conception of subjectivity. Nietzsche, Freud, and Lacan all probe the role of the unconscious, of drive, and desire in subjectivity. They raise questions concerning the eroticism of the subject, and the subject's relation to pain, loss, and guilt. Some feminists use these post-Kantian theories to explore the implications of Kant's moral law from a psychological perspective, and to investigate the differences between men's and women's relation to the "law." For example, Sarah Kofman argues that the nature of men's respect for women, implied in Kant's ethical writings, bears the trace of the originary relation of respect—for example, a child's respect for her/his mother. According to Kofman, this relation implies a desire to hold women at a distance in order not to be crushed by their power or to reveal their weakness. But the price one pays for this respectful distance is the loss of sensual pleasure, which characterized Kant's own celibate life.[35]

Other feminists focus on Kant's theory of imagination in the *Critique of Judgment* in order to substantively revise his earlier theories of subjectivity and autonomy. They explore, for example, how Kant's account of aesthetic pleasure contributes to understanding the role of feelings in the development of moral subjectivity.[36] For example, Jane Kneller follows Hannah Arendt's reading of the *Critique of Judgment* to show that Kant's notion of common sense—*sensus communis*—implies that community is crucial for his understanding of autonomy. From this point of view, impartiality need not mean detachment from or indifference to particular perspectives, but an ability to think in the place of everyone else. Kneller argues, furthermore, that Kant's aesthetics open up the possibility not just of thinking with others, but of feeling with others, and thus creates a space for imagination and feeling in moral subjectivity that can be used to revise Kant's earlier account.[37] In the same spirit, Marcia Moen reads the *Critique of Judgment* as offering an analysis of intersubjectivity—as providing a role for feeling in his account of *sensus communis* and in his turn to the body as the locus of feeling.[38]

CONCLUSION

Finally, in answer to the question posed in my title, is the relation between feminism and Kant one of antipathy or sympathy, my answer is: both. Or perhaps more precisely: it depends on who is answering. If a reader of Kant finds herself/himself inclined more sympathetically or more critically to Kant, this may depend on a number of factors: it may depend on the persuasiveness of rational argumentation. But it may also depend on certain predispositions within the reader. The reader might find herself/himself judging Kant on such factors as the triumph and humility of comprehending an elaborate philosophical system, or the desire for a structure amidst the uncertainties of contemporary life, or the anger at entrenched misogynist views and at any thinker who gives evidence of such views. Thus, it is not possible to "objectively" decide the case, for or against Kant, from a feminist perspective.

In evaluating the feminist debates on Kant, I will close with the following questions: What do feminist interpretations of Kant contribute to Kant scholarship? And what do they contribute to feminist philosophy? Feminist readers of Kant, whether sympathizers or critics, have transformed the inherited terrain of debate. Rather than dealing merely with Kant's internal philosophical criteria, as scholars typically have done, feminist readers have taken concerns arising from feminist philosophy as points of departure in their analyses of Kant. In this context, questions about embodiment, emotion and imagination, community and power relations have become central in debates about Kant. Feminist interpretations are an example of the rejuvenation of philosophy that occurs when women become participants in a dialogue that historically has excluded them.

Feminist readings of Kant also make an important contribution to feminist philosophy more generally. Such readings are part of the important task of historical self-knowledge. As Elizabeth Spelman points out in *Inessential Woman*,[39] if feminists do not know adequately the historical tradition from which they seek to distance themselves, they risk repeating the very premises that they ostensibly reject. Moreover, feminists engaged in reading Kant contribute to a more sophisticated and nuanced theorizing about epistemology, ethics, and aesthetics than can occur in a historical vacuum. Feminists have moved far from an earlier dismissal of Western male philosophers as patriarchal, and hence of no interest for feminist philosophy. Rather, feminist philosophers currently recognize that however much one may identify a philosopher as masculinist, one still needs to engage either positively or critically with this tradition. Moreover, the diversity of feminist interpretations of Kant are a contribution to the more general theoretical recognition of the multiplicity of feminist perspectives. One can no more justify a unitary truth in feminist philosophies than one can in masculinist philosophies.

Feminist readings of Kant, like any self-conscious hermeneutical engagement both with the world of the text and with one's own contemporary realities, create philosophy anew. Thus we should remember that when women become scholars—and enter the "public" exercise of reason, they do not grow beards (as Kant joked). But they do open paths for rethinking the contents and methods of education and intellectual discourse more generally. It is to this larger project that feminist readings of Kant seek to contribute.

NOTES

1. This essay was originally based on my introduction to *Feminist Interpretations of Kant* (University Park: Pennsylvania State University Press, 1997). It then become the basis of another essay, "Feminist Perspectives on the Western Canonical Tradition: Kant," in *Companion to Feminist Philosophy*, ed. Alison Jaggar and Iris Young (Oxford: Blackwell Press, 1997), but in this final stage must be viewed as the beneficiary of that essay.

2. Elizabeth Grosz, "Contemporary Theories of Power and Subjectivity," in *Feminist Knowledge; Critique and Construct*, ed. Sneja Gunew (London: Routledge, 1990), 60.

3. Ibid., p. 61.

4. See, for example, Marcia Baron, "Kantian Ethics and Claims of Detachment," in *Feminist Interpretations of Kant*, ed. Robin May Schott (University Park: Pennsylvania State University Press, 1997) and Adrian Piper, "Xenophobia and Kantian Rationalism," *Philosophical Forum Quarterly* 25. 1–3 (Fall/Spring 1992–93): 188–232 (also reprinted in Schott, 1997).

5. See Hannelore Schroder, "Kant's Patriarchal Order," in Schott, 1997, and Robin May Schott, "The Gender of Enlightenment" in *What is Enlightenment?*

18th Century Answers and 20th Questions, ed. James Schmidt (Berkeley: University of California Press, 1996; reprinted in Schott, 1997).

6. E.g., Schroder and Schott. Even readers sympathetic with Kantian ethics, like Marcia Baron, take issue with much that he says about women ("Kantian Ethics and Claims of Detachment").

7. Seyla Benhabib, *Critique, Norm, and Utopia* (New York: Columbia University Press, 1986), 45.

8. See John H. Smith's interesting discussion of the Enlightenment debates in "Reading Kant with Sade with Lacan: The Limits and Lost Cause of the Enlightenment," 7ff. (manuscript). Department of German, University of California, Irvine.

9. Ibid., p. 10.

10. See Christine Di Stefano discussion in "Dilemmas of Difference," in *Feminism/Postmodernism*, ed. Linda Nicholson (New York.: Routledge, 1990), 75.

11. Jane Flax, "Postmodernism and Gender Relations," in *Feminism/Postmodernism*, p. 42. Flax writes, "The way(s) to feminist future(s) cannot lie in reviving or appropriating Enlightenment concepts of the person or knowledge."

12. Ibid., 43.

13. See, for example, my book, *Cognition and Eros; A Critique of the Kantian Paradigm* (University Park: Pennsylvania State University Press, 1993).

14. Adrian Piper, "Xenophobia and Kantian Rationalism."

15. See *Cognition and Eros*.

16. See Iris Young's discussion of impartiality in, *Throwing Like a Girl and Other Essays in Feminist Philosophy and Social Theory* (Bloomington: Indiana University Press, 1990), 96.

17. Seyla Benhabib, "The Generalized and the Concrete Other," in *Situating the Self; Gender, Community and Postmodernism in Contemporary Ethics* (New York: Routledge, 1992), 156–57.

18. Immanuel Kant, *Foundations of the Metaphysics of Morals*, trans. Lewis White Beck (Indianapolis, Ind.: Bobbs-Merrill, 1959), p. 18. *Kants Gesammelte Schriften*, Ausgabe der Königlichen Preußischen Akademie (Berlin, 1903–), 4:403.

19. Herta Nagl-Docekal, "Feminist Ethics: How It Could Benefit from Kant's Moral Philosophy," in Schott, 1997.

20. Sally Sedgwick, "Can Kant's Ethics Survive the Feminist Critique?" *Pacific Philosophical Quarterly* 71 (1990): 60–79; reprinted in Schott, 1997.

21. Claudia Card, "Women's Voices and Ethical Ideals: Must We Mean What We Say?" *Ethics* (October, 1988), 99:1, 125–35.

22. See Marcia Baron, "Kantian Ethics and Claims of Detachment," in Schott, 1997.

23. Jean Rumsey, "Re-Vision of Agency in Kant's Moral Theoy," in Schott, 1997.

24. I do not mean to assert there is any single, essential position by which a reader who is also a woman interprets. Rather, I point to the fact that women might be especially disturbed by such passages, just as blacks are especially disturbed by racist comments, and Jews by antisemitic ones. Men, of course, may also find such passages disturbing, as many white people also find racist comments deplorable.

25. Kant, *Anthropologie in pragmatischer Hinsicht*, in *Kants Gesammelte Schriften*, Ausgabe der Königlichen Preußischen Akademie (Berlin, 1907), 7:306. *Anthropology from a Pragmatic Point of View*, trans. Lyle Dowdell (Carbondale and Edwardsville: Southern Illinois Press, 1978), p. 221.

26. Kant, *Anthropologie in pragmatischer Hinsicht*, in *Kants Gesammelte Schriften*, 7:307. *Anthropology from a Pragmatic Point of View*, p. 221.

27. Kant, *Beobachtungen über des Gefühl des Schonen und Erhabenen*, in *Kants Gesammelte Schriften*, 2:229–30. *Observations on the Feeling of the Beautiful and the Sublime*, 132–33.

28. Kant, *Beobachtungen über das Gefühl des Schonen und Erhabenen*, in *Kants Gesammelte Schriften*, 2:231–32. *Observations on the Feeling of the Beautiful and the Sublime*, 132–33.

29. Kant, *Anthropologie in pragmatischer Hinsicht*, in *Kants Gesammelte Schriften*, 7:307; *Anthropology*, p. 222.

30. Hannelore Schroder, "Kant's Patriarchal Order," in Schott, 1997.

31. Barbara Herman, "Can It Be Worth Thinking About Kant on Sex and Marriage?" in *A Mind of Her Own; Feminist Essays on Reason and Objectivity*, ed. Louise M. Antony and Charlotte Witt (Boulder, Colo.: Westview Press, 1993), 55–57.

32. See *Cognition and Eros*, for an example of this view. See also Kim Hall, "*Sensus Communis* and Violence: A Feminist Reading of Kant's *Critique of Judgement*," in Schott, 1997.

33. Jane Flax, "Postmodernism and Gender Relations in Feminist Theory," in *Feminism/Postmodernism*, 41–43.

34. See *Cognition and Eros*, chap. 9.

35. Sarah Kofman, "The Economy of Respect: Kant and Respect for Women," from *Le Respect des femmes* (Paris: Galilee, 1982), reprinted in Schott, 1997.

36. See Jane Kneller's article, "The Aesthetic Dimension of Kantian Autonomy," in Schott, 1997.

37. Jane Kneller, "The Aesthetic Dimension of Kantian Autonomy," in Schott, 1997.

38. Marcia Moen, "Feminist Themes in Unlikely Places: Rereading Kant's *Critique of Judgement*," in Schott, 1997.

39. Elizabeth Spelman, *Inessential Woman; Problems of Exclusion in Feminist Thought* (Boston: Beacon Press, 1988), 6.

II

Kant and Contemporary
Social Issues

6

Sharon Anderson-Gold

Crimes against Humanity

A Kantian Perspective on International Law

Most ethical theorists believe that some form of international community is essential to humanity's survival and moral development. It can be argued that the interdependence resulting from the impacts of modern technology and the development of a world market have extended the moral principles of social responsibility beyond the confines of civil society. In the late eighteenth century, Immanuel Kant forecast the inevitability of this "cosmopolitan" development in his essay "Idea for a Universal History from a Cosmopolitan Perspective" and declared its object, an international community of nations, a moral goal in "Perpetual Peace." We have seen the emergence in the twentieth century of organizations designed to give practical significance to the Kantian ideal of an international community united by international law and dedicated to the promotion of human rights. At the same time, we have seen the emergence of terrorism and ethnic conflicts that threaten the viability of such organizations and their ideal of community.

Contemporary conflicts like the Bosnian civil war with its policy of "ethnic cleansing" damage the fragile hope that human rights will be universally recognized and respected. Such conflicts raise, in a particularly acute form, the question of the nature and extent of the obligations of the members of an international community for the protection of human rights and for the maintenance of peace. Should member nations intervene in such conflicts or does the right to self-determination of independent nations provide immunity from inter-ference even when the combatants adopt policies that violate the basic human rights of whole segments of ethnic populations? This paper will consider the traditional Kantian doctrine that international law requires noninterference in the internal affairs of nations even when the official policies of a government involve the systematic violation of human rights or what today we would call "crimes against humanity." Because Kant maintains that political subjects have no coercible rights against their sovereign, it has been inferred that either there are no human rights in addition to civil rights or those human rights are "vacuous." In either case, it would seem that human rights that are anything other than politically defined appear to be a without a systematic basis in Kant's account of rights. Something, then, must be missing in Kant's account of the relationship between law and ethics. How can a moral philosophy whose foundation lies in the concept of humanity as an "end-in-itself" with a dignity beyond price result in an account of rights that are essentially "relativized"? My object will be to reconstruct a Kantian account of the relationship between law and ethics that will support a positive doctrine of human rights and a limited principle of political intervention.

As A. J. M. Milne notes in *Human Rights and Human Diversity*,[1] the idea of human rights is one of the most prominent in contemporary political rhetoric. To accuse a regime of violating human rights is a very serious charge. The claim that certain rights belong to human beings in all places and all times is supported by no less august a document than the United Nations Universal Declaration of Human Rights (1948), which states: "Everyone is entitled to all the rights and freedoms set forth in this Declaration without distinction of any kind such as race, color, sex, language, religion, political or other opinion, national or social origin, property, birth or other status."[2] Given that the "rights and freedoms" specified in this document are inaccessible to the majority of human kind, Milne asks, what does it mean to provide an account of human rights that is irrelevant to the condition of most of humanity? If human identity is in part constituted by cultural and social conditions, how should the facts of cultural diversity affect an adequate account of human rights? Are human rights everywhere the "same" and if not what does it mean to demand respect for human rights?

One of the major theses of *Human Rights and Human Diversity* is that human rights must be contextualized and cannot be expected to be the same in content and scope everywhere.[3] For example, material conditions will dictate whether a given political community will be able to provide a particular resource such as universal health care as a political or civil right. We cannot expect the same level of material entitlements across political societies. Therefore, the claim that all human beings are "entitled" to the same level of health care might better be interpreted as a call for assistance to developing nations from those more advanced rather than as an explication of a current right. At any rate, one cannot claim that an underdeveloped nation has violated the human rights of its citizens in failing to provide a material good that it cannot afford.[4]

However, according to Milne, the "contextualization" of human rights goes even deeper and provides for differences in the scope and content of civil right *within* particular political societies based upon different status positions.[5] What is "fair" and "equal" is relative to these positions. It is presumed that these status positions arise from some division of labor that is in the best interest of the community as a whole and that the community's natural interest is in maintaining the best way of life for each status position. As long as the particular interpretation given to a system of rights provides each participant with an opportunity for a decent existence, Milne argues that rights do not have to be equal and the fact that they are not equal is not a sufficient reason to believe that human right has been violated. A caste system or a gender stratified society could pass Milne's test without violation of human rights. This assumes that the community is in some sense "united" in its acceptance of these differences, and that only a "polarized" society is in danger of a systematic violation of human rights. This leaves a great deal of power to define what is "decent" in the hands of the dominant group and equates a lack of active resistance with acceptance. Such systems, however, do not meet a Kantian standard for justification of inequalities. Kant maintains that it must be possible for those who are occupying inferior social/economic positions to "work their way" out of these positions.[6] The benefit of the community cannot override respect for humanity in each *individual* as an end in itself in a Kantian analysis. Neither a caste nor a gender-stratified system meets this condition.

Nonetheless, Milne recognizes that the idea of *human* rights must have some basic minimum standard defining what it is to have a social and civil status and that standard must be universally valid both throughout and across political societies. If there are any universally valid forms of human rights it becomes possible for governments to suppress them, or worse, fail to recognize them. Milne does, for example, consider slavery and racial discrimination to be incompatible with human rights. In general physical differences are not relevant to issues of human rights and (with the exceptions noted above) tend to lead to the polarization of the community. His argument for why, nonetheless, interference in the internal affairs of a racist regime is unacceptable is not a direct inference from the contextualization argument. Milne summarizes the dilemma in the following question: "Can what is wrong according to international morality ever be right according to universal morality?" and answers "Only if war against the offending state is a lesser evil than the violation of human rights of which that state is guilty."[7] International morality, which demands noninterference in the internal affairs of other nations, supports the community of nations. Since war by its nature endangers the international community, war as a means of gaining respect for human rights, Milne concludes, is likely to be the greater evil than the violation of them in a particular state. But if "endangers" here merely means that war can threaten the physical survival of particular nations, then the argument is not sufficiently morally grounded. The argument would then be essentially a consequentialist argument weighing the probabilities of escalating violence leading to the breakdown of peace. Is it the physical survival of humanity as a natural species that is an end in itself? Or is physical survival a moral obligation because humanity as a moral species is an end in itself? If it is the latter, then, to demonstrate that one is morally obligated to support any international institution, it must also be necessary to demonstrate that this *institution is connected to the development of humanity as a moral species.* For it is only as a moral, and not merely as a natural species, that humanity is intrinsically valuable and an end-in-itself.

However, one could at this juncture represent the violation of the political right to self-determination as an attack on the legal basis of the international community. This would bring the argument into line with the traditional Kantian doctrine that the prohibition on interference in the internal affairs of a sovereign nation must be viewed as the primary obligation on legal grounds. This is a very serious argument, yet the conclusion in the form of an absolute prohibition on political intervention is challengeable. I believe that an argument can be made that a limited principle of political intervention is implicit in the *concept of law* that provides the legal basis of an international community. If I can show that in Kant's own terms, the *ethical basis of international law* requires that states *qua* moral persons respect the human rights of their subjects as a condition for their participation in the "rights of nations," then I believe a limited principle of political intervention follows. Because human beings are not directly "citizens" of international communities, there appears to be a "gap" in terms of the moral principles that generate the legal obligation of individuals to civil society and the moral principles that generate the legal obligations of political societies to one another. But that "gap" is more apparent than real. For although it is true that organized power is differently situated within civil society and within international communities, this does not affect the fundamental principle of human right from which all obligations of any type are generated.

Implicit in the concept of an international community is the principle of political self-determination, that is, the right of an organized group of people to govern itself without interference from other organized groups. This right is more basic than the specific political and civil rights that are derived from specific forms of government and specific constitutions. Political and civil rights do in fact vary in both content and scope within the international community and this variation can be said to reflect the basic right of a people to political self-determination. When, then, can it ever be said that a government has violated its citizens rights? Citizens of democratic republics will value active political participation especially in the forms of free public speech and assembly. Does the lack of such participation in other states constitute just cause for political intervention on the part of democratic republics to change the deficient political constitutions? What role do human or pre-political rights play in limiting the variation in civil rights that a government can rightfully impose? What sorts of grounds are just cause for suspension of the political right of self-determination? What is a basic human right? How is it recognized? I would like to demonstrate that the basic human right to external freedom generates all forms of political society and lies as much at the basis of international community as at the basis of civil community. Basically, I will argue that there are no political rights (specifically no national immunity rights) where there are no human rights.

An international community presupposes some universal form of human right. Nations can be morally obligated to respect the independence of other nations only if there is some universal or basic human right to self-determination. Because humanity is a moral species, the moral capacity for self-determination requires that a system of external freedom or legal right be secured. Civil law secures this right for individuals, international law secures this right for politically organized groups or states. At the same time, the independence of such states permits a political "contextualization" of human rights that inevitably results in variation in their legally defined scope and content. However, no "contextualization" of human rights is compatible with "crimes against humanity," which I shall define as the categorical denial of the humanity of a particular group of individuals and the systematic suppression of their human/political right to freedom from arbitrary interference. I will focus on this form of freedom because while with some reservations I have accepted Milne's argument that within nonpolarized communities cultural diversity may justify different social-status positions, the very notion of a social position requires that individuals be secured from arbitrary interference. When individuals are denied that which is essential to having any secured social or political status, there is in fact no limit to the violence that can be taken against them. Therefore, "crimes against humanity," while often referring to genocide or the systematic murder of populations, includes also systematic violations of persons (rape) and property (and systematic denials of access to property). Unlike the legal limitations on freedom that can vary greatly between political societies and within legally defined status groups within political society, "crimes against humanity" strip individuals of all social-civil status, permitting if not requiring their complete annihilation. Such violations signal the denial of moral personhood and thus humanity in its moral sense. State policies that promote or protect "crimes against humanity," I shall contend, do not fall under the immunity protection from interference by other states even though noninterference is a corollary of the independence granted by international law.

So far I have been arguing that our humanity is the basis of a fundamental right to be secure in our persons from arbitrary interference on the part of others. But what is it about humanity as such that provides such a justification? In the *Religion*, Kant maintains that the predisposition to personality is an original and inextirpable constituent of human beings from which the capacity to be subject to the moral law arises.[8] As such it is both a necessary and sufficient condition for the imputation of rights and obligations. The minimal condition for inclusion in the moral community is, then, not any specific cultural achievement, social status, or personal talent but simply a certain "receptivity" that Kant regards as basic to humanity. Is this "receptivity" an empirical quality that could be subjected to an investigation and found wanting? Could whole racial and ethnic groups be discovered to be without this essential characteristic? Since Kantian anthropology appears to be constructed out of a regressive analysis of the conditions necessary to describe a moral subject and since morality is not itself an empirical concept, a research protocol sufficient to prove that some subgroup of a *species exhibiting moral subjectivity* is without this vital quality appears to be transcendentally constrained. Kant's moral philosophy is in fact based squarely on this ethical-anthropology, which is reflected in the postulate that humanity is an end in itself and the source of all duty. What does this mean?

Fundamentally, in Kant's view, all duties are duties to humanity. This claim is derived from an analysis of the conditions of the possibility of morality as a categorical imperative. The formulation of rules of action, or imperatives is an intrinsic part of practical life. When the "author" of such an imperative is also its "subject," the resulting obligation can be categorical or absolutely binding if and only if the subject is an *end-in-itself*. Through the capacity to obligate oneself, to formulate universal principles, subjective existence demonstrates intrinsic value. Were it not for this stipulation, that humanity, in each subject, is an *end-in-itself*, the fact that I can formulate or author a principle might as well serve to release as to bind me to its purpose. Thus, autonomous self-legislation, reveals the subject as an end-in-itself and this in the very first instance constrains and shapes the legislating will. The binding quality of a moral principle is what Kant refers to as its modality, that is, its categoricalness. For Kant, the concept of a "hypothetical" morality is a non sequitur. Hypothetical imperatives formulate only the rules governing the relationship of means to ends but they do not provide any doctrine of "ends." Without a doctrine of ends they provide no necessary constraint to any action. According to Kant, if morality constrains (and Kant thought that this was beyond question), it constrains "categorically" and it can constrain categorically because the author/subject is an *end-in-itself*.

Autonomy then, is a fundamental attribute of a moral subject. But freedom from arbitrary interference is an essential corollary of both moral and legal autonomy. The capacity for self-legislation carries with it an entitlement to external freedom that can only be rightfully constrained according to universal principles maximizing external freedom. Therefore, every human subject has an innate right to freedom from arbitrary interference, where "arbitrary" in a Kantian system is defined in terms of a restriction on the *maximum possible system of freedom*, which is reciprocally limited and binding. This is compatible with some degree of cultural diversity but provides a critical criteria in the form of a maximization principle that is independent of the social structure. This innate right is not a "civil" right. It is a necessary condition for the possibility of any political obligation at all. Since everyone has the moral obligation to refrain from arbitrary interference with others but cannot adequately do so unless also so secured, everyone has the obligation to enter into a civil society. Civil society then comes into existence in the moral domain only as a consequence of the universal will to be secured from arbitrary interference. Any interference that is not reciprocally limited and reciprocally binding is prima facie arbitrary. Any system of legal right that does not strive toward the maximum is morally deficient.[9] Having derived the authority of civil society from the innate right of the subject to be free from arbitrary interference, there cannot be a morality or a civil authority that does not guarantee this minimum human right.

Although government can take many forms, according to Kant the civil condition is characterized by a threefold relationship between governor and governed. Only a "legal subject" can be obligated to obey positive law. The concept of a legal subject requires that all subjects be secured freedom (as a human being), equality(as a subject of the state), and independence (as a citizen).[10] Once these conditions are met, specific civil and political rights will depend upon the form of government, its constitution and its positive legislation. This means that while the scope and content of human rights will vary in terms of political expression, the idea of universal human rights is embedded within the structure of the civil condition as well as within the structure of the international community. But what if the law is specified in such a way that not all human persons are recognized as legal subjects?[11] Such a legal system, while internally coherent, would still be morally deficient by Kantian standards. Are we to regard such states as "moral persons"? And even if we were to accept this rather weak analogy with human persons, are not such states by their very failure to recognize the basic rights of all persons in violation of moral law? Isn't international law also to be understood as standing in relation to moral law? Are not such states in violation of international law?

In his work, *Kant's System of Rights*, Leslie Mulholland recognizes this fundamental tension between the legal and the moral realms.[12] He maintains that there is a problem in Kant's system of rights in that Kant maintains that the first principle of the doctrine of rights is analytic and does not depend upon any ethical elements. The distinction between law and ethics allows for the differentiation between the sphere of coercible duties (legal obligation) and those that require the adoption of an end (ethical obligation). Legal duties are coercible in that the rightfulness of the action does not depend upon any intention or motive of the agent. They can therefore be externally constrained in a manner consistent with ethics. This distinction is extremely important to the development of the innate right and the entire sphere of external freedom. However, unless strict law is derived from a prior ethical principle that provides an *ethical interpretation for the concept of "person,"* it is not clear that all human beings must be considered as persons in the law. According to Mulholland, that all human beings are persons is not an analytical principle derivable simply from the definition of a subject of rights and obligations. That all human beings are persons is an *a priori* synthetic principle derived from the concept of humanity as an end in itself. "If law is separated from ethics, however, there is no ground for insisting that all beings who in the sphere of ethics have the status of person, must also have this status in law."[13] The question for Mulholland, then, centers around how we can demonstrate that law cannot be separated from ethics, that any system of law that does not acknowledge the innate right of all persons (where all human beings by virtue of their consciousness of their freedom and capacity to be obligated) is inherently deficient. Contrary to Kant's own conclusions in this matter, Mulholland argues that unless the innate right of those subject to law includes the title to coerce the executive to acknowledge that right, the separation of law and ethics is fatal.[14] While granting that subjects have the moral title to attempt to secure their rights captures the moral requirement that law be reciprocally binding, it doesn't quite speak to the issue of the interest of the international community in violations of human rights. As a practical matter the power of the state may be such that resistance is ineffective and leads only to more extensive violations. And inasmuch as it may be tempting to view such violations primarily as "internal harms" not affecting the relationships between nations, it is necessary to demonstrate in addition in what sense "crimes against humanity" are harms to the international community.

The obligation to enter political society is fundamentally a moral obligation because it is the direct consequence of the obligation to secure one's innate right to freedom. This ends the state of nature for any specific group of individuals. But organized political groups remain in a state of nature wherein their rights in relation to one another remain provisional unless they too explicitly enter into a lawful condition. That lawful condition, a federation of free states united under a law of nations, is built upon the same moral principle of the universal right to freedom that justifies the sovereignty of individual nations. Kant maintains that every form of association must be governed by the principle of external freedom (public law).

"Hence, not only municipal Law, but also a Law of nations, may be thought of as belonging to the general concept of public Law. Because the surface of the earth is not unlimited in extent, both kinds of Law inevitably lead to the Idea of international Law or world Law. Consequently, if just one of these possible forms of juridical condition lacks a principle circumscribing external freedom through laws, then the structure of all the others will unavoidably be undermined and must finally collapse."[15]

This is to say more than that each nation must respect the liberty rights of every other nation. It means also that the integrity of the civil condition depends upon the subordination of its system of law to principles of international law "if just one of these . . . lacks a principle," and so forth. Kant states explicitly that public law contains the principle that mutually and reciprocally constrains all forms of external freedom. I have argued that public law (the principle of external freedom) at its most basic level must guarantee that all human persons are free from arbitrary interference. Unless all human persons are protected by public law then there cannot be a *universal juridical condition that is the object of public Law.* Although Kant's remarks on world law are rudimentary, the idea of world community is such as to require that every human person even foreign traders, strangers, potential immigrants, and so on be treated with hospitality because even though such persons do not have a positive right to colonization this "does not nullify the right of a citizen of the earth to attempt (to establish) a community with everyone and to visit all the regions of the earth."[16] All that is necessary to be a "citizen of the earth" is to be an "inhabitant," there are no national/ethnic/racial restrictions on the obligations of hospitality. Although the law of nations includes the "rights of war," these rights are strictly delimited both in respect to what a state can do with its own subjects and with respect to what a state can do to an enemy population. Kant explicitly denies that any state can rightfully view its subjects in the nature of either animals or property to be used for its own purposes. "This kind of an argument . . . absolutely cannot be applied to a human being, and especially not to a citizen."[17] Even with respect to an enemy population Kant states: "To a state against which a war is being fought, defensive measures of every kind, except those that would make a subject of that state unfit to be a citizen are allowed. If it were to employ such measures, it would thereby make itself unfit to be considered a person in relation to other states in the eyes of the Law of nations (and as such to participate in equal rights with the other states)."[18] Under the law of nations, states are regarded as "moral persons" in the way that individuals are moral persons even in a state of nature, but there is this interesting difference that this form of law is concerned not only with the relationship of one state to another "but also with the relationship of individuals in one state to individuals in another and of an individual to another whole state."[19] Apparently, the fact that persons reside in different states does not cancel the claims of the juridical condition. Thus, even in war, soldiers cannot rightfully (even if so commanded) violate the human rights of enemy noncombatants. What holds true between subjects of different nations must hold true in civil conflicts. Clearly, then, neither the sovereignty of a nation nor its right to lawful self-determination provide a moral shield for actions that violate basic human rights. A federation that could tolerate violations of basic human rights would be fostering only the power rights of nations or dominant ethnic groups but not the moral principles that provide the justification for sovereignty or even for the rights of war. That type of toleration would surely "undermine" the moral structure of its lawful members because it attacks the universal juridical condition that is ultimately the aim of the federation itself. Thus, if the moral value of an international community is derived from human rights rather than simply from the pragmatic value of peace, then it is not clear that interference to end a violation of human rights is the greater evil. This argument holds for those violations of human right that are contrary to the existence of a universal juridical community. Since racial, ethnic, and gender differences cannot be used to define human rights, they cannot become the basis for denial of human rights. Nations that engage in such actions are themselves in violation of international law, hence "unfit to be considered a person in relation to other states" or "to participate in equal rights with other states."

While not every form of political community will provide for the right to vote and contest elections or the right to health care or social security, every political community must secure to all human persons the status of "legal person" with its protections and immunities. "Crimes against humanity" such as genocide and ethnic cleansing cannot be "legal" because they entail the destruction of the "legal subject" to whom the obligation to obey the law is addressed. This puts such groups of individuals into a state of war with their "governors" and justifies revolutionary activity. Does it also justify interference by other nations in the internal affairs of communities engaged in racial or ethnic conflict? Can other communities use force to assist a beleaguered group? If some groups are denied their human/political rights by the governments of the area in which they reside do they then become "legal orphans?" But if the violence is not "legal" to begin with, what prohibition can there be against assistance?

"Crimes against humanity" are considered by some to be legal paradoxes because it is maintained that human beings can only claim political protection insofar as they are legal subjects not in virtue of their humanity per se. One cannot, it is maintained, be directly, the legal subject of an international community. Because "crimes against humanity" are by definition arbitrary interferences permitted (or even required) by law, they destroy one's legal standing and deny one's human right. Such individuals are in effect legally "orphaned" by the government within whose jurisdiction they reside. They become in effect "foreigners" without a government of their own. Without a government of their own there is no political power that is obligated to act on their behalf. By this reasoning, if there is a "crime," there is no one authorized to correct the wrong. Something is wrong with this reasoning.

Generally speaking, crimes are harms done to the community as well as to the individual. That is why individuals who have been harmed cannot abolish the crime by waiving their "right" to retribution. The injustice remains and requires adjudication by the civil authority. Is this the case simply because crime is a "legal" category? Is the injustice an artifact of the civil law? Fundamental human rights are not artifacts of civil law. If they were, the civil condition would carry no specifically moral sanction. Violations of fundamental human rights would be punishable by the community in a pre-civil condition. Every individual has a right to aide in distress and what counters an unjust action (interference with the freedom of another) is defined by Kant as just.[20] Civil law only becomes obligatory because there is a natural law requiring that these rights be secured. Natural law then is the foundation of the title of civil authority; it is not sublated into civil law. But natural law is also the foundation of the law of nations. It is therefore reasonable to conclude that sovereigns lose their immunity right under the law of nations if they violate natural law. Crimes against humanity because they destroy the basic juridical condition that makes any law obligatory are harms to the international community as much as to the politically suppressed group. This entails not only that it would not be wrong to assist the suppressed group but that the international community has a positive ethical obligation to aide. Since we have already argued that governments guilty of such crimes have no immunity right, in this context ethical obligation is not in opposition to legal obligation. This ethical obligation requires that nations adopt the "rights of humanity" as their end and act in accordance with this end *without being coerced to do so.* Not being coerced to do so, a nation may act unilaterally if this is not in conflict with other obligations. But, since obligations to one's own citizens, allies and the international community generally preclude unilateral action, justified interference will require a consensus among like-minded nations. While my argument for a limited principle of political intervention is drawn from the "rights of humanity," it dovetails nicely with a similar argument by Harry van der Linden. Arguing for a limited principle of political intervention as essential to the duty to promote international peace, van der Linden offers the following guidelines: "that the intervention must be essential for political success; that nonviolent intervention rather than military intervention should be chosen . . . ; that the intervention should accord with the will of those on whose behalf it takes place; and that the intervening agent should seek support for its action within the world community."[21] These policies are designed to minimize the danger of the escalation of violence, which although not the whole would clearly be an important part of a moral international politics.

While in general noninterference is important to the long-term goal of ending all war, the primary objective of the federation is to secure a universal juridical condition. Political rights exist only as an extension of human right. Justice cannot be secured where human right is violated. Just as virtue must be the ground of happiness, it is justice that will in the long run secure peace. There is no necessary relation between peace and justice. The denial of basic human rights is not a "contextualization" issue. It destroys the right of the government to claim immunity from interference. Where does this leave the question of the "lesser evil" as Milne puts it? Milne claims that war cannot be the lesser evil because it necessarily violates human rights, presumably the immunity right to independence. But in this case there is no immunity right to be violated. If natural law is the basis of the law of nations, it must be possible for a sovereign nation to forfeit its immunity right just as individuals who commit crimes under civil law forfeit theirs. On the other hand, I would maintain that it is not possible for the international community to tolerate "crimes against humanity." If basic human rights are anything less than universal, if the international community can readily tolerate "local" violations while benefiting from a general peace, then the terrorist strategy of exporting violence so that peace will no longer be worth the "price," will continue to make a certain twisted sense.

In conclusion, while differing cultural/economic conditions may make a variation in scope and content of human rights acceptable within some basic definition of what it is to be a subject of rights, the idea of humanity as a moral species is presupposed in any analysis of human rights and international community. If it is the case that the idea of human rights underwrites the constraints on international interference and on the conditions of war, then there must be some basic sense of human rights that is more fundamental to the possibility of international community than the prohibition on interference itself. With respect to this basic definition of human right there can be no merely "local" violation that is not also a threat to the idea of international community. I would maintain that "ethnic cleansing" and in general "crimes against humanity" are actions that governing powers cannot undertake without violation of the basic conditions of international community. If it is permissible to define basic human rights through ethnic inclusion or exclusion, then the very principles formulated to maintain community peacefully through prohibition of interference/coercion/war are reduced to merely pragmatic considerations designed to protect the interests of particular groups. In order that these laws and prohibitions carry serious moral weight, they must in their very formulation pledge security to humanity *qua* humanity.

While international law is no doubt pragmatically connected to humanity's survival, unless humanity's survival is itself a moral concern, the derivation of human rights from the idea of an international community is in turn merely "pragmatically" grounded.

While from an historical perspective the capacity of the international community to conceptualize the task of securing basic human rights may be just emerging, already public consciousness of its significance transcends merely pragmatic concerns. Having formulated the moral foundations of international law in the principle of humanity, we cannot regress to a policy that permits violations of human rights. In these cases our moral interests are our "vital" interest. While pragmatism is compatible with morality to a point, the material ends that human beings seek, peace and security, are ultimately only possible as a result of the moral development of the species. The full natural perfection of the species is thus possible only if humanity is also a moral species.

NOTES

1. A. J. M. Milne, *Human Rights and Human Diversity* (Albany: State University of New York Press , 1986), Introduction.

2. Ibid., 1–2

3. Ibid., 9

4. If however, a society's resources are very unevenly distributed and many people have no access to the basic means to secure a living, this condition may not be met. A Rawlsian formula could be used to determine whether or not existing inequalities are justified or require redistribution.

5. Milne, *Human Rights*, 167.

6. Immanuel Kant, *Kants Gesammelte Schriften* (Berlin, 1914), 6:315; *The Metaphysical Elements of Justice*, trans. John Ladd (Indianapolis, Ind.: Bobbs-Merrill, 1965), 80.

7. Milne, *Human Rights*, 171.

8. Kant, *Kants Gesammelte Schriften*, 6:26–28; *Religion within the Limits of Reason Alone*, trans. Theodore M. Greene and Hoyt H. Hudson (New York: Harper & Row, 1960), 21–23.

9. Since striving toward the maximum amount of freedom may be constrained by various material conditions including the competing power of other organized groups, this duty may be treated as one of "broad" rather than "strict" obligation. That is the manner in which Kant discusses the duty of the sovereign to reform the constitution. Milne discusses different degrees of freedom in terms of the "enlightenment" of the society. This raises some interesting questions concerning the nature of the obligations of one society

toward another in terms of "enlightenment" that are beyond the scope of this paper.

10. Kant, *Kants Gesammelte Schriften*, 8:273–313; *On the Old Saw: That Might Be Right in Theory But It Won't Work in Practice*, trans. E. B. Ashton (Philadelphia: University of Pennsylvania Press, 1974), 58.

11. Although Kant allows that not all political subjects may be active citizens, he requires that the laws "must not be incompatible with the natural laws of freedom and with the equality that accords with this freedom, namely, that everyone be able to work up from this passive status to an active status" and also that passive citizens can demand that they be treated by others in accordance with the laws of natural freedom and equality. Passive citizens, although they do not actively guide the law, enjoy the rights of legal subjects. *Kants Gesammelte Schriften*, 6:315; *The Metaphysical Elements of Justice*, 80.

12. Leslie Mulholland, *Kant's System of Rights* (New York: Columbia University Press, 1990), Introduction.

13. Ibid., 171.

14. Kant recognizes the right of political subjects to criticize positive law but grants wide latitude to the sovereign for interpretation of the people's rights with respect to issues of welfare. This is an appropriate subordination of welfare to law. However, basic human rights, in particular the right to freedom of expression which Kant regards as the shield of all rights, ought to be regarded in a different manner than welfare rights. By categorically denying the people a title to coerce the sovereign to recognize their basic rights, Kant does not adequately mark this difference. It is on this level that the title to coerce cannot be waived and the separation of law and ethics is fatal.

15. Kant, *Kants Gesammelte Schriften*, 6:311; *The Metaphysical Elements of Justice*, 76.

16. Ibid., 6:353; Ladd, p. 126.

17. Ibid., 6:345; Ladd, p. 118.

18. Ibid., 6:347; Ladd, p. 120.

19. Ibid., 6:343–44; Ladd, p. 115.

20. Ibid., 6:260; Ladd, p. 36: "the use of coercion to counteract it, inasmuch as it is the prevention of a hindrance to freedom, is consistent with freedom according to universal laws; in other words this use of coercion is just."

21. Harry Van der Linden, "Kant: The Duty to Promote International Peace and Political Intervention," *Proceedings of the Eighth International Kant Congress*, 1995, volume II, part I, pp. 74–75.

7

Sidney Axinn

World Community and Its Government

The present political situation, a pause in the world's major hot and cold wars, gives us a rare interval in which to consider the matter of world government. As Edmund Wilson once put it, "this is the time to think . . . because as soon as a war gets started, few people do any more thinking about anything except demolishing the enemy."[1]

In the course of considering the need for a single world government, this paper will consider the problem of nationalism, the delights of equality, Hobbes the pacifist, Kant on world government, nationalism as cultural lag, the morality of community attachments, and the locus of morality . . . which community? The thesis of the paper is the obvious: it is time for the world community to be under the legal and military force of a single world government.

THE PROBLEM OF NATIONALISM

Shall we continue with the present world order, the system of sovereign nations? That's the issue, and we may not have an indefinite time to consider it. Why is the status of nations of concern? Because of two facts about them: (1) as Stephen Nathanson put it, "a nation is a demilitarized zone,"[2] and (2) nations go to war. The first point makes

119

them desirable; the second makes them dangerous and undesirable. The problem is to have the first without the second.

THE DELIGHTS OF EQUALITY

It was common sense, up to the end of World War II, to assume that there are powerful nations and weak nations. Further, safety consisted in being a citizen of a powerful nation. These old pieces of common sense no longer hold. Instead of powerful nations and weak nations, there is now an impressive degree of equality. Thomas Hobbes gave us a serious definition of equality: Individuals are equal when the weakest can kill the strongest. (We all know the citation.) *When the weakest nation can kill the strongest, nations are also equal.* At least, equal in one very significant respect. Just as with individuals, insult any one of them and you are in danger! The real insult, of course, is that none of them can protect its citizens any longer.

It should be obvious that, as our hero essentially put it, the weakest nation can kill the strongest, "by secret machination, or by confederacy with others."[3] There are no defenses against nuclear weapons, and almost none against chemical and biological weapons. That the emperor had no clothes, in the story, was amusing: that the great nations have no defenses is the urgent community issue . . . and we must say so whether or not it is in bad taste.

Instead of considering the problems involved in forming a single world government, political and diplomatic attention and effort have gone into the matter of reducing the number, or eliminating, nuclear weapons. There seems to be no serious reason to expect more than trivial or nominal progress on these lines. However, even if these efforts succeeded, the world would still face dangers almost as great as those of the present. Two new kinds of weapons were developed in World War II: (1) atomic weapons; and (2) ICBMs, inter-continental ballistic missiles. Even if all the world's nuclear weapons and warheads were to disappear, there would remain the possibility that almost any two nations could each completely destroy the major cities of the other in less than twenty minutes. Fitting the ICBMs with "conventional" warheads would still leave us in that situation. While we may well prefer a death by explosives without radiation rather than one with radiation, the main problem remains. The problem, of course, is war.

Oddly enough, we all know the solution to the problem of war. Its not a new subject for mankind, and the leading political philosophers have not ignored it. Hobbes and Kant have given us clear and forceful analyses, and they come to the same conclusion. The solution is a world legal system, a world government. I think we know this, but seem not to have the courage to say so and act on it. Perhaps it may help to overcome our lack of courage if we review the arguments that Hobbes and Kant gave, and follow their application to the relationship between sovereign nations.

HOBBES, THE PACIFIST

Hobbes's analysis of the need for government, for a legal system, is as well known as anything in political theory. I hope I may be excused for rehearsing the familiar: the Hobbes experts are urged to skip this section . . . and even beginning students in political philosophy have been presented with the essentials of Hobbes's position. My point is to stress his exact application to international relations.

To be dependent on oneself for one's own protection, that is, to be sovereign, is to be in great danger. A world in which all parties are individually sovereign is a world of "nature," an anarchist situation in which life . . .while it lasts . . . is miserable. The only solution is to have "a common power set over them . . . with right and force sufficient to compel performance" (Leviathan, chapter XIV). Does this apply to nations as well as individuals? Indeed so. I don't argue that one finds this in Hobbes's text: only that his text applies exactly to the current relations between sovereign nations. And I am hardly the only one to make and stress this point.

Hobbes starts his chapter XIII of the Leviathan with the classic argument for the equality of men, noted above. Men are not to be treated as equals because they have immortal souls, or because of abstract morality or personhood, or because they are made in the image of God, or because they love each other, and so on, but simply and urgently because "the weakest has strength enough to kill the strongest, either by secret machination, or by confederacy with others that are in the same danger with himself." The nations of the present world are essentially in the same sort of equality with each other. The weakest nation, with nuclear weapons, has strength enough to kill the strongest. It is no longer the case that there are strong nations and weak nations, *militarily.* Nuclear weapons are now the great equalizer, a phrase once applied to the invention of guns and gunpowder.

Hobbes's argument starts with the premise of the equality of the individuals in the state of nature, and nations now satisfy that premise. He then adds the premise of egoism: "of the voluntary acts of every man, the object is some good to himself" (chapter IV). Nations satisfy this requirement, quite obviously. Hobbes's distinction between war and peace certainly holds: when there is no common power to be feared, men, and nations, must rely on themselves for security . . . and are therefore at war with all others. Peace is the situation between two or more parties in which they rely on someone else for security. He gives the classic description of a cold war in his comments on "a posture of war" (chapter XIII): "in all times, kings, and persons of sovereign authority, because of their independency, are in continual jealousies, and in the state and posture of gladiators: having their weapons pointing, and their eyes fixed on one another; that is, their forts, garrisons, and guns upon the frontiers of their kingdoms; and continual spies upon their neighbors" (chapter XIII). As one says in Japan, "so, so, so."

What follows from this is obvious. "To this war of every man [*read nation*] against every man [*nation*], this also is consequent: that nothing can be unjust. The notions of right and wrong, justice and injustice, have there no place. Where there is no common power, there is no law; where no law, no injustice. Force and fraud are in war the two cardinal virtues" (chapter XIII). The essential motive that inclines us to give up this anarchy and seek peace is not an abstract love of justice, but, as he puts it succinctly, "fear of death" (ibid.). In parallel, the rational motive that should lead us to give up the individual sovereignty of nations is fear of death.

It was once reasonable to hold that if one gave loyalty to the king, the king could and would provide safety from enemies. Enemies foreign and domestic. Now, we find that our kings simply can not do that. No king, no government can provide safety against the delivery of nuclear weapons. Present delivery systems, the ICBMs and submarine-launched missiles particularly, have no defense. Even if some unlikely Star Wars defense is produced, it is reckoned to be much less than perfectly effective. And even Star Wars defenses do not take into consideration the assembly within a nation of nuclear weapons by terrorist or other agencies. Or launching from submarine or other near-border sites.

Giving loyalty to the king has always had to be balanced against the risk that the king, himself, may be assassinated. This is hardly anachronistic. It was said, fairly recently, that the president of the United States is the most powerful person in the world. However, even those who have carried that title have been affected in a rather material way by Hobbes's notion of equality. Consider Presidents Kennedy, Ford, and Reagan: one was shot at and not hit, one shot at and hit but not killed, one shot and killed. This record is no embarrassment to Hobbes's position: many governments are much more successful in keeping their chief executives alive, as well as their ordinary citizens. I mention it as a reinforcing example of the notion of equality. And to raise the question of the value of a narrow patriotism as protection in the actual world.

The world has, as we all know, atomic and nuclear weapons that may be delivered by a wide variety of means—not only delivery by air (aircraft and rockets), ship (surface and submarine), and artillery . . . but also local final assembly on site. In addition to these devices, biological and chemical weapons are now included in some of the "undeveloped" nations' arsenals (as well as our own).

Do we have the obvious case for a single world government in this situation? A recent news report suggests that Iran may soon be in possession of nuclear weapons, with help from Argentina and China. Suppose that every nation or almost every nation on the globe were to posses nuclear weapons and delivery capabilities. Would the present anarchy still be tolerable, be preferable to the risks of an evil world government? One response heard is that it has worked for over forty years since the invention of the atom bomb. However, this is no more persuasive then the old fallacy that if playing Russian roulette with a loaded pistol has been accompanied by excellent health, the game ought to be continued.

After agreeing that a legal system is required in international relations, and that an effective legal system can only come from a single world government, there is still the great complexity of choosing the structure of that government. On this matter, another advocate of a world legal system can be usefully considered.

KANT ON WORLD GOVERNMENT

Kant has given us two different answers to the question of the structure of a world legal system. Strangely, only one of these is noted by most commentators on his political views. In certain texts, Kant holds for "a lawful federation [voluntary?] under a commonly accepted inter-national right," rather than "a state which is . . . a cosmopolitan commonwealth under a single ruler."[4] There is also his well-known recommendation for a League of Nations. However, he usually makes clear that there must be "enforceable public laws to which each state must submit."[5] Enforceability, of course, requires a compulsory rather than a voluntary system. Is the world order to be a voluntary or a compulsory system? A collection of sovereigns, or just one? We want more than a mechanical counting of passages to decide his view; we want an internal analysis of the position.

Because they are rarely considered, I'll stress the texts that give Kant's arguments in favor of a single world government, and some of the details about how to achieve that result.

In his well-known paper of 1793 on Theory and Practice, we find a passage that one might call *Der Sperling* argument.

No state is for a moment secure from the others in its independence and its possessions. The will to subjugate the others or to grow at their expense is always present, and the production of armaments for defense, which often makes peace more oppressive and more destructive of internal welfare than war itself, can never be relaxed. And there is no possible way of counteracting this except a state of international right, based upon enforceable public laws to which each state must submit (by analogy with a state of civil or political right among individual men). For a permanent peace by means of a so-called *European Balance of Power* is a pure illusion, like Swift's story of the house which the builder had constructed in such perfect harmony with all the laws of equilibrium that it collapsed as soon as a sparrow alighted on it. But it might be objected that no states will ever submit to coercive laws of this kind, and that a proposal for a universal federation, to whose power all the individual states would voluntarily submit and whose laws they would all obey, may be all very well in the theory of the Abbe St. Pierre or of Rousseau, but that does not apply in practice.

For my own part . . . we should proceed in our disputes in such a way that a universal federal state may be inaugurated, so that we should therefore assume that *it is possible.*"[6]

The "balance of power" theories are ridiculed: only an international or world government with "coercive laws" can solve the problem. And he makes strong use of the analogy to the state of civil and political rights among individual men. Along with Hobbes in the individual case, the solution is not a debating society but a "universal federal state." Neither individuals nor states are willing to give up their own ability to use force, but Kant relies "upon the very nature of things to force men to do what they do not willingly choose."[7]

This is no isolated passage in Kant. We find the same thing in his work on Justice, in *The Metaphysics of Morals.*[8] In that place he adds the remark that a single state composed of nations would "extend over vast regions, it would be too large to govern." If it were too large to govern, it would fail to protect its members. For this reason he says that the idea of permanent peace cannot be realized, but still should be aimed at and approached.

However, we now have many new features that Kant did not consider. Whether or not an area is too large to govern is a technical question of fact. At this point in history, the military power of a single nation can and does patrol the entire globe. Therefore, Kant's assumption is now simply wrong. The earth can be governed by a single power. And there is more than one candidate for that position.

What kind of international federation did Kant take to be desirable? He answers,

> A congress . . . is merely a free and essentially arbitrary combination of various states that can be dissolved at any time. As such it should not be confused with a Union (such as that of the American states) that is founded on a political constitution and which therefore can not be dissolved. Only through the latter kind of union can the Idea of the kind of public Law of nations that should be established become a reality, so that nations will settle their differences in a civilized way by a judicial process, rather than in the barbaric way (of savages), namely through war."[9]

Here we get a rough idea of Kant's model for a world government, the constitutional union of the American states. Presumably, when this was written in 1797, Kant had some familiarity with the U.S. Constitution. He must have been impressed with article I, section 10, paragraph 3, "No state shall keep troops or ships of war in time of peace . . . or engage in war, unless actually invaded, or in such imminent danger as will not admit of delay." It certainly would require great changes to make the U.S. Constitution a proper basis for a world government. However, Kant has recommended that we establish such a world government on that "kind of union." For Kant, as for Hobbes, a world government is to be compulsory, not voluntary. A voluntary government is a contradiction in terms.

NATIONALISM AS CULTURAL LAG

Why is there so much resistance on almost all sides to the idea of a single world government? Why such sturdy loyalty to sovereign states that can no longer defend their own citizens?

The old term "cultural lag" seems most accurate. Of course, one can imagine a world government that would be extremely undesirable. Kant himself, in "Perpetual Peace," holds that a single despotic ruler would bring "the burial ground of freedom."

A bit inconsistent here. If the world can't be governed, it can't be governed despotically. But we no longer have the objection that the world is too large to govern. On the contrary, we fear that it might be governed too closely; and that is sometimes given as an objection to the idea of world government.

Recently, an impressive number of studies of international relations have appeared. Haskell Fain's *Normative Politics and the Community of*

Nations[10] is one of the latest and most interesting. It is particularly strong in its analysis and proposals for protecting civil rights in a world of complicated international treaties. Earlier thoughtful studies that have gained attention were by Stanley Hoffman, Richard Falk, Henry Shue, and Charles Beitz, to mention just a few in English. Regularly there appears a comment like the disclaimer that Haskell Fain gives in his first chapter: "world government? Wright did not advocate it, *nor does any serious scholar.*"[11] A brief disclaimer, given without any special argument.

One wonders why "no serious scholar" desires it. Is the very idea of a world government too horrible or too obscene or too naive to deserve even a brief refutation? To pay attention to the idea of world government does risk the charge of disloyalty to one's own country. Odd, at a stage of history in which, as the cliché has it, the world has become one economic unit. The heads and other officials of major states meet regularly to deal with mutual problems . . . the exchange rates, trade, terrorism, population, ecology, and so on. To live in a single economic world and refuse even to consider a single political world is to be guilty of cultural lag! I hope that at least those professionally involved in law and social philosophy will not continue to ignore the demands of a unified world law.

As Hobbes has explained, when the weakest can kill the strongest . . . it is time for an international legal system . . . a single world government. Following Kant, we may hope for it. Following common sense, we must talk about it, plan it, and produce it.

THE MORALITY OF COMMUNITY ATTACHMENTS

Is there a morally serious charge of disloyalty in proposing to place one's nation under the protection of an international government, under the protection of that international government's military forces? No more so than is the surrender of the physical protection of one's family to the local government's police force . . . and the national government's military. Even the NRA membership are ultimately Hobbesians: We all are.

Must there be an end to communities that wish to preserve their own cultures . . . their languages, religions, economic and political ideologies, attachments of all sorts? Only when they carry military consequences. But one must expect that there will be shifting relationships between national interests and the interests of the world government. The parallel in U.S. history would be the line, the moving line, between states rights and federal rights; and we need not produce one final utopian answer to where that line must always be. Such legal, political and social questions will keep our political philosophers, jurists, and politicians in business indefinitely!

THE LOCUS OF MORALITY—WHICH COMMUNITY?

It has been argued that isolated individuals have no actual framework for morality, that abstract theory produces no gut attachments. Attachments, including moral attachments, require actual communities. Certainly, moral pronouncements that are made as if people had no community responsibilities, no community loves and hates, do seem empty. One knows that something essential is missing, just as an analysis of human biology with no notice of sex might be taken to have skipped over something of possible importance. However, the moral advantages of community attachments must also be paired with their liabilities.

Consider the point that Ernst Cassirer made in *The Myth of the State*:

> As a matter of fact in all primitive societies ruled and governed by rites, individual responsibility is an unknown thing. What we find here is only *a collective responsibility*. Not the individuals but the group is the real "moral subject." The clan, the family, and the whole tribe are responsible for the actions of all the members. If a crime is committed it is not imputed to an individual. By a sort of miasma or social contagion, the crime spreads over the whole group. Nobody can escape the infection. Revenge and punishment too are always directed to the group as a whole. In those societies in which the blood feud is one of the highest obligations it is by no means necessary to take revenge upon the murderer himself. It is enough to kill a member of his family or his tribe. In some cases, as for instance in New Guinea or among the African Somalis, it is the eldest brother rather than the offender himself who is killed. (Italics added)[13]

Cassirer, in the quote above and other places, takes guilt by association to be a primitive hangover. As he views history, only individual responsibility is the basis for civilized morality. The problem, of course, is to gain the benefits of community attachment without the "primitive" reflexes that Cassirer reminds us are still not far below the surface. At least formally, one must agree that both hate by association and love by association are morally unpersuasive.

Attachment to *the widest possible human community* provides the moral framework that Oldenquist and others insist on . . . and yet avoids the primitive response of guilt by association. Where nationalism is merely primitive tribalism, it has small moral claims. Where nationalism makes cultural, personal, social, and economic contributions beyond the primitive, it can remain morally cherished. Nations that refuse to give up their military sovereignty deserve Cassirer's, and our, contempt. Considering ways and means of giving up national sovereignty is not the only game in town . . . but almost, and this is an urgent time to play it.

In the last paragraph of the powerful argument for his philosophy of history, Kant insisted, "our descendents . . . will naturally value the history of earlier times . . . only from the point of view of what interests them, i.e., in answer to the question of what the various nations and governments have contributed to *the goal of world citizenship*, and what they have done to damage it.[14]

NOTES

1. In the introduction to Edmund Wilson, *Patriotic Gore: Studies in the Literature of the American Civil War* (New York: Oxford University Press, 1962).

2. Stephen Nathanson made this point in a discussion at the meeting of the Concerned Philosophers for Peace, Temple University, October 1989. For his views on several aspects of nationalism, and his thoughtful analysis of Alasdair MacIntyre's Lindley Lecture on patriotism, see his "In Defense of 'Moderate Patriotism,'" *Ethics* 99.3 (April 1989: 535–52).

3. Hobbes, *Leviathan*, chap. XIII, "Of the Natural Condition of Mankind."

4. "On the Common Saying, 'This May be True in Theory, But it Does Not Apply in Practice,'" in Hans Reiss, ed., *Kant's Political Writings*, trans. H. B. Nisbet (Cambridge: Cambridge University Press, 1970), 90.

5. Ibid., 92.

6. Reiss, *Kant's Political Writings*, 91–92.

7. Ibid., 92.

8. *The Metaphysics of Morals*, trans. John Ladd, Indianapolis, Ind.: Bobbs-Merrill, 1965, 123–24. (from *Kants Gesammelte Schriften* [Berlin: Königlichen Preusischen Academie der Wissenschaften, 1902], 350).

9. In his work on Justice, ed. by Ladd, cited, 124–25 (from *Kants Gesammelte Schriften* [Berlin: Königlichen Preusischen Academie der Wissenschaften, 1902], 351).

10. Philadelphia: Temple University Press , 1987.

11. Haskell Fain, *Nortmative Politics and the Community of Nations*, Philadelphia: Temple University Press, 1987, 15.

12. For this viewpoint, see Andrew Oldenquist, "Loyalty," *Journal of Philosophy* 79.1 (April 1982:173–93).

13. Ernst Cassirer, *The Myth of the States* (Garden City, N.Y.: Doubleday, 1946), 358.

14. "Idea For a Universal History from a Cosmopolitan Point of View," *Kants Gesammelte Schriften* [Berlin: Königlichen Preusischen Academie der Wissenschaften, 1902] trans. Lewis White Beck, in *Kant on History*, ed. L. W. Beck (Indianapolis, Ind.: Bobbs-Merrill, 1963). My emphasis.

8

Charles W. Mills

Dark Ontologies

Blacks, Jews, and
White Supremacy

To what extent can the ideas of Immanuel Kant, or at least of some kind of modified Kantianism, be useful in helping us to understand the problems of race, and the racial and ethnic tensions, that continue to plague the modern world? For minority philosophers working on race there are, of course, general conceptual obstacles to the appropriation of *any* of the classic figures of the Western canon. After all, Western philosophers have not historically been interested in theorizing about these issues; their writings may reflect racism, but they do not analyze it.[1] In the case of Kant's work, however, the challenge is particularly acute because both the potential payoff and the apparent obstacles are so great. On the one hand, the decline of utilitarianism and the apparent failure of Marxist socialism have led to the triumph of a rights-based person-centered liberalism, making Kant arguably the most important moral/political philosopher of the modern period.[2] So if a Kantian framework could be employed for theorizing race, this would obviously be of great benefit to those working on such issues. On the other hand, how could a philosophy celebrated for proclaiming the irrelevance to full personhood of anything but rationality have anything useful to say on a subject as seemingly morally irrelevant and "phenomenal" as race?

In this essay, I want to outline a strategy for bringing race and Kantian—or perhaps "Kantian"—theory together. My specific focus will be on the dynamic of black-Jewish relations, but though I see this as an object of interest in its own right, its ultimate value for us will be the instrumental illumination it sheds on a background political structure whose contours are barely acknowledged, let alone mapped, in mainstream Anglo-American political philosophy: white supremacy. For most white philosophers, race (if it is noticed at all) is essentially conceptually residual, a "deviation" from ideal practice to be theoretically handled through discussions of affirmative action, compensation, reparations, and so forth. I will suggest that racial privilege as itself a normatively backed political system needs to be taken far more seriously by white moral/political philosophers as we approach the twenty first century, and that Kantian theory can be adapted to provide a philosophical blueprint of its architecture.

Ontologies Light and Dark

Tensions between the African American and Jewish American communities, a constant subterranean presence in recent decades, surfaced once again with the infamous November 1993 Khallid Muhammad speech at Kean College, in which Jews were accused of being "bloodsuckers" of the black community. This was, of course, only one of a long series of unhappy episodes, going back in the most recent cycle to the 1960s (though ultimately older), which have worsened relations between black and Jewish Americans: the Nation of Islam's publication of *The Secret Relationship between Blacks and Jews*; the murder of Yankel Rosenbaum in Crown Heights; Jesse Jackson's "Hymietown" remark; the firing of Andrew Young by the Carter White House for unauthorized meetings with the PLO; Israel's suspected role in giving apartheid South Africa the technology to acquire nuclear weapons; the 1968 teachers strike in New York; and, more generally, the perceived prominence of Jewish intellectuals in the neoconservative ideological backlash to the movements and causes of the 1960s and '70s (including affirmative action), with its well-publicized conversions, apostasies, and *mea culpas*. Op-ed pieces, conferences, books and anthologies, on the subject, all continue to multiply, and an exhibition on black-Jewish relations sponsored by the Jewish Museum in New York toured the country some years ago in an attempt to build bridges.[3]

I want to take a different approach to analyzing this by now familiar issue, an approach that relies on a reconceptualization of the polity as a *racial* one. My strategy for appropriating Kant to this end will utilize the interrelated notions of "personhood" and "respect," the conceptual apparatus central to his moral/political universe. For Kant's work is the best articulation of the moral egalitarianism we associate with the Enlightenment, the American and French Revolutions,[4] and the rise of modernist individualism: the once-daring idea, exploding the old social hierarchies of antiquity and feudalism—patrician and plebeian, noble and serf—that all humans are moral equals, *persons*, and so, as autonomous moral agents, equally worthy of respect. "Kant's entire moral philosophy can be understood as a protest against distinctions based on the far less important criteria of rank, wealth, and privilege. . . . Kant's is an ethics of the people, of moral egalitarianism. . . . Respect is an attitude due equally to *every* person, *simply* because each is a person, a rational being capable of moral self-determination."[5] Indeed in the *Groundwork* and *The Metaphysics of Morals* we find (at least ideally) an inspiringly ecumenical conception of personhood so far removed from the phenomenal world of prejudice and ethnocentrism (or anti-Copernican geocentrism) that even intelligent aliens from another planet can be persons, since the crucial feature for equal moral status is rationality.[6] If we speak of a "social ontology," then—a mapping of the basic units of a social universe—we can say that in Kant we have the social ontology of an ideal Enlightenment liberalism, the polity as a *respublica noumenon*, a world of abstract individuals equally deserving of respect, and characterized by their freedom, equality, and independence.

So much for the familiar Kantian ideal world, the world toward which he hoped we were progressing. What, however, about the reality? To get a sense of this we need to turn to a radically different figure, someone from the oppositional black tradition also concerned with the moral idea of "respect," but with an understandably different perspective on it. Consider the Jamaican political activist Marcus Garvey (1887–1940), who died in obscurity but is celebrated today as the organizer and leader of the largest black political movement in history.[7] At the height of its global influence in the 1920s, the organization he founded—the Universal Negro Improvement Association—"could boast over 1,200 branches in over 40 countries, with 700 branches flourishing in the United States alone," others being spread across the Caribbean, Central America, Canada, and Africa, making Garveyism a "subversive" ideology of significant concern for many of the governments of the white world.[8] Garvey's anticolonial and antiracist political program failed in his own lifetime, but his ideas would live on to inspire subsequent generations of African and African American activists. And his basic message to the millions of Africans "at home and abroad" who read his *Negro World* newspaper and tried to follow his political guidance was: "A race without authority and power is a race without respect."

For the reality is, of course, that the world in which Garvey was politically active—the world of the early twentieth century, as indeed the world for many previous years, and some would argue the world even today—was *not* in conformity with the raceless Kantian ideal. Instead, what one could term *global white supremacy*, the domination of the planet by white people, was the norm.[9] In the United States itself, there was the official system of segregation known as "Jim Crow," with systematic disenfranchisement of blacks, thousands of unpunished lynchings, inferior housing and education, pervasive job discrimination, and a color line running through most everyday transactions in life (separate and inferior dining, traveling, and entertainment facilities) and extending even into death (separate hospitals and cemeteries).[10] Elsewhere, the world was dominated by European colonialism, which in 1914 "held a grand total of roughly 85 percent of the earth as colonies, protectorates, dependencies, dominions, and commonwealths,"[11] a political system justified by an ideology of "master" and "subject" races.[12] And everywhere in lay and academic opinion, popular consciousness and respectable scholarship, the inferiority of nonwhites, particularly blacks, was taken to have been "scientifically" established—whether by craniometry, Camper's facial angle, recapitulationism, Social Darwinism, or IQ theory.[13]

In this world it would be quite wrong to assume that the Enlightenment Kantian social ontology—people as abstract noumenal individuals equally deserving of respect—was the norm, with a few unfortunate deviations. Rather, the *opposite* was the case. The norm was the routine restriction of full personhood to whites, and the consignment of nonwhites to a subordinate moral status. Garvey's linking of race to respect thus becomes perfectly understandable as a recognition of the state of affairs that actually obtained, the realization that the Kantian ideal was *not* taken seriously where nonwhites were concerned. Far from race being deemed irrelevant to personhood, it was precisely skin color, hair, and facial features that were used to categorize people and determine their moral standing. So this could be said to be the "dark ontology" that is the unacknowledged dark side of the Enlightenment ideal. Simply put: one set of rules for whites, another for nonwhites. All persons are equal, but only whites (and really only white males) are persons.

The claim is, then, that whatever the merits of the Enlightenment social ontology of Kant as an ideal, the reality is this dark ontology. It could be said to be triply "dark." Firstly, it is dark in the sense of being color-coded, consigning nonwhites to a lower rung on the ontological ladder. Secondly, it is dark in the sense of being sinister, a social ontology of domination and subordination. And finally, it is dark in the sense of being largely unacknowledged in Western political theory. Little theoretical attention has been paid to the fact that the polity, and Western moral/political philosophy, were structured in this way, so that one might get the impression that the ideal had generally historically been realized, with admittedly some unfortunate deviations. (So there is an analogy here to the "dark matter" in the universe, that can be detected only by inference, by the way it bends light and twists gravitational fields. Or think of the term "black economy" to describe the underground economies of some Third World countries, where in some cases the unofficial economy of drugs and smuggling is the *real* economy, and the official economy is a myth.)

We can represent these ontologies diagrammatically as in figure 1, using "personhood" and "respect" as the conceptual common denominator.[14] This provides a simple and straightforward way to translate race into the vocabulary of mainstream political philosophy. On the one hand is the official ontology of the ideal Enlightenment, where abstract raceless and colorless individuals are treated as persons deserving of equal respect. On the other hand is the actual dark, "naturalized" social ontology,[15] the ontology of the divided Enlightenment, characterized by an "exceptionalism in European thought about the non-West," an "Enlightenment dichotomization" in its normative theories.[16] This is the social ontology of the world of slavery, colonialism, and segregation, where concrete individuals are seen as raced and colored and treated differentially accordingly. If the former is the world of abstract Kantianism, the latter can be said to be the world of *"Herrenvolk Kantianism."* I adapt this term from the sociologist Pierre van den Berghe's description of white settler states such as the United States, Australia, and South Africa as *"Herrenvolk* democracies," polities that are democratic for the master race, the *Herrenvolk,* but not for the subordinate race(s).[17] Extrapolating this scheme to moral theory, then, I suggest we can imagine a *Herrenvolk* ethics, a set of moral rules that prescribes a different schedule of norms—rights, duties, privileges, liberties—for different subsets of the human population according to racial demarcation. So if idealized Kantianism has a population of raceless persons among whom symmetrical relations of mutual respect are supposed to obtain, then we could say that naturalized *Herrenvolk* Kantianism has a population partitioned between white persons and nonwhite subpersons, with *a*symmetrical relations between them. Persons give each other respect, but give *dis*respect to subpersons, who in turn, to show that they know their place in the scheme of things, are normatively required to show racial deference to persons. So for nonwhite subpersons, it is disrespect rather than respect which is the norm, the "default mode," of this system. For blacks in the West—*contra*

Figure 8-1. Official Kantianism: Ideal Enlightenment Ontology

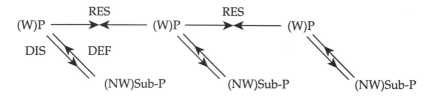

POPULATION: Abstract individuals

Raceless persons give each other mutual respect *as* individuals.

Personhood and self-respect are taken for granted, have no connection with race.

Herrenvolk Kantianism:
Actual Dark (Unacknowledged) Enlightenment Ontology

POPULATION: Raced individuals, white persons, and nonwhite sub-persons

White persons give each other mutual respect *as* whites, but give racial *dis*respect to nonwhite sub-persons, who in turn are required to give racial deference to whties.

For nonwhites, personhood and self-respect have to be fought for, and are intimately tied up with race.

---

official, ideal Kantianism—this *Herrenvolk* ethic means that moral standing and race, whiteness/personhood/respect and blackness/subpersonhood/disrespect, have been inextricably tied up together for hundreds of years.

Finally, I want to consider the objection that, however interesting such a model may be, it has very little to do with Kant and Kantianism, even in a scare-quotes sense, so that my attempt to locate it in this framework is essentially misguided.[18] I think there are two points to be made in reply.

The first is that in the application of "contemporary Kantian social philosophy" to the real world, it is the *naturalized* rather than the idealized ethic that we need to grapple with and understand in our efforts to change people's moral consciousness and behavior (which is presumably the ultimate point of moral philosophy). And even if Kant himself had said nothing at all about race in his work, one could still see this as derivatively "Kantian" insofar as notions of personhood, respect and self-respect have, though in a racialized form, been central to this consciousness and behavior. As an academic exercise, mapping the internal normative logic of (an idealized) Kant's views on personhood and respect will always be valuable in its own way. But when it comes to actually engaging with and transforming human social practices, we also need a corollary recognition of how systematically divergent from the ideal these practices have been, and what theory has guided these divergences. For such a remedial moral project, one needs to map not so much the idealized normative logic (by now surely very familiar) as the *non*-ideal naturalized logic of these notions *as concretely instantiated* in the actual theories and practices of the racially privileged population in the West.

But the second point is that it turns out that Kant himself had a hand in *both* ontologies; it is not the case that his work only inspired the laudable ideal theory from which others' lamentable practice then fell short. For if Kant can be regarded as the father of modern moral theory, he is also known to some—a fact that will probably astonish many Anglo-American philosophers—as the "founder of the modern concept of race."[19] This embarrassing attribution will not be found in the average contemporary philosophy textbook or anthology, but the judgment is not new, and the evidence seems to support it. Radical and minority philosophers have, perhaps, more of a motivation to uncover such passages, given their conviction that even seemingly abstract and "pure" philosophy has too often been infected by racism and Western imperialism. But Kant is not some minor and obscure figure; he is, as emphasized, the increasingly preeminent moral/political philosopher of the modern period, and it is surprising that there has not been more attention to this aspect of his work in establishment mainstream theory.

There is, to begin with, his notorious statement in the 1764 *Observations on the Feeling of the Beautiful and Sublime* that "so fundamental is the difference between [the black and white] races of man . . . it appears to be as great in regard to mental capacities as in color," so that "a clear proof that what [a Negro] said was stupid," was that "this fellow was quite black from head to foot."[20] Often cited by black philosophers as a paradigm example of impure reason that stands in need of critique, this passage could, nonetheless, be dismissed as no more than a "pre-critical" lapse. More problematic for such an interpretation, however—as David Theo Goldberg points out[21]—is his later 1775 essay "On the Different Races of Man" ("Von den Verschiedenen Rassen der Menschen"), in which he outlines a classic hereditarian, anti-environmentalist account of innate racial difference that essentially anticipates post-Darwinian "scientific" racism.[22] In George Mosse's summary of this essay: "Racial make-up becomes an unchanging substance and the foundation of all physical appearance and human development, including intelligence."[23]

But the most detailed account of the centrality of race to Kant's thought, *including* his "critical" philosophy, is to be found in a recent article by Emmanuel Eze.[24] Drawing on both translated and untranslated work, and greatly developing the discussions of previous authors, Eze shows that Kant's moral theory really needs to be understood in the context of his anthropology and physical geography, subjects on which he lectured for forty years, thus including his mature "critical" period. For Kant, it turns out, there is a natural color-coded racial hierarchy of (reading from top to bottom) white Europeans, yellow Asians, black Africans, and red Americans, with corresponding differential capacities for moral educability. Europeans are basically self-starters; for Asians there is some hope, though they cannot grasp abstract concepts; Africans can at least be morally educated as slaves and servants, with the help of a split bamboo cane (Kant offers some advice on how to beat Negroes, given the obstacle to their moral education posed by the thickness of their skins); and Native Americans are just hopeless, and cannot be educated at all.[25] Thus, as Eze concludes, Kant can be regarded as putting the empirical racial classifications of Carolus Linnaeus on a sophisticated theoretical foundation: race is actually a transcendental.[26] "The black person, for example, can accordingly be denied full humanity since full and 'true' humanity accrues only to the white European. For Kant European humanity is *the* humanity par excellence."[27] So Immanuel Kant, the theorist of abstract noumenal persons deserving of equal respect, is simultaneously one of the founders of the dark ontology of *sub*persons and racial *dis*respect that black activists such as Garvey have traditionally had to fight against.[28]

RACE AS A POLITICAL SYSTEM

My suggestion, then, is that only by recognizing the existence of this background system of political domination and its accompanying social ontology can we really begin to understand the troubled relationships between blacks and Jews.[29] If we see these problems solely in terms of individual prejudice and bigotry, free-floating attitudes, and cultural predispositions, we will miss crucial realities that need to be incorporated into an adequate explanation. In other words, we need to talk about race as itself a political system, and the differential and evolving relations of blacks and Jews to it. We need to put this relationship in a historical context and ask where Jews are located with respect to this system, where blacks are located with respect to this system, what psychology is tendentially produced in people by these different locations, how social cognition of the system is shaped by these different locations, what form ethnic affirmation and racial self-identification characteristically take under these conditions, and how moral assertions of personhood and demands for respect typically play themselves out, given this background dark ontology.

Now as mentioned, part of the problem, certainly in mainstream political philosophy and to a large extent in political theory more generally, is that we lack a developed theoretical vocabulary and conceptual framework for this enterprise. Categories, distinctions, and theorizations do not crystallize out of nowhere; they have to be developed by people who think long and hard about the matter, make mistakes, try out ideas, correct themselves, have an epistemic community to go back and forth with on theoretical innovations. Cognition is, *contra* the Cartesian paradigm, essentially social, reliant on an already-developed network of concepts and paradigms. Without a constituency with a motivational interest in developing this understanding, and with the educational training to facilitate it, certain realities will remain largely uninvestigated and unmapped. Cognitive psychologists have documented the remarkable extent to which our perception of the world is theory-driven rather than data-driven.[30] We have macro- and micro-theories about how things work and tend to filter, process, and assimilate information accordingly. Perceptions that are not in keeping with, or are actively contradictory to, pre-existing theories tend either to be ignored or to be suspended as puzzling anomalies, viruses epistemically quarantined from the body of existing theory, which eventually perish for want of a sustaining conceptual environment. Whites have generally taken their domination of the planet for granted and so have either ignored it or positively valorized it, not seeing it as a negative system of oppression whose mechanisms need investigation. Nonwhites have generally been cognitively disadvantaged by being either deprived of formal education or socialized into a white conceptual framework whose internal logic is refractory to an investigation of these realities. And where attempts *have* been made to develop oppositional understandings of the racial order, they have generally been marginalized by mainstream thought.

So the result is that the body of critical theory on the racial structuring of the polity cannot compare in depth, detail, and sophistication to the tremendous volume of work which, by taking *whites* as the norm, assumes an essentially "raceless" system. Yet, as George Mosse has written: "Racism as it developed in Western society was no mere articulation of prejudice, nor was it simply a metaphor for suppression;

it was, rather, a fully blown system of thought, an ideology like Conservatism, Liberalism, or Socialism, with its own peculiar structure and mode of discourse," indeed "the most widespread ideology of the time."[31] For hundreds of years race was a political system in its own right: it was through race that whites came to understand their identity, their position in the world, their manifest destiny, their civilizing mission, their burden, their entitlements and privileges, their duties and responsibilities. The term "white supremacy" is usually associated with localized regimes, for example the American Old South and apartheid South Africa. But as I pointed out earlier, it is obvious that in a broader sense, the history of the world has long been a history of white supremacy, in that Europeans basically controlled the globe and were the privileged race, the *Herrenvolk*. "[As late as the 1940s the world] was still by and large a Western white-dominated world. The long-established patterns of white power and nonwhite non-power were still the generally accepted order of things. . . . [W]hite supremacy was a generally assumed and accepted state of affairs in the United States as well as in Europe's empires."[32] Historian of antisemitism Léon Poliakov argues that the horrors of the death camps produced an expedient amnesia about this truth in the postwar European intelligentsia, so that the centuries-old centrality of racist ideology to the *mainstream* of Western thought was erased, and attributed instead to scapegoat figures such as Arthur de Gobineau and Houston Chamberlain: "A vast chapter of western thought is thus made to disappear by sleight of hand, and this conjuring trick corresponds, on the psychological or psycho-historical level, to the collective suppression of troubling memories and embarrassing truths."[33]

Thus we need to add to the traditional vocabulary of modern Western political theory—absolutism and constitutionalism, dictatorship and democracy, capitalism and socialism—such concepts as white supremacy, pigmentocracy, a *racial* polity. For even if we assume complete good faith and sincere commitment on the part of whites to eradicate the legacy of this system of *de jure* racial privilege, the world of European expropriation, slavery, and colonialism, there will be a period of continuing *de facto* white advantage, sustained by—if nothing else—cultural lag, institutional momentum, accumulated wealth, and attitudinal inertia. Whites on the whole will generally be privileged with respect to nonwhites, in terms of economic opportunities, political input, and dominant cultural representations. (There are, of course, class and gender differences in both populations that for the sake of simplicity I am going to ignore.)

Let's look at race as a *politically constructed categorization*, then, the marker of locations of privilege and disadvantage in a set of power relationships. (Thus one recent book actually talks about *The Invention of the White Race*.)³⁴

1. Race is essentially *relational* rather than monadic—there have to be at least two groups characterized as races for the categorization to be motivated. (One could say that without two races, there could not be one race.)

2. Race is *dynamic* rather than static—the relations between races change over time, as do the rules for racial membership.

3. Race is only *contingently* tied to phenotype: a given appearance is neither necessary nor sufficient for inclusion in the privileged race R1, or the disadvantaged race R2. The Japanese, for example, have been classified as honorary whites (in South Africa under apartheid), so phenotypical whiteness was not necessary to be white. On the other hand, there are peoples who would today be thought of as uncontroversially white—the Irish, Slavs, Mediterraneans, Jews—who have in the past been seen as borderline whites, or sometimes even nonwhites. And in the United States, where genealogical criteria are crucial, there are people who are phenotypically white, who could "pass" for white, who, by the "one-drop" rule, count as black.

4. Race is usually "vertically" defined, in terms of hierarchy and subordination, with R1 over R2 over R3. Although it is certainly logically possible for investigation to be carried out for purely taxonomical reasons, the motivation for the project has usually been to arrange the "races" in some kind of moral/evolutionary/intellectual/aesthetic hierarchy.

5. For individuals of a given phenotype, race may vary both *temporally*, in a given system (shifting membership rules over time, as discussed above) and *geographically*, through entry into a different system (different membership rules in different racial systems). People of mixed black and white heritage who count as "browns," "mulattoes," or even "whites" by local Caribbean and Latin American rules will then become black in the United States.

6. Race is *unreal*—in the biological/anthropological sense, race does not really exist, and though the categories continue to be used, most scientists agree that it is actually a category like phlogiston.³⁵

7. Race is *real*—in the sociohistorical/political sense, race does exist as a categorization with a massive effect on the shaping of people's psychology, culture, socioeconomic opportunities, life chances, civil rights, and so on.

8. Race as a system has to be *maintained* through constant boundary policing against both the contestation of members of subordinate races who seek inclusion in the privileged race, and, more radically, those who wish to dissolve the system altogether.
9. Finally, although there are local systems with different rules, historically the most important *global racial system* has been the system of white domination, structured on a white/nonwhite axis.

Now given such a background, where the basic divide is between privileged whites and disadvantaged nonwhites, the crucial question obviously becomes: Who gets to be white? And to anticipate the following discussion, the simple answer is: Blacks never get to be white, while Jews get to be white, or nearly white, most of the time.

The Position of Blacks in This System

First, the straightforward case, that of blacks. This case is straightforward because blacks have the dubious honor of being the paradigm representatives of the darkness in these dark ontologies. In the racial taxonomies drawn up by Europeans from the seventeenth century onward, blacks are almost always at the bottom, the last quasi-human link (or sometimes the missing link) in the Great Chain of Being before it descends unequivocally into the animal kingdom.[36] Kant's derogatory judgment has already been mentioned, but (confining ourselves just to philosophers) there is also Hume's, which it echoes, that "negroes, and in general all the other species of men" are "naturally inferior to the whites," Voltaire's polygenist conclusion in "The People of America" that blacks (and Native Americans) are a different species, unrelated to Europeans, whose understanding is "greatly inferior," "not capable of any great application or association of ideas," and Hegel's denial in *The Philosophy of History* that sub-Saharan Africa *has* any history, so that since Negroes are "capable of no development or culture," European *slavery* at least has a civilizing influence: "we may conclude slavery to have been the occasion of the increase of human feeling among the Negroes."[37] The native peoples of the Americas are also disparaged in Western theory, of course, appearing in most of the classic social contract theorists' writings as the paradigm "savages" of the state of nature. But they at least get to be "noble savages" some of the time; blacks are almost always *ignoble* savages. Similarly, whereas in the case of other nonwhites there has sometimes been a grudging

European valorization of their civilizations, as with China and India, there has almost never been a corresponding respect for African civilizations, and black African claims to the most famous civilization on the continent, that of Ancient Egypt, continue to be contested.[38] So conceptually linked are blacks with the ground floor of racial hierarchies that when other nonwhite races of higher status are being contingently forced downward because of conjunctural circumstances, the process is sometimes described by race relations theorists as "niggerization."

What explains this unhappy distinction? One argument is that on practically all the major theories offered to explain white racism, blacks are the antipodes, the polar opposites, to whites, so that—to the extent that these theories are complementary, and *multiple* causation may be involved—there is a devastating confluence of mutually reinforcing causes:

1. *Culturalist explanations.* It has been argued that the historic source of white racism lies in a combination of religious intolerance and cultural predispositions to see nonwhites as alien, Other. The medieval battles against Islam are then the precursors of the racism that would accompany European expansionism into the world. African religions were seen as devil-worship, black culture, and customs viewed as "mumbo-jumbo," paradigmatically bizarre.[39]

2. *Psycho-sexual explanations.* There are also explanations focusing on the *body*, and the psychological associations, linked with European, particularly English, color symbolisms, of nonwhite flesh.[40] And of all human bodies, blacks' are the farthest from the Caucasoid somatic norm, not just in color but also in hair texture and facial features. So whereas at various times other races have on occasion been seen as physically attractive, sexually "exotic," the black body has usually been portrayed in grotesque and negative terms, caricatured and denigrated in seventeenth- and eighteenth-century illustrations of European travelers' tales, the later representations of "scientific" racism, American postbellum "blackface" imitations, nineteenth- and twentieth-century cartoons and advertising.[41]

3. *Politico-economic explanations.* Finally, Marxist explanations of racism attribute it to the ideological need to rationalize the political/economic projects of privileged classes.[42] African slavery thus arguably demands the most severe kind of racism, since slavery reduces people to things, property, and requires their depersonalization for the atrocities necessarily accompanying it.

Moreover, blacks are the only people to have been enslaved *as a race*—African slavery, unlike the systems of ancient Greece and Rome, was tied to phenotype—so that African features became the stigmata of subordination.

Overall, then, blacks have been at the bottom of these dark ontologies, or, more strongly, have usually *defined* where the bottom is. Other races have shown more mobility, and have been able to move up the ontological ladder. But for centuries Western consciousness has been imprinted with the image of blacks as the paradigm subpersons: ugly, uncivilized, of inferior intelligence, prone to violence, and generally incapable of serious contributions to global culture.

THE POSITION OF JEWS IN THIS SYSTEM

Now let us compare this with the position of Jews. In medieval Christendom, Jews were traditional outcasts, victims of the Inquisition, pogroms, expulsions, forced conversions, massacres. But this persecution was carried out under the sign of the cross. Though there are some precursors of what we would today call racism—for example, the fifteenth-century deployment in Spain of the criterion of *limpieza de sangre*, or "purity of blood," against *marranos*, those Jews who sought exemption through conversion[43]—religion rather than race is the central category of identification. It is really only with the advent of the modern period, the rise of secularism, and the diminished significance of faith as a social marker, that race becomes for Europeans a central category of other- and self-understanding. Although, as I pointed out at the start, the bourgeois revolutions flatten the normative social hierarchies within Europe itself, producing in the ideal limit the noumenal Kantian individual, an ontological gap begins to open up (in what is also the "Age of Discovery") between Europe and *non*-Europe. A social ontology gradually crystallizes around *race* in which Europeans/"whites" are opposed to, and raised above, the rest of the world.[44]

And in this social ontology, Jews basically get to be white. This is not to say that they are *fully* white—as Winthrop Jordan has pointed out, "If Europeans were white, some were whiter than others."[45] Internal fine-grained *intra*-European exclusionary distinctions continue to be made, coinciding often with subordinated minority status, or with undeveloped nation or region, and giving rise to more restrictive conceptions of entitlement: Teutonism, Anglo-Saxonism, Aryanism. And some of these, of course, would later be drawn upon by private racist groups (or in the case of the Nazis, a group that gained state power) to rewrite a more exclusionary definition of whiteness. But for the official, state-backed racial system the fundamental conceptual cut, the main line of cleavage in this global dark ontology, is that between white European and nonwhite non-European. And Jews generally end up on the white side of the line. As George Mosse notes: "The Jews were either ignored by anthropologists during most of the eighteenth century or considered part of the Caucasian race, and still believed capable of assimilation into European life. . . . Ideas of cosmopolitanism, equality, and toleration operated for the Jew as they could not for the Negro; after all, the Jew was white. . . . Indeed, only after the mid-nineteenth century was racism applied to Jews with any consistency. No one seemed to feel such [ambivalence] toward blacks. Blacks, unlike Jews, had a fixed lowly position in the 'great chain of being,'" a position "close to the animal world."[46] Thus in the racial taxonomies that were increasingly devised in the period, Jews were generally subsumed under whites, not identified as a separate category. So though European Jewry continued to be the victims of prejudice and ostracism, they benefited from being *European*, from being citizens of the continent that increasingly dominated the world. They benefited materially, as all Europeans did, from European imperialism. They benefited culturally, by being considered as citizens of the superior global culture. And they benefited "ontologically," being classed with the privileged global race of whites. Within this framework, then, one could argue that from the modern period onward, Jews really become nonwhite only under the Third Reich, which was precisely why the Nuremberg Laws came as such a shock to German Jewry.

Even in Europe, then, the situation of Jews differed from that of nonwhites. But in North America, which is the site of the racial system that concerns us, the contrast was even sharper. Here, of course, the legacy of medieval Christendom was much weaker, and new political systems were erected on the expropriation of Native American civilizations. So from the start, there was an explicit commitment to an egalitarianism of a *Herrenvolk*, racially exclusivist kind, which—more clearly than in the Old World, where nonwhites were part of the distant empire—was structured around an axis of crucial differentiation from the *domestic* nonwhite population. And, again, Jews counted as whites. Particularly in the United States, where mass turn-of-the-century Jewish immigration from the Eastern European Pale of Settlement coincided with the formal introduction of Jim Crow/*de jure* segregation after the 1896 *Plessy v. Ferguson* Supreme Court decision, Jews were juridically categorized as white. The signs read "White" and "Colored," not "White," "Jewish," and "Colored." This is not by any means to deny the stigmatization of Jews by the Klan, the wave of antisemitism in the 1920s that led to a restrictive rewriting of the immigration laws, the prevalence of discrimination in the form of restrictive housing covenants, job advertisements that specified "Christian" applicants, exclusion from private clubs, and university admission quotas. But it is to point out the qualitatively worse character of oppression for those *formally* subordinated by the racial polity. Of the thousands of U.S. lynchings from the 1880s to the 1930s, for example, only one victim (Leo Frank in 1915)[47] was a Jew. The ontological whiteness of Jews gave them an edge that gradually enabled them to assimilate and enter the Northern industrial economy in a way that the millions of black migrants from the sharecropping South were not able to emulate.

With the discrediting of antisemitism after the war, the Jewish success story comes to its remarkable climax in the present financial standing of American Jewry, while for blacks, by contrast, the civil rights victories over formal segregation in the 1950s and '60s have not produced a comparable material success. Now uncontroversially white (except in the eyes of racist fringe groups), favored by the system, many Jews can no longer see that system's continuing racial character. In comparing black American to Jewish American history, they look at their own success and ask why blacks can't achieve the same, an analysis encouraged by the dominant school in U.S. race relations theory, which assimilates race to ethnicity and represents the black experience as a variant of the traditional immigrant European experience.[48] Increasingly, there is the feeling that blacks are really asking for special treatment. But as two sociologists, Douglas Massey and Nancy Denton, have recently argued in their *American Apartheid*, to understand the causes of the continuing existence of a black "underclass" today, one needs to realize that from the 1920s onward, no European immigrant group in the big American cities suffered a rate of ghettoization that reached even the *lowest* degree blacks suffered, so that in a sense the term "ghetto" can be properly associated only with black Americans.[49] It is the difference between the fates of a religiously stigmatized, but *white*, minority, still part of the European family, and the *nonwhite* minority who after hundreds of years in North America remain strangers at the gate, the paradigm representatives of subpersonhood. So one could say that Jews in the West essentially become white from the modern period onward, become nonwhite for a restricted period under the localized racial system of Nazism, suffering racial mass murder, and then become white again in Europe after the war. And this is quite different from the ontological trajectory of blacks, who, because of their original location as chattel in a slave system, are nonwhite practically from the beginning and remain so today.

COMPARISON OF BLACKS AND JEWS

The point of my argument, then, is that it is a mistake just to assimilate the histories of blacks and Jews, as many well-meaning liberals do, pointing to a common experience of suffering and racism, and then expressing bewilderment at the tensions between them. There are similarities in the histories, to be sure, but there are also significant differences that need to be taken into account. And many of these differences stem, I suggest, from their differential location in this racial system and its social ontology. The idea here is not to get into one of those repellent "Holocaust competitions" ("My Holocaust was worse than yours"). As philosopher Laurence Thomas, himself a black Jew, has argued, the differing goals and structure of American slavery and the institutionalized genocide of European Jewry obviate totalizing comparisons anyway, apart from the inherent odiousness of such an exercise.[50] Rather, the aim is to try to *explain* the divergence in the subsequent fates of the two groups. Some of these important similarities and differences may be summarized in the following table.

BLACKS AND JEWS:
SIMILARITIES AND DIFFERENCES[51]

Similarities

1. Both peoples have been forcibly displaced from their original homelands.
2. Both have a history of slavery.
3. Both have been the victims of state apparatuses of subjugation: oppressive laws, government-sanctioned ideologies of inferiority.
4. Both have been the victims of mass murder at the hands of white, Christian, Western civilization.
5. Both have been theologically stigmatized, Jews being represented as Christ-killers, Africans represented as devil-worshippers.
6. Both have been morally stigmatized in Western culture as paradigm outsiders, scapegoats, pariahs.
7. Both have been aesthetically stigmatized, so that women of both groups have sometimes changed or tried to soften their "racial" features to facilitate sexual competition with the *shiksa*/white woman.
8. Both have been discriminated against in North America in employment, housing, education.

9. Both continue today to be the victims of individual hate-crimes: personal attacks, defacements of houses of worship, cross-burnings.

10. Both draw on the Old Testament to make sense of their experience—Jews viewing it as a literal account, blacks as an analogy (though some blacks do see themselves as the "real" Jews).

11. The language of oppression and redemption used by Jews has sometimes also been employed by blacks: "Egyptian bondage," "ghetto," "Diaspora," "Exodus," "promised land," "children of Zion."

12. They have sometimes been depicted in racist literature (Klan, Nazi, Aryan Nation) as cooperating to overthrow and take over white Western civilization.

13. They have actually cooperated in the founding and staffing of civil rights organizations (the NAACP, the National Urban League) and alliances against racist laws and practices in the United States.

14. Both populations are politically generally more liberal than the white Gentile majority.

15. Early-twentieth-century Pan-Africanism and Zionism have significant similarities as redemptive nationalist political movements, seeking, respectively, black liberation/African decolonization and a homeland for the Jews (Garvey himself was sometimes characterized as a "Black Moses").[52]

Differences

1. Jews were displaced from their homeland, but generally retained their identity, traditions, family structure, and cultural control of their lives. "Black" is itself a *new* identity forged out of the forced bringing together in the West of many different African peoples with no common language, whose families were often broken up by slavery, and who were until recently largely deprived of literacy and told that they had no real culture or history.

2. The enslavement of Jews occurred thousands of years ago; the enslavement of blacks was a reality little more than a century ago, and is thus a much more powerful *living* memory in shaping contemporary consciousness.

3. Jews were enslaved at a time when slavery was standard

practice throughout the world, and there was no special "racial" link; blacks were enslaved during the modern period, when slavery was dead or dying out in the West, so that "slavery acquired a color" and black features became the racial stigmata of subordination.

4. Israel received reparations from Germany for the crimes of the Jewish Holocaust; African Americans and Caribbeans have yet to receive reparations from the American government or Europe generally for the crimes of slavery and the African Holocaust. (In fact, it was the former slaveowners who, after emancipation, were compensated for the loss of their property.)

5. Though the Christian church has a long, culpable history of antisemitism, the mainstream Western religious tradition is still a *Judaeo*-Christian tradition, not an *Afro*-Christian tradition.

6. Correspondingly, Judaism is today respected as one of the main global religions (with Christianity, Islam, Hinduism); African religions are generally not respected, and most blacks in the West are themselves converts to Christianity (though often in a syncretized version).

7. European Jews are phenotypically sufficiently similar to other Europeans that in North America they can assimilate with a change of name ("Funny, you don't look Jewish"). In the felicitous phrase of one writer, Jews have "protective coloration."[53] Thus under the Third Reich, when Jews were classified as racial subpersons, *Untermenschen*, they were forced to wear the yellow Star of David so that they could be identified as such. Blacks, by contrast, are identifiable by phenotype no matter how they try to assimilate; their permanent subpersonhood is written on their faces.

8. Because of the phenotypical closeness of Jews and Gentile whites, as against blacks and whites, the perceived need (given the internalization of a racist aesthetic) for transformative cosmeticization is much more foundational and pervasive for the black body than for the Jewish body (a technologically unrealizable change of skin, to begin with, as against occasional rhinoplasty, "nose jobs").

9. The classic racist stereotypes differ crucially in that Jews are generally credited with (sometimes supernormal) intelligence, while blacks are traditionally represented as bestially subnormal. Thus the most famous antisemitic document, the forged *Protocols of the Elders of Zion*, credits Jews with the ability

to plan and carry out the takeover of the world. Insofar as racist propaganda allocates blacks a contributory role in such an enterprise (however worthy), by contrast, it is only as foot soldiers, muscle.

10. From the time "race" becomes an important category in the European colonization and settling of North America, Jews have generally been socially categorized as "white," albeit stigmatized "off-whites." Blacks, on the other hand, have always been "nonwhite," indeed the *paradigm* nonwhites upon whose subordination the system has been based.

11. In North America today, Jews are economically successful, while blacks continue to be at or near the bottom of the ladder.[54]

12. In North America today, Jews are successful and influential in the worlds of "high" intellectual culture (the academy, scholarly books, highbrow fiction, literary magazines) and middlebrow culture (Hollywood movies, television); blacks continue to be greatly underrepresented in both spheres. Where blacks have made a significant contribution to popular culture—in black or black-derived music (jazz, blues, rock and roll), which has been the single greatest force in shaping American popular music—their lack of *economic* control over the industry has meant that they have often not reaped the rewards they deserved for their work.

13. As a result of this preeminence, the Jewish community—in the words of Laurence Thomas—have greater "group autonomy," cultural control of representations of themselves, than blacks do.[55] There is a fundamental asymmetry, by which Jews are regarded as the foremost interpreters of their own experience in a way that blacks are not, and by which far more Jews are seen as experts on the black experience than vice versa.

14. The tragedy of the Jewish Holocaust is commemorated in popular culture (movies, TV), and thus imprinted on mass consciousness,[56] in a way that the African Holocaust is not, though the effects of the latter continue to make themselves felt in the degraded position of Africa and African Americans in the world today. A show like *Roots*, the 1977 television dramatization of the Alex Haley novel (which was in its time, admittedly—and is still now, twenty years later—the highest-rated miniseries ever),[57] is the exception rather than the norm. In general, there has been relatively little serious exploration of the ordeals of slavery and Jim Crow, despite their obviously fundamental shaping effect on both black and white

Americans. The most famous big-budget Hollywood films about slavery and the postbellum period either overtly demonize blacks (the 1915 *Birth of a Nation*) or romanticize plantation life from the whites' perspective (the 1939 *Gone With the Wind*). In addition, demeaning portrayals of blacks as servile "Toms," comic "coons," and threatening "bucks" were routine for decades in Hollywood movies (and continue to some extent to appear in disguised form today) long after antisemitic portrayals of Jews ceased to be permissible, an indication of the differential status of the two groups in the white racial polity.[58]

15. In North America, the Jewish community is on the whole far better politically organized than the black community, a reflection variously of class differences, a greater degree of assimilation, and (given black disenfranchisement) a longer history of political activism. In addition, in the United States for many decades, Jews were a prime source of funding for black civil rights organizations, on the one hand a tribute to the antiracist commitments of many Jews, but on the other, the foundation of a differential power relationship. The overall result is that Jewish-black political relations have generally *not* been peer-to-peer relations but have been viewed by many blacks as paternalistic.

16. Israel is seen as part of the West; the decolonized African nations are not.

17. In the postwar period, after the revelations of the death camps, racist ideology of the antisemitic kind ceased to be respectable in the West. By contrast, anti*black* racist ideology never died, and from the late 1960s onward has had a dramatic resurgence in the form of IQ theory (alleged lower black intelligence)[59] and some interpretations of sociobiology (alleged greater black propensity for violence).

18. The overall judgment of historian George Mosse: "[I]f, under the shock of the holocaust, the postwar world proclaimed a temporary moratorium on anti-Semitism, the black on the whole remained locked into a racial posture which never varied much from the eighteenth century to our time. . . . Moreover, nations which had fought against National Socialism continued to accept black racial inferiority for many years after the end of the war."[60]

19. The overall judgment of philosopher Lawrence Blum: Blacks are both vulnerable and subordinated; Jews are vulnerable, but they are not subordinated.

NARRATIVES OF IDENTITY AND
OPPRESSION, NEGOTIATIONS OF PERSONHOOD

Against this background, I want to try to explain the dynamic of the degeneration of black-Jewish relations, and its source in the differentiated ways in which personhood is characteristically negotiated in a racial polity.

The logic of the racial polity is that personhood cannot be taken for granted by everybody. In the ideal Kantian ontology, the presumption is that all humans are persons, so that this is our starting point, and one expects respect as a matter of course. But in a system of white domination, supported by a dark ontology of master and subordinate races, members of the subordinate races will routinely *not* get respect. It will be an immanent part of the culture and social structure that they get a *dis*respect that is not at all contingent but, especially in the *de jure* phase of racial subordination, is mandated by the system as part of its reproductive dynamic. In other words, treating nonwhites as equals would jeopardize the racial order, violating the *Herrenvolk* ethics that is its moral economy. So this dark ontology has to be continually maintained through transactions at the boundaries. Correspondingly, the most salient feature of the experience of those classified as subpersons in this system will be the need, for their own self-respect, to assert their personhood, to contest the racial disrespect that they routinely receive. For if they just accept it without protest, they are accepting the official definition of themselves as less than human, not really persons.

In a section of *The Metaphysics of Morals* titled "On Servility," Kant points out that a person's feeling of "his inner worth" and "inalienable dignity" "instills in him respect for himself" and likewise demands "*respect* for himself from all other rational beings in the world": "He can measure himself with every other being of this kind and value himself on a footing of equality with them. Humanity in his person is the object of the respect which he can demand from every other man, but which he must also not forfeit. . . . And this *self-esteem* is a duty of man to himself."[61] But in the racial polity, where historically servility is precisely what *has* been expected and required of subpersons, their demands for equal respect from the population of official persons will be actively resisted, and their duty to themselves of self-esteem will be much harder to fulfill. Personhood, respect, and self-respect thus have to be *fought* for by nonwhites in a way that they do not for whites, or for abstract individuals in the race-free polity of an ideal Kantianism.[62] And to the extent that whites remain committed to a racist self- positioning of superiority over nonwhites, their own self-respect and personhood will be jeopardized by this contestation from below. So the reciprocal interlinkage of definitions of personhood in terms of race may give rise to a zero-sum game of conflicting ontologies. Relations between blacks and Jews, paradigm nonwhites and borderline whites, need to be examined against this background.

For blacks in North America, the basic conceptual divide, the one around which their lives have historically been structured, will naturally be that between whites and blacks. They will be less attentive to differences among whites—language, customs, religion, and so on—because their experience has been that these differences are eventually rendered irrelevant by the objective logic of the racial system. The rules of the American racial order, predicated on the subordination of the expropriated reds and the enslaved blacks, offer even borderline whites—the Irish, Slavs, Mediterraneans, Jews—the chance of whitening themselves.[63] In fact, the experience of ethnic oppression in Europe could have contradictory psychological outcomes. Although it did make some immigrants more sensitive to racial oppression in their new home, for others it had the converse effect. Precisely because their status was shakier, precisely because their group had originally been beyond the pale, they were sometimes *more* eager to demonstrate their whiteness,their worthiness to be admitted into the club. Most of the millions of newcomers embrace the system with the militant assertion of their bona fides as legitimate white people fully deserving of respect.

The strategy of negotiating personhood therefore characteristically plays itself out differently in these two locations—unambiguously nonwhite, ambiguously white. One could say that it is the difference between outside outsiders and inside outsiders. For blacks, with no hope of attaining whiteness, the tendency will be to challenge the system of racial privilege and racialized personhood itself. Because of their antipodean location—the standpoint of chattel seeing Western civilization from the bottom—black critics are be forced in radical directions to make sense of their experience and to attain respect. For Jews, on the other hand, the situation is significantly different, in that they have a choice. As victims of Christian persecution in the Old World, they could agitate for the dismantling of the system of racial persecution in the New, demanding that respect and personhood be de-linked from race. And, to their credit, Jews have been the European ethnic group most active in the founding and staffing of civil rights organizations in the United States. But as Europeans, whites, they *also* had the option of entering the racial system, even if the barriers were higher for them than for some other groups. And as Cornel West points out: "Like other European immigrants, Jews for the most part became complicitous with the American racial caste system."[64]

Moreover, as Europeans, even borderline ones, their standpoint is from within the system, so they have difficulty seeing the project of the West *from outside*, as epistemically privileged blacks, along with Native Americans the West's primary victims, have always been able to do. For them, the dominant narrative is the history of persecution of Jews by Gentiles and the basic conceptual division that between Jews and Gentiles (of all colors). They recognize, of course, that blacks have been subordinated within Christian civilization, but their personal experience naturally sensitizes them more to antisemitism than to antiblack racism. It is unsurprising, then, that though some Jews were antiracist activists, most were content to assimilate to majority white Gentile society and, in some cases, to collaborate in the creation of the *Herrenvolk* cultural products necessary to maintain the racial order. For these Jews, the dominant strategy for negotiating personhood is to insist, against antisemitic slanders imputing to them an alien nature, on their Europeanness, their rightful membership in the West, with either no awareness of or indifference to the way in which Europeanness has itself come to be tied up with claims to white supremacy.

I think black hostility to Jews needs to be seen within this context. My suggestion is that the historic black struggle against white oppression generates, as an ideational accompaniment, conspiracy theories centered on race, and that over time Jews increasingly become the prime suspects.

Fredric Jameson suggests that the conspiracy theory is a kind of half-baked Hegelianism, a degraded attempt to think the whole.[65] There is a lot to this, but I would add that it is an attempt to think the whole that also has the political and psychological virtue of *highlighting human agency*. This is particularly important for subordinated groups, since there is a general tendency in complex modern societies for their human-made character to disappear, so that their causality becomes impersonal, fetishized, like a force of nature. Things happen, but no one is to blame. Or, even worse, blame for group subordination is attributed to the group itself (their culture, their innate biological deficiencies, etc.). The conspiracy theories of the oppressed refuse this causal evisceration, or causal misdirection, by expressly categorizing the group's plight as a state of *oppression* (which presupposes the hostile agency of other humans). *Racial* conspiracy theories are then a subset of conspiracy theories in general, involving the racial identification of the oppressed and oppressor group and the imputation of some kind of racial motivation to the latter.

Now it is important to realize that racial conspiracy theories are nothing *new*, and that in fact historically the most influential of such theories have come from the dominating groups themselves. If we think back to the various colored perils that have historically haunted the white imagination—the Red (Indian) Peril, the Yellow Peril, the Black Peril—then clearly there are the racial conspiracy theories of rulers worried about the insurrection of their subjects. Europeans in the late nineteenth and early twentieth centuries worried about race wars of revenge produced popular literature about nonwhite alliances to challenge colonial white supremacy. As Gary Okihiro points out, "Fundamentally . . . the idea of the yellow peril does not derive solely from the alleged threat posed by Asians to Europeans . . . but from nonwhite people, as a collective group, and their contestation of white supremacy," and thus an idea "expounded most vehemently at the height of imperialism and at the start of Third World nationalism and decolonization."[66] In the United States, similarly, the intellectual legacy of the Indian wars and the watchfulness for slave uprisings generated what Gary Nash and Richard Weiss call *The Great Fear: Race in the Mind of America.*[67] Books such as Lothrop Stoddard's *Rising Tide of Color against White World-Supremacy* were favorably reviewed and influential in the 1920s.[68]

So racial conspiracy theories come in many versions. The racial conspiracy theories of the oppressed, blacks in particular, draw on the undeniable fact—no paranoid fantasy, this—that colonialism, the slave trade, segregation, and so forth were developed and institutionalized through the concerted and planned actions of whites. These things did not just happen; they were made to happen. In these historical cases, of course, no reasonable person could deny the role of racism. But in contemporary mainstream social theory's analyses of the plight of blacks in the United States, racism tends to drop out as an explanation, with increasing recourse instead to the "culture of poverty," genetic propensity, and transformations of the local and global economy with racially differentiated, though not racially motivated, effects. Black popular discourse, in contrast, generates detailed theories explaining, for example, political assassinations, the prevalence of drugs in the ghetto, the origins of AIDS, the targeted marketing to a black clientele of particular products (cigarettes, soft drinks, fast-food stores, footwear, sportswear, and so on), and the perceived persecution of elected black officials and black celebrities in the United States (Marion Barry, Mike Tyson, Michael Jackson, O. J. Simpson, to name the most recent), as the result of white conspiracies.[69] Such theories have the psychological and political function of insisting on the continuing existence of racism as a causal factor determining black lives, and representing the plight of blacks as something avoidable, something that is the result of oppressive human causality, of individual choices and public policy decisions made one way rather than another. The causality may be short-circuited, structural trends voluntarized, the locus of ultimate responsibility misidentified, details or the central thesis completely wrong, but in a sense this is irrelevant: what collectively they do is to reaffirm the *human*-created character of the black situation.

My suggestion, then, is that a lot of black hostility to Jews can be cognitively explained as an insistence on the continuing existence of a system of racial disadvantage for which Jews are at least partly just a symbol. Traditional antisemitism is, among other things, a set of conspiracy theories about Jewish attempts to capture Christian virgins, pollute Gentile blood, take over the world, and so on. So there is, so to speak, a preexisting *legitimized* trope in mainstream culture with a slot for Jews as the prime agents of a sinister, behind-the-scenes, globally efficacious social causality. Black antiwhite feeling and theory, seeking a template to categorize, understand and protest black oppression, and traditionally inclined toward conspiracy theories with real roots in historical fact, intersects with the formal structure of conventional antisemitism. But the content and motivation are then obviously significantly different from those of the classic European variety.

Moreover, this unfortunate cognitive synthesis is encouraged by the ambivalences and shifts in black-Jewish relations arising out of the two groups' divergent positions in the white polity, especially the increasing assimilation and material success of Jews since World War II, which, together with the rise of black nationalism and (sometimes) separatism, pulls the two politically apart. Because established WASP capital and exclusivist ethnic networks blocked Jewish immigrants' access to certain investment opportunities, professions, and neighborhoods, available jobs and economic roles brought them differentially into contact with blacks, so that white oppression then often wore a Jewish face. The cognitive impact is deepened by the fact that Jews are already somewhat differentiated from other whites, and as cognitive psychologists have shown, "vividness" is a factor in determining what sticks in our head, what we remember.[70] So this then gives rise to a specifically black antisemitism that seizes on the Jews as the key agents responsible for ongoing black subordination. In James Baldwin's famous judgment: "Negroes are anti-semitic because they're anti-white."[71] Jews here serve as a confused cognitive proxy for the real target—the system of racial political power, and a set of exclusionary mechanisms that, with the demise of *de jure* racism, is much harder to identify. Affirming black personhood and racial self-respect requires a narrative of racial exploitation to pre-empt dominant narratives of racial inferiority; narratives of racial exploitation become racial conspiracy theories; and Jews, especially Jews whose situation in North America have dramatically improved over the century and who have turned politically right, become the paradigm conspirators.

From the Jewish side, of course, things seem quite different. To begin with, some Jews will simply be racist, an unsurprising development given their assimilation into a culture that for hundreds of years took black inferiority for granted. But even liberal, antiracist Jews will understandably be hurt, puzzled, and outraged when they seem to hear from blacks, people with whom they have allied in the past, the same language and rhetoric that they have heard for centuries from traditional antisemites. A detached analysis of such a psychological phenomenon is obviously easier to develop when one is not oneself likely to be a victim of the phenomenon in question. When Jews hear that black American youths in Crown Heights chanted "Kill the Jew!" before Yankel Rosenbaum was stabbed to death, it must send a shudder down their spine, bringing back memories of the Russian Cossacks, the East European pogroms, the Nazi *Kristallnacht*. When they hear Khallid Muhammad accusing Jews of controlling the Federal Reserve Board, it must bring back memories of the *Protocols of the Elders of Zion* and the accusations of a Jewish conspiracy to take over the world. When they hear that they are responsible for the African slave trade, it must bring back memories of the medieval Christian portrayal of Jews as the main source of all human evil. Within a narrative of Jews versus Gentiles, within a framework where a Jew's personhood and right to respect and equitable treatment characteristically have to be asserted against Gentile attack, the color of the accusers is less significant (except to sharpen the pain) than the familiar message.

Jewish self-respect therefore demands the denunciation of those who, yet again, are singling out the underdog Jews for special blame. But within the conflicting narrative of whites versus blacks, this denunciation is read by *blacks* as the white racists' familiar denial of responsibility for their racist policies of oppression, and the persecution by the powerful of those courageous enough to speak the truth and expose their role. So *black* self-respect demands that one stand up to the agents of white racism, the architects of the dark ontology, and prove one's personhood by not buckling and giving in to white criticism. The result, obviously, is a disastrous clash of narratives and negotiations of personhood, in which the ranks close, the categories lock into place, the reflexive tropes harden, and the affirmation of self-respect increasingly manifests itself in racial accusation. Rival conceptions of the social order and racially conflictual views of personhood collide and feed on each other, establishing a self-sustaining degenerative cycle of mutual recrimination, in which each side's self-conceived moral duty of affirming their humanity constitutes proof for the other precisely of their *immorality* and *inhumanity*.

CONCLUSION

I have focused on the narrow question of blacks and Jews, but of course the problem of racial and ethnic conflict in the world today is much broader. What is the solution? The threat of the balkanization of the polity into competing tribal groups, with all for each and none for all, may suggest that these local particularistic identities are now too dangerous to be persisted with, and should perhaps be dispensed with altogether in the name of an encompassing universalism. But the problem, at least in the West, is that historically this kind of universalism has itself usually turned out to be a white particularism in disguise, in that it is really the "other" ethnic/racial groups (the groups who are designated *as* "ethnic," *as* "minorities," *as* raced) who have to give up their ethnicity/race and assimilate to the majority population. So what we really need to strive for is a rainbowed rather than an abstract—in effect a white—universalism. Moreover, ethnic and racial identities are not going to be given up as long as they condense narratives of history and origin, meaning and personhood. The challenge, as Cornel West points out, then becomes the moral *rethinking* of these identities so that they can be disarmed, stripped of the exclusionary commitments that lead to antagonism and conflict: the revision of what it means to be white, black, Jewish. And the main obstacles to such a revision are not conceptual—there is no intrinsic consistency problem with the simultaneous valorization of different ethnic/racial identities—but *political/psychological*, that is, whether as a matter of contingent fact, given present patterns of subjugation, such a moral transformation is really likely.

The crucial issue is therefore the connection between racial/ethnic identity and the structure I have delineated. These group identities will continue to come into conflict not out of logical necessity but through their shaping and reshaping by a context of relative access to and blocking from economic opportunities, cultural image-making, and political input. As long as a structure of racial privilege exists in the United States (and elsewhere), claims to racial identity will essentially be coded ways of affirming and challenging differential privilege. Affirming whiteness in this context means affirming white entitlement to privilege; affirming blackness means challenging black exclusion. Appeals to moral toleration of difference will do no good if the system remains intact, because no matter how subjectively sincere people's intentions, the objective structure will keep recoalescing the identities in their old antagonistic form. Race will become an innocent identity, and will be most safely affirmed precisely when there is no longer any need to affirm it, when there is no connection between race and structural advantage or disadvantage. In an ideal Kantian world, unlike the world of *Herrenvolk* Kantianism, respect will be detached from race, and its present explosive moral charge will be defused.

But achieving such a world—bringing into existence Kant's *respublica noumenon*—requires us to look honestly at the world that actually exists. Kant's "two viewpoints" dichotomization assumes that our freedom as noumenal moral agents to do our duty can always overcome empirical disinclination, that we can always see and do the right thing.[72] Contemporary Kantians are justifiably more dubious about such a metaphysics of moral agency, recognizing the many ways in which our upbringing and this-worldly empirical obstacles can deform our moral development, impeding recognition and performance of our duty. The point of identifying and mapping a *Herrenvolk* Kantianism, as I have done, is not, of course, to endorse the actual, naturalized, non-ideal practice of the past and present, but to make ourselves self-consciously aware of the history and structure of these practices and how they have affected and continue to affect our moral psychology. Solving the problem of how to get there from here, of how to realize the ideal, requires an accurate delineation of the obstacles on the route. Epigrammatically, one could say, following Justice Blackmun, that the ideal of a world *beyond* race can be reached only by going *through* race, not by trying to go *around* race.[73] Less figuratively: white moral and political philosophers need to recognize the centrality of race to the past few hundred years of global history, and how white domination has shaped not only the moral topography of our world but their own moral theorizing and moral practice. To reflect these realities, we need, as Onora O'Neill has argued, theories that abstract without idealizing, that register the radical historical differences between agents rather than subsuming them under abstract, colorless individuals.[74] And in constructing such a theory, we can greatly benefit, I suggest, from drawing on black and Third World oppositional traditions, the theorizing about race of those persons whose personhood has historically been denied because of race.

In conclusion, then, to the black community, to my own community, I would say this. The narrative of oppression we have inherited from hundreds of years of slavery and subjugation in the West is in danger of degeneration, and needs to be redirected against the appropriate target. We betray those who gave their lives in the struggle against racism if we ourselves embrace racist and antisemitic ideas. The Jewish community are not the enemy; the enemy is white racism and the present legacy of an historically exclusionary racial structure. To the extent that *some* Jews are now actively complicit with this structure, they should of course be criticized. But there is no genealogical connection between this structure and the Jews; they did not create it, and they themselves have been victimized by it. Nor should criticisms be global accusations that ignore the history of the many Jews who have fought against racism, anti-black as well as antisemitic. To accuse Jews as a group of such conspiracies puts us morally on the same level as traditional white racists—Nazis and Klansmen—and deprives us of the moral authority the black community, as victims rather than victimizers, have traditionally had. The assertion of black personhood and the demand for black respect, far from leading us to condone black wrongdoing and black antisemitism in the name of black solidarity, require us to condemn them for the sake of our own self-respect.

To the Jewish community, I would say this. While always keeping alive the memory of the Jewish Holocaust and recognizing the continuing danger of antisemitism, including black antisemitism, you need to update the traditional narrative of Jewish victimization. Late-twentieth-century North America is not the Third Reich, nor is it likely to be transformed into it. Although individual blacks may commit antisemitic acts, blacks as a group do not have power, so that this kind of ideational and behavioral racism cannot be put on the same plane of social significance as the *institutional* racism, directed primarily against people of color, of the centers of political and economic power. Nor should the justifiable criticism of the former be used as a pretext to blind oneself to the existence of the latter. History moves on, and one's group narratives, negotiations of personhood, and moral responsibilities must keep pace accordingly. If because of the horrors of Nazism we think of Jewishness as being classically in part a disadvantaged location in a system of racial power, then we could say that in North America the real "Jews" have never been the Jews. The real "Jews" are Native Americans. Or the real "Jews" are blacks. In an anthology published many years ago, Rabbi Alan Miller, a member of the Jewish Reconstructionist Movement, made this very point: "[The black man] is the one who, on the American scene, has been the persecuted. He is, in truth, the American 'Jew.'"[75] In North America today, it cannot realistically be claimed that Jews are part of the *Untermenschen*.

So there is an ironic turn-around that is surprising only to those who see race as fixed rather than fluid. On this continent, whether one speaks angrily of white supremacy or more gently and nonconfrontationally of white privilege, the system of racial advantage is divided on an axis of white/nonwhite, and Jews are on the privileged side of that line. Difficult and astonishing as it may be to accept, then, unthinkable and incongruent as it is with the defining Jewish narrative, the fact has to be faced that Jews in the West are now unequivocally part of the privileged race. As Nat Hentoff says in his introduction to the same anthology: "We are, all of us who are white, the *goyim* in America."[76] Updating your narrative means realizing this fact, and recognizing that—in addition to your own heroic efforts—part of the reason for your success on this continent is that doors have been opened for you that were closed to nonwhites. Whatever your personal feelings and political views, you are objectively socially advantaged by your racial characterization. So your moral responsibility, now, as privileged members of society—indeed, the moral responsibility of all whites of good will—is to throw your political and organizational weight behind the opening up of these doors to everyone, so that whiteness, blackness, and Jewishness will be equally connected to— and thereby equally disconnected from—personhood; all races and ethnicities will have an equal chance in a nonracial polity; and the shameful dark ontology inherited from the shadowed and divided Enlightenment will disappear in a blaze of egalitarian light.

NOTES

Support for writing this essay was provided by the Institute for the Humanities, University of Illinois at Chicago. I have benefited from the comments of two anonymous reviewers for SUNY Press. This is a somewhat revised version of a paper, "Dark Ontologies," I presented as a public lecture on May 2, 1994, at the Joint Symposium and Public Lecture Series on "Race and the City," cosponsored by the University of Toronto Philosophy Department and the Holy Blossom Temple of Toronto. (The other lecture was given by Professor, and Rabbi, David Novak of the University of Virginia.) The main motivation for the event was the unfortunate deterioration in black-Jewish relations in Toronto after a revival of the Jerome Kern/Oscar Hammerstein II musical "Show Boat" (based on the 1926 Edna Ferber novel) was launched, over angry black protest, at the inaugural 1993 opening of a Jewish cultural center in the city.

1. Charles W. Mills, "Non-Cartesian *Sums*: Philosophy and the African-American Experience," *Teaching Philosophy* 17. 3 (1994): 223–43.

2. Kant's place in the history of ethics has, of course, long been secure. He is "arguably the most important moral philosopher in the modern period"; Roger J. Sullivan, *Immanuel Kant's Moral Theory* (New York: Cambridge University Press, 1989), xiii. His dramatic rise in stature in Anglo-American *political* theory is more recent, originally stimulated by the Kantian themes in the book usually credited with reviving postwar Western political philosophy, John Rawls's *A Theory of Justice* (Cambridge, Mass.: Harvard University Press, 1971). The trajectory over the past quarter-century can be tracked by comparing Hans Reiss's 1968 introduction to his first edition of Kant's political writings

with his 1989 postscript to the second edition: "Kant, at least in English speaking countries, is not generally considered to be a political philosopher of note." "Kant's standing as a political thinker has been substantially enhanced in the English-speaking world since this volume went to the printers just over two decades ago. More and more scholars are willing to rank him among the leading figures in the history of political thought." Hans Reiss, ed., *Kant: Political Writings*, 2nd ed., trans. H. B. Nisbet (1970; reprinted, New York: Cambridge University Press, 1991), 3, 250.

3. There is an anthology of articles, with illustrations from the exhibition, accompanying it: *Bridges and Boundaries: African Americans and American Jews* (New York: George Braziller in association with the Jewish Museum, 1992), ed. Jack Salzman, with Adina Back and Gretchen Sullivan Sorin. See also Paul Berman, ed., *Blacks and Jews: Alliances and Arguments* (New York: Delacorte Press, 1994). An older but still valuable collection is Nat Hentoff, ed., *Black Anti-Semitism and Jewish Racism* (New York: Richard W. Baron, 1969). Some of the articles in the Salzman anthology date back to the 1940s, demonstrating how longstanding the issue really is: see, for example, Kenneth B. Clark, "Candor about Negro-Jewish Relations" (1946), in Salzman, 91–98.

4. "Kant has rightly been called the philosopher of the French Revolution" (Reiss, Kant, 3) though paradoxically he rejected the right to revolution himself: (ibid., postscript, section VII).

5. Sullivan, *Moral Theory*, 197.

6. *Kants Gesammelte Schriften*, Ausgabe der Königlichen Preußischen Akademie (Berlin: Georg Reimer, 1903), 4:385–463; *Groundwork of the Metaphysic of Morals*, trans. H. J. Paton (1948; reprinted, New York: Harper & Row, 1964). *Kants Gesammelte Schriften*, 6:203–491; Immanuel Kant, *The Metaphysics of Morals*, trans. Mary Gregor (New York: Cambridge University Press, 1991). One needs to distinguish "ideal Kantianism" from Kant's own views since, as Reiss reminds us, Kant himself had "a very narrow conception . . . of what kind of individuals can be expected to achieve maturity and autonomy of political judgment," a conception that in fact excludes the *majority* of the population (Reiss, Kant, 257). For Kant's relegation of women to the status of "passive citizens," see Susan Mendus, "Kant: 'An Honest but Narrow-Minded Bourgeois?'" in *Essays on Kant's Political Philosophy*, ed. Howard Lloyd Williams (Chicago: University of Chicago Press, 1992), 166–90.

7. *The Philosophy and Opinions of Marcus Garvey*, 2 vols., ed. Amy Jacques-Garvey, with an introduction by Robert A. Hill (1923, 1925; reprinted, New York: Atheneum, 1992); E. David Cronon, *Black Moses: The Story of Marcus Garvey and the Universal Negro Improvement Association*, 2nd ed. (1955; reprinted, Madison: University of Wisconsin Press, 1969); John Henrik Clarke, ed., *Marcus Garvey and the Vision of Africa* (New York: Vintage Books, 1974); Rupert Lewis and Patrick Bryan, eds., *Garvey: His Work and Impact* (Kingston, Jamaica: ISER, UWI, 1988).

8. Rex Nettleford, "Garvey's Legacy: Some Perspectives," in Lewis and Bryan, Garvey, 312.

9. V. G. Kiernan, *The Lords of Human Kind: Black Man, Yellow Man, and White Man in an Age of Empire* (1969; reprinted, New York: Columbia University Press, 1986); Charles W. Mills, "Revisionist Ontologies: Theorizing White Supremacy," *Social and Economic Studies* 43.3 (1994): 105–34.

10. C. Vann Woodward, *The Strange Career of Jim Crow*, 3rd ed. (1955; reprinted, New York: Oxford University Press, 1974); George M. Fredrickson, *White Supremacy: A Comparative Study in American and South African History* (New York: Oxford University Press, 1981).

11. Edward W. Said, *Culture and Imperialism* (New York: Alfred A. Knopf, 1993), 8.

12. Frantz Fanon, *The Wretched of the Earth*, trans. Constance Farrington (1961; reprinted, New York: Grove Press, 1968).

13. Stephen Jay Gould, *The Mismeasure of Man* (New York and London: W. W. Norton, 1981).

14. Mills, "Revisionist Ontologies."

15. For a discussion of the enterprise of "naturalizing" ethics, see Alvin I. Goldman, "Ethics and Cognitive Science," *Ethics* 103.2 (1993): 337–60.

16. Philip D. Curtin, introduction, *Imperialism* (New York: Walker, 1971), xiii; Pierre L. van den Berghe, *Race and Racism: A Comparative Perspective* (New York: Wiley, 1967).

17. Van den Berghe, *Race and Racism*. The "democracy" is, of course, further qualified by exclusions of gender.

18. One of the anonymous SUNY Press reviewers commented that my contribution was "very interesting but not at all applicable directly to Kant."

19. The judgment of the German anthropologist Wilhelm Mühlmann, *Geschichte der Anthropologie* (Frankfurt a.M., 1968), 57; cited in Léon Poliakov, "Racism from the Enlightenment to the Age of Imperialism," in *Racism and Colonialism*, ed. Robert Ross (The Hague: Martinus Nijhoff, 1982), 59.

20. *Kants Gesammelte Schriften*, 2:253–55; Immanuel Kant, *Observations on the Feeling of the Beautiful and Sublime*, trans. John T. Goldthwait (Berkeley and Los Angeles: University of California Press, 1960), 111–13.

21. David Theo Goldberg, *Racist Culture: Philosophy and the Politics of Meaning* (Cambridge, Mass.: Blackwell, 1993), 32, 241n.45.

22. *Kants Gesammelte Schriften*, 2:427–43; Immanuel Kant, "On the Different Races of Man," in Earl W. Count, ed., *This Is Race: An Anthology Selected from the International Literature on the Races of Man* (New York: Henry Schuman, 1950), 16–24.

23. George L. Mosse, *Toward the Final Solution: A History of European Racism* (1978; reprinted, Madison: University of Wisconsin Press, 1985), 31. See also Kant's 1785 "Bestimmung des Begriffs einer Menschenrasse," in *Kants Gesammelte Schriften*, 8:89–106.

24. Emmanuel Eze, "The Color of Reason: The Idea of 'Race' in Kant's Anthropology," in *Anthropology and the German Enlightenment*, ed. Katherine M.

Faull (Lewisburg, Pa. Bucknell University Press, 1995), 196–237. Eze cites an earlier essay by Christian Neugebauer, "The Racism of Kant and Hegel," in *Sage Philosophy: Indigenous Thinkers and Modern Debate on African Philosophy*, ed. H. Odera Oruka (Leiden: E. J. Brill, 1990), 259–72. One of Neugebauer's main sources is a German compilation by E. Henscheid, *Der Neger* (Frankfurt G. M., 1985).

25. Eze, "Color of Reason," 209–15.

26. Ibid., 215–19.

27. Ibid., 217.

28. This is not to say that Kant would necessarily have endorsed all the practices of European domination. In one passage of *The Metaphysics of Morals*, for example, he characterizes as a "vacuum" those lands "uninhabited by civilized people," but peopled rather by "savages" (American Indians, Hottentots, the inhabitants of New Holland) not in "a rightful condition." But though he understands the temptation for Europeans "to found colonies" by force or fraud and thus "establish a civil union with them," thereby fulfilling "the end of creation," he explicitly repudiates "this veil of injustice (Jesuitism), which would sanction any means to good ends" (*Kants Gesammelte Schriften*, 6:266; *Metaphysics of Morals*, 86–87). So the question of the extent to which Kant himself could be categorized as a *"Herrenvolk* Kantian" is too complex to be resolved here, and would require a systematic survey of his writings that confronted, rather than ignored and evaded, the role race plays in his moral/political theory and philosophy of history. A defender might argue that his polarized moral universe, divided simply between persons and non-persons, leaves no conceptual room for *sub*persons, and that as long as a basement level of rationality has been achieved, nonwhites would count as full persons. But the racial hierarchy cited above raises questions about this. With respect to gender, feminists have long pointed out that the introduction of the "active citizen/passive citizen" distinction shows how easily the formal commitment to respect for all persons can be evacuated of content: see Susan Mendus, "Kant," note 6. The characteristics Kant lists as typical of passive citizens—lack of civil personality, dependence upon the will of others, inequality (e.g., *Kants Gesammelte Schriften*, 6:314–15; *Metaphysics of Morals*, 126)—would certainly all have been seen as completely applicable to the status of blacks in the New World.

29. Reference throughout, of course, is to European Jews.

30. Richard Nisbett and Lee Ross, *Human Inference: Strategies and Shortcomings of Social Judgment* (Englewood Cliffs, N.J.: Prentice Hall, 1980). See also the opening chapters of Paul Thagard's *Conceptual Revolutions* (Princeton, N.J.: Princeton University Press, 1992), in which he emphasizes the importance of conceptual change in belief revision.

31. Mosse, *Final Solution*, ix, 231.

32. Harold R. Isaacs, "Color in World Affairs," in *White Racism: Its History, Pathology and Practice*, ed. Barry N. Schwartz and Robert Disch (New York: Dell, 1970), 474–86.

33. Léon Poliakov, *The Aryan Myth: A History of Racist and Nationalist Ideas in Europe*, trans. Edmund Howard (1971; reprinted, New York: Basic Books, 1974), 5.

34. Theodore W. Allen, *The Invention of the White Race*, vol. 1: *Racial Oppression and Social Control* (London and New York: Verso, 1994).

35. In the famous judgment of Frank B. Livingstone: "There are no races, there are only clines [continuously varying phenotypical traits]." "On the Nonexistence of Human Races," in *The "Racial" Economy of Science: Toward a Democratic Future*, ed. Sandra Harding (Bloomington and Indianapolis: Indiana University Press, 1993).

36. For a discussion, see Cornel West, "A Genealogy of Modern Racism," in *Prophesy Deliverance!: An Afro-American Revolutionary Christianity* (Philadelphia: Westminster Press, 1982), 47–65.

37. David Hume, footnote to the 1753–54 edition of his essay, "Of National Characters," first published in 1748; cited by Winthrop D. Jordan, *White over Black: American Attitudes toward the Negro, 1550–1812* (1968; reprinted, New York and London: W. W. Norton, 1977), 253; Voltaire, "The People of American," cited in Thomas F. Gossett, *Race: The History of an Idea in America* (1963; reprinted, New York: Schocken, 1965), 44–45; Georg Wilhelm Friedrich Hegel, introduction, *The Philosophy of History*, trans. J. Sibree (New York: Dover, 1956), 91–99.

38. Martin Bernal, *Black Athena: The Afroasiatic Roots of Classical Civilization*, vol. 1: *The Fabrication of Ancient Greece, 1785–1985* (New Brunswick, N.J.: Rutgers University Press, 1987).

39. See, for example, Jordan, *White over Black*.

40. Jordan, *White over Black*; Joel Kovel, *White Racism: A Psychohistory* (1970; reprinted, New York: Columbia University Press, 1984).

41. Jan Nederveen Pieterse, *White on Black: Images of Africa and Blacks in Western Popular Culture* (Amsterdam, 1990; reprinted New Haven and London: Yale University Press, 1992). Those more sympathetic to politicoeconomic explanations, however, such as Pieterse himself, argue that there are clear temporal shifts in the Western iconography of blacks, and that universally negative images came to prevail only *after* a certain period (the rise of the Atlantic slave trade).

42. Oliver Cox, *Caste, Class and Race* (New York: Modern Reader, 1948); Cedric J. Robinson, *Black Marxism: The Making of the Black Radical Tradition* (London: Zed Press, 1983); David Roediger, *The Wages of Whiteness: Race and the Making of the American Working Class* (London and New York: Verso, 1991).

43. Kirkpatrick Sale, *The Conquest of Paradise: Christopher Columbus and the Columbian Legacy* (New York: Knopf, 1990); David E. Stannard, *American Holocaust: The Conquest of the New World* (New York and Oxford: Oxford University Press, 1992).

44. Kiernan, *Lords of Human Kind*.

45. Jordan, *White over Blacks*, 254.

46. Mosse, *Final Solution*, 14.

47. Salzman, *Bridges and Boundaries*, 183–85.

48. For example, Nathan Glazer and Daniel Patrick Moynihan, *Beyond the Melting Pot*, 2nd ed. (1963; reprinted, Cambridge, Mass.: MIT Press, 1970). For a critique, see Stephen Steinberg, *The Ethnic Myth: Race, Ethnicity, and Class in America*, rev. ed. (1981; reprinted, Boston: Beacon Press, 1989), and *Turning Back: The Retreat from Racial Justice in American Thought and Policy* (Boston: Beacon Press, 1995).

49. Douglas S. Massey and Nancy A. Denton, *American Apartheid: Segregation and the Making of the Underclass* (Cambridge, Mass.: Harvard University Press, 1993).

50. Laurence Mordekhai Thomas, *Vessels of Evil: American Slavery and the Holocaust* (Philadelphia: Temple University Press, 1993).

51. Apart from the authors actually cited, these points have been derived variously from the three anthologies mentioned earlier—*Black Anti-Semitism and Jewish Racism*, *Bridges and Boundaries*, *Blacks and Jews* (especially the chapter by Julius Lester, "The Lives People Live," 164–77)—and my own thoughts on the matter.

52. Cronon, *Black Moses*.

53. Bruce Wright, *Black Robes, White Justice* (New York: Lyle Stuart, 1987), 53.

54. During the years 1972–89, the average household income of Jewish Americans was 1.55 times the U.S. national average. Blacks, by contrast, were near the bottom, at 0.68 of the national average. Source: National Opinion Research Center, Cumulative General Social Survey, 1972–1989, cited in Christopher Jencks, *Rethinking Social Policy: Race, Poverty, and the Underclass* (Cambridge, Mass.: Harvard University Press, 1992), 28.

55. Laurence Thomas, "Group Autonomy and Narrative Identity: Blacks and Jews," in Berman, *Blacks and Jews*, 286–303.

56. In a personal conversation with me, however, Roger Gottlieb has argued that the narrative structure of the multiple-Academy Award-winning film *Schindler's List* (1993) tacitly testifies to the power of continuing anti-semitism, in that the focus is on the morally agonized German, whereas the Jews whose story it should really be are basically a backdrop.

57. I am indebted to my colleague Sandra Bartky for reminding me of this.

58. Donald Bogle, *Toms, Coons, Mulattoes, Mammies & Bucks: An Interpretive History of Blacks in American Films*, rev. ed. (1973; reprinted, New York: Continuum, 1989). See also, more recently, Daniel Bernardi, ed., *The Birth of Whiteness: Race and the Emergence of U.S. Cinema* (New Brunswick, N.J.: Rutgers University Press, 1996), and Michael Rogin, *Blackface, White Noise: Jewish Immigrants in the Hollywood Melting Pot* (Berkeley: University of California Press, 1996).

59. See, most recently, Richard J. Herrnstein and Charles Murray, *The Bell Curve: Intelligence and Class Structure in American Life* (New York: Free Press,

1994), which endorses a basically hereditarian analysis of the well-documented fact that the average black score on IQ tests is about one standard deviation (fifteen points) below the average white score. Note also—with respect to point no. 9, above, of the "Differences" between blacks and Jews—the authors' observation (275) that "Jews—specifically, Ashkenazi Jews of European origins—test higher than any other ethnic group." For a critique, see *The Bell Curve Debate: History, Documents, Opinions*, ed. Russell Jacoby and Naomi Glauberman (New York: Random House, 1995).

60. Mosse, *Final Solution*, 235–36.

61. Kant, *Gesammelte Schriften*, 6:434–35; *Metaphysics of Morals*, 230–31.

62. See, for example, Bernard R. Boxill, "Self-Respect and Protest," in *Philosophy Born of Struggle; Anthology of Afro-American Philosophy from 1917*, ed. Leonard Harris (Dubuque, Iowa: Kendall/Hunt, 1983), 190–98; and Michele M. Moody-Adams, "Race, Class, and the Social Construction of Self-Respect," in *African-American Perspectives and Philosophical Traditions*, ed. John Pittman (New York: Routledge, 1996), 251–66.

63. Noel Ignatiev, *How the Irish Became White* (New York and London: Routledge, 1995); Karen Brodkin Sacks, "How Did Jews Become White Folks?" in *Race*, ed. Steven Gregory and Roger Sanjek (New Brunswick, N.J.: Rutgers University Press, 1994), 78–102.

64. Cornel West, "On Black-Jewish Relations," *Race Matters* (Boston: Beacon Press, 1993), 101–16.

65. Fredric Jameson, *Postmodernism, or The Cultural Logic of Late Capitalism* (Durham, N.C.: Duke University Press, 1991), 38.

66. Gary K. Okihiro, *Margins and Mainstreams: Asians in American History and Culture* (Seattle: University of Washington Press, 1994), 120, and, more generally, chapter 5, "Perils of the Body and Mind," 118–47.

67. Gary B. Nash and Richard Weiss, eds., *The Great Fear: Race in the Mind of America* (New York: Holt, Rineheart and Winston, 1970).

68. Lothrop Stoddard, *The Rising Tide of Color against White World-Supremacy* (New York: Charles Scribner's Sons, 1920). For a discussion, see Gossett, *Race*, chapter 15. As Gossett points out (397), Stoddard's book makes a brief appearance in F. Scott Fitzgerald's *The Great Gatsby*, disguised as *The Rise of the Colored Empires* by one "Goddard."

69. Patricia A. Turner, *I Heard It through the Grapevine: Rumor in African-American Culture* (Berkeley and Los Angeles: University of California Press, 1993).

70. Nisbett and Ross, *Human Inference*.

71. James Baldwin, "Negroes are anti-semitic because they're anti-white," *New York Times Magazine*, 9 April 1967; reprinted in Berman, *Blacks and Jews*, 31–41.

72. Sullivan, *Moral Theory*, appendix I. But see Nancy Sherman, *Making a Necessity of Virtue: Aristotle and Kant on Virtue* (New York: Cambridge University Press, 1997), for the view that the traditional hyper-rationalist picture of

Kantian ethics is misleading, and fails to appreciate the significance of his writings on moral psychology.

73. In the 1978 Supreme Court decision in *Regents of the University of California v. Bakke*, Justice Blackmun made the subsequently oft-quoted observation that "[i]n order to get beyond racism, we must first take into account race."

74. Onora O'Neill, "Justice, Gender, and International Boundaries," in *The Quality of Life*, ed. Martha Nussbaum and Amartya Sen. (Oxford: Clarendon Press, 1993), 303–23.

75. Rabbi Alan W. Miller, "Black Anti-Semitism—Jewish Racism," in Hentoff, 101.

76. Nat Hentoff, *Black Anti-Semitism*, xvii.

9

Nelson Thomas Potter Jr.

"The Principle of Punishment Is a Categorical Imperative"[1]

KANT'S VIEWS

There has been a considerable renaissance in retributivism as a theory of the justification of punishment in the second half of this century. Retributivism is often defended as if it were a particularly hardy moral intuition, a basic free-standing moral principle that is underivable from any broader theory or set of principles. In this vein it is often "supported" through the presentation of outrageous and horribly cruel crimes, especially against persons, particularly murder, in order to elicit what may be thought to be the natural and appropriate emotional response, a response of anger, indignation, and desire for retribution.[2] Under such accounts the retributive idea has little to do with ethics thought of as a rationally defended systematic theory.[3]

In the history of retributivism, Kant has a prominent place. He was one of the classic defenders of a tough retributivism, at a time when the new humaneness and teleology in the theory of punishment was making its first headway with the help of (equally classic) Enlightenment writers like Beccaria. I wish to show that Kant did not regard retribution as a basic, underivable moral principle; rather, he is concerned, as far as possible, to find a rational basis for the idea of retribution, and to relate it closely to the root ideas of his moral philosophy: the categorical imperative (CI), and the idea of respect for persons. Kant's theory of punishment has been discussed usually as a series of statements that have been considered for their *implications* for the justification of punishment; it is less often considered with respect to its basis in the broader Kantian practical philosophy.

Kant uses the phrase "a categorical imperative" usually to refer to a specific obligation that is derived from *the* categorical imperative. Thus for example, "Refrain from making any lying promises" is a categorical imperative that is established by the argument presented in the second of Kant's well-known four examples in the *Grundlegung zur Metaphysik der Sitten*.[4] So when Kant writes that "The principle of punishment is a categorical imperative" (MS, 6:331), he is telling us that this principle (*a*) makes an unconditional moral demand, not one that may be altered for the sake of someone's convenience or preference, and (*b*) that it can be derived from some version of *the* categorical imperative. The title quotation also refers to the *principle* of punishment, which Kant identifies as the *lex talionis* (MS, 6:232). The *lex talionis* is usually identified with the formulations derived from Mosaic law, "An eye for an eye, a tooth for a tooth, a life for a life."[5]

Punishment is in Kant's view a topic in the philosophy of law or right (*Recht*). Punishment is imposed not by individuals, but by courts and judges, and it is therefore a practice that presupposes the existence of the state. Kant argues in some detail that we have a moral obligation to leave the state of nature and to enter a civil commonwealth, because it is only in a state or commonwealth that external justice, especially with respect to rights to hold property, can be assured and enforced. The state then exists as the enforcer of the rights of citizens.[6]

Kant's theory of the state and its proper functions, and of the law of property and of punishment, are all statements of moral ideals. Kant understands that actual states will at best approximate to such ideals, and at worst, will fail to exemplify some or all of these ideals.[7] We should remember that in the discussions that follow Kant is talking about developing an ideal, and we can think about the issue of punishment in a similar vein by asking to what extent Kant's ideal is embodied or not in arrangements for handling crime and punishment in present-day societies.[8]

Because the discussion of punishment is part of the *Rechtslehre*, what we are applying is not the familiar categorical imperative as stated in the *Grundlegung*: "Act only on that maxim through which you can at the same time will that it should be a universal law" (G, 4:421). Rather we will be using the more restricted version that is appropriate for *Recht*, which Kant calls "The Universal Principle of Law (*Recht*)":

"An action is *right* if it can coexist with everyone's freedom in accordance with a universal law, or if on its maxim the freedom of choice of each can coexist with everyone's freedom in accordance with a universal law." (MS, 6:230; the quotation marks are in Kant's text)

The kind of freedom referred to is external freedom. Inner freedom of thought and motivation is beyond the reach of *Recht*. Also, with respect to inner freedom, individuals could not come into conflict. The concern of the principle of right is the ways in which one individual's use of freedom may interfere with that of another individual.[9]

It will be noticed that the quoted principle contains the phrase, familiar from the CI, "universal law." This is the main part of the principle that establishes the connection with the original CI. The universal principle of law is a more specific version of the general CI, a version limited to external actions that might affect others. The restatement of the law in terms of coexistence of everyone's freedom is a paraphrase of the "universal law" idea. My breaking a promise will be right only if my freedom to break the promise can coexist with a similar freedom on the part of everyone else to break such promises. Since in Kant's view, such freedoms of each and every person to fail to keep promises cannot coexist, then such an action cannot be right, that is, in accord with the universal principle of right. The universal law formulations of the CI are principles of justice or fairness, and in that sense they are also principles of *equality*. Kant immediately presents an argument to show that "there is connected with Right by the principle of contradiction an authorization to coerce someone who infringes upon it" (MS, 6:231). A little later he concludes, "Right and authorization to use coercion mean one and the same thing" (MS, 6:232). This authorization amounts to an authorization to punish individuals guilty of actions that violate the law, for punishment turns out to be the only kind of coercion that Kant discusses.[10]

The motivation within the doctrine of *"Recht"* is not the inner motive of duty that Kant has emphasized so much in the *Grundlegung* and the second Critique. But since Kant insists that a moral precept must always be paired with a motivation adequate to make it effective in human choice (see MS, 6:218–19), we here introduce the threat of coercion and punishment to take the place of inner moral motivation, which we are not relying on in *Recht* (MS, 6:232). The laws against rape or against speeding on the interstate do not appeal to our better nature in asking us to refrain; they warn us that if we violate (and are caught and convicted) we will be punished, and the fear of punishment provides the incentive. Hence, according to Kant's way of proceeding here, in the realm of *Recht*, the concern with action is limited to the external, that which can affect another, and hence that which can bring us into conflict with the wishes and indeed with the rights of another.[11]

When Kant begins his main discussion of punishment (MS, 6:331ff.), he juxtaposes two ideas, that of equality and that of the law of retribution (*lex talionis*), as follows (I quote at length):

> But what kind and what amount of punishment is it that public justice makes its principle and measure? None other than the principle of equality (in the position of the needle on the scale of justice), to include no more to one side than to the other. Accordingly, whatever undeserved evil you inflict upon another within the people, that you inflict upon yourself. . . . But only the *law of retribution (lex talionis)*—it being understood, of course, that this is applied by a court (not by your private judgment)—can specify definitely the quality and the quantity of punishment; all other principles are fluctuating and unsuited for a sentence of pure and strict justice because extraneous considerations are mixed into them. (MS, 6:332)

The proper measure of the punishment, namely, equality, restores the equilibrium that existed before the crime, and that was first disturbed by the crime.

The fact that he understands the criterion for punishment in this quote in terms of the idea of equality means that Kant intends the criterion as an application of the categorical imperative. In supplementary comments added in the second edition, he writes, in a similar vein, that only the *lex talionis* "is by its form always the principle of the right to punish since it alone is the principle determining this Idea a priori." (The CI is itself *a priori*.) The phrases used to spell out the CI, "universal law," "coexistence," and so on all imply equality; the idea of equality is perhaps most explicit in Kant's general ethics in the spelling out of the idea of the kingdom of ends in the *Grundlegung*. The first formulation CI is a principle of justice or fairness, and by invoking the idea of equality in settling on the proper amount of punishment we are seeking through the punishment to restore the preexisting equality of consideration.[12]

So, Kant's insistence on the *lex talionis* is inspired by his thought that punishment itself ought to be an application of the CI. We find a standard for the appropriate quantity and quality of punishment only in the basic idea of the CI itself, the idea that we are all moral equals.[13]

Now let us look more closely at this derivation, in particular the idea that the punishment is to be quantitatively and qualitatively a sort of mirror image of the crime. One of the merits of this idea, as we've seen, is that it makes manifest to the person punished the appropriateness of a certain quality and quantity of punishment. And yet the proposition that the punishment should mirror the crime is something other than a mere analysis of the concept of punishment. Alternative statements of moral principle here, though perhaps all incorrect, seem conceivable: that the punishment should double, or be half the quantity of the crime, or that the punishment for *any* moderately serious crime should be death, or that each criminal conviction must entail the confiscation of exactly half of one's property. The possible principles here are endless, and this is a clue that the *lex talionis* is synthetic rather than analytic. And yet there seems to be something special and intuitively plausible about the *lex talionis*, as opposed to any of the possible alternatives. In Kant's scheme of philosophical possibilities, this might suggest that the *lex talionis* is synthetic *a priori*. That in fact seems to be exactly what Kant believed.

He begins to develop this idea in a remarkable passage that develops an analogy between the realm of external freedom, and the mathematical/physical world:

> The law of reciprocal coercion necessarily in accord with freedom for everyone under the principle of universal freedom is, as it were, the *construction* of that concept, that is, the presentation of it in pure intuition a priori, by analogy with presenting the possibility of bodies moving freely under the law of the *equality of action and reaction*. In pure mathematics we cannot derive the properties of its objects immediately from concepts but can discover them only by constructing concepts. Similarly, it is not so much the concept of Right as rather a fully reciprocal and equal coercion brought under universal law and consistent with it, that makes the presentation of that concept possible. (MS, 6:233)

This analogy between the model of the physical world, which was at the center of Kant's attention for so long in the earlier years of his philosophical development, and the political model of the reciprocal rights of persons thought of as externally related to one another in space is important. The Newtonian law that is most closely connected in this analogy with the idea of punishment is the law of the equality of action and reaction, Newton's third law, a principle that Kant thought of as a synthetic *a priori* principle.[14]

Hence, in Kant's view, the principle of punishment is indeed synthetic *a priori*, by analogy with the geometrical/physical construction of bodies in space, and hence is necessary and invariable, like any categorical imperative. Just as Newton's laws allow for zero tolerance in variation of effect, given the cause, so likewise appropriate punishment must fit the crime exactly, according to the *lex talionis*. But whence in the physical model comes the practical ideal that the punishment must be *qualitatively* identical to the crime? Kant does not answer this, but I suggest that the analogy for quality is vector direction of reaction. Given the status of Newton's third law, we can understand why Kant sought no further derivation of the principle of punishment, regarding it rather as a sort of practical axiom or basic law.

Kant in the *Groundwork*, as is well known, said that violations of perfect duties are actions such that "their maxim cannot even be *conceived* as a universal law of nature without contradiction" (G, 4:424). On the other hand, the "general canon" for all duties, perfect and imperfect, is that "we must *be able to will* that a maxim of our action should become a universal law" (G, 4:424). Nevertheless, many violations of duties that we wish to call perfect duties seem to involve the failure of the broader criterion only.[15] This seems to be the case with respect to Kant's clearest example of the application of the principle of law, his claim that a hereditary nobility is contrary to *Recht* (see MS, 6:329; compare "Theory and Practice," 8:291–93, 297–98), for Kant's point is that a person excluded from such an advantage could not vote for such an arrangement, that is, could not will such a law. This example is discussed further below in the section entitled "Other Examples of Application."

Now we can see more clearly the sort of "derivation" claimed for the principle of punishment. There is no contradiction in conception in a system that would have the punishment double the crime, or in a system that would punish the entire range of possible crimes with equal severity, that is, with the same punishment. After all, the *lex talionis* is synthetic *a priori*, and therefore its denial is not self-contradictory. Nevertheless the *lex talionis* is the only true application principle here, in Kant's view. Analogously, nature might, without contradiction, be such that for every action the reaction doubles it,[16] or it might be such that the interior angles of a triangle are greater than 180 degrees. However, the true synthetic *a priori* proposition in each case is different, stating what we know as Newton's third law and the familiar theorem of Euclid.

So, although there is no incoherency or contradiction in having the punishment double the crime, or halve the crime, such alternative principles could not be willed by everyone. The subject being punished could not rationally will excessive punishment, and those benefiting from deterrence or those who are crime victims or friends of crime victims could not rationally will punishment that was too light. The *lex talionis*, proposing as it does *equality* of crime and punishment, is simply an extension or instantiation of the universal principle of law, which itself is already a principle of equality or fairness. With punishment, the key moral concept of equality (of initial distribution, or of regard before the law) is simply extended to state a principle for responding to publicly wrongful actions.

Kant's Partial Retributivism

Kant is a partial retributivist only, because the function of the institution of punishment is to provide deterrence of antisocial acts.[17] Punishment hence has a teleological function, a goal: Punishment serves the function of protecting the rights of all of us, by providing crime control through deterrence. The nonteleological side of punishment pertains to determining the proper quantity and quality of punishment, determining the proper distribution of punishment for those who have violated the law. This is not determined teleologically, but formally, by the principle of equality, as embodied in the *jus talionis*. This means that we may not adjust the amount of punishment to enhance deterrence, or to achieve the most efficient balance between enforcement costs and the costs of crime.[18]

The actual examples of the *lex talionis* that Kant provides sound to us quite harsh. Probably for that reason there was little problem within the punishment theory as Kant thought of it, of having the *lex talionis* indicating punishments that would be inadequate in their deterrent effect. More often there would be "overkill," if I may use that expression, from the point of view of deterrence; that is, the punishment would be more harsh than the needs of adequate deterrence would require. We need to consider these questions of the adequacy of the "match" between deterrence needs and the punishment dealt out by the *lex talionis*, because the criteria for each are entirely independent of each other in a partial retributivist theory like that of Kant, and it appears that they could relate to each other in ways that would cause trouble. The most likely sort of trouble I think will seldom occur, namely, that the *lex talionis* mandates a punishment that is inadequate for the purposes of deterrence.[19]

The Right to Punish

What is Kant's chief concern in presenting a criterion to determine the appropriate level of punishment? His concern, expressed over and over again, is that the punishment be appropriate from the point of view of the person who is receiving the punishment. Sometimes this concern is expressed in the claim that the punishee could not reasonably dispute the justice of the punishment. The phrase "the right to punish" (from MS, 6:363), as Kant uses it, also suggests concern with the punishee, for he is the individual against whom this right would be exercised. After mentioning the right to punish, Kant concludes:

> To inflict *whatever* punishments *one chooses* for these crimes would be literally contrary to the concept of *punitive justice*. For the only time the criminal cannot complain that a wrong is done to him is when he brings his evil deed back upon himself, and what is done to him in accordance with penal law is what he has perpetrated on others, if not in terms of its letter at least in terms of its spirit. (MS, 6:363)

Hence, the *lex talionis* alone assures that the rights of the punishee are not violated. Again, Kant writes,

> Moreover, one has never heard of anyone who was sentenced to death for murder complaining that he was dealt with too severely and therefore wronged: everyone would laugh in his face if he said this. (MS, 6:334)[20]

In addition, there is another important qualification on the imposition of punishment, which also comes from concern for the personhood of the punishee. When such a person is executed, the punishment "must still be freed from any mistreatment that could make the humanity in the person suffering it abominable" (MS, 6:333). In this brief statement Kant opposes torture executions.

Since punishment, as our title quotation has indicated, is a categorical imperative, it should not be surprising to find it so bound up in Kant's thinking with the idea of respect for persons. Punishment must respect the rights of the punishee. Any theory of the justification of punishment, as a part of moral theory, must have an important concern about the harm inflicted on the punishee.

Too Much/Too Little

It is easy enough to understand that punishment must not exceed the limits of what is appropriate, and that, when it does so, it would be a violation of the moral rights of the punishee. But it is more difficult to understand why punishment *short* of the maximum may not be permitted. Just how and why would it be a violation of anyone's rights for a convicted murderer to be sentenced to a long prison sentence? Yet Kant strongly speaks out against lesser sentences, and in one of his most infamous statements, urges that death penalties against convicted murderers should be carried out even when it could serve no purpose:

> Even if a civil society were to be dissolved by the consent of all its members (e.g., if a people inhabiting an island decided to separate and disperse throughout the world), the last murderer remaining in

prison would first have to be executed, so that each has done to him what his deeds deserve and blood guilt does not cling to the people for not having insisted on his punishment; for otherwise the people can be regarded as collaborators in this public violation of justice. (MS, 6:333)[21]

This sort of passage strongly suggests that Kant is a thorough retributivist, rather than a partial one, as was claimed above, for in the circumstances described, the deterrent function of punishment would seem to be nonexistent. It appears that the only reason for executing the murderers is to let justice be done (= a retributivist rationale), since there would be no continuing society that would experience the benefits of deterrence that would in other circumstances flow from such executions.

Kant himself never addresses this point, so what I suggest here is a speculative extension of what I take to be Kant's basic ideas. There are two points of justification Kant may have in mind here:

1. The crime is murder, and the scales of justice are not restored until there is an execution. Not executing might seem to make the murder *victim* something less than an equal of the murderer, since the victim is dead and the murderer is allowed to live. In other cases, when a serious crime is punished lightly, the crime victims feel badly treated, and discriminated against. Anything less than full retaliation, it might be said, denies justice and equality to the victim.
2. Joel Feinberg quoted some of these extreme statements from Kant in his "The Expressive Function of Punishment,"[22] saying that such passages marked Kant as an expression theorist. The expressive function is no part of Kant's official theory, but if he did hold to it and it explains such statements, then he would be saying these things because he felt it was important to denounce, through the act of punishment, the injustice of the crime, and to reassert the innocence of the victim. However, the expressive function mostly reduces to a deterrence aspect, which is irrelevant in determining appropriate quantity and quality of punishment.

It is true that Kant thinks of the *lex talionis* as being an exact, precise standard that ideally at least allows zero tolerance. Punishment according to the proper standard of the CI should be neither too little nor too much. Such comments by Kant also may point toward the idea that the failure to carry out appropriate punishment is a violation of a duty to *oneself*, which would reflect a lack of inner integrity or self-respect. To fail to punish to the proper degree is to fail to have an adequate hatred of criminal conduct; such an idea, which seems implicit in Kant, brings him close to being an exponent of the expression theory.

Notice that the application of the CI to derive a standard of punishment is different from the familiar four examples in the G, and other similar examples elsewhere in Kant's moral philosophy. It is different because it does not have the agent deliberating about the moral acceptability of her or his own maxim. Rather, the CI is used, not in a context of personal choice and deliberation, but in order to make an abstract moral judgment about the appropriate level (and, in Kant's view, quality) of punishment. Such a judgment would be relevant to the actions of and hence of interest to the sentencing judge, the legislator, the punishee, the crime victim, or the mere interested moral observer, in relation to their different roles.

In review, Kant's retributivism does not at all present the common idea that retribution is a basic, axiomatic, underivable moral intuition or emotion. The *lex talionis* is instead derived from the categorical imperative itself, and for this reason includes as central to it the CI idea of respect for persons, including the person to be punished. This is an abstract derivation of a moral precept, characteristic of the *Rechtslehre*, rather than a personal deliberation about one's own maxim, and hence about one's own course of action that is characteristic of Kant's ethics. Also, Kant is not a pure retributivist; the state institutions of punishment are to serve the indispensable function of crime control. In all of these ways Kant, unlike many more recent writers, "rationalizes" his retributive theory of punishment. The famous outbursts, especially about the need to execute all the condemned murderers before a society disbands, cannot be entirely understood within the scope of Kant's "rationalized retributivism," but I hope that understanding how Kant tries to justify his version of retributivism can help to make them seem less outrageous. Kant thinks that punishment cannot be less than the *lex talionis* requires, perhaps because such a punishment would reflect a lack of equal respect for the crime victim, and also a lack of adequate hatred of the wrongdoing being punished.[23]

RELATED MATTERS

Now that we have presented the outline of Kant's views on punishment, emphasizing how they are derived from the categorical imperative, we will pursue some related topics.

Punishments Incompatible with Humanity

As mentioned above, Kant rejected torture executions, saying that capital punishment "must still be freed from any mistreatment that could make the humanity in the person suffering it into something abominable" (MS, 6:333). This thought, that exotic torturous forms of execution such as drawing and quartering should not be permitted, is at least one of the thoughts that moved the writers of the U.S. Bill of Rights to forbid "cruel and unusual punishments" in its Eighth Amendment.

In the early 1970s the question of whether capital punishment in and of itself may be contrary to the U.S. Constitution because it constitutes cruel and unusual punishment was the question before the U.S. Supreme Court, and in *Furman v. Georgia* (408 U.S. 238 [1972]) the Supreme Court did reject capital punishment as it then existed as unconstitutional. The five justices who formed the majority in Furman were divided, however. Two, Brennan and Marshall, thought that in principle capital punishment was unconstitutional. Three other justices were only addressing capital punishment laws as they then existed, and some of them were later convinced to join the majority in 1976 in *Gregg v. Georgia* (428 U.S. 153 [1976]), in upholding a new form of law that tried to guide the discretion of the sentencing authority (judge or jury) by listing mitigating and aggravating circumstances in the light of which that sentencing authority would decide between death or a lesser penalty. Our present interest, however, is in Brennan's more absolutist opposition to the death penalty as found in his Furman opinion. I quote at length:

> Death is truly an awesome punishment. The calculated killing of a human being by the State involves, by its very nature, a denial of the executed person's humanity. The contrast with the plight of a person punished by imprisonment is evident. An individual in prison does not lose "the right to have rights.". . . A prisoner remains a member of the human family. . . . An executed person has indeed "lost the right to have rights." As one 19th century proponent of punishing criminals by death declared, "When a man is hung, there is an end of our relations with him. His execution is a way of saying, 'You are not fit for this world, take your chance elsewhere.'"
>
> In comparison with all other punishments today, then, the deliberate extinguishment of human life by the State is uniquely degrading to human dignity.

The language of Kant and of Brennan is not precisely the same, but this conclusion seems unavoidable: the reasons that Kant gives for rejecting torture executions (while defending capital punishment) are the same as those Brennan gives for opposing capital punishment in every case. Such treatment is incompatible with the humanity of the person being punished. Brennan and Kant disagree only concerning the scope of the state punishments that are forbidden. The only additional difference (which here makes no difference) is that whereas Kant is expressing a moral ideal, Brennan is writing as a Supreme Court justice with the authority to interpret constitutional language, which is itself usually understood as embodying certain moral ideals.

Now some may urge that the worst murderers have no humanity to preserve. Kant would have disagreed with that, it seems, since he never considered the possibility of beings with human shape but without human potential. Jean Hampton briefly considers this possibility in "The Moral Education Theory of Punishment," but does not discuss it.[24] Against this idea, it may be said that whenever we wish to proceed to murder or genocide in some semipublic fashion, we do so by dehumanizing those who are to die, as the Nazis did; so the hypothesis, whether correct or incorrect, presents special dangers of potential for misuse. Like Hampton, we will have to dismiss this possibility without at present considering it further.

How are we to decide who is correct, Brennan or Kant? How broad is the correct scope of the "inhumanity objection"? Does it cover only torture executions or does it cover all executions? As thus stated, it seems to me an unmanageable question that may not admit of a generally convincing unique correct answer. In any case, answering this question convincingly is also a project beyond the scope of this paper.

Suppose Brennan were right. Then Kant would have to make do with some lesser punishment such as long-term imprisonment for such "capital crimes" as murder or treason. Similar problems arise in connection with punishments Kant proposes in a second-edition appendix to the *Rechtslehre*. These additional examples are to make the point that although one may not be able to find a qualitatively similar punishment, one can find a punishment that brings back upon the criminal his own conduct "if not in terms of its letter at least in terms of its spirit" (MS, 6:363). Kant writes:

> The punishment for rape and pederasty is castration (like that of a white or black eunuch in a Seraglio), that for bestiality, permanent expulsion from civil society, since the criminal has made himself unworthy of human society. (MS, 6:363)

The U.S. Supreme Court has ruled out banishment as violative of the "cruel and unusual punishment" clause (*Trop v. Dulles*, 356 U.S. 86

[1958]), and the mutilation of castration is one that many might wish to reject on similar grounds.[25]

Lex Talionis

A related problem, in spite of Kant's suggestions for punishments "in the spirit" of the crime, is whether there are *qualitatively* appropriate punishments for all crimes. Kant has an ingenious suggestion for the appropriate punishment for theft:

> But what does it mean to say, "If you steal from someone, you steal from yourself"? Whoever steals makes the property of everyone else insecure and therefore deprives himself (by the principle of retribution) of security in any possible property. He has nothing and can also acquire nothing; but he still wants to live, and this is now possible only if others provide for him. But since the state will not provide for him free of charge, he must let it have his powers for any kind of work it pleases (in convict or prison labor) and is reduced to the status of a slave for a certain time, or permanently if the state sees fit. (MS, 6:333)

If we accept this account, then we have a large class of crimes taken care of by something like imprisonment at hard labor: all property crimes, including all theft, fraud, and burglary. The contemporary American universal solution for criminal behavior of imposing long prison sentences thus gains some endorsement from Kant with respect to a large share of those now in prison.

But other crimes remain problematic. What about drug dealing? First we must decide what the gravamen of this offense is, and that would be no easy matter. What about tax evasion? Or perjury? The problem of finding appropriate mirror-image punishments is more acute in the case of crimes such as these, which may not have an individual victim. What about assault? Do we assault the offender back? What about escape from custody? The task of finding a punishment for each type of crime that is a quantitative and qualitative mirror of the crime seems to be not possible of accomplishment, especially when the demand for *qualitative* similarity is included. Even in the case of theft, where Kant urges imprisonment at hard labor, we should ask, "How long?" Will the answer depend on the amount stolen? Double time for double money? The task of constructing perfectly equivalent punishments for each crime seems beyond human capability. We could surely accomplish such a task only by loosening the ties between crime and punishment, along the lines proposed in Hyman Gross's schema for determining appropriate punishment, where the scale of crimes is arranged and opposite it is a scale of punishments.[26] Crimes must be arrangeable at least ordinally, something that is difficult enough. The scale of punishments will have a certain pitch. But as Gross describes it, there is no single "verifiable" point of contact between the two scales; if there were, this would give us confidence about the correct match of other point-pairs on the two scales. A defender of *lex talionis* like Waldron does so without seeking for such a perfect, zero-tolerance match between crime and appropriate punishment.

Kant discusses a large number of examples that in his view affect appropriate punishment. He seems particularly interested in class distinctions, which he thinks will make a difference in determining appropriate punishment. These examples, which taken together are somewhat puzzling and difficult to make sense of because of their variety, are listed here to make it clear that Kant is sometimes less doctrinaire with his examples than in his more abstract pronouncements. For example, after insisting fervently that death is the only appropriate punishment for murder, he presents no fewer than three examples that are in his view justified *exceptions* to this rule! ((4), (5), and (6), below). In contrast (3) seems to be presented as a complicated argument for the death penalty for treason. (1) Kant writes of a person of high rank verbally insulting a person of lower rank. Punishment: the offender must publicly apologize, and kiss the hand of the insulted one, which will produce in him a humiliation similar to the one he produced (MS, 6:332). (2) Again, he writes of a high-status person striking a low-status person. Punishment: The offender must apologize and also must undergo solitary confinement involving hardship (MS, 6:332–33). (3) A complicated case of men of honor and scoundrels being tried together for treason (MS, 6:333–34). (4) Another complicated case where almost everyone who was a citizen was an accomplice in the murder. Solution: All should be sentenced to death, but then reprieved by executive decree, and given a lesser punishment, perhaps banishment (MS, 6:334). The cases of (5) the mother murdering her illegitimate child (MS, 6:336) and of (6) killing a fellow soldier in a duel. In both cases the killing has been motivated by a sense of honor, which would suggest a lighter penalty. Kant's puzzling solution to both cases is that death remains objectively the appropriate penalty, though it appears to be unjust for reasons that are obscure to me (see MS, 6:336–37).

In conclusion, we can say that Kant's abstract theory of punishment sets a very high ideal: the punishment must be perfectly matched to the crime, both quantitatively and qualitatively. There is a suggestion that, ideally at least, there should be zero tolerance, in the sense that we should be able to specify precisely what the appropriate punishment is.

Only if there is zero tolerance will the punishment be defensible to the person being punished, thereby making its appropriateness clear to her.

Punishment as Expressive and as Moral Education

This aspect of Kant's theory of punishment makes it seem similar to two theories of punishment that have been more recently proposed: the expressive theory of punishment (Feinberg) and the moral education theory (Hampton).[27] All three views, in somewhat different ways and for somewhat different reasons, emphasize the *symbolic* character of punishment. The expressive theory, already mentioned above, emphasizes the authoritative denunciation of the offender and his action that is accomplished through the punishment. The moral education theory emphasizes the aim of improving the moral character of the person punished through the punishment's delivering a moral message. In Kant's view the punishment is symbolic, but the primary recipient of the message is the person punished, and the message is: "This hard treatment is appropriate." Hampton is opposed to the death penalty as incompatible with the goal of moral-education,[28] and Kant gives little hint that he wishes or expects to produce learning in the person punished. If such an expectation were central to the institution of punishment, rather than a happy by-product in some cases, then Kant would have introduced teleological considerations into the heart of his account of punishment. If the punishment is to have a general deterrent effect, others must know of it, and probably must judge it appropriate; to this extent Feinberg (and Scheid and Byrd) is correct in judging Kant to be a deterrence theorist. But in Kant's own view deterrence is a secondary (though still essential) effect, with the primary concern being the appropriateness of the punishment in relation to the punishee.

Other Examples of Applications

Kant does not have very many examples of explicit application of the categorical imperative in the context of *Recht*. Perhaps the theory of property is another such application, at least at certain points. I will not pursue this example now, since it would involve considerable complexity. A more manageable example for our purposes is Kant's argument against the privileges of a hereditary class of nobility. Like Kant's theory of property, it also involves the key requirement of potential universal advance consent.

Kant states the requirement of advance consent most fully in "Theory and Practice" (1793, KGS 8:273–313), where he describes it as "a *mere idea* of reason, one, however, that has indubitable (practical) reality" (KGS 8:297):

> Specifically , it obligates every legislator to formulate his laws in such a way that they *could* have sprung from the unified will of the entire people and to regard every subject, insofar as he desires to be a citizen, as if he had joined in voting for such a will. For that is the criterion of every public law's conformity with right. If a public law is so formulated that an entire people *could not possibly* agree to it (as, e.g., that a particular class of *subjects* has the hereditary privilege of being a *ruling class*), it is not just; however, if *only* it is *possible* that a people could agree to it, it is a duty to regard that law as just, even if the people are presently in such a position or disposition of mind that if asked it would probably withhold its consent. (KGS 8:297; also see 8:289–300; and MS, 6:328–29)

This criterion is similar to what Kant in the *Groundwork* calls "the general canon for all moral judgment of action" (G, 4:424), namely, that "we must *be able to will* that our action should become a universal law" (G, 4:424). It is *not* an instance of the more specific test used in connection with the case of the lying promise, namely, that "Some actions are so constituted that their maxim cannot even be *conceived* as a universal law of nature without contradiction" (G, 4:424). One can speculate that such *Recht*-applications present another partial picture of the idea of the Kingdom of Ends that Kant presents in the *Grundlegung*, though Kant never tells us so. Clearly, the requirement of general will–like universal consent is an alternative statement of the "universal law" conception that is found in many formulations of the categorical imperative.

This general criterion, together with the sample application to reject hereditary nobilities, represents another sample application of the Kantian principle of law, together with another description of the application process. The exercise takes place entirely in the realm of ideas, and the results of any such exercise would be conclusions about the normativity or lack thereof of actual positive laws and social institutions.

Does this general criterion work for the case of Kant's theory of punishment? Consider the following as a sketch for a Yes answer: Who is the person whose reason is not likely to consent to punishment? Answer: the one being punished. So, in justifying punishment we must focus our attention on that one, and assure ourselves that we can justify the punishment to *him*. So the general criterion explains Kant's approach to the justification of punishment.[29]

Probably the main difference between such examples and the more familiar four examples in the *Grundlegung* is that the latter *ethical* applications deal with the agent's *maxims*, and hence have a background assumption about the agent's motivation that is absent in the applications of *Recht*. Moral principles of *Recht* are always mere impersonal precepts, with the motivation left unspecified, and also the direction to specific agents left unspecified. Maxims, reflecting as they do the agent's personal choices of actions, ends of action, and motives of action are absolutely central to the realm of inner freedom that Kant calls "ethics."[30] But judgments concerning *Recht* involve no such reference to the agent's personal choices or motives.[31]

Conclusion

The main aim of this paper has been to examine Kant's views on punishment in relation to the most central ideas of his moral philosophy, especially respect for persons, but also the ideas of the categorical imperative, and of justice and equality. Kant's views on punishment are not isolated and separable from his other ideas on ethics and politics. Arguably, this should make his views on punishment seem more interesting than they otherwise might seem, for they are shaped by the most powerful and attractive ideas that make his ethical theory as a whole a matter of so much philosophical interest. The harsh retributivism that lies on the surface of these texts is tempered by deeper-lying teleological themes: the benefits of deterrence of antisocial actions in preserving our rights, and the moral teleology of the idea of respect for persons. This discussion, also enriched with a brief consideration of Kant's argument against hereditary nobility, broadens our understanding of how the categorical imperative is to be applied outside of ethics, in the area of *Recht*.

NOTES

1. MS, 6:331. MS stands for *Metaphysik der Sitten* by Kant (1797–98). G stands for *Grundlegung zur Metaphysik der Sitten* (1785). Later references to Kant's writings are given in the text; after an abbreviation for the work, these references contain volume and page of the passage in in Prussian Academy edition of Kant's works: *Kants gesammelte Schriften, herausgegeben von der Deutschen* (fomerly *Königlichen Preußischen*) *Akademie der Wissenschafter*, 29 volumes (Berlin: Walter de Gruyter [and predecessors], 1902), hereafter KGS. Most English translations of works referred to include these page numbers marginally. For translations from MS I use Mary Gregor's translation.

2. For example see Michael S. Moore, "The Moral Worth of Retribution," in *Responsibility, Character, and the Emotions*, ed. Ferdinand Schoeman (Cambridge: Cambridge University Press, 1987). Moore even makes use of that popular master of inflammatory rhetoric Mike Royko to make the ressentiment family of feelings seem to be morally attractive. It has sometimes even been urged that there may be an evolutionary basis for retribution, because a strategy of being initially open to cooperation with new persons, and then responding in a friendly fashion to friendly responses, and in unfriendly fashion to unfriendly responses (and it is here that we have the retribution-like response) may have by this time in our species-history as social animals been hardwired into us. See Robert Axelrod, *The Evolution of Cooperation* (New York: Basic Books, 1984).

3. For more on this see Michael Davis's *Make the Punishment Fit the Crime* (Boulder, Colo.: Westview Press, 1992), chapter 2, "The Relative Independence of Punishment Theory."

4. What is directly established by the procedure of applying the categorical imperative is the acceptability or not of the *maxim* of action that is being tested. But if a lying promise maxim is shown to be unacceptable in a CI test then there is or seems to be a rather direct inference to the following being a categorical imperative: "Do not make lying promises."

5. See Exodus 21:23–25, where the full quote is: "And if any mischief follow, then thou shalt give life for life, eye for eye, tooth for tooth, hand for hand, foot for foot, burning for burning, wound for wound, stripe for stripe." Cf. Numbers 35:21; Leviticus 24:17–20. For an excellent recent discussion of this idea, see Jeremy Waldron, "Lex Talionis," *Arizona Law Review* 34 (1992): 25–51.

6. This is admittedly an optimistic view of the state, or perhaps better an idealized view of the state. But Kant's view on this obligation to leave the state of nature, and on his absolute prohibition of revolution no matter how unjust the state, seems to be that any state at all is better than the state of nature.

7. For example, Kant was a republican, and an opponent of heriditary nobility. He lived in an authoritarian state that was something quite different from a republic, and was surrounded by political societies that had hereditary nobilities; in fact, further, he was as a university professor an employee of the state, and he made his peace with it, and expressed in his writings his commitment to obey its commands. For a discussion of the appropriate respective realms of obedience and scholarly freedom see the essay "What Is Enlightenment?" and also "Strife of the Faculties," both KGS 9.

8. Kant makes this point when, after offering a republican definition of the state, which, so far as it is in accord with the pure principles of Right, forms an Idea of the state: "This Idea serves as a norm (*norma*) for every actual union into a commonwealth (hence serves as a norm for its internal constitution) (MS, 6:313). As such it provides us with a standard for use in criticizing existing institutions and practices. We must strive after realizing this ideal: "it is that [ideal] condition which reason, *by a categorical imperative* [Kant's emphasis] makes it obligatory for us to strive after" (MS, 6:318).

9. For example, A's hitting and injuring B interferes with B's freedom, though it may be something that A wants to do. A's taking B's food and eating it himself again interferes with B's intended use. A complete discussion of the retributive idea would also include crimes that may not have specific victims, such as tax evasion or perjury. Although there is a mention of a "maxim" above, as in the earlier statements of the CI in the *Grundlegung*, and maxims are inner entities that state people's intentions and motives, the only concern of this principle of the *Rechtslehre* is with external action.

10. Advance prevention is of limited usefulness; burglars and rapists, for example, usually take care to avoid the presence of others who might interfere. Kant gives us a Newtonian analogy for the importance of the concept of equality:

> The law of a reciprocal coercion necessarily in accord with the freedom of everyone under the principle of universal freedom, is, as it were, the *construction* of that concept, that is, the presentation of it in pure intuition a priori by analogy with presenting the possibility of bodies moving freely under the law of the *equality of action and reaction*. (MS, 6:232)

The phrase "a fully reipricol and equal coercion" (MS, 6:232) that Kant uses in explicating this idea surely means not that everyone is coerced equally, but more like this: that everyone is subject to coercion to an equal extent, whenever he or she has performed the same sort of punishable act.

11. If wealthy A offers starving B money for food, he affects him, and his failure to offer help affects him negatively. But B has no right to A's assistance, and hence A's obligations in such cases are discussed not in the *Rechtslehre* portion of the *Metaphysik der Sitten* but in the *Tugendlehre* portion.

12. Equality of consideration may be illustrated as follows: A murders B, and is subsequently punished by being executed. The status quo ante was that A and B were equal in being alive; the status quo post is that they are equal in both being dead. The original equality is impossible to restore, since that could happen only by bringing the dead (A) back to life. But the formal equality that existed before also exists again after the punishment, and so there is a sort of restoration of equality.

13. Notice that Kant's scales of justice comparison is merely quantitative; Kant indicates he also wishes the punishment to be *qualitatively* identical as well, and in fact he defends capital punishment for murder by saying that "There is no *similarity* between life, however wretched it may be, and death, hence no likeness between the crime and the retribution, unless death is judicially carried out upon the wrongdoer" (MS, 6:333). I believe that Kant will have difficulty defending his insistence that the punishment be similar in quality as well as in quantity, but defense of this thesis will have to await another paper.

14. See Michael Friedman, *Kant and the Exact Sciences* (Cambridge, Mass.: Harvard University Press, 1992), 44.

15. This surprising result is perhaps clearest in Barbara Herman's essay, "Murder and Mayhem," reprinted as chapter 6 of *The Practice of Moral Judgment*, ed. Barbara Herman (Cambridge, Mass.: Harvard University Press, 1993).

16. I say this although any departure from the equality of action and reaction is a violation of conservation principles that are very basic to physics. If the reaction doubled the action, for example, then we would have a creation of new energy out of nothing, and the possibility of a perpetual motion machine, for instance.

17. For development of this interpretation see Don Scheid, "Kant's Retributivism," *Ethics* 93 (1983): 262–82; Sharon Byrd, "Kant's Theory of Punishment: Deterrence in its Threat, Retribution in Its Execution," *Law and Philosophy* 1 (1989): 151–200; and the author's own "Kant on Obligation and Motivation in Law and Ethics," *Jahrbuch für Recht und Ethik* 2 (1994): 95–112.

18. For example, some law that is difficult to enforce, such as vandalism, we might enforce by punishing the few we catch with excessive severity; this might be less costly than beefing up enforcement, and catching more people in the act, which might have a deterrence-enhancing effect equal to the other policy, while being more expensive. The now familiar utilitarian idea of *maximizing* efficiency of deterrence is an idea that comes into common currency only in the nineteenth century, so in Kant we have the idea of deterrence, but no idea of maximizing deterrence. In any case, such a maximizing idea is quite at odds with Kant's approach in this area.

19. Where the mandated punishment is inadequate, we might call the principle the *lax talionis*. What should count as "adequate" deterrence is a nice question. It cannot mean a punishment adequate to deter any would-be criminal, for this would mean no punishment would be adequate. How can any punishment be adequate to deter a would-be malefactor who believes, no matter how irrationally, that he will not get caught, or who is not at all thinking about possible consequences of his punishable act? Such actions seem to be "undeterrable." Very roughly, a punishment will be "adequate" in deterrent effect if it would deter most deterrable criminal acts of a given kind.

20. Even in the second Critique, where Kant only briefly introduces the subject of punishment for a paragraph, he mentions the concern about the right of the punishee:

> For even though he who punishes can do so with the benevolent intention of directing his punishment to [the ultimate happiness of the one being punished], it must nevertheless be justified as punishment, i.e., as mere harm in itself, so that even the punished person, if it stopped there and he could see no glimpse of kindness behind the harshness, would yet have to admit that justice had been done and that his reward perfectly fitted his behavior. (KpV, 5:37)

21. Maybe Kant got carried away here. He sometimes gets carried away when he is writing against an opponent. (Cf. the response to Benjamin

Constant in "On a Supposed Right to Lie . . .") His juices have been brought to a boil by Marchese Beccaria (referred to at end of MS, 6:334), who opposed capital punishment, and he is tempted into an overstatement in his reply. It is tempting to say this, but this explains away rather than explaining the passage. I think personally, however, that this remains a part of the correct explanation of such extreme comments.

Kant makes a similar statement against lessening punishment earlier. It is the rest of the sentence that our title-quotation comes from:

> The principle of punishment is a categorical imperative and less woe to him who crawls through the windings of eudaemonism in order to discover something that releases the criminal from punishment or even reduces its amount by the advantage it promises, in accordance with the Pharisaical saying, "It is better for *one* man to die than for an entire people to perish." (MS, 6:331–32)

So if such extreme remarks are a slip of the pen, or a temptation in the heat of a response, they are repeated slips or temptations.

22. Reprinted in Feinberg's *Doing and Deserving* (Princeton, N.J.: Princeton University Press, 1970), 95–118. Insofar as Kant has in mind the physical construction model of bodies in space in thinking of punishment, this model limits comparison with conceptions of punishment as expressive. Deterrence in the physical analogy would be like the natural consequences of an equal reaction = punishment restoring the original equilibrium of a given body with others, rather than the effects of authoritative denunciation and its psychological (e.g., deterrent) effects on others.

23. I have hinted at the difficulties, in my view, of defending, or even of working out and presenting, a version of the *lex talionis* that provides for both quantative and qualitative likeness between crime and punishment. If the requirement of qualitative likeness is dropped, arguably the *lex talionis* becomes little more than the retributive idea that the punishment should fit (a quantitative concept) the crime. I will discuss Kant's presentation of the *lex talionis*, and the numerous examples he includes later in this chapter.

24. See her comment directly after her footnote 22. The killing of human beings when it is done after the model of the destruction of excessive numbers of dogs or cats, or badly injured horses, for example, would be something other than punishment. Such actions would be clearly incompatible with any positive claims concerning the humanity of the individual being thus killed.

25. Proposals for castration are often presented as an alternative to life in prison to be undertaken only with the consent of convict. Even so, it raises troubling issues. Another problem with the punishment for "bestiality" is that it approximates to being a victimless crime that adversely affects the freedom of no other person; it seems that it would at worst be a violation of a duty to oneself, especially given Kant's views on the moral standing of animals.

26. See his "Culpability and Desert" from *Archiv für Rechts und Sozial-philosophie* 19 (1983). This essay is reprinted in most editions of *Philosophy of*

Law, 4th ed., ed. Joel Feinberg and Hyman Gross (Belmont, Calif.: Wadsworth, 1991), 669–76, or example.

27. Feinberg, *Doing and Deserving*; Jean Hampton, "The Moral Education Theory of Punishment," *Philosophy and Public Affairs* 13.3 (1984): 208–38. Compare Herbert Morris,"A Paternalistic Theory of Punishment," *American Philosophical Quarterly* 18.4 (October 1981). Insofar as Kant has in mind the physical/geometrical model of objects in space in equilibrium in thinking of punishment, the comparison of Kant's views with the moral education view will be limited. According to the geometrical model individual agents are thought of simply as Newtonian bodies; hence the idea of the "education" of such bodies is quite foreign to the analogy.

28. See the discussion around footnote 22 of Hampton, "The Moral Education Theory of Punishment."

29. Look at Kant's interesting discussion of issues related to this point at MS, 6:335. There Kant is replying to Beccaria's criticism of the death penalty that provision for such could never be contained in the original contract, because individuals could never consent there to lose their own life in case they murdered someone. Kant's reply is to make a distinction between the aspect of the person that would so consent (*homo noumenon*) and the aspect that would not (*homo phenomenon*): "The chief point of error (*proton pseudos*) in this sophistry consists in its confusing the criminal's own judgment (which must necessarily be ascribed to his *reason*) that he has to foreit his life with a resolve on the part of his *will* to take his own life, and so in representing as united in one and the same person the judgment upon a right [*Rechtsbeurteilung*] and the realization of that right [*Rechtsvollziehung*]" (MS, 6:235). There is a further discussion of issues concerning application and consent earlier in this paper.

30. See the author's "Maxims in Kant's Moral Philosophy," *Philosophia* 23.1 (July 1994): 59–90, for further discussion of these points.

31. Sidney Axinn gave me useful comments on an early draft of this essay. A shorter version of it was presented to the Pacific Division of the American Philosophical Association on March 31, 1995, with useful and provocative comments by Jacqueline Marina and from the floor. Most important, very helpful critical comments were given me on the penultimate draft of the paper by Don Scheid, and all along the way I discussed the project with my colleague Mark van Roojen.

10

Thomas Auxter

The World of Retribution

When commentators survey the various conceptions of criminal justice in the Western tradition, they typically refer to Immanuel Kant's moral philosophy as the paradigm case of a retributivist theory. Indeed, they often cite Kant's famous comment about the moral necessity of executing murderers, including those who would otherwise remain isolated on a remote island: "Even if a civil society were to dissolve itself by common agreement of all its members (for example, if the people inhabiting an island decided to separate and disperse themselves around the world), the last murderer remaining in prison must first be executed, so that everyone will duly receive what his actions are worth and so that the bloodguilt thereof will not be fixed on the people because they failed to insist on carrying out the punishment; for if they fail to do so, they may be regarded as accomplices in this public violation of legal justice."[1] This is supposed to illustrate what it would be like to believe that only retribution can satisfy the demands of justice for criminals and that no other idea of criminal justice can be a legitimate basis for punishment or pardon. Readers are led to believe that within a Kantian framework retribution is required in order to uphold the most basic moral values.

Kant specialists who discuss the idea of retribution have not sought to challenge this prevailing view.[2] The standard response has been to

191

explain why retribution is the only morally legitimate idea of punishment. Recently some scholars have made an effort to "soften" the idea of retribution by elaborating and narrowing the conditions under which it would apply.[3] While this does make Kant appear to be less severe and uncompromising in his views on punishment, it underscores the idea that retribution is essentially bound up with Kantian moral principles and is even required in order to explain the meaning of Kant's practical philosophy. By making the theory of retribution appear more rational within a Kantian framework, recent commentators have supported the view that retribution is truly at the center of a critical approach to morality.

Does Kant's moral philosophy stand or fall on his theory of retribution? I argue that it does not depend on any such assumption and that adoption of the retributivist principle forces us to abandon some Kantian moral efforts that would otherwise appear promising. To be sure, Kant was a retributivist. I agree with scholars who say that the retributivist principle was important to Kant and that he believed it fit neatly within his overall architectonic. Nevertheless, it is left for us to decide whether Kant was right about the status of the theory of retribution within his moral philosophy and what principles or theories a Kantian would have to sacrifice to maintain the theory of retribution.

How do we identify the retributivist theme in Kant's thought? Kant describes "the retributive principle of returning like for like" as a law according to which one "can determine exactly the kind and degree of punishment."[4] A person is "deserving of punishment" for "any undeserved evil" inflicted on someone else. Justice demands that the one who inflicts evil receive injury and suffering in return. But the principle of retribution is not limited to human justice. It is also the basis of divine justice inasmuch as the highest good conceivable to us is the otherworldly condition in which happiness is exactly proportionate to virtue. While human retribution applies only to intentional acts demonstrably harmful to others, divine retribution applies to every decision an individual makes that has a bearing on the formation of moral character. On this view we should always try to reward virtue with happiness. However, because human powers of judgment are limited, we must wait for God to even up the score in most cases in which people have benefited from vice. In other words, the retributive strain runs more deeply through Kant's philosophy than it might appear from a quick survey of his writings on human justice. It even affects the way he defines the highest good in his writings on the relationship between moral theory and cosmic justice.

Yet the fact that the retributivist theme turns up in a fundamental concept like the highest good is not as decisive as it might seem at first.

The origin of this religious idea of retribution is not a mystery: Kant lived in a society and a culture in which the influence of institutionalized Christianity was considerable. It is clear enough how the idea of reward for virtue came to have the status of a moral intuition and why Kant might have wanted to show that he could accommodate this intuition within a critical approach to morality that otherwise might seem threatening. But the doctrine of the highest good as an otherworldly reward for virtue is not crucial for Kant's theory of experience.[5] The fact that he omitted this concept of the highest good from every formulation of the categorical imperative, as well as from the interpretation of typical moral dilemmas, shows how dispensable the concept is for practical judgment. Thus we are not required to believe that retribution is morally necessary simply because it is an ingredient in the concept of the highest good. If one's goal is to show that retribution is inextricably linked to the most basic principles of Kant's practical philosophy, it will not suffice to argue that retribution is grounded in the concept of the highest good, inasmuch as the status of the highest good is itself a controversial issue. The question remains: Is retribution required in order to uphold basic Kantian moral principles?

I

Why did retribution *look* like the moral world to Kant? We have already considered one answer in the context of discussing the highest good: the conventional interpretation of Christianity conferred the status of a moral "intuition" upon the idea of reward for virtue, and Kant made an effort to show that the critical philosophy could accommodate this "intuition" (through the back door of the "Transcendental Dialectic" of the *Critique of Practical Reason*). This happened in spite of the fact that the critical philosophy is supposed to be about the critical examination of conventional wisdom, not the certification of it.

No doubt institutionalized religion is an important factor. Kant always had an uneasy truce with this element of society. But there is more to it than this. Kant faced the problem of what it means to be human in a world that had become grossly inhuman: the world of punishment administered by the European aristocracy prior to the French Revolution. In order to get a concrete idea of what it was like for Kant to think about alternatives for criminal justice, it is necessary to have some idea of what the criminal justice system of his own time was like.

The power of punishment is a power widely and frequently abused in Western history. In Kant's time the Constitution Carolina Criminalis

(1532) was still in effect in the German states. This code imposed the death penalty for a wide range of "crimes"—including sin and possession by the devil. Enforcement of the code was vested with aristocrats who were free to use it to secure power and solidify privilege. People were punished for religious and moral "offenses," depending upon the desires of those who stood to gain by abuses of power. Confessions gained through torture counted as evidence.

The French Revolution brought with it a wave of reforms on such criminal justice issues across much of Europe. In Prussia the reform movement resulted in the Preussisches Landrecht (1792), which limited the arbitrary enforcement of penalties. It should be stressed that Kant sympathized with the French Revolution in general and with the reforms in the Prussian penal code in particular. In fact, Kant identified with the spirit and values of the French Revolution to such an extent that he carefully followed the reports of each turn of events, thought about the issues raised concerning human equality, and wrote his conclusions into the principles and formulations of the critical philosophy during his last decade of active publishing. For this reason German idealism, following Kant's lead, is sometimes called "the philosophy of the French Revolution."[6]

Kant thought that it was wrong to punish human beings for what one person believed to be the state of another's soul. According to the principles of the critical philosophy, the condition of the soul is unknowable. Thus the penal code of the time was wrong *both* because it lent itself to abuse by self-interested parties *and* because even the most well-intentioned and knowledgeable judges could not claim to administer justice on this level.

Kant's solution to these social and theoretical problems was to look for a "scientific" theory of punishment that would fit in with the tendencies and sensibilities of the age to favor "enlightened" explanations over those associated with religious superstition and fanaticism. He latches onto a Newtonian solution: each action calls for an equal and opposite reaction—no more, no less, no excesses. This is what equality would come to mean in criminal justice. In effect, Kant redefined equality in the domain of criminal justice. His goal was to stop the excesses in punishment by designing a system that is scientific and rigorous. In this way Kant hoped to eliminate the highly subjective factors that invite abuse and maintain inequality.

Taking Newtonian mechanics as a model for science, Kant imagined a world in which people would only be punished for the ostensible suffering caused to others by their law-breaking activity. A theory of strict retribution makes punishment scientific in this way, demanding as a condition of justice that people are punished for precisely the suffering caused by an illegal action, defined as a behavior, not as a disposition or state of the soul.

Considering the severity of the penal code at the time Kant was developing a critical approach to crime and punishment, it is understandable why Kant would reach for a "scientific" doctrine, one carrying the prestige and stamp of approval of an "enlightened" age, barely emerging from widespread ignorance and cruelty. Yet this does not mean that a later age must take this expression of a critical approach to be what a more thorough examination would produce as a result. I believe the origins of such a theory of punishment should make us doubly suspicious of it—of its birth as an alternative to cruelty and of the limitations that inevitably follow. This is hardly a generic or prototypical experience on which to build a critical conclusion—except by contrast, which is precisely what Kant achieved with his theory of retribution.

In today's context, it is more difficult to understand that Kant saw retribution as a progressive idea, in keeping with the values and movement of the French Revolution. We need to remember that an entire generation of progressive legal scholars was inspired by Kant to seek reform on all aspects of the law with the value of equality in mind. Kant's theory of retribution was progressive for its time. But this does not mean that it is morally progressive *for a later time*. Suppose it were to happen later that a growing conservative movement wanted to reverse decades of efforts to eliminate inequalities. Suppose this movement found retribution convenient as an article of faith at a time when people were uneasy about the increased extent of crime. Suppose the success of this movement focused attention and used up resources on lawbreakers while social and economic inequalities remained as before or grew worse. In this case it would be wrong to appropriate Kant's theory for a defense of retribution. It would be wrong to cite Kant as "the classical defender" of retribution when retribution meant no such thing to Kant. In each case retribution is part of a larger package.

By the middle of the twentieth century, retribution had a very different meaning from what it meant to Kant in the wake of the French Revolution. In fact, retribution seemed to be discredited and on its way out in most Western societies. In Europe, only the fascist countries (Germany, Italy, and Spain) actively used the death penalty, the most obvious and palpable symbol of a full and unabashed commitment to retribution. The defeat of fascism in 1945 meant the abolition of the death penalty in Germany and Italy. Fascism also provided vivid recent examples of the major roles retribution and revenge had to play in a monstrous political movement that became so powerful it finally took the entire world to stop it.

In the 1950s, research in Europe and the United States repeatedly demonstrated that there was not one example where the introduction or abolition of the death penalty made a significant difference in the murder rate (as reported annually by region). Ongoing research questioned the effectiveness of the death penalty in any of the countries keeping statistics on the issue. At the same time literary figures like Arthur Koestler and Albert Camus made it clear enough how much the death penalty dehumanizes all of us. By the end of the fifties almost all European countries and several states in the United States had abolished or discontinued use of the death penalty as a pointless and degrading form of revenge that played into the hands of dangerous political forces.

But by the end of the century we find retribution making a surprising comeback—in some way linked to the ascendancy of conservative political forces generally. Getting tough on crime means the death penalty, more prisons, and a kind of righteous anger that says they are getting what they deserve, and maybe it will teach them a lesson.

The conservative view that the meritorious deserve the material goods of life finds its complement in the retributive view that the wicked deserve to suffer. Moreover, a conservative politics of "getting tough on crime" creates a climate inviting theories that purport to show "getting even" is the right thing to do—no matter how much evidence is adduced showing this idea to be a failure in the realm of human relations and social development. The academic world finds itself in a state of amazement: ideas of retribution have become intellectually respectable again. Theories of retribution appear and rationalize the grim results.

How should we interpret these changes in meaning from one time to another? What should we make of the fact that retribution can bring a measure of equality in one period and yet serve to slow down and even reverse equality in another? Should we say that an advocate of retribution-as-equalization in Kant's time is defending retribution-as-stratification today? Can we say that the meaning of the proposal of retribution remains unchanged throughout this period of history? Is it true that Kant is the "classical" defender of *any* of the proposals for retribution we find before us now? A critical philosophy needs to ask critical questions about the historical choices we face.

II

Doubts about the meaning and status of retribution in Kant's theory should lead us to ask questions about the relationship between retribution and the most fundamental moral principles of the critical philosophy. How important is retribution for Kant's *system* of moral philosophy?

Kant's main argument for the moral necessity of retribution occurs in his discussion of penal law in the *Rechtslehre*:

> What kind and what degree of punishment does public legal justice adopt as its principle and standard? None other than the principle of equality (illustrated by the pointer on the scales of justice), that is, the principle of not treating one side more favorably than the other. . . . Only the Law of retribution (*jus talionis*) can determine exactly the kind and degree of punishment.[7]

Kant bases his case for retribution on the principle of equality, on the requirement that people be treated equally. Indeed, the phrase he uses interchangeably with "retribution" is "returning like for like," suggesting that equal treatment is the foundation for the concept of retributive punishment. While this argument strategy avoids the problems associated with the concept of the highest good discussed earlier, it is still subject to other problems. The two most serious problems are: (1) When noncriminals "return like for like" to the criminal, have they acted morally or have they entered into the patterns of conduct of the criminal? and (2) Can the behavior demanded by retribution be made consistent with the social behavior Kant advocates when he discusses the ideal for conduct in the realm of ends? Let us now consider how Kant might answer these questions.

At first glance it seems plausible that criminals have taken unfair advantage of others and that the principle of equal treatment entitles others to expect that the state, which is charged with providing guarantees of equal treatment, will even the score. Kant makes this argument when he asserts that the state should punish in such a way that one person is not treated more favorably than another. Moreover, commentators who follow Kant in this line of argument emphasize that the moral authority of the state stems from this function of establishing reciprocity, which entails criminal punishments that are compatible with the concept of reciprocity as equalization of the benefits and burdens of membership in society.[8]

Yet there is still a problem with what we can morally authorize the state to do in our names. Retributive punishment is supposed to induce suffering in the criminal equal to the suffering the criminal caused. The conceptual problem with this idea is well known: variations in personal histories, attitudes, and values make it virtually impossible to decide what would count as equal suffering. The problem is a real one for Kant because he based the argument for retribution on the principle of equality, *and* he made it clear that this involves equal discomfort and equal humiliation.

Aside from the conceptual problem with equalization of suffering, should we desire equal suffering, even if we could achieve it? The dilemma is pointed up by a statement made by a recent attorney general of the state of Florida (which houses one of the largest death row populations in the United States) concerning how the state should act in the days before an execution. The state, he said, should withdraw on a day-by-day basis all privileges from the one who is to be executed. Each day the state should take away some portion of the food, some provision for personal hygiene, some amount of exercise and living space, and some mode of contact with the outside world. Only by this means, he said, could we recreate in the killer the terror and desperation of the victim. The goal, he concluded, is to squeeze the life out of the killer on a very gradual basis so the maximum suffering can be exacted before the execution, and we can thereby approximate what the killer did to the victim.

How would Kant respond? To be sure, Kant insisted that we never degrade the humanity in ourselves or in the criminal through the act of punishment.[9] Some commentators believe that Kant meant to rule out torture and mutilation with this stipulation.[10] But Kant already argued that we *ought* to produce equal suffering in the criminal, and he stated emphatically that any reduction of the amount of it is tantamount to abandoning the commitment to legal justice, meaning "it is no longer worthwhile for men to remain alive on this earth."[11] Consequently, he left himself very little room to add stipulations about the decent treatment of criminals. He may have believed that there is no moral authorization to rape the rapist because that would involve accepting the values of the criminal and degrading humanity. He may have believed such crimes are "committed against humanity itself"[12] and therefore should not be repeated because they are abhorrent and would further degrade humanity. But is not repeating the act of killing also abhorrent and degrading? And if we truly believe in the equalization of suffering, how can we resist the proposal to squeeze the life out of the killer, or any other proposal to increase the suffering and humiliation of the criminal, in order to approach the suffering of the victim? How, indeed, can we avoid adopting the values and duplicating the activities of the offender, if we are charged with exacting equal pain? Is this what it means to enter the world of retribution? What, then, is left of our desire to respect "humanity itself" and to avoid activity that would degrade the humanity in us?

Retribution leads us in the direction of immoral activity and undercuts the moral authority with which we act. This is, I believe, the most obvious and telling point that a Kantian can make against retribution. But just as telling, if not immediately apparent, is that a commitment to retribution precludes the development of human moral identity along the lines proposed in the realm of ends version of the categorical imperative.

When Kant discusses the realm of ends in the *Grundlegung*, he spells out what it means to treat human beings with respect (as ends in themselves). What would it be like if this were a general rule for society? The realm of ends is the most comprehensive moral ideal of what this would involve. Kant calls it a "complete determination" of the moral law and "a very fruitful concept" for the effort to bring consciousness of the moral law "nearer to intuition . . . and so nearer to feeling."[13] Since this was the goal of proposing alternative formulations of the moral law in the first place, the realm of ends is the fulfillment of the process of spelling out the meaning of the moral law.

When Kant expands on the meaning of the realm of ends, he explains it in terms of the idea of mutual adaptation:

> If we abstract from the personal difference of rational beings and also from all content of their private ends, we can think of a whole of all ends in systematic connection, a whole of rational beings as ends in themselves as well as of the particular ends which each may set.[14]

Here Kant asks us to "abstract from the personal difference of rational beings." In other words, he is asking us to disregard ("negatively attend to"[15]) the moral difference in personality (the difference in moral culpability) in order to appreciate and cultivate the moral identity rational agents share. The "systematic connection" can only occur if we discontinue the divisive process of praising and blaming for virtues and vices we imagine are there and bring into existence "a whole of rational beings as ends in themselves." This "purposive unity," as Kant calls it in the first Critique, is based on affirming, rather than judging, the moral worth of all who enter into it. If we also disregard "the *content* of private ends" (emphasis added), we will conceive of a systematic union that stresses adaptation to the activities and ends of others (the *form* of private ends).

Although Kant is frequently criticized for his formalism, that is, for his sketchy formal notion of universally permissible behaviors that offer little guidance on what social ideal is rationally desirable, his realm of ends formulation provides a positive ideal of mutual adaptation. It is not enough simply to abstain from violating the rights of others when pursuing the content of private ends. We must continually adjust individual "forms" of private ends so that they will relate systematically to a "well-formed" whole. In other words, these activities will complement each other within "a whole of all ends"— including "the particular ends which each may set."

This "purposive unity" was anticipated at the end of the first Critique and reaffirmed and developed in the discussion of the ectypal world in the second. The same immanent conception of mutual adaptation was also incorporated into his "moral teleology" at the end of the third Critique when he identified "the final purpose we must aim at in this world" as *"the highest good in the world* that we can achieve through freedom."[16]

Kant also elaborates on the meaning of "a whole of all ends" in the third Critique when he discusses the nature of teleological judgment. He points out that when people transform (*unternommenen*) themselves into a moral community, they become part of an organization (*Organisation*) of life. Indeed, they fashion their lives according to this moral idea.

> In such a whole every member should surely be end as well as means, and because all work together toward the idea of the whole, each should be determined as regards place and function by means of the idea of the whole.[17]

We find here both the idea of respect for the humanity of all others and the idea of an on-going process of mutual adjustment so that the whole (moral community) is possible.

If an organic process of mutual adaptation is central to the critical philosophy, what does this mean for criminal justice in society? With the exception of retribution, there is room for every one of the major ideas of criminal justice. The moral ideas of mutual respect and co-evolution are compatible with the criminal justice goals of (1) isolation of violent offenders, (2) deterrence, (3) rehabilitation, and (4) restitution. If we value human beings as human beings, we do not subject them to violence by failing to separate violent offenders from others. Isolation is a legitimate goal for violent offenders so that their behavior can be contained. It should not be necessary to argue that this shows respect for what is human in us. If we want to cultivate our humanity, we cannot be indifferent to changes in human arrangements that deter crime and reduce victimization. Deterrence is a legitimate goal because we do not want human beings to be attacked. If we ignore the rehabilitation of offenders, how can we expect them to have a chance at a human life, and how can we expect to have authentically human relations with them after they are released? *Rehabilitation* is desirable because people who cannot "live again" among us cannot become part of a moral community when they are released. If we do not engage in *restitution*, reconciling victims and victimizers with each other and with the community, how can we say we are on a path of mutual adaptation in accordance with a moral idea of the whole? Although restitution is a theory that applies only to nonviolent crimes, it is important to note that such acts have always been the vast majority of crimes committed. There is no reason why a Kantian framework should preclude addressing this issue.[18] With these considerations in mind, we need to reevaluate ideas of criminal justice within the larger context of the critical philosophy.

Each of the major theories of criminal justice speaks to legitimate human concerns. All of them find a place within a developed critical approach to experience in which the idea of "a whole of all ends" is taken seriously. The single exception is the one theory that demands to be the only theory that counts, namely, retribution.

What does retribution involve? How are the activities of retribution related to efforts to bring into existence a realm of ends? Does retribution have a place in the movement toward the realm of ends?

Regardless of whether we are talking about retribution on a cosmic scale or merely within a legal framework, there are certain inescapable presuppositions.[19] The first assumption is that we must consider deeds as individual achievements. Otherwise, it is possible to punish someone for something she or he did not do. This means that moral agents need to interpret their experiences in ways that separate and keep distinct the deeds of various individuals. In effect, we are giving agents "moral" incentives to become atomic individuals, and in an important sense, to remain isolated from other agents. Furthermore, the very process of judging—whether it is done by an "official" judge or by others who contemplate (or criticize) the process—involves adopting a "detached," external standpoint for "impartial" judging. Consequently, to the extent that we advocate retributive punishments, we introduce a social distance between judges and the judged. Finally, the appropriateness of the judgment is itself a matter of debate, and differences in judgment become the basis for further invidious and pernicious differences among agents.[20]

The process of mutual alienation built into retribution cannot be made compatible with the process of creating a realm of ends, because the former requires emphasizing and intensifying moral differences among individual agents while the latter requires cultivating a common moral identity. The former presupposes an ontology of discrete individuals who *must* remain discrete in order for the "moral" process of retribution to occur. The latter requires disregarding moral differences to create a "purposive unity" based on moral identity. It should be apparent that retribution locks us into patterns both alien to and prohibitive of life in the realm of ends.

If the Kantian advocates of retribution want to defend the morality of seeking to "even the score," they can still claim that the distant goal of the realm of ends can only be reached *after* all acts of retribution have been completed. They could argue that a comprehensive series of retributive acts is a precondition for entering the realm of ends. But if that is the case, it is incumbent on them to explain how two seemingly incompatible processes of moral progress are finally related and why a moral philosophy that otherwise rules out radical separations of ends and means must make an exception for retribution.

We have considered why retribution is not suitable as a theory of criminal justice for Kant's moral philosophy and why it would be desirable to have a new theory for this purpose. Nevertheless, some of the characteristics Kant ascribes to a theory of retribution should be elements of *any* more adequate Kantian theory of criminal justice. The fact that "getting even" does not right wrongs does not mean that there is no other way to do this. Restitution, for example, is a theory of criminal justice expressly dedicated to this task. It is also important to develop a theory recognizing a human being as a human being rather than as merely an instrument for the purposes of others. Although retributivists claim that their theory is uniquely suited to this purpose, they introduce their own curious form of instrumentalism when they celebrate retribution because it satisfies the demands of "bloodguilt" and "bloodlust." Although retributivists claim devotion to the values of "pure" respect and "pure" equality, they find themselves slipping into the vocabulary of a "pure" (supposedly purifying) revenge against those who "deserve to suffer."

There is more to respecting human beings than can be entertained by any theory that invites an endless series of retaliatory acts. But to come to this awareness students of Kant's philosophy must unlearn what they have come to take for granted about theories of criminal justice other than retribution, namely, that alternatives are all merely paths to the goal of social utility and are therefore to be dismissed. When we develop Kantian versions of restitution, rehabilitation, isolation of violent offenders, and deterrence, we will be more securely on our way toward the realm in which human beings are treated as ends in themselves.

III

An examination of the historical context within which Kant advocated retribution (section I) should lead us to call into question several common assumptions about Kant and criminal justice, including the idea that the moral choice of retribution was the same for Kant as it is for us. At a minimum, we should expect more careful historical work before conclusions are drawn and consequences are suffered of the magnitude of a retributivist takeover of the fundamental values of human life. Before proceeding with the agenda and machinery of retribution, there are critical questions about history that must be asked in order to understand the meaning of the choice before us.

We have also seen (section II) that there are troubling questions about the status of retribution within the critical system of moral philosophy. Retribution brings with it the idea of a moral world composed of autonomous atomic individuals who ought to see their lives as fundamentally and finally about rewarding and punishing each other on the basis of individual desert. This moral ontology of retribution enforces a world order that is radically different from the moral world in which human beings respect the humanity in themselves and strive to create a social realm, a community, in which the humanity of everyone is recognized, affirmed, and developed. It should be clear enough by now that there is a critical choice before us about which world we will enter when we say we are creating the moral world. Whatever retribution means historically, it presents a dramatic either/or choice for what human beings will make of the moral world today. How we face human life and how we develop the critical philosophy hinge on this choice. I have argued that when we enter the world of retribution, we leave the moral world.

While we are rethinking the meaning and status of retribution, we may want to rethink revenge. Kant's position is that retribution and revenge are separate matters and should be kept that way. He views revenge as a pathological reaction and retribution as a measured response.[21] Feelings of revenge can only serve to undermine the administration of criminal justice.[22]

It is instructive to compare Kant's position with positions of the latest generation of retributivist thinkers. It is a curious fact that the "new retributivists," those in the twentieth century who follow Kant's arguments for retribution and use them (*sub specie a eternitatis*) to bolster their own theories, depart from Kant on this crucial point. Although Kant emphasizes that retribution should only be carried out based on the value of respect for human beings and that the feeling of revenge corrupts moral judgment and draws us away from the legitimate task at hand, Kant's followers today want to build feelings of revenge into the foundations of their ideas of what should be done to criminals. This gives revenge a special moral status Kant could not endorse. I will focus on the arguments of two of the new retributivists,

Jeffrie Murphy and Michael Moore, each of whom writes and teaches within both the fields of philosophy and law. I believe their arguments reveal something about the connection between retribution and revenge that could have caused Kant, if he had noticed it, to move away from retribution and toward the moral center of his own philosophy on issues of punishment.

In "Getting Even: The Role of the Victim,"[23] Jeffrie Murphy attempts to ground feelings of revenge in "our commonsense beliefs," which he dates back to the time of Homer. Indeed, Murphy introduces his essay with the words of Achilles:

> Not if his gifts outnumbered the sea sands
> or all the dust grains in the world could Agamemnon
> ever appease me—not till he pays me back
> full measure, pain for pain, dishonor for dishonor.
> *Iliad* IX.383–86

Murphy argues that there is nothing wrong with desiring and expecting equal suffering, down to the last detail, for injuries suffered and that moral common sense delivers this conclusion, although our "Christian liberal culture" insists that "such psychological states are either unambiguously evil or unambiguously sick."[24] But Murphy thinks that most people, even if unwilling to provide verbal endorsement of such a view, do in fact find it acceptable in principle for victims to resent and hate those who victimize them. He adds, "Perhaps Christianity's victory over pagan common sense is largely verbal."[25] In Murphy's view, the moral common sense that we find in legitimate "retributive hatred" expressed today has a precedent and historical foundation in feelings of revenge in ancient Greek society. It is only because "a Christian liberal culture" intervened causing us to suppress these feelings that we have a prejudice against seeing the intimate connection between revenge and retribution. The burden of proof, he believes, is on those who would deny the ancient and common moral wisdom that retribution is legitimately the institutionalization of revenge.

There are several problems with this version of retribution. I will comment only on the most serious one, namely, the problem with appealing to Homer as a moral foundation and source of inspiration. Homeric moral values are less "ancient" and enduring than commonly supposed. Homer, whether one poet who dictated the *Iliad* and the *Odyssey* or thirty poets who previously passed along this epic poetry in an oral tradition, is usually thought to be not much earlier than a millennium B.C.E. Much older is "the ancient religion" to which Socrates refers (with a sense of reverence) in the *Politeia*. The "old ways" in Plato's time were still present in the words and experiences at Eleusis. The initiation at Eleusis occurs at least another half millennium before Homer. In other words, for "the ancients" there was a more ancient moral wisdom than what we find in Homer. In Homer we find the values of patriarchy, domination, cleverness, intrigue, and revenge. At Eleusis we find the values of respect for all others and respect for the humanity that is in us. Socrates saw Homer for the moral impostor that he was. He even finds it humorous that anyone should be inspired by a worldview that portrays the gods as fighting each other. Socrates identifies with the morality of the ancient religion.[26]

If we consider moral values in historical context, we make room for a conclusion that differs from the one Jeffrie Murphy draws in "Getting Even." We can appreciate early Christianity (in some forms) as a resurfacing of the most ancient moral common sense, uncorrupted by the values of domination represented by Homer. In other words, there is nothing about "the gentle spirit"[27] (Kant's words) of Christianity that is incompatible with "the ancient religion."

Since Kant thought that this gentle spirit was also compatible with the spirit of his own moral philosophy, it seems worthwhile to ask about the "breath of life" (*psyche*) that animates Eleusis, moves through dialogue with Socrates, awakens "the gentle spirit" of Christianity and takes modern form in Kant's imperatives to respect the humanity of everyone and develop the humanity that is in us. However we describe this spirit or the forms it takes, it is not the spirit of retribution.

How ancient is the world of retribution? Are feelings of revenge natural and inescapable—elements of the most ancient moral approach to life? Or, is the world of retribution limited to certain epochs when revenge becomes the goal of life? What becomes of human beings who enter this world? It is impossible to evaluate retribution as an institution (the institutionalization of revenge) without answers to these critical questions. Yet commentators in the Western tradition usually act as if retribution were somehow grounded and validated because it is as ancient as Homer and is found as a central theme throughout this tradition of epic poetry. They do not consider the possibility that Homer is shallow ground—no place to stake something as serious as a moral identity, no place to find the values to guide us through a life in which human beings live well together. If the "new retributivists" rest on a foundation of Homer, they lose moral authority for their arguments as the moral reputation of Homer declines under the scrutiny of post-Victorian scholarship.

The other "new retributivist" we will briefly consider here, Michael Moore, has no trouble finding a moral foundation for feelings of revenge, and he does not need Homer to do it. In fact, he does not need to go out of the present to ground retribution. Mike Royko is enough to do it.

Who is Mike Royko? He is a newspaper columnist cited by Michael Moore in "The Moral Worth of Retribution"[28] as a living example of the kind of moral outrage we should properly feel and express when confronted with the details of brutal murders. Royko's stock-in-trade is recounting in painful detail the grisliest murders of the time. Readers of Royko's syndicated newspaper column are whipped into a frenzy of bloodlust for the death of the killer—after they have fully satisfied their morbid curiosity, of course. Michael Moore actually includes Royko in his references and dwells on a Royko example in order to get the juices of revenge going.

Moore wastes no time in introducing examples from Mike Royko in order to explain what we should properly feel about retribution. After announcing an argument strategy of seeking to "justify a moral principle by showing that it best accounts for those of our more particular judgments that we also believe to be true," he immediately turns to "some examples Mike Royko has used to *get the blood to the eyes* of readers of his newspaper column"[29] (emphasis added). A series of examples from Royko, followed by arguments, followed by more examples from Royko, constitute the basis for "our more particular judgments." These judgments are supposed to lead us (with blood in our eyes?) to the "deontological" conclusions that society has "a duty to punish" and that "we have an obligation to set up institutions so that retribution is achieved," no matter what the practical consequences might be.

If building a moral mandate for a course of action depends on the ability of the proponent "to get blood to the eyes" of an audience, then there is something wrong with the approach. Taking the plunge into a world of pathological behaviors rules out balancing all relevant considerations and choosing an option that respects and develops the humanity in all of us.

Noticing the extent to which some of the current arguments for retribution depend on a belief in the moral legitimacy of revenge should prompt us to think again about why Kant warned us not to mix revenge with retribution. Kant believed that feelings of revenge are pathological. Such feelings take over human life and drive it in a direction people would not otherwise choose. Choices and acts become unfree. Reason can no longer balance all relevant considerations and deliver a result that bears the marks of autonomous decision making. Human beings suffer a fate instead of choosing one.

There are yet other questions about the meaning of "getting even" that raise doubts about the morality of retribution. "Getting even" is supposed to right wrongs by evening the score or bringing the scales of justice back into balance—through the agency of equal and opposite reactions. Is this quantitative and mechanical model of what balance involves appropriate for the sphere of human relations? Is a Newtonian model of social relations appropriate for a world that no longer holds Newtonian mechanics to be ultimately and finally true of the physical realm, much less of any other realm? For that matter, does it fit in with key elements of the critical philosophy itself? Is it consistent with the systematic observation of the phenomena/noumena distinction? With the injunction (Third Antimony) not to impose physical world models on the moral world? With the discussion (in the Paralogisms) that calls into question the idea that the soul is an atomic individual (with hard boundaries) capable of reduction to mechanical, external relations with others?

Is there an alternative conception of balance that makes more sense of human relations in general and of criminal justice in particular? Is there an idea of balance more in keeping with Kant's defense of rational autonomy against pathological feelings like revenge? Is there a notion of balance that is more compatible with the ideal of mutual adaptation in the Kantian realm of ends? A comprehensive examination of possible answers to these questions takes us beyond the scope of this essay. I will simply close by offering a suggestion drawn from the earlier comparison between Homeric and Socratic moral values.

The ideas of *sophrosynē* and *dikē* that Socrates derives from ancient wisdom traditions form the basis for a different conception of balance. *Sophrosynē* involves tempering each activity to every other activity and is the coordination and integration (through the use of reason) of all activities in a life well-lived. *Dikē* is the dynamic equilibrium we create in social relations by adopting the same approach. The goal is to balance activities with each other on both the individual and social levels. When Socrates says it is wrong to harm others, or it is wrong to seek revenge against those defeated in war, he is explicitly rejecting the Homeric view that justice requires "the full measure" of retaliation for injuries suffered.[30] Instead, we should be asking what is required for human development to proceed based on the values of *sophrosynē* and *dikē*. It makes sense to restore life, as far as possible, to the level of activity experienced before wrongdoing occurred, not to exhibit and cultivate feelings of "retributive hatred."

This idea of balance fits in well with Kant's desire not to be overtaken by revenge (or any other pathological reaction, for that matter). It also makes sense of the concept of mutual adaptation as a moral process that we find in the realm of ends formulation of the categorical imperative.[31] How, then, do we rethink criminal justice with this idea of balance in mind? The line of investigation proposed earlier, namely, to think about the compatibility (in Kantian terms) of all theories of criminal justice (minus retribution), now seems more promising. Retribution, which is based on a dubious idea of balance, is the one theory that excludes the recognition and explication of the full meaning—in human terms—of other theories of criminal justice. If we dismiss the imperative to "get even," we make way for each of the remaining theories to be adjusted to the others in a developed (non-pathological and balanced) moral life of mutually adjusted activities.[32]

NOTES

1. Immanuel Kant, *Die Metaphysik der Sitten* (*The Metaphysics of Morals*), *Kants Gesammelte Schriften*, Ausgabe der Königlichen Preußischen Akademie der Wissenschaften (Berlin, 1902–), 6:333 (102). The Akademie edition will be cited as "KGS." The volume number is followed by page numbers of the original and the translation (latter in parentheses).

2. By "challenge" I mean offering detailed criticisms or formulating an alternative theory rather than merely registering disagreement.

3. See Jeffrie G. Murphy, *Kant: The Philosophy of Right* (New York: St. Martin's, 1970) and *Retribution, Justice and Therapy* (Dordrecht: Reidel, 1979). See also Don E. Scheid, "Kant's Retributivism," *Ethics* 93 (1983): 262–82. Jeffrie Murphy argues that retribution cannot rightfully be exacted from criminals until genuine reciprocity exists in a society. Don Scheid argues that Kant is a "partial retributivist," instead of a "thoroughgoing retributivist," because retributive punishments are dispensed to control crime and guarantee individual liberty, rather than to ensure that the wicked suffer. Both Murphy and Scheid restrict the conditions under which retribution is appropriate and thereby reduce the number of instances in which retribution can legitimately be applied. Jeffrie Murphy changed and developed his position in *Retribution Reconsidered* (Dordrecht: Kluwer, 1992)—finding and affirming a closer link between retribution and revenge. One problem with his more recent position is discussed in section III.

4. Kant, *Die Metaphysik der Sitten*, KGS 6:332 (101).

5. Thomas Auxter, "The Unimportance of Kant's Highest Good," *Journal of the History of Philosophy* 17 (1979): 121–34, and "The World View of the Moral Consciousness," *Kant's Moral Teleology* (Macon, Ga.: Mercer University Press, 1982), 81–101.

6. See T. Mertens, "Kant's Renewed Interest in Progress: On Enthusiasm and the French Revolution." *Tijdscha Filosof* 56.1 (March 1994): 73–106. Nevertheless, Kant is on record as being opposed to violent political revolution.

7. Ibid.

8. Herbert Morris, *On Guilt and Innocence* (Berkeley: University of California Press, 1976).

9. Kant, *Die Metaphysik der Sitten*, KGS 6:363.

10. Jeffrie G. Murphy, *Retribution, Justice, and Therapy*, 85.

11. Kant, *Die Metaphysik der Sitten*, KGS 6:332 (101).

12. Ibid., 363.

13. Kant, *Grundlegung zur Metaphysik der Sitten*, KGS 4:436 (54).

14. Kant, *Grundlegung zur Metaphysik der Sitten*, KGS 4:433 (51).

15. Kant, *Logik*, KGS 9:45.

16. Kant, *Kritik der Urtheilskraft*, KGS, 5:448–50.

17. Ibid., 375.

18. See Mark S. Umbreit, *Crime and Reconciliation* (Nashville, Tenn.: Abingdon Press, 1985).

19. When we are considering retribution on a cosmic scale, we need not assume that God would be the only one to judge. Some advocates of Kant's conception of the highest good, e.g. John Silber, believe that everyone should constantly reward virtue and punish vice in those whom they encounter— regardless of whether any laws of the state have been violated. See John Silber, "Kant's Conception of the Highest Good as Immanent and Transcendent," *Philosophical Review* 68 (1959): 469–92; "The Importance of the Highest Good in Kant's Ethics," *Ethics* 73 (1962–63): 179–97; and "The Copernican Revolution in Kant's Ethics: The Good Re-examined," *Kant-Studien* 51 (1959–60): 85–101. For criticisms of Silber's position (including the idea that we can know the extent to which others are virtuous), see Lewis White Beck, *A Commentary on Kant's Critique of Practical Reason* (Chicago: University of Chicago Press, 1960), 244–45; Jeffrie G. Murphy, "The Highest Good as Content for Kant's Ethical Formalism," *Kant-Studien* 57 (1965–66): 102–10; and Thomas Auxter, "The Unimportance of Kant's Highest Good," *Journal of the History of Philosophy* 17 (1979): 121–34.

20. For a more detailed analysis of the dynamic of judgement in the process of retribution, see Thomas Auxter, "Kant's Conception of the Private Sphere," *Philosophical Forum* 12.4: especially 301–2.

21. Kant makes the point that revenge is pathological as early as the 1770s in his university lectures on ethics. In his discussion of "Reward and Punishment" he states: "Punishments must be in keeping with nobility of mind. . . . They must not be insulting or contemptuous; otherwise they induce an ignoble type of character." Later in the lectures, when he covers the topic of "Vengeance," he makes it clear that he is speaking about the character of the agent of the action at least as much as the one who suffers from it: "to insist on one's right beyond what is necessary for its defense is to become revengeful. We become implacable and think only of the damage and pain which we wish to the man who has harmed us, even though we do not thereby instill in him greater respect for our rights. Such desire for vengeance is vicious." Immanuel Kant, *Lectures on Ethics*, trans. Louis Infield (New York: Harper & Row, 1963), 57, 214.

22. When Kant refers (in the *Rechtslehre*) to executions by torture, he criticizes the practice because it violates the humanity of the criminal: "the

death of the criminal must be kept entirely free of any maltreatment that would make an abomination of the humanity residing in the person suffering it" (KGS 6:333 [102]). This is similar to the way people today usually pose questions about the permissibility of vengeful actions taken against murderers: Will it violate whatever humanity is left in the killer? Then attention becomes focused on another question: *Is* there any humanity left in the killer? In my view this is a red herring when we discuss issues of revenge. The most telling studies of the death penalty as the institutionalization of revenge, namely, Arthur Koestler's "Reflections on Hanging" and Albert Camus' *Reflections of the Guillotine*, ask a different question: What becomes of the humanity of the rest of us when we engage in these practices? I ask a related question: When we enter the world of retribution, *is* there any humanity left in us? I have discussed this issue in "Killers and Killers of Killers," a paper presented at the Conference on Capital Punishment, Georgia State University, February 1980.

23. Jeffrie G. Murphy, "Getting Even: The Role of the Victim," *Punishment and Rehabilitation*, ed. Jeffrie G. Murphy (Belmont, Calif.: Wadsworth, 1994).

24. Ibid., 133

25. Ibid., 136

26. The contrast between Homeric and Eleusinian moral values is obscured by the fact that the initiation at Eleusis changed significantly when the Athenian state began administering the mysteries sometime prior to the sixth century B.C.E. With Homer, and even more with the transformation of Athenian life into the image of Homer, there is a reduction of Eleusinian symbols to patriarchal, ethnocentric, and hegemonic terms. Without taking this history into account, it is easy to accept common misconceptions about the initiation, e.g., that foreigners were excluded, and miss the key differences between Homeric moral values and the values of the "ancient religion." In this way we find Homeric moral values ensconced and defined as what is essentially and primordially Greek.

For accounts of the initiation at Eleusis and its influence on Greek life, see Walter Burkert, *Greek Religion* (Cambridge, Mass.: Harvard University Press, 1985); C. Kerenyi, *Eleusis: Archetypal Image of Mother and Daughter* (Princeton, N.J.: Princeton University Press, 1967); and J. W. Roberts, *City of Sokrates* (London: Routledge and Kegan Paul, 1984). Roberts observes that "The Platonic Sokrates never alludes to his own initiation, but he uses the language of the Mysteries" (p. 135). For a statement of the conventional view that Plato's moral theory is compatible with Homeric moral values, see Arthur W. H. Adkins, *Merit and Responsibility: A Study in Greek Values* (Oxford: Oxford University Press, 1960). For a critique of the status of women in Homeric poetry, see Eve Browning Cole, "Women, Slaves, and `Love of Toil,'" *Engendering Origins: Critical Feminist Readings in Plato and Aristotle*, ed. Bat-Ami Bar On (Albany: State University of New York Press, 1994), 127–44. For a statement of the differences between Homeric and Sophist moral values on the one hand and Socratic and Platonic moral values on the other, see Wendy Brown, "'Supposing Truth Were a Woman . . .': Plato's Subversion of Masculine Discourse," *Feminist Interpretations of Plato* (University Park: Pennsylvania State University Press, 1994), 157–80.

27. Immanuel Kant, "The End of All Things," *Perpetual Peace and Other Essays*, trans. Ted Humphrey (Indianapolis, Ind.: Hackett, 1983), 103.

28. Michael Moore, "The Moral Worth of Retribution," *Responsibility, Character, and the Emotions*, ed. Ferdinand Schoeman (Cambridge: Cambridge University Press, 1987), 179–219.

29. Ibid., 183–84.

30. See Plato, *Politeia* I and X, and *Gorgias* 469–527.

31. This reading of Kant's philosophy makes it much easier to identify and develop the values that are at the heart of the Western moral tradition, in contrast with the Victorian model of Kant scholarship (still prevalent) that wants to find warring schools of thought (teleological versus deontological versus utilitarian) in Western ethics. I discuss the more general problem of the Victorian "hangover" of twentieth century ethics in "The Process of Morality," *Hegel and Whitehead: Contemporary Perspectives on Systematic Philosophy*, ed. George R. Lucas Jr. (Albany: State University of New York Press, 1985), 219-38. In that essay I also suggest how we might make sense of the *continuity* of the Western moral tradition—with Socratic, Kantian, and utilitarian moral values interpreted as stages in a process of moral development. I give a detailed account of the teleological dimensions of Kantian ethics in *Kant's Moral Teleology* (Macon, Ga.: Mercer University Press, 1982). Finally, I discuss the question of revenge in relation to the meaning and direction of the critical philosophy in "The Revenge of the Thing in Itself," 1993 Conference of the German Studies Association, Washington, D.C., October 10, 1993.

32. Portions of this essay were published previously in a paper, "Kants Theory of Retribution," *Akten des Siebenten Internationalen Kant-Kongresses*, Kurfurstliches Schloss zu Mainz, 1990, ed. von G. Funke (Bonn: Bouvier, 1991). I am especially grateful to Otto Johnston for pointing to many of the historical details (including information concerning Kant's influence on an entire generation of legal scholars) that fill in the context for an estimation of the significance of retribution for Kant's time. Ellen Haring, Richard Haynes, Gillian Nassau, Michael Radelet, Patrick Riley, Pete Self, and Roy Weatherford gave helpful comments and suggestions that led to significant changes in the text. Nelson Potter allowed me to see early versions of "'The Principle of Punishment Is a Categorical Imperative,'" which appears in this volume. His careful explication of Kant's views helped me to appreciate the importance of a Newtonian model for the expression of a theory of retribution.

11

Harry van der Linden

A Kantian Defense of Enterprise Democracy

To those familiar with Kant's political philosophy, the very title of this paper may seem puzzling, or even as expressing a highly implausible idea. After all, Kant himself supported the emerging capitalist economy of his own time and saw the economic dependency of workers on their employers not as a focus for economic change but rather as a ground for denying them the political right to vote.[1] Proponents of enterprise democracy, to the contrary, commonly come from the socialist tradition and hold that workers should have the right to democratically control their companies, following the principle of "one person, one vote." Moreover, they often argue that one reason in support of enterprise democracy is that it increases political participation. So the question arises: How can any defense of enterprise democracy reasonably be called "Kantian"?

In the first section I will show that Kant's categorical imperative (focusing on the "universal-law" and "humanity as-an-end-in-itself" formulas) grounds the moral demand for democratic firms.[2] This justifies my claim of offering a *Kantian* defense of enterprise democracy: The very idea was beyond Kant's intellectual horizon, as is clear from his view that wage-earners should not have even the political right to vote, but his normative ethics can be used convincingly to ground this ideal.

My claim of providing a Kantian defense of enterprise democracy would be weakened if there were *basic* features of Kant's practical thought inconsistent with this ideal. It is, of course, impossible to show exhaustively here that this is not the case. I will develop in the second section only one argument to this effect: the socialization of productive property required by enterprise democracy is not inconsistent with the normative premises of Kant's defense of the right to private property. My broader aim in the second section is to sketch and defend in more detail a model of enterprise democracy (operating within a market economy) that accords with Kantian ethics. I will do so partly by way of addressing some common objections to this economic ideal.

THE CATEGORICAL IMPERATIVE AS NORMATIVE BASIS FOR ENTERPRISE DEMOCRACY

In a recent article Barbara Herman notes that "a neglected issue in Kant interpretation" is that a "satisfactory moral theory should offer more than an algorithm for permissibility." She explains: "It is not enough to get a version of the CI procedure [Categorical Imperative in its universal-law formulation] going that can spit out the expected, correct results. . . . [A]ctions (or maxims) should be rejected for reasons that explain what is wrong with them. Being told that we may not act on maxims that we cannot will that everyone act on does not explain enough."[3]

Herman's observation is well taken. We need a reason why it is morally wrong to act on nonuniversalizable maxims. And this means that we also need to explain why we should be committed to the "CI procedure." That this rather obvious point often has been overlooked is because it is wrongly assumed that Kant's ethics as a deontological ethics precludes that moral actions are guided by some goal.[4] I will argue that the ultimate value of the CI procedure is that virtuous maxims involve respect for rational nature and, more broadly, include a moral commitment to the goal of a harmony of all human beings (i.e., the "realm of ends"), while nonuniversalizable maxims imply disvaluing rational nature and this harmony of human beings. I will also show that my argument does not make Kant's ethics consequentialist because, on my account, the determination of morally right action or practice is a question not so much of finding what optimally realizes some end(s) but rather of establishing maxims that uphold or mirror the ideal of a harmony of human beings.

Kant himself explicitly states that the purpose of the moral law is to make possible a harmony of human beings. In clear anticipation of the universal-law formula, Kant argues in his pre-critical *Lectures on Ethics* that "truthfulness" is "in accord with every purpose; it is in harmony with the will of others, and everyone can guide his conduct by it." Lies, however, "contradict each other and are inconsistent with my purposes and with those of others." Kant continues:

> Moral goodness consists, therefore, in the submission of our will to rules whereby all our voluntary actions are brought into a harmony which is universally valid.
>
> Such a rule, which forms the first principle of the possibility of the harmony of all free wills, is the moral rule. . . . Our actions must be regulated if they are to harmonize, and their regulation is effected by the moral law. (27:257–58/17)[5]

Now the task for Kant was to discover and explicate the moral law or basic moral principle that can effect such a harmony of free wills.

Kant offers his solution in his later work, *Foundations of the Metaphysics of Morals*. The basic idea of his solution is that if all of us follow the demand of the universal-law formula to act only on those maxims that all of us can adopt, a harmony of human agents will emerge. In the words of H. J. Paton: "Kant's view is clearly that coherence of rational wills can be based only on obedience to one and the same universal law as such, and that without this there can be no genuine coherence." Paton adds: "If this is so, in seeking to obey universal law as such we are seeking to realize the condition of coherence among rational wills."[6]

The two most basic aspects of the harmony of free wills are universal respect for autonomy and universal mutual promotion of individual ends. Kant argues that in testing our maxims on the basis of the universal-law formula, we will come to place moral constraints upon the pursuit of our individual ends, because some maxims concerned with this pursuit are nonuniversalizable. Kant's classic example is the maxim of falsely promising to pay back a loan intended for private need in order to get the loan.[7] One cannot rationally will that everyone would adopt this maxim because the resulting general distrust would make one's false promise ineffective. Now Kant holds that if all of us guide the pursuit of individual ends only by maxims that everyone can adopt, then this pursuit would no longer lead to conflict. Thus one purpose of the universality test is that it makes us construct a moral ideal: the moral order of a harmony of human beings as a state of equal external freedom for all. For Kant, the ultimate significance of this aspect of the harmony of free wills is, however, not that it makes individual happiness possible, though this is important, but that it facilitates autonomous or moral decision making. Accordingly, within the harmony of free wills human agents respect one another as autonomous or legislative selves, seeking conditions that are conducive to moral autonomy.

The universal-law formula also leads to the imperative that we ought to promote *directly* one another's happiness. Kant argues that the maxim of not promoting the ends of others cannot be rationally willed as a universal law, for it would imply that one would lack the help of others as a necessary means to one's own happiness. To strengthen Kant's argument, it may be noted that even though the wealthy and fortunate person may be willing to forego the aid of others by adopting a maxim of nonbeneficence, it would still be irrational for her to adopt this maxim because her happiness would be much more difficult to realize in a world in which the quality of life of most people would be worsened by a general refusal to help one another. A second purpose of the universal-law formula, then, is that it leads to the aspect of the harmony of free wills that agents in this moral order will actively seek to contribute to the realization of one another's ends.

So the answer to Herman's query why maxims must pass the universality test is that maxims that fail the test involve a denial of the moral ideal of the harmony of free wills as a society of universal mutual promotion of individual ends and universal respect for autonomy.[8] Or, to put it otherwise, acting on nonuniversalizable maxims is wrong irrespective of possible negative consequences because in acting on such maxims we are choosing an immoral order. Conversely, commitment to the "CI procedure" is a commitment to the harmony of free wills, and actions with moral worth are precisely those actions based on maxims that keep this ideal in view.

This latter claim easily can be misinterpreted. A first misunderstanding is that the claim is given a consequentialist twist so that morally right action is interpreted as opting for the action that is estimated to be most effective in bringing about the harmony of free wills. On Kant's account, however, there might be situations in which acting on immoral rather than virtuous maxims is most effective in bringing about the moral ideal. This signifies that upholding an ideal in one's actions is altogether different from the consequentialist approach of viewing right action, or practice, as searching for the optimal realization or promotion of some end(s). The consequentialist will ask: "Which action or practice has the best consequences?" The Kantian will ask: "What kind of world are you constructing through your maxim aimed at some good(s) once your maxim is universalized? Is this world consistent with the ideal of the realm of ends?" One crucial practical difference between the two approaches is that the consequentialist will hold (or, at least, is logically committed to hold) that restriction of the freedom or rights of only some people for the benefit of many others is justified, whereas this would be wrong for the Kantian because it would be inconsistent with the ideal of the harmony of free wills.

A second misunderstanding is that "upholding an ideal" is interpreted as not encompassing the commitment to promote the realization of the ideal. As Paton indicates in the above, Kant holds that virtuous agents will make the overall purpose of the moral law their own end— that is, they will see it as their duty to bring about the harmony of free wills.[9] Kant's nonconsequentialist message here, then, is that the means chosen for promoting this ideal must mirror the ideal, or that the standards of the moral ideal must guide the labor of realizing the ideal.[10]

The humanity-as-an-end-in-itself formula of the categorical imperative states: "Act so that you treat humanity, whether in your own person or in that of another, always as an end and never as a means only" (*Foundations*, 4:429/47). This formula is often read as demanding "respect for persons"—that is, we must treat ourselves and others as beings with a rational nature. Kant's first illustration of how to apply the formula suggests, however, a more comprehensive interpretation. Kant states that he who considers suicide should ask himself "whether his action can be consistent with the *idea of humanity* as an end in itself" (my emphasis). Now considering Kant's well-known claim that the various formulations of the categorical imperative are only so many different expressions of one and the same law, we should infer that this idea of humanity is the same as the harmony of free wills. In other words, the idea of humanity refers to ideal humanity, a humanity unified by general obedience to universal law as such. Accordingly, the humanity-as-an-end-in-itself formula may be rephrased as demanding that we always uphold, or mirror, ideal humanity in our actions. Thus there is a close link between this formula and the universal-law formula, for they both demand that we act only on maxims that can become universal laws, or laws of a unified humanity or harmony of free wills.

All this is not to say that the humanity-as-an-end-in-itself formula does not imply that we must have "respect for persons."[11] Certainly, Kant often claims that we must treat rational nature as an unconditional end. His basic insight, I think, is that in acting only on maxims that can become universal laws, we uphold the freedom of others to set and pursue their own ends (including their happiness and moral autonomy), and thus we are treating others as rational agents or persons with unconditional value. That is to say, in acting in harmony with the notion of ideal humanity, we are also respecting "humanity" in a second and derivative sense: We are treating what is truly human (i.e., what separates us from other animals), rational nature, "agency," or our capacity to set and pursue ends, as an unconditional end. Conversely, in acting on maxims to which other human beings cannot assent, we are treating these others as mere means to our individual ends, denying their "humanity," rational nature, or capacity for self-determination. Kant's earlier example of falsely promising to pay back a personal loan in order to get the loan illustrates the point. In deceiving others in this manner, one is, in effect, denying that they are ends in themselves, or legislators who should test their own maxims on the basis of the universal-law formula, for one makes them assent to a maxim that is not the real maxim. It may be noted, moreover, that Kant derives the duty to promote the individual ends of others from the idea that we must treat rational nature as an unconditional end: this duty is an instance of seeking to further the flourishing of rational nature and its ends. What is lost, however, in the "respect for persons" reading of the humanity-as-an-end-in-itself formula is that to respect rational nature as an unconditional end is to will oneself and others as legislators of the ideal moral order, promoting the conditions of autonomy and universal happiness; it is to will ideal humanity or the harmony of free wills. The "respect for persons" reading neglects the moral ideal that Kant's ethics projects.

For Kant, the ideal of the harmony of free wills also should guide duties to oneself. He holds, for example, that suicide is usually not consistent with the "idea of humanity," meaning that in destroying one's humanity for the sake of one's inclinations one is disvaluing the ideal of the harmony of free wills. Consider also the grounding of the duty to develop one's talents. One reason that one cannot rationally will that the failure to develop one's talents become universal law is that this would imply that the necessary means for one's own happiness would be lacking. However, the more important reason is that general development of talents is needed for cultural progress, and Kant saw this kind of progress as indispensable to the incremental historical realization of the harmony of free wills.[12]

Kant's summary in the *Foundations* of the different formulations of the categorical imperative affirms my interpretation. Kant states here (4:436–37/54–55) that all maxims that accord with the moral law have a form (universality), a material (human agents as ends in themselves), and a complete determination (consistency with the realm of ends, i.e., the harmony of free wills). The threefold division corresponds to the categories of quantity as developed in the first Critique: unity, plurality, and totality (B 106; A 80). It follows that the purpose of general obedience to the moral law is to make possible a unified plurality, that is, a totality. The unity (form) is universal law as such. The plurality (material) consists of human agents and their individual ends. The former applied to the latter creates a moral totality (the complete determination), ideal humanity. Correlating with the two aspects of the plurality, this totality, the harmony of free wills, has two basic aspects (discussed earlier): universal mutual promotion of individual ends and universal respect for autonomy.

Kant's explication of the moral law that must make possible a unified humanity has at least two major weaknesses. Their correction opens the road toward enterprise democracy.

The first weakness is that Kant seems to have viewed the determination of universal laws, or approximations thereof, primarily as an activity that each individual can successfully perform by herself in isolation from others.[13] In accordance, Kant often claims that the demands of the moral law are clear to any conscientious person.[14] This monological picture, however, is somewhat balanced by Kant's passionate plea in "What Is Orientation in Thinking" for freedom of speech. In reply to the contention that oppressive political power can never take away the freedom to think, Kant states: "But how much and how accurately would we *think* if we did not think, so to speak, in community with others to whom we *communicate* our thoughts and who communicate their thoughts to us!"[15] Here, then, Kant seems to recognize that at least free communication is essential for arriving at not only moral truth, but also empirical knowledge. A similar inconsistency can be found in Kant's political philosophy. On the one hand, he supports representative democracy, thus recognizing that the voting process as a dialogical activity is a *sine qua non* for determining representative laws. On the other hand, Kant does not object to a monarchy (on a temporary basis, at least), because the conscientious monarch can legislate along representative lines.[16]

The second weakness is based on the fact that Kant holds that the moral ideal—the realm of ends—cannot be institutionally expressed and must be seen as an "inner" unification of good wills, a "church invisible."[17] Kant is, to some extent, correct here in that the realm of ends as a harmony of *virtuous* beings can never become fully visible because we can never know for sure whether actions are merely in accord with duty or done out of duty. But the point should not be exaggerated, for there is less reason to doubt that a series of actions in accordance with duty is rooted in a virtuous disposition than to doubt this with regard to any given individual action. It seems, therefore, reasonable to assume that the closer we approach a situation in which people through their actions promote universal happiness and the possibility of autonomy for all, the closer we get to the moral ideal of the realm of ends. The real practical significance of the claim that we can never be sure about the moral value of our actions is that we should operate on the idea that moral progress is always possible, whether it be on the individual or collective level. At any rate, what is crucial to note here is that one effect of Kant's view of the realm of ends as a church invisible is that he does not consistently develop his ethics as a social ethics in which it is argued that it is our duty to bring about ideal institutions. To be sure, this criticism should not be pressed too far, for Kant argues at various places in his work that the moral ideal can emerge only within the framework of the republican state and the federation of states (which must guarantee universal external freedom), thus grounding the social duty to bring about these political ends.[18] Moreover, Kant holds that it is important to modify the visible church so that it can better fulfill its function of preparing the way for the church invisible. Yet, in failing to argue that all our institutions must instantiate or approximate the realm of ends, Kant neglects to address systematically the question whether a capitalist economy is compatible with this ideal. Relatedly, he fails to give the duty to bring about a world in which human agents promote one another's ends any real direct content beyond the demand that we all fulfill the individual duty of beneficence.[19]

To overcome the first weakness, we must argue more consistently and emphatically than Kant did that dialogical and institutional action is needed to arrive at universal laws. Consider again political will-formation. Kant's notion of the conscientious ruler who can know the will of the people is to be rejected. Voting, political discussion, political action, political education, and recognition of conflicting interests are all needed to come to (approximations of) universal laws. This means that each individual must be seen as a co-legislator rather than as an isolated legislator, and that direct or participatory democracy, where feasible, should replace representative democracy. It also means that the political system must guarantee for all the conditions that enable one to be a co-legislator. As Kant himself recognized, even though he was not fully consistent in this regard, the categorical imperative demands a *constitutional* democracy that protects various basic civil and political rights as conditions of participatory autonomy. I may add that for states to arrive at universal laws regulating international conduct, more dialogical and institutional action is required than Kant envisioned in his peace proposal.

Analogous remarks apply to economic institutions. With regard to issues that foremost concern employees, corporate managers often make decisions inconsistent with the will of the employees, as is exemplified by arbitrary dismissals, unsafe work conditions, intrusive electronic monitoring, lack of health care, and other such wrongs common to capitalist economies. What is needed in order to better approximate decisions that can meet the consent of all employees is that they contribute to making these decisions. Accordingly, the categorical imperative demands that workers become co-legislators in their companies and have various economic rights that protect their conditions of participatory autonomy or co-legislatorship, such as the rights to occupational safety and health, free speech, privacy, and due process. Further, even if one grants the improbable claim that within the modern business corporation the decisions of higher management generally accord with the will of the employees, it is still the case that the employees are treated as "means only" because they are systematically denied the opportunity to co-determine the rules governing their company and work. Corporate managers also often make decisions that violate public interest and thus cannot meet public consent, and it is typically only after these decisions have led to harmful consequences that to some extent they become the subject of public scrutiny. Enterprise democracy will ameliorate these problems because, among other reasons, there is a much greater overlap of the interest of employees and the public interest than is true of the interest of corporate managers, and the process of decision making will be more open. (I will later consider the question whether direct input of people from outside companies is needed, as well.)

Enterprise democracy also seems to be the answer to the second weakness of Kant's explication of the moral law, namely, his neglect of addressing the question of how the ideal of mutual promotion of individual ends can be best institutionally realized. I will explore in the next section several reasons why the worker-managed economy fares better in terms of this ideal than does our corporate economy. One reason is that there will be greater material equality in the democratic economy because the workers will collectively decide the wage differentials in their companies (within the constraints set by the market) and also share in the profits. Other reasons are that participatory autonomy in democratic enterprises increases work satisfaction and is conducive to the adoption of industrial policies better in accordance with the needs of most consumers.

We can conclude, then, that the realm of ends as the ultimate end of the moral law makes the ideal of enterprise democracy imperative. The aspect of universal respect for autonomy is to be further explicated as requiring that we all become participants of the economic, as well as political and cultural, institutions in which we function, for only thoroughly democratic institutions can approximate universal laws and respect human agents as co-legislative or autonomous selves. The aspect of universal mutual promotion of individual ends is to be further developed as demanding that we create our economic institutions so that they optimize the satisfaction of the ends of their participants and, ultimately, of all human beings. With regard to either aspect, the worker-managed economy, but not our corporate economy, approximates the ideal.

OBJECTIONS AND REFUTATIONS: A FURTHER EXPLORATION OF ENTERPRISE DEMOCRACY

Perhaps the most common objection to enterprise democracy is that it is not feasible because most workers lack the competence for managing their firms. Another common objection is that this economic ideal is not really viable because workers will generally lack sufficient motivation for democratic decision making due to the fact that it is very time-consuming and occasionally frustrating.

To address these objections, at least three basic levels of decision making should be distinguished.[20] The first level concerns the day-by-day conditions of one's job and includes decisions on such issues as work pace and schedule, distribution of specific tasks, and minor improvements in production or services. The second level consists of particular decisions concerning grievances, selection of new members to the self-managed firm, demotion and promotion, leaves, and other personnel matters. The third level involves decisions that more or less have an impact on the whole democratic enterprise, such as adoption of new personnel policies and regulations, introduction of new technology, distribution of profits, and investment and product diversification decisions.

Competence and motivation are not serious problems with regard to the first two levels. Workers are, of course, capable of controlling their own immediate working environment, and they have a clear incentive for doing so because it will significantly improve job satisfaction due to the fact that it will enable them to opt for greater variation in tasks and a more flexible work schedule. Control over work conditions also seems conducive to greater self-respect due to increased responsibility and complexity of tasks, more human interaction, and increased appreciation by fellow workers. Further, elected employee committees can either oversee or directly handle decisions on the second level, depending on the issues involved. Competence, once again, seems no major issue, but occasional impatience and frustration with committee work might occur. One would suppose, however, that workers will find it worth paying this price, considering that they will gain a great reduction in arbitrary personnel decisions that are all too common in our corporate economy.[21]

Empirical studies of democratic enterprises confirm these observations in that these studies show that participatory practices concerning matters of direct significance to workers increase their productivity.[22] This increased productivity due to better morale and job satisfaction partly explains why democratic firms in our society often are more productive than capitalist firms.[23] It also makes it not surprising that more and more conventional corporations have provided employees with some say concerning their work or personnel issues by creating, for example, quality control circles, autonomous work groups, and peer-review boards for resolving employee grievances.[24]

The main problems seem to be competence and motivation on the third level: The issues are typically more complex here and for the most part farther away from the immediate interests of many workers. The problem of competence can be rephrased as the challenge of so creating relations between workers and experts in technology and business that the idea of enterprise democracy can still be upheld. How this can best be accomplished depends partly on the size and type of firm. What is at least feasible in terms of competency and consistent with the idea of enterprise democracy is that workers either directly elect and remove (upper) management or elect a supervisory board for this purpose. Managers will then decide many third-level issues, but some of these issues (e.g., profit distribution and new personnel policies and regulations) will be decided by occasional firmwide worker meetings or voting. Likewise, the democratization of technological control is feasible in that workers, or their representatives, can decide the goals and values guiding the development and introduction of new technology in their firms. Even the actual design of new technologies within these parameters should not be seen as the sole prerogative of technical experts, for workers might provide valuable input on basis of their direct familiarity with relevant technologies.[25]

In sum, workers are able to participate meaningfully in decisions that more or less concern their entire firms, and this will be increasingly so the more they improve their democratic skills and enlarge their understanding of technology and business operations. But will they opt for this? There is empirical evidence in support of an affirmative answer, even though the interest of workers in participatory decision making in company issues seems less strong than their interest in participatory practices on the shop floor level.[26] However, the very fact that there is some significant participatory interest in company issues is encouraging, for it is the case that the findings are based on workers primarily socialized in nonparticipatory environments, and it seems reasonable to assume that interest in participation will increase once workers are socialized in an established worker-managed economy.[27]

Theory must guide practice (i.e., the construction of the democratic economy), and it is, therefore, still important to ask of normative defenses of enterprise democracy whether they provide in theory adequate motivational reasons for participation on the third level. Here I believe that the Kantian approach shows its distinct character and strength. Some commonly assumed, or explicitly stated, motivational grounds for participation are increased self-respect, self-realization (the overcoming of self-alienation caused by being a mere cog in the machine), improved material conditions (due to the sharing of profits and to smaller wage differentials), and the intrinsic rewards of democratic decision making itself. All these grounds are significant but might not always be sufficient. The intrinsic rewards of democratic decision making are rather limited for some people and not always forthcoming. Self-esteem and self-realization can be gained in activities other than work—for some people even more successfully so. Further, the change toward worker-managed firms is unlikely to improve the material conditions of all workers, and even if one assumes material improvement for all, there is still the problem that the increase may not be significant enough or that one may decide to take a free ride on the participatory efforts of others. The Kantian approach addresses these dilemmas by stressing that active participation is a question not just of rights and improving one's own condition but also of responsibility, duty, and moral concern for others. From a Kantian perspective, it is a prima facie duty to help to shape both the internal and external decisions of one's firm so that autonomy and happiness are promoted in general. Nonparticipation means that one's fellow workers are not positively respected as co-legislators. It also means that one neglects the tremendous impact of the decisions of individual firms on local communities and even on society as a whole. One executes with fellow workers these decisions but one fails to co-legislate them. Thus one displays a lack of responsibility and moral concern for others. The Kantian approach, then, also emphasizes *moral* motivational reasons for participation, and the strength of this is that moral reasons (for participation) are commonly viewed as overriding nonmoral reasons (for nonparticipation). In other words, Kantian ethics seems especially suitable for guiding the construction of the worker-managed economy, because in making an appeal to moral grounds for participation— which might be reinforced by company mission statements that emphasize moral responsibility and goals—we can expect participation to be forthcoming where none would occur if an appeal had been made to nonmoral grounds alone. More broadly, the Kantian approach is attractive and effective in making participation part of moral development: the autonomous self is a co-legislative self.

Proponents of democratic enterprises generally agree that these firms should operate in a market economy. Enterprise democracy cannot flourish in the centrally planned economy because this economy precludes that enterprises themselves make any substantive decisions concerning, for example, product diversification, volume, pricing, and employment. There are many other objections to the centrally planned economy, such as that it is inefficient, leaves consumers with too little choice, and concentrates too much power in the state. Indeed, contemporary socialists have increasingly embraced the market, realizing that within the socialist tradition—and Karl Marx is a prime example—the capitalist market economy and the market economy as such are often equated, so that a rejection of the former seems to necessitate a rejection of the latter.

A much more difficult and controversial issue concerns the appropriate form of ownership of worker-managed firms. One possible arrangement is that each worker owns a share of her firm's capital, giving her a right to vote. A clear disadvantage of this arrangement is that shares may become prohibitively expensive. This would create a strong incentive for permitting the hiring of wage workers, leading to exploitative and nondemocratic relations within the firm. Another concern is that members of the firm, upon leaving their company, would sell shares to outsiders, gradually dissolving enterprise democracy.[28] Besides, individual share ownership will cause inequalities in wealth inconsistent with the Kantian ideal of mutual promotion of individual ends.

These problems are avoided by collective ownership of the firm's assets by the workers: There are now no individual shares to be bought or sold, and whoever works for the firm has a right to vote and co-determine how the profits are to be distributed. Collective worker ownership, however, also has some disadvantages. A first problem is that workers might opt for foregoing investments that pay off in the long term, choosing instead for receiving more income for themselves in the short term.[29] (Note that the increased value of a firm benefits workers only if they sell their company.) Other problems are that workers may defer too long the liquidation of unviable companies, that they may be too conservative risk-takers with regard to the formation of new companies or product lines, and that they may be neither willing nor able to borrow the money for starting companies with a very high capital requirement per worker.[30]

There is no agreement among economists of enterprise democracy how serious these problems are and how they can be best solved. One common basic proposed solution is to place ownership of productive assets in the hands of local banks or investment agencies. Firms then rent capital from the investment agencies at the market rate of interest and must sustain its value. The investment agencies also foreclose unviable firms and promote the formation of new firms or product lines. Enterprise democrats have elaborated this basic proposal in various ways: the investment agencies may be public, receiving their funds by taxing worker-managed firms, or they may be private enterprises funded by personal and government savings as well as by equity shares owned by private individuals, democratic firms, and the government.[31] Other variables are that the investment agencies may be guided by nationally or regionally developed economic plans, be fully worker-managed, or have boards with representatives from connected capital-renting democratic enterprises, individual investors, and the government.

In my view, an advantage of public investment agencies is that they can be subjected to politically determined investment guidelines, but a related problem is that these agencies may make investment decisions that are politically expedient and economically unsound.[32] On the whole, competing private investment companies may be more inclined to neglect the general interest in making investment decisions than is the case for public investment agencies, but this might be offset by creating boards with representatives from their different stakeholder groups, such as their capital-leasing democratic enterprises and the local community. Both types of investment agencies, and especially the public variant, raise the worry of concentration of economic power if they own all or most of the productive assets of society, enabling them to unduly restrict the autonomy of democratic enterprises. So, all in all, it seems best that the worker-managed economy be pluralistic in terms of ownership: Firms may be collectively owned by their workers, or their capital may be leased from public or private investment agencies, or in some cases a combination of these might even be appropriate. The collectively worker-owned firms may get their capital from borrowing from public or private sources or from reinvesting their surplus. With regard to reinvesting surplus, the option might be chosen to let workers as individuals share in a financially limited way in the increased value of productive assets as long as they are members of the firm (i.e., nonvoting and nontrading limited shares). This would somewhat dilute collective ownership, but increase the incentive to invest. In all cases, the preferred ownership form should depend on the nature and size of the firm's activities and the choice of its members. It should further be noted that, ultimately, much more practical experience and theoretical reflection is needed to settle the question of exactly which forms of ownership are optimal for enterprise democracy.[33] What also supports a pluralistic approach is that different societies may need to adopt different intermediate forms of ownership on the road to the ideal, reflecting their different points of departure.

Enterprise democracy requires that private productive property ownership be socialized. On the traditional account of private productive property, which no longer fully applies to our capitalist economy, the owners have the right to manage the assets, as well as the right to their value (when the assets are sold) and the right to the surplus generated by their use. In the worker-managed economy, the right to manage and the right to surplus belong collectively to the workers of the democratic firms, while to right to the value of capital will be both private and collective. So the question emerges: How can a defense of enterprise democracy reasonably be called "Kantian" in light of Kant's legitimation of private property? A brief look at the basic premises of Kant's justification of private property will show that the notion of socialized productive property is not "un-Kantian."

In *Metaphysical First Principles of the Doctrine of Right*, part I of *The Metaphysics of Morals*, Kant defines property ownership as follows: "Something external is mine if I would be wronged by being disturbed in my use of it *even though I am not in possession of it* (not holding the object)" (6:249/71). The point of this definition is that ownership must be distinguished from mere physical possession: When a house is rightfully your property it yours even when you are away. For Kant, the legitimation of ownership is basically a question of how first or original acquisition of external objects is possible, because acquisition through voluntary transfer can be justified only if ownership of the goods transferred can be justified. The justification of original acquisition of external objects, in turn, is basically a question of how original acquisition of land is possible, because ownership of a piece of land in effect entitles one to the (unowned) things on the land. Moreover, ownership of external objects is not possible without land ownership. The reason for this is that without land ownership a first person could justifiably physically occupy the land on which a second person owns an object and was not physically present, and this first person would then be justified in removing or destroying this object (see 6:261–62/83).

Original acquisition of a piece of land takes place through first physical occupation by one person and must impose upon on all others the obligation not to take this land, for otherwise the acquisition is mere usurpation. For Kant, this obligation (like all duties of justice) is grounded only if it accords with the rational will of each person, that is, the "united will." The "civil condition," or social contract, expresses the united will, and so Kant argues that "[t]herefore something external can be *originally* acquired only in conformity with the Idea of a civil condition, that is, with a view to it and to its being brought about"

(6:264/85). Kant adds: "Hence *original* acquisition can be only *provisional. Conclusive* acquisition takes place only in the civil condition." In other words, Kant holds that land is rightfully originally acquired when it is appropriated with the presumption that the act of acquisition accords with the united will as it is expressed in a civil constitution. It is only when a civil constitution is actually in place that provisional ownership can become definite.

The united will can "grant" provisional ownership only if the united will is the original owner of all land in the first place. This *"original possession in common"* should not be confused with some temporal or factual *"primitive possession in common"*; rather, it is a "practical rational concept" (6:262/84). Likewise, the institutionalization of the rule of law and, with it, the transformation of provisional ownership into conclusive ownership, presupposes that the united will has full authority over the land. Now Kant held that since the united will has this authority, it would be right for the state, if it would accord with the united will, to revoke laws that favor the continuity of large feudal estates or holdings of the church. Kant supported redistribution of land for the sake of political democracy: This redistribution would create small property owners who would thus become their own "master" as a precondition for the right to vote.[34] By the same token, it would be permissible on Kant's view that the united will would opt for resocialization of private productive property for the sake of enterprise democracy (assuming that appropriate compensation is provided).

To support further that socialization of productive property is not necessarily an "un-Kantian" idea, it should be noted that Kant himself indirectly grants its legitimate possibility by arguing that actual collective possession of the land as in the case of nomads in Mongolia is justified if it can be seen as arising "from a contract by which everyone gave up private possessions" (6:251/73; see also 265/86).[35] Additionally, it is essential that Kant's legitimation of property is not confused with the traditional liberal defense of the right to private property as a moral right prior to the social contract, for this defense indeed contradicts my argument for socialized productive property. That Kant is far away from the traditional liberal defense is underlined by his remarkable claim that all property of his own time "will always remain only provisional unless [the social] contract extends to the entire human race" (i.e., the realization of the league of nations) (6:266/87).

It has been shown that for the workers themselves democratic firms offer a much closer approximation of the realm of ends as a society of universal respect for autonomy and mutual promotion of individual ends than is true of conventional firms. To recapitulate and expand the argument somewhat, democratic firms provide all workers with the opportunity for decision making and thus enable the development of participatory autonomous individuals. Some delegation of tasks to various experts seems inevitable, but, even so, the final responsibility for the main decisions of their companies remains within the hands of the workers because management is accountable to the workers and can be removed. Other benefits are a greater sense of community among workers, more varied and satisfactory work for many, and protection of significant worker rights for all as a precondition of their co-legislatorship. The material conditions of many workers also might improve, because it is to be expected that workers will opt for smaller income differences and a fairly egalitarian distribution of profits. In existing producer cooperatives a common ratio of top and minimum income is 3:1 or smaller,[36] and we may assume that this ratio will become smaller in the worker-managed economy when democratic companies no longer need to compete with conventional corporations for attracting management. The democratic economy will fall short of egalitarian ideals because, among other reasons, different profit margins between industries and high demand for, but low supply of, some skills will continue to create economic inequalities. Yet, certainly, these inequalities will be small as compared to the extreme economic inequalities of capitalist society, and so a final improvement in the situation of workers will be that the material resources required for effective participation in the political process will be more equally distributed in society. One would expect that this will significantly increase the workers' voices in shaping the political will, especially since worker-managed firms will strengthen their democratic skills and also might be conducive to their increased political interest (as an aspect of having developed more democratic characters).[37]

What has not yet really been shown is that worker-managed firms are superior to corporate firms in terms of promoting the well-being and autonomy of local communities and also society at large. Here one might object that it is to be expected that worker-managed firms in a competitive market-economy will act like capitalist corporations, pursuing all too often their own interests at the cost of broader interests.

There are several reasons for holding that the worker-managed firm will fare better in respect to promoting universal autonomy and well-being. A first reason pertains to the expansion of firms. In a competitive market economy, democratic firms have an adequate incentive to invest so as to better meet consumer demand, especially so if capital can be leased from investment agencies. Unlike their capitalist counterparts, however, democratic firms do not have a strong incentive to expand continually because it would only mean that greater profits are shared with more workers. Thus one would expect that democratic firms will be smaller than capitalist firms, which is advantageous for effective workplace democracy. Likewise, it may be anticipated that when worker-managed companies grow rather large they will transform their divisions into independent companies for the sake of democracy, assuming that technical efficiency does not require otherwise.[38] However, the advantage crucial to note here is that worker-managed firms will engage in much less aggressive and manipulative selling techniques, decreasing the endless promotion of the consumerist lifestyle so typical of capitalist society.[39] This will not only contribute to the well-being and autonomy of the average consumer, but it will also free resources needed for those who lack the minimal material and educational means for a happy and autonomous existence. A related benefit might be that it will motivationally facilitate workers to opt for less work and more free time, an option that also goes against the economic interest of capitalist firms but can be feasibly realized within worker-managed firms.[40]

We may further infer that workers as the final decision-makers in worker-managed firms generally will make economic decisions more in accordance with the interests of most consumers and citizens than the decisions made by present corporate executives because the interests of workers are more representative of the interests of most consumers and citizens.[41] For example, workers who choose for following minimal antipollution standards only pollute their own backyards, and it is difficult to see how they would ever decide for the kind of plant relocations that continue to devastate our local communities. By the same token, one would expect an increased use of the human resources of economic enterprises for improving the educational system and cultural life of the local community.

A final comparative strength is that worker-managed firms eliminate several factors that contribute to corporate wrong-doing in our society involving such harms as unsafe goods and production processes endangering the public.[42] In democratic firms the gap between upper management and the average worker will be much smaller, making it much less likely that economic harms will occur or continue to be inflicted because management fails to detect the harms or because workers fail to inform management about them due to fear of dismissal, lack of knowledge, or indifference arising from having no real job responsibility. In general, since workers will have much more control in democratic firms, we may assume on their side increased moral responsibility for, and awareness of, possible economic harm. The same is to be expected of upper management once they become answerable to workers. And a last reason why enterprise democracy is conducive to less economic harm is the openness of democratic decision making, making it difficult for reports of economic harm to remain hidden under the carpets of upper management, as is common in cases of corporate harm.

Democratic enterprises are not the cure for all economic ills. The workers of these firms do have economic interests that may collide with the general interest: the myth of the invisible hand of the capitalist market economy should not be replaced by a myth of an invisible hand of the worker-managed market economy. Additional measures are necessary to create an economy conducive to participatory autonomy and human flourishing. Day care on site, paid leaves for birth and family emergencies, flexible career tracks, and the like must be available for equal opportunity of participatory autonomy. Community representatives on the governing boards of some large democratic firms might be necessary in order to protect the interests of local communities. Public enterprises at state, regional, and city levels are imperative with regard to industries and services that tend to be monopolistic, are vital to the economy at large, or may be unprofitable: airports, railroads, ferries to remote islands, mail, electricity, water, and so on. In these enterprises management should be accountable to both workers and public agencies. The economy should be pluralistic in an additional way: Very small companies owned and managed by one or some private individuals might be beneficial to those who seek temporary employment or do not feel at home in participatory environments. These companies may also be important for innovation and quick response to new market demands. People should be able to work for themselves.[43] Some long-term industrial planning, adopting more stringent regulatory laws, increasing the number of services and goods outside market mechanisms, and providing more international aid all seem essential for the economy that accords with the realm of ends. Some of these measures limit the autonomy of worker-managed firms, but this is justified: workers and elected managers should have the full right of control with regard to decisions that primarily effect themselves; however, with regard to decisions that have a major impact on the conditions of autonomy and well-being of others, the right to manage might need to be shared in some form with representatives of stakeholder groups outside the companies. More broadly, since no company is an island, its decisions may be constrained by the political process (regulatory law, and so on).

To conclude, I wish to emphasize that there are limits to the attempt to construct economic institutions so that they "inevitably" will promote universal autonomy and happiness. Once we assume that human beings are primarily selfish agents, a decent economy seems out of reach. The more reasonable—and Kantian—assumption is that human agents are interested in making and pursuing universal laws when favorable social circumstances prevail. In other words, the assumption is that human beings will take on the task of moral autonomy once they have real opportunities for doing so. Enterprise democracy, as sketched here, provides such opportunities for all in the economic realm. It may be once more noted, though, that my view of the democratic economy, like any reasonable model of the good economy, must be seen as open-ended: How a decent economy is to be created is a question of ongoing theoretical reflection and practical experience. Even Kant's practical philosophy as a normative basis for enterprise democracy may need modification beyond my broadening his notion of autonomy as participatory autonomy and my extrapolating his demand for universal mutual promotion of individual happiness as an institutional demand. Kant offers a rich conception of the morally good life, but says too little about human happiness in general. In my evaluation of the capitalist economy, I have suggested that a life of community, meaningful work, and self-expression is superior to a life of isolated consumption. This certainly fits with Kant's understanding of the morally good life, and I think that a further analysis of human flourishing within a still-pluralistic framework will ultimately only strengthen (as a second-level justification) the case for enterprise democracy. What I hope to have shown here is that Kantian ethics itself can already take us a long way.

NOTES

1. In Kant citations, the first number refers to the volume number of the Prussian Academy edition of his collected works (*Kants Gesammelte Schriften*, Berlin: 1902–), the second number refers to the page number of this edition, and the third number refers to page number of the English translation used. For Kant's claim that wage-earners should not have a right to vote, see *On the Common Saying: "This May Be True in Theory, but It Does Not Apply in Practice,"* in Hans Reiss, ed., *Kant's Political Writings*, trans. H. B. Nisbet (Cambridge: Cambridge University Press, 1970, 1991), 7:295–96/77–78.

2. I draw in the first section from my *Kantian Ethics and Socialism* (Indianapolis, Ind.: Hackett, 1988) and my "Cohens sozialistische Rekonstruktion der Ethik Kants," in *Ethischer Sozialismus: Zur politischen Philosophie des Neukantianismus*, ed. Helmut Holzhey (Frankfurt am Main: Suhrkamp, 1994). I now do not use Hermann Cohen's work to link Kantian ethics and enterprise democracy, but my Kant interpretation is influenced by Cohen and other Marburg neo-Kantians.

3. "Murder and Mayhem," in *The Practice of Moral Judgment* (Cambridge, Mass.: Harvard University Press, 1993), 115. This article first appeared in *The Monist* 72 (July 1989): 411–31.

4. Cf. Thomas Auxter, *Kant's Moral Teleology* (Macon, Ga.: Mercer University Press, 1982), x.

5. Trans. Louis Infield (Indianapolis, Ind.: Hackett, 1980).

6. *The Categorical Imperative* (New York: Harper & Row, 1967), 140.

7. See *Foundations of the Metaphysics of Morals*, trans. Lewis White Beck (Indianapolis, Ind.: Bobbs-Merrill, 1959), 4:423/40. Kant actually uses here the natural-law formula, but the applications of this formula and of the universal-law formula significantly overlap with regard to duties to others.

8. Herman's own answer is that nonuniversalizable maxims involve the "error of 'devaluing' or 'discounting' rational agency." See *The Practice of Moral Judgment*, 127. It will soon become clear that our main difference is that only my view *also* stresses that non- universalizable maxims are wrong due to their denial of Kant's moral ideal of the realm of ends.

9. Kant himself frequently states that we have a duty to promote the highest good (*summum bonum*) as a combination of universal virtue and happiness. In *Kantian Ethics and Socialism*, chap. I and chap. II, section 2, I show that this duty *insofar as it falls within our ability to fulfill it* is identical to the duty to realize the harmony of free wills.

10. This guideline should not be confused with the directive that we should act as if we are already living in the moral ideal, ignoring the evil in our world. Kant seems to follow this latter directive when he claims that international intervention is always wrong and that we should not lie to an aggressor who asks us the whereabouts of his intended victim. In my view, the standards of the moral ideal are in such situations in conflict with one another—e.g., truth-telling and protecting people from harm—and we must then act on the standard most fundamental to the ideal. Mirroring the ideal in such situations also means that we should not deny the validity of the ideal through our conduct and that we should leave room for possible future endeavors toward the ideal. Kant himself seems to endorse these ideas in his argument that a defensive war might be just if various immoral means, such as assassins and poisoners, are not used. See further my "Kant, the Duty to Promote International Peace, and Political Intervention," in *Proceedings of the Eighth International Kant Congress,* ed. Hoke Robinson (Milwaukee, Wis.: Marquette University Press, 1995), vol. II, part I, 75–76.

11. My analysis of the imperative of "respect for persons" has benefited from Thomas E. Hill Jr., *Dignity and Practical Reason in Kant's Moral Theory* (Ithaca, N.Y.: Cornell University Press, 1992), essay 2, "Humanity as an End in Itself"; Christine M. Korsgaard, "The Right to Lie: Kant on Dealing with Evil," *Philosophy & Public Affairs* 15 (1986): 325–49; and Onora O'Neill, *Constructions of Reason* (Cambridge: Cambridge University Press, 1989), essay VII, "Universal Laws and Ends-in-Themselves." Our main interpretative difference is that I emphasize much more that this imperative puts forth the realm of ends as both

a limiting constraint on, and aim of, moral action. Only my interpretation accords with the central role of the doctrine of the highest good in Kant's practical philosophy, which is convincingly explicated by Yirmiahu Yovel, *Kant and the Philosophy of History* (Princeton, N.J.: Princeton University Press, 1980). Cf. note 9, above.

12. See *Critique of Judgment*, trans. Werner S. Pluhar (Indianapolis, Ind.: Hackett, 1987), 5:433/321. Kant's idea of the cultural facilitation of moral progress is discussed in Patrick Riley, *Kant's Political Philosophy* (Totowa, N.J.: Rowman and Littlefield, 1983), chapter 4.

13. Jürgen Habermas raises (and overstates) the same criticism in his communicative ethics.

14. See *Foundations*, 4:404/20. See also *Critique of Practical Reason*, trans. Lewis White Beck (Indianapolis, Ind.: Bobbs-Merrill, 1956), 5:8n/8n.

15. *Kant's Political Writings*, 8:144/247.

16. See "A Renewed Attempt to Answer the Question: 'Is the Human Race Continually Improving?'" Part II of *The Contest of Faculties*, in *Kant's Political Writings*, 8:88 and 91/184, 187.

17. See *Religion within the Limits of Reason Alone*, book III, division 1, sections 4 and 7.

18. See my *Kantian Ethics and Socialism*, 6–11. See also Robert B. Pippin, "On the Moral Foundations of Kant's *Rechtslehre*," in *The Philosophy of Immanuel Kant*, ed. Richard Kennington (Washington, D.C.: Catholic University of America Press, 1985).

19. Kant holds that the state has the right "to constrain the wealthy to provide the means of sustenance to those who are unable to provide for even their most necessary natural needs." See *The Metaphysics of Morals*, trans. Mary Gregor (Cambridge: Cambridge University Press, 1991), 6:326/136. However, this idea clearly falls short of the ideal of mutual promotion of individual ends within the realm of ends.

20. I modify here three similar levels drawn by John J. McCall, "Participation in Employment," in *Contemporary Issues in Business, Ethics*, ed. Joseph R. DesJardins and John J. McCall (Belmont, Calif.: Wadsworth, 1985, 1990), 166.

21. One striking example is that more than 150,000 employees are fired yearly (in the United States) without good cause. See Lewis L. Maltby, *A State of Emergency in the Workplace* (1990), 3. This brief report of the American Civil Liberties Union describes the lack of rights in the American workplace.

22. For a summary of some recent studies, see David Schweickart, *Against Capitalism* (Cambridge: Cambridge University Press, 1993), 100–3.

23. Some other factors are that democratic firms have a lower turnover rate and that their workers are prepared to monitor each other's job performance (because they all will profit from increased productivity). For a fuller discussion, see Samuel Bowles and Herbert Gintis, "A Political and Economic Case for the Democratic Enterprise," in *The Idea of Democracy*, ed.

David Copp, Jean Hampton, and John E. Roemer (Cambridge: Cambridge University Press, 1993), 390–92. It is nonetheless the case that more or less democratic firms often have not flourished in capitalist societies. Some explanations are that failed firms were based on nonsocialized forms of ownership, encountered financing problems, had to compete for managers with capitalist firms, and evolved from failed capitalist companies. In short, many causes of failure are ones that will no longer exist for democratic firms in the environment of market socialism. See further Bowles and Gintis, ibid., pp. 392–94, and Robert A. Dahl, *A Preface to Economic Democracy* (Berkeley: University of California Press, 1985), 130–32. The issue also receives a valuable discussion in Jon Elster, "From Here to There; or, If Cooperative Ownership Is So Desirable, Why Are There So Few Cooperatives?" *Social Philosophy & Policy* 6 (Spring 1989): 93–111. In my view, however, Elster too hesitantly supports the economic viability of democratic enterprises.

24. Participatory programs in capitalist corporations have met with success notwithstanding that employees have expressed such motivational obstacles as the beliefs that these programs do not give a real say to them and are intended to better exploit them and weaken union power. See Sharon McCarthy, "The Dilemma of Non-participation" and George Strauss, "Workers' Participation and U.S. Collective Bargaining," in *International Handbook of Participation in Organizations*, vol. 1: *Organizational Democracy: Taking Stock*, ed. Cornelis J. Lammers and György Széll (Oxford: Oxford University Press, 1989). Workers' interest should be even greater in the worker-managed economy since it eliminates these motivational obstacles. It will also eliminate lack of interest due to temporary employment.

25. Cf. Carol C. Gould, *Rethinking Democracy* (Cambridge: Cambridge University Press, 1988), 279, who offers a valuable discussion of how technology can be democratized within worker-managed firms.

26. See Louis Putterman, "After the Employment Relation: problems on the Road to Enterprise Democracy," in *Markets and Democracy: Participation, Accountability and Efficiency*, ed. Samuel Bowles, Herbert Gintis, and Bo Gustafsson (Cambridge: Cambridge University Press, 1993), 140. His conclusion is partly based on the comprehensive study by David I. Levine and Laura D'Andrea Tyson on the productivity effects of participation, in *Paying for Productivity*, ed. Alan S. Blinder (Washington, D.C.: Brookings Institution, 1990).

27. Cf. Dahl, *A Preface to Economic Democracy*, 98, who makes the same point with regard to mixed research findings concerning the claim that participation in democratic enterprises increases interest in political participation.

28. See further Dahl, *A Preface to Economic Democracy*, 140–41, and Jon Elster and Karl Ove Moene, eds., in their introduction to *Alternatives to Capitalism* (Cambridge: Cambridge University Press, 1989), 22–25.

29. See further Saul Estrin, "Workers' Co-operatives: Their Merits and Their Limitations," in *Market Socialism*, ed. Julian Le Grand and Saul Estrin (Oxford: Clarendon, 1989), 180–81.

30. For the first two of these problems, see Thomas E. Weisskopf, "Challenges to Market Socialism: A Response to Critics," *Dissent* (Spring 1992): 250–61, esp. 255, and also his "A Democratic Enterprise-Based Market Socialism," in *Market Socialism: The Current Debate*, ed. Pranab Bardhan and John Roemer (Oxford: Oxford University Press, 1993), 123. For the final problem, see John E. Roemer, *A Future for Socialism* (Cambridge, Mass.: Harvard University Press, 1994), 47. Roemer argues for a market socialism without significant enterprise democracy.

31. The first alternative basically accords with David Miller, *Market, State and Community: Theoretical Foundations of Market Socialism* (Oxford: Oxford University Press, 1990), 309–12, and Schweickart, *Against Capitalism*, 70–77; the second alternative is offered by Estrin, "Workers' Co-operatives: Their Merits and Their Limitations," 187–91. Similar proposals are briefly discussed in Roemer, *A Future for Socialism*, 47–48.

32. Cf. David Miller, "A Vision of Market Socialism," *Dissent* (Summer 1991): esp. 412.

33. Cf. Roemer, *A Future for Socialism*, 20: "Socialists should want those property rights that will bring about a society that best promotes equality of opportunity for everyone. One cannot honestly say, at this point in history, that one knows what those property rights must be."

34. See *The Metaphysics of Morals*, 6:324–25/134–35 and *On the Common Saying: "This May Be True in Theory, But It Does Not Apply in Practice,"* 7:296/78.

35. I am indebted here to Leslie A. Mulholland, *Kant's System of Rights* (New York: Columbia University Press, 1990), 275, 294, who offers a fine discussion of Kant's grounding of the right to property.

36. See Estrin, "Workers' Co-operatives: Their Merits and Their Limitations," 171–72.

37. See Dahl, *A Preface to Economic Democracy*, 94–98. Cf. note 27, above.

38. Cf. Schweickart, *Against Capitalism*, 97–98.

39. Cf. Schweickart, *Against Capitalism*, 120–22.

40. Shortening working hours reduces unemployment, and any labor shortages are disadvantageous to capital in terms of increased wages and more difficult to enforce "labor discipline." Lengthening working hours is advantageous because, among other reasons, it reduces the total company costs of fringe benefits. For a fuller discussion, see Juliet B. Schor, *The Overworked American: The Unexpected Decline of Leisure* (New York: Basic Books, 1991), chap. 3, who also shows that Americans (more than West Europeans) have suffered from lack of leisure time. Workers in democratic enterprises are free to opt for less income and more leisure time for the sake of a more fulfilling life.

41. Cf. Dahl, *A Preface to Economic Democracy*, 100.

42. See also my "Cohen, Collective Responsibility, and Economic Democracy," *Il Cannocchiale: Rivista di Studi Filosofici* (1991): 345–60, esp. 355–56, 359–60. Published by Edizioni Scientifiche Italiane, Naples.

43. That the good economy needs various kinds of productive units is also argued by Alec Nove, *The Economics of Feasible Socialism Revisited* (London:

HarperCollins, 1983, 1991). Nove offers the valuable guideline that we must balance a diversity of preferences of workers concerning how to organize their labor and production with the interests and needs of consumers (see pp. 211–12), but I worry that he places too much emphasis on the category of state-controlled and state-owned firms.

12

Gerald F. Gaus

Respect for Persons and Environmental Values

I. THE "INVIDIOUS HUMANISM" OF KANTIAN LIBERALISM?

One, perhaps dominant, strand in contemporary liberal moral and political theory draws inspiration from Kant.[1] According to this "deontological" or "Kantian liberalism," "society, being composed of a plurality of persons, each with his own aims, interests, and conceptions of the good, is best arranged when it is governed by principles that do not *themselves* presuppose any particular conception of the good."[2] Because, on this view, each is an autonomous chooser of his own ends in life, respect for the person and autonomy of another demands that we refrain from imposing our view of the good life on him. Only principles that can be justified to all respect the personhood of each.

Individual freedom, economic justice, racial and sexual discrimination, civil disobedience, rights to privacy—on these issues, the Kantian liberal's commitment to respecting persons and their visions of the good life leads to (what are, at least to many) reasonable and attractive prescriptions.[3] But when it comes to the treatment of animals and, especially, the nonsentient environment, Kantian liberalism—like Kant's theory itself—strikes many as inadequate. Christina Hoff, for one, believes that there is a "seamier side" to "Kant's ethical humanism." If ethics is exclusively about what is required for moral persons to respect themselves and each other, we cannot owe duties *to* plants and animals. The result, she says, is that Kant's "invidious humanism" "altogether excludes animals from the moral domain."[4] Kantian ethics would thus seem to be the exemplar of what Richard and Val Routley call "person chauvinism":

> It would be *bad*, to say the least, if Western ethics, in its various strands, were to turn out to rest on human, or person, chauvinism. For Western ethics would then have no better foundation than, and open to the same sorts of objections as, moral codes based on other sorts of chauvinism, e.g. on familial, national, sexual, racial or socio-class chauvinism-in particular it would be open to the objection that it discriminated against nonhumans in a prejudicial and unwarranted way, and would thereby stand condemned.[5]

Is, then, Kantian liberalism's basic principle of respect for persons (and their differing values) hostile to the inclusion of environmental values in the moral realm? Answering this question turns out to be surprisingly complex. Section II examines a basic and widely embraced Kantian liberal argument. We shall see that, indeed, such a Kantianism puts supreme value on agency and project pursuit, and this makes it well-nigh impossible to adequately protect environmental values. Section III, however, argues that much contemporary Kantian liberalism goes astray because it misconstrues the nature of personhood and autonomy; I shall defend an alternative understanding that I believe is truer to Kant's own conception. Section IV then shows how this reformulated Kantian liberalism can take environmental values seriously. Nevertheless, section V acknowledges that this proposal will not satisfy the demands of many environmental philosophers. We shall see that the fundamental commitments of Kantian liberalism preclude its being considered an environmental ethic.

II. KANTIAN LIBERALISM 1:
RESPECT FOR PROJECT PURSUERS

A Basic Kantian Liberal Argument

Bernard Williams provides an excellent sketch of a basic, and I think popular, sort of Kantian liberal argument.[6] The point of departure is that persons are rational agents, and this in itself implies that they have certain desires. "Is there anything that rational agents necessarily want? That is to say, is there anything they want (or would want if they thought hard enough about it) merely as a part or precondition of being agents?"[7] Well, as an agent one necessarily *acts*: action, as distinguished from some mere piece of behavior such as a sneeze, is purposive. One seeks to bring about a result that one views as good or desirable. On this view, then, the rational agent is necessarily a pursuer of valued goals and ends. Consequently, because one values these goals one also disvalues interferences with action that thwart the pursuit of values. Agents (so the argument runs) thus necessarily view freedom from interference (with their actions) as good. More than this, it is claimed that, because freedom is necessary to one's agency, one must demand of others that they not interfere. One thus claims a right to non-interference; making such a claim on others, one is also bound to acknowledge that they have similar rights against you.[8]

To respect another is, as Stephen L. Darwall says, to give "appropriate consideration or recognition to some feature" of that person in one's deliberations about what to do.[9] Now because, on this view, the crucial feature of a person is her status as agent—as a pursuer of valued ends who demands freedom and other goods necessary to agency—it follows that to respect another is to give appropriate consideration to *this* fact. To respect others is to respect them *qua* agents or project pursuers with attendant interests in freedom and well-being. The projects of an agent, says Stanley Benn,

> are an exteriorization of himself, projections, indeed, of himself into the world; his identity as a person, qualifying for respect not only from others but also from himself, depends on his sense that they are indeed his own, informed by interests which together constitute him an intentional agent with an enduring nature, not simply a stream of experiences, even of remembered or envisaged experiences. . . .
>
> The respect due between persons is anchored, then, in the recognition of one another as subjects of interests in this sense, making on each the same demand for forbearance and consideration that each makes on other project makers. One may believe the other's project quite worthless in itself. Its claim to respect rests not on its being valuable and worthy of one's concern, or even on one's interest or benevolent concern for its author but simply on its being a person's project.[10]

"Thus," concludes Jeffrey Reiman, "it is rationally required that we each limit our actions at that point at which all can pursue their sovereign interests to the maximum compatible with the same for everyone. We recognize the truth of the *moral imperative of respect*."[11]

Now since these Kantian liberals conceive of persons as project pursuers, they are apt to think of *autonomous* persons as particular sorts of project pursuers. To be sure, contemporary liberals typically begin with the observation that "autonomous" derives from the Greek words for "self" and "rule" or "law." But, though they speak of a *nomos* of which one is the author, what they have in mind is a *life* of which one is, in some sense, the author. "The fundamental idea in autonomy is that of authoring one's own world without being subject to the will of others."[12] An autonomous person employs her critical faculties to evaluate her aims and projects in such a way that they are truly hers, rather than simply imposed by, or unreflectively taken over from, others. "What makes an individual the particular person he is," writes a well-known liberal philosopher of autonomy, "is his life plan, his projects. In pursuing autonomy, one shapes one's life, one constructs its meaning. The autonomous person gives meaning to his life."[13] Autonomy then is an excellence that project pursuers can achieve; as such, autonomous agents are worthy of our esteem.[14] Autonomous agents thus are to be respected and promoted.[15]

The Greening of Kantian Liberalism

Such an ethic is not particularly friendly to the protection of environmental values. The crucial moral category is that of agency *qua* project pursuit: if respect for such agents is the root of all morality, it would seem that moral duties can only be owed to project pursuers. Moreover, to the extent that Kantian liberals do embrace teleological, value-promoting considerations, the supreme value—autonomy—is an excellence of project pursuit. If one is not an agent pursuing projects, one seems excluded from the moral realm. Nevertheless, at least two paths from Kantian liberalism to environmental ethics have been attempted.

Environmental Degradation and Respect for Agents

Pretty obviously, the welfare of agents, and their ability to achieve the excellence of autonomy, are setback by a wide variety of environmental degradations. Pollution is the most obvious case. If, as Kantian liberals insist, damaging your neighbor's body or health manifests disrespect, then so does health-endangering pollution of the biosphere. As John Passmore stresses, "there is no moral innovation in the view that one ought to pay for damages to one's neighbour; all that is new is the wider application of the ideas both of 'damage' and of 'neighbour'."[16] The importance of this should not be belittled: many of the environmental issues of widest concern today (e.g., global warming) are those that are detrimental to agents in precisely this way. And the Kantian liberal can go further: not only restrictions on pollution, but policies to conserve the environment for future generations, are defensible. If we are to respect future generations, we must not hand on to them a depleted and ravaged world.[17]

Nonetheless, this route is not apt to satisfy environmentalists. Ultimately, this approach can only protect animals, plants, or species by showing that they are resources for agents—instruments for agents that must be preserved for the sake of the projects and plans of those agents. But, insist environmental philosophers such as Holmes Rolston III, environmental ethics is *not* to be understood as

> an ethics of resource use; nor one of benefits, costs, and their just distribution; nor one of risks, pollution levels, rights and torts, needs of future generations, and the rest—although these figure large within it. Taken alone, such issues enter an ethic where the environment is *secondary* to human interests. The environment is instrumental and auxiliary, though fundamental and necessary. Environmental ethics in the *primary*, naturalistic sense is reached only when humans ask questions not merely of prudential use but of appropriate respect and duty.[18]

Rolston and other environmentalists seek an ethic according to which the environment is intrinsically valuable—valuable in itself—and so not to be valued simply an instrument for successful project pursuit. And it seems that this is impossible for Kantian liberalism.[19]

Stretching the Concept of Agency

If Kantian liberalism restricts moral citizenship to agents, the obvious tack for environmentally minded Kantians to take is to stretch the notion of an agent so as to include many nonhuman life forms. I do not have in mind the view—subscribed to by Stanley Benn—that some nonhuman animals such as dolphins may satisfy all the normal criteria for agency or personhood.[20] Rather, the argument being considered here revises the concept of "agency" so that it becomes widely applicable to the nonhuman world. It has been maintained, for example, that a human agent demands noninterference and respect because she seeks to achieve her good. But, if so, then the critical feature for agency is pursuit of one's good. Human agents pursue what they value, believe to be good, etc. Now other creatures, it is said, also pursue their own good, although, unlike humans, they may not self-consciously do so. But they too require noninterference and respect if they are to achieve their good—though, of course, they cannot demand them as their due.

Thus Thomas Scanlon believes that morality includes beings with a good, who possess a point of view that is sufficiently akin to ours for us to grasp their good, and compare it to our own, that is, human, perspective. As Scanlon sees it, this excludes tomato plants, forests, and ant colonies, but includes all beings that can feel pain.[21]

Paul Taylor would extend the moral community much further. Taylor distinguishes between human ethics (ethical relations among humans) and environmental ethics (ethical relations between humans and nature). The former embraces the basic Kantian liberal understanding of morality as based on respect for persons understood as autonomous pursuers of their own unique value-systems.[22] Environmental ethics, he argues, is structurally similar, being based on a principle of respect for nature. Each individual organism, he maintains, is

> a teleological (goal-oriented) center of life, striving to preserve itself and realize its good in its own unique way. To say it is a teleological center of life is to say that its internal functioning as well as its external activities are all goal-oriented, having the constant tendency to maintain the organism's existence through time and to enable it successfully to perform those biological operations whereby it reproduces its kind and continually adapts to changing environmental events and conditions.[23]

All animals and plants, Taylor believes, have a good of their own, because they can be benefited or harmed. Consequently, they are owed respect, which implies human duties of nonmaleficence, noninterference, and fidelity.[24]

Why Respect the Good of Others?

Taylor's ambitious extension of respect-based ethics raises to the fore a question never properly answered in our basic Kantian liberal argument. Why does the fact (if it is one) that plants (or, indeed, other people) have goods necessarily matter to us? That Alf has a good is apt to matter to Alf (though, quite sensibly, we can say that Alf ignores what is good for him and does something else). But it is unclear why this fact about Alf—that he cares for his good—should lead him to act respectfully toward Betty, much less toward trees.[25] Three rather different arguments may be appealed to at this juncture.

First, it might be suggested that because Alf wants to pursue his good, he wants non-interference, and he gets this from Betty by agreeing not to interfere with her. Now this is certainly *an* argument from project pursuit to mutual restraint, but it is more Hobbesian than

Kantian: agents reach a modus vivendi.[26] And if this is indeed the crucial argument, it promises little for animals, and even less for the environment: it is pointless to try to reach an agreement for mutual restraint with such entities.[27] To be sure, one might conceive of environmentalism as based on a sort of modus vivendi between humans and nature: for the sake of our own continued survival, humans consent to a sort of contract with nature, ensuring the continued survival of both parties. But surely in this context the idea of a contract is simply metaphorical: no contract *with* nature is possible, for *nature* cannot be the subject of duties. Stripped of its metaphorical trappings, this sounds very much like a nature-as-resource argument: in order to secure the continued welfare of humans, the prudent course of action is to conserve and protect nature.

A second strategy is to argue that we should respect other agents because they are valuable and capable of autonomy. But value is a precarious foundation for equal respect, for agents differ in their valuable features. Certainly they differ in their autonomy. To base respect on value, but to equally respect what is of less and what is of greater value is, on the face of it, inappropriate.[28] Indeed, it seems unjust, for those who have achieved greater value deserve greater respect. And if, as in Kantian liberal theory, the ultimate aim is to ground equal basic rights on respect for persons, claims to differential respect threaten to undermine the entire theory.[29] Those employing this argument are thus driven to dubious assertions that either in some sense all agents are equally valuable, or that above a certain threshold, differences in autonomy, and so on are somehow irrelevant to how much respect is due an agent.[30] Whatever plausibility such assertions might have when applied to the worth of human agents evaporates when extended to animals and the environment. Taylor has been widely (and rightly) criticized for his claim that all living beings have equal inherent worth—and so "we are left with the conclusion that the claim to human superiority [e.g., over plants] as regards inherent worth is a widely accepted but totally unfounded dogma of our culture."[31] A theory driven to the claim that Einstein or Gandhi has the same inherent worth as a dandelion or a microbe is, to understate the point, somewhat counterintuitive.

Lastly, and most Kantian, it might be insisted that Alf, wanting others to refrain from interfering with his actions, is committed to prescribing a universal rule that no one is to interfere with the actions of another. Williams observes:

> What the argument claims is that I must either give them [i.e. others] the right to interfere with my freedom or withhold that right from

them. The argument insists, in effect, that if I am to be consistent, I must make a rule to the effect that others should not interfere with my freedom, and nothing less than this rule will do. But the rule, of course, just because it is a general rule, will equally require me not to interfere with their freedom.

But why must I prescribe any rule? If I am in the business of making rules, then clearly I will not make one enjoining others to interfere with my freedom, nor will I make one permitting them to do so. But there is another possibility: I do not regard myself as being in this business, and I make no rule either way. I do not have to be taken as giving permission. . . . As the egoist Max Stirner put it: "The tiger that assails me is in the right, and I who strike him down am also in the right. I defend against him not my *right*, but *myself*."[32]

Why (as Taylor recommends) should we treat animals as we now do persons rather than (as Stirner recommends) treat persons as we now do animals? What needs to be explained—and what our basic Kantian liberal argument leaves mysterious—is why the latter option is closed to us.

III. KANTIAN LIBERALISM 2:
RESPECT FOR MORAL PERSONS

Rational Agency

Let us return to the starting point of our basic Kantian liberal argument: an agent, it was said, necessarily *acts*: action, as distinguished from a mere piece of behavior such as a sneeze, is purposive. Contemporary Kantian liberalism—at least the version we have thus far been considering—understands this as a supposition that persons are pursuers of goals (conceptions of the good, values, projects, etc.) and so desire freedom. It is here, right at the outset, that the basic Kantian liberal argument takes a misstep by (mis)understanding the essential purposiveness of action as teleological. Not all action seeks, in any significant sense, to achieve goals.[33] To give just one well-known example, public choice theorists have repeatedly demonstrated that voting in elections is an irrational means to achieve political goals; the probability that one's vote will matter is "vanishingly small," rendering any possible payoff (in terms of goal achievement) "also minute."[34] And because so many social theorists embrace the goal-oriented characterization of rational agency, they conclude that voting must be irrational. But there is another obvious possibility: although voting does not achieve one's political goals, one still has reason to vote as, say, an expression of one's political allegiance. Action is necessarily purposive not in the sense that it is inherently goal-directed, but because it is intentional, that is, it is undertaken for reasons.[35] To be sure, an agent is not always conscious of his reasons; indeed, he may be unable to fully explicate them when asked.[36] Nevertheless, if we wish to explain and understand an action, we must consider the beliefs, values, and so on of the agent, and how they provide him with certain sorts of reasons to act. To be sure, it always can be said that an agent has the goal of acting this way rather than that, but by "goal" here all we mean is that one intends to act—one acts for reasons. Depicting this as acting to achieve a goal suggests that one is acting for a particular sort of reason—that is, a teleological one.

Suppose we know that entity α did something, Φ. I shall say that, if Φ-ing is to be understood as an action, the explanation must maintain that Φ was caused by α's beliefs and the associated reasons for action.[37] If the explanation assigns no causal role to α's beliefs, then Φ is not an action. Consider some possible values for α and Φ:

α	Φ
(1) the car's engine	stalled in traffic
(2) the tree	shed its leaves
(3) the bacteria	attacked the body
(4) the mosquito	bit Alf
(5) the dog	knocked its empty food bowl
(6) Betty	deconstructed Kant's *Groundwork*

It would be a rare explanation of (1)–(4) that would refer to the beliefs and reasons of the α in the explanation of Φ.[38] Some, I suppose, might be tempted to talk of the mosquito's belief that she could get a nice meal from Alf's arm, but it is hard to take this too seriously. In contrast, it does not seem at all far-fetched to explain the dog's knocking its bowl in terms of its desire to eat, and it's belief that if it knocks the bowl loudly enough food will be forthcoming. Of course, this can be disputed: an advocate of operant conditioning may explain the dog's behavior in an entirely different way, such that it is not understood as an action. Of course behaviorists are tempted to do that for (6) too, but most of us are fairly certain that the proper (causal) account of this requires reference to Betty's beliefs and values.

Private and Public Reasoners

That dogs meet one condition for agency does not imply they are agents; philosophers typically specify other conditions which serve to restrict agency to (a subset) of the class of humans, and perhaps a few of the higher mammals.[39] And in this they are, I think, right. However, for my present purposes I shall characterize agency extremely broadly: very roughly, let us say that something is an agent if its behavior can typically be explained as intentional.[40] Now we might distinguish two sorts of agents. The first type acts exclusively on its own beliefs, values, emotions and desires. If dogs are agents, they are of this sort. A dog is exclusively devoted to satisfying its own desires and appetites. This is not to say that it never desires to please others—for example, its master—but that, too, is a desire of its own. We might say that agents of this sort are fully embedded in their own perspective: all their actions flow from the way the world seems to them. I shall call these purely *private reasoners*.[41]

Now, prima facie, it would seem that all agents are purely private in this way. On what other basis can one act except on one's own beliefs, values, and so forth? And in one sense this is true: one cannot entirely transcend one's own viewpoint. However, some agents have three capacities absent in our purely private reasoners: (1) they are able to consider the viewpoint of others, and understand what reasons those others have; (2) they are able to reason with others from a common standpoint that provides everyone with reasons; and (3) they are able to act on the basis of this standpoint. This involves what Kant called the "public use of reason"; it requires that we "think from the standpoint of everyone else."[42] The crucial feature of moral persons, as opposed to purely private agents, is that they can employ public reason by searching for a common standpoint, and once finding this perspective, act on it.

Considerable evidence suggests that normal humans develop into public reasoners, though the degrees to which they develop this capacity vary.[43] The first logical step in becoming such a reasoner is awareness that one's own reasons are not definitive for everyone: they have their own reasons that may well be very different from yours.[44] One recognizes, in essence, that practical reason is personal and differentiated.[45] But such recognition alone does not make for a public reasoner; it seems that a psychopath can recognize such differentiatedness, but this only leads him to employ his private reason strategically, taking account of the different reasons upon which others act in order to better get what he wants.[46] Public reasoners can reason with others, in the sense that they can arrive at reasons that are shared—they are reasons verified from a common standpoint. And this is no mere theoretical capacity; public reasoners can act on the basis of reasons identified from this public perspective.

Respect for Moral Persons as Public Reasoners

To respect others as moral persons is, in essence, to treat them appropriately given their status as public reasoners: that is, on the basis of reasons they can embrace.[47] To respect others is, then, to adopt a public standpoint when making demands and in other dealings with them: we employ considerations that are accessible to other moral persons and provide them with genuine reasons to act. In contrast, one who acts solely on her private reason in dealings with others treats them as mere instruments for, or obstacles to, the successful completion of her projects: she does not confront them as moral persons who are reasoned *with*.

Why should I treat a moral person in this way, rather than just acting on my private reason in my dealings with her? As Stirner asks, why not treat a moral person as if she were a tiger? This "why should I be moral?" question, often asked by philosophers, assumes that somehow the default option is to ignore public reason, and we need to be *argued into* treating others and ourselves as public reasoners. This, I think, is to get things precisely backwards. Understanding ourselves and others as public reasoners is so deeply woven into our understanding of ourselves and the social world that it is almost impossible to imagine being argued *out of it*. When I trust my friend, argue with my parent (or my child), am indignant at being mistreated by a stranger or resentful[48] when my colleagues take advantage of me by having me teach all the large lectures, I suppose all the time that they are able to see things from my point of view, and exhibit a fault if they simply ignore my view and act solely on their own reasons. In all these relations I routinely suppose that they have a reasons to Φ, which does not translate into simply (*a*) I can predict that they will Φ or (*b*) Φ-ing is entailed by their desires, concerns, projects or values or (*c*) I can coerce them into Φ-ing. These may all be true of my dog: I can predict that my dog will sit for a treat, that it desires to sit for a treat, or that it can be coerced into sitting. But, besides all this, we suppose that other moral persons can act on publicly justified principles. Indeed, it is most difficult to imagine a social life thoroughly purged of this conception of others. Such a world would be populated by agents relying only on their private reason, unable to ascend to a public point of view. Hobbes's state of nature is one approximation to this intensely private world. Indeed, that each individual relies only on her own private judgment is at the root of the conflict in the state of nature.[49] To employ a metaphor of Kant's, among such purely private reasoners disagreements about what is to be done could result in (intellectual or physical) struggles or battles, but there could be no debate, no appeal to the public tribunal of reason.[50] Social life would be reduced to a series of strategic interactions, again, in a way akin to Hobbes's state of nature.[51]

The Social Contract, Public Reason, and Autonomy

I have been arguing, then, that moral persons are capable of public reason. They are capable of transcending their private concerns by acting on principles that can be justified to all. The public justification of such principles can be usefully understood as a social contract. Kant described the "original contract" as an idea of reason according to which there is "a coalition of the wills of all private individuals in a nation to form a common, public will."[52] Kant, of course, conceived of the social contract as a distinctively political idea, but contemporary Kantians such as Rawls extend the notion of the contract to the moral sphere.[53] The notion of a social contract is an apt way to express the search for a public perspective among individuals, each devoted to different values and goals. Although, as I have argued, it is erroneous to conceive of personhood itself as essentially goal-directed, it is nevertheless true that in our pluralistic culture, individuals are devoted to a dizzying diversity of values, goals, and projects. If these individuals are to respect each other's moral personality, they cannot impose their private judgments on each other. Rather, they must arrive at what Rawls calls a "public conception of justice": principles that everyone embraces and knows that all others embrace.[54] Moreover, the contract metaphor suggests that in a deeply pluralistic society, in which it is unlikely that individuals will converge on any specific values or ways of living, public reason is apt to articulate a compromise; the only terms that everyone can accept are those that reasonably, but not maximally, advance the values of all.[55] Rawls's description of the social contract as "a pact of reconciliation" or the result of a "bargain" is apt.[56] Agents who take their private projects and values seriously, yet are committed to respect for the moral personality of others, are led to a public morality that adequately advances the values of all.[57]

Focusing on public reason points us toward a conception of autonomy very different from that which we explored above. We saw that the often-repeated explication of an "auto-nomos" agent as one imposing a law, a *nomos*, on himself, does not fit well with recent liberal philosophers' stress on a self-created life. But reflect now on an agent who recognizes and acts on the dictates of public reason: such an agent imposes on herself maxims that constrain her private reason. This corresponds to Kant's understanding of an autonomous agent as one who gives universal (i.e., public) laws to which he is subject.[58] Both agents who consult solely their private reason, and those who are ruled by the private reason of others, fail to exercise their autonomy. Thus understood, our capacity for autonomous action simply *is* our ability to embrace public reason; as O'Neill emphasizes, "[a]utonomy does not presuppose but rather constitutes the principles of reason and their authority."[59] Autonomy, then, is not an excellence of agency, it is rather what *constitutes* our moral personality.[60] Thus understood, Kant's claim that the "principle of autonomy . . . is the sole principle of morals" is not only intelligible but true.[61]

IV. ENVIRONMENTAL VALUES AND PUBLIC REASON

The Participants in Public Reason

Now it may seem that, in the end, this account of respect for persons is no more friendly to environmental values than was the agent-as-project-pursuer version. Indeed, it appears more hostile. Although it is pretty implausible to conceive of all life forms as quasi-agents, seeking their good, it is even more outlandish to conceive of them as participants in public reason. I suppose some may imagine what it would be like to reason with kangaroos and gum trees, but it remains relevant that we do not conceive of them as moral persons (because they aren't moral persons), and so nothing in our current way of understanding our world commits us to such thought experiments. In any event, public reason depends on shared concepts and understandings of the world, and these clearly do not obtain between us and the nonhuman inhabitants of earth.[62]

Public reason thus presupposes certain sorts of beings (capable of autonomy) with a certain understandings of the world; nonhuman life cannot participate in this discourse. But Williams is surely right that (*pace* the Routleys) such "speciesism" is not to be understood as an ethical flaw, as are racism and sexism:

> A concern for nonhuman animals is indeed a proper part of human life, but we can acquire it, cultivate it, and teach it only in terms of our understandings of ourselves. Human beings both have that understanding and are the objects of it, and this is one of the basic respects in which our relations to each other must always be different from our relations to other animals. Before one gets to the question of how animals should be treated, there is the fundamental point that this is the only question that there can be: how they should be treated. The choice can only be whether animals benefit from our practices or are harmed by them. This is why speciesism is falsely modeled on racism

and sexism, which really are prejudices. To suppose that there is an ineliminable white or male understanding of the world, and to think that the only choice is whether blacks or women should benefit from "our" (white, male) practices or be harmed by them: this is already to be prejudiced. But in the case of human relations to animals, the analogues to such thoughts are simply incorrect.[63]

Persons and Patients

The attempt to stretch the notion of moral personhood to include large parts of the nonhuman world must, then, be dismissed as confused. However, having better grasped what respect for persons requires, we—unlike those endorsing respect for persons as project pursuers—are not driven to it. According to the Kantian liberal view with which we began (section II), to respect a person was to respect her as a project pursuer; on this view respect for persons translates into granting to others the freedom from interference and other goods requisite for their successful pursuit of projects (and the development of their autonomy *qua* excellence in agency). Such an ethic affords protection only to agents, and (indirectly) the resources for agents' projects. If *that* is how we understand an ethic of respect for persons, then indeed the only way to provide protection for noninstrumental environmental values is to somehow expand the category of agents to include nonhuman life. But I have suggested that this posits much too close a connection between personhood and project pursuit. On the view I have proffered, to respect another as a moral person is to regulate one's relations with her according to a *nomos* reached through public reason. But it is not to be supposed that the only considerations relevant to public reason deal with the conditions for project pursuit. No doubt in a culture such as ours they will be of central importance, but it is surely too strong to suppose that the agenda for public reasoning is restricted to this single item.

Many moral persons value the environment, not merely instrumentally, but intrinsically—simply for itself. Consider the value of a species, such as one of the snail darters.[64] Now there are indeed instrumental arguments for preserving such species, including a general concern to preserve genetic diversity as a resource for future scientific and economic innovations.[65] Nevertheless, many who are committed to the preservation of snail darters do not value them as in any way useful to humans, but simply because they are perceived as valuable in themselves. And by this I do not mean that they think snail darters are valuable because they take pleasure in contemplating them (although that too would be a source of value); rather, I mean that they esteem snail darters because of their worthy characteristics.[66] Now such people insist that the preservation of environmental values should be on the public agenda. That is, they will insist that the social contract, specifying public principles that all can embrace, must take account of the value of species. If the social contract ignores environmental values, these moral persons can reasonably object that they do not have adequate reason to comply with it. In this case, the principles regulating social life are not ones they can autonomously adopt (they are private reasons masquerading as public reason); as such, these principles would fail to respect the moral personality of these environmentally minded persons.

The crucial point, then, is that the social contract specified by public reason is not to be restricted to the way persons can affect each other's agency. If all the parties to the social contract cared only about their own agency, then reasoning with each other—providing each other with reasons to accept the contract—would indeed be restricted to considerations that relate to what promotes agency. But people's concerns are much wider: many care about the environment as well as their own agency. Consequently, when reasoning with environmentalists, their deep valuing of the environment cannot be disregarded. Consequently, how moral persons are to treat nonpersons becomes a matter for public reason.[67]

Liberal Pluralism and Environmental Values

Alf, an environmentalist, may thus insist that the moral principles reached through public reason protect endangered species. The protection of these species is, he believes, valuable in itself. So far, so good. But now he confronts Betty, another member of his community, who sees little or no value in the preservation of snail darters. What are they to do? Hopefully, their first response is to reason *with* each other. Alf will seek to show Betty the value of preserving the species. But while we can expect some success here, often enough our attempt to show others the appeal of an intrinsic value—be it in music, art, food, films, or whatever—comes to naught.[68] Suppose Betty simply fails to see the point in halting a major hydroelectric project so that some hitherto unnoticed species of fish can survive. What is Alf now to do?

The environmentalist, I think, is apt to insist that the snail darter simply *is* objectively intrinsically valuable. And, as Rolston says, "Value generates duty."[69] If, then, snail darters are intrinsically valuable, we all have a duty to protect them, and anyone who fails to recognize this duty must be flawed. In the end, I suspect the environmentalist would conclude that we should simply go ahead and protect the snail darter, Betty's evaluative blindness notwithstanding. Now if this is indeed the environmentalist's position, it entails the rejection of the basic premise of Kantian liberalism. As we saw at the outset, basic to the Kantian liberal project is that moral principles should not presuppose the validity of any particular conception of what is of value. Kantian liberalism supposes that citizens exhibit lively, rational disagreement about what is of value: indeed, they insist, there simply are no answers to valuational issues that provide all with reasons to act.[70] Consequently, such liberals are committed to the view that treating each with respect requires that no citizen's values be declared intrinsically superior to others.[71]

Thomas E. Hill Jr. advances a somewhat different proposal. Hill suggests that an anti-environmentalist—one who "has no qualms" about destroying the environments when doing so is free of "adverse effects of human beings and animals"[72]—is in some way defective. Although indifference to nature is "not itself a moral vice, it is likely to reflect either ignorance, a self-importance, or lack of self-acceptance which we must overcome to have a proper humility."[73] On Hill's view, one who does not care at all for nature is likely in the grips of self-importance, of measuring "the significance of everything by its relation to oneself and those with whom one identifies."[74] Thus the character of the anti-environmentalist seems flawed; Betty's anti-environmentalism flows from certain deficiencies, which are the root of moral vices. On one interpretation of Hill's argument, he advances the following principle:

> If X is sufficient for Y and necessary for Z, and if Y is morally objectionable, then the presence of Z is morally objectionable.

That is, if some trait X (e.g., self-importance) is sufficient to yield a morally objectionable condition (e.g., one who is deficient in moral awareness) and if X is also necessary for another trait Z (e.g., anti-environmentalism), then the presence of Z is morally objectionable. The moral objectionability works, as it were, backwards from Y to X, then from X to Z. Thus formulated, I think, the principle is plausible; but it is very demanding. It requires that X be sufficient for Y *and* necessary for Z. The are very strong claims, and it seems doubtful that they can be made out in our environmentalist case. To assert that self-importance is sufficient for immorality and necessary for anti-environmentalism seems pretty implausible.

It may seem that a weaker, probabilistic, interpretation of the principle would suffice:

> If X is likely to produce Y and Z is unlikely to occur without X, and if
> Y is morally objectionable, then the presence of Z is morally
> objectionable.

But the principle is now not very compelling. For example, it can plausibly be claimed that self-interest is likely to produce immoral behavior, and that the market is unlikely to occur without self-interested behavior. Does this mean that the market is morally objectionable? Well, suppose that the market is just the place where self-interested behavior is turned to the public benefit; it is the exceptional case where private vices are turned into public virtues. If so, that self-interest is likely to produce immoral behavior would hardly constitute a criticism of the market.

Other formulations of the principle are possible, and I shall not pursue these detailed criticism further. More generally, Hill is explicit that underlying his environmentalism is a substantive idea of human excellence.[75] But it is just such rich ideals of human excellence that Kantian liberals insist cannot be publicly justified. For Hill there really is something defective in a person who looks at Niagara Falls, and whose reaction is "Lots of water falling off a cliff—too bad it is all wasted, and we can't use it for irrigation or something."[76] Not only must this be seen as a defective response but, given the commitment to public reason, its defectiveness must be held to be publicly verified. Kantian liberalism is deeply skeptical of this latter claim: these sorts of evaluative issues are a continuing subjects of reasonable dispute. It seems most unlikely that the relevant environmental values or character ideals can be publicly verified as beyond reasonable dispute.[77]

For the reformulated Kantian liberalism I have sketched here, the environmental values can only be one among others in the public justification of principles. Environmentalists are correct to maintain that the principles arrived at in public reasoning must take account of their values; but so can the valuers of science, ballet, and country and western. In the end, then, even the staunchest valuer of the environment must acknowledge that respecting the personhood of others— providing them with considerations that are reasons for them— requires compromise. Environmental values must be protected, but so must the others. In a liberal society such trade-offs are not simply pragmatically necessary, but are entailed by respect for the personhood of others.[78]

So while environmental values must be taken seriously by a justified morality and a just polity, they do not trump other values such as economic growth, recreation, or artistic values. Just environmental policies will reflect a compromise among these competing values. And, as Passmore notes, this implies that environmentalists will not always have the strongest moral case, even when a species or a wilderness area is seriously threatened.[79]

V. KANTIAN LIBERALISM AND ENVIRONMENTAL ETHICS

I am under no delusion that this proposal will be welcomed by many environmental philosophers. Most environmentalists are convinced that they *really* know what is of value, and they understandably enough reject as outrageous the claim that respect for persons forbids this value being imposed on the blind who fail to appreciate it. (So too does the aesthete often disparage the liberal as a protector of—and probably one of—the Philistines.) "It is at this point," Passmore points out, "that the cry is loudest for a new ethic" that offers environmental objects a moral status in no way derivative of their relations to human beings.[80] Before concluding, let me briefly consider the difference between Kantian liberalism and an environmental ethic of the sort called for by Rolston and others.

Rolston, it will be recalled (section II) insists that a true environmental ethic is not "an ethics of resource use; nor one of benefits, costs, and their just distribution; nor one of risks, pollution levels, rights and torts, needs of future generations, and the rest." It is not, in short, an ethic that provides protection to environmental values as merely instrumental to human interests or welfare. Now our reformulated Kantian liberalism *does* meet this condition for an environmental ethic. Environmental values need not be instrumental to any human interest or need; environmental objects are acknowledged to have value in themselves. But Rolston would hardly be appeased by this.[81] For the view I have been articulating seems to imply that the practical importance of an environmental value derives from some moral person embracing it. If some value V is ignored by all moral persons—if no one embraces it—then it is of no moral importance. Thus, even though the reformulated Kantian liberal account does not assume an instrumental stance towards environmental value, it certainly seems to assign it a *derivative* place.

Yet on any intelligible view of the place of value in morality, there is a fundamental sense in which the moral import of a value always derives from some moral person recognizing it, allowing it to guide his action and standing up for it. Even the most objective of values cannot stand up for itself in moral discourse. Morality is a practice among moral persons—any consideration can only enter into it through them. A value that is in principle unrecognizable by any moral person can be of no practical importance; in this way the moral importance of any value is necessarily derivative of its recognition by persons. Still, it may be said, a theory based on respect for persons renders environmental values derivative in an especially strong sense: in public reason, what is of importance is not, say, that snail darters are valuable, but that *Alf values* snail darters, or recognizes their value. "The relation is," as Rolston points out, "three-place."[82] If Betty recognizes a reason to preserve snail darters, it is because she is committed to respecting the moral personality of Alf. From an "interspecific viewpoint," Rolston charges, such an ethic is "submoral."[83]

We need to distinguish two cases: when Alf can induce others to appreciate the intrinsic value of the snail darter, and when he is unable to do so. In the former case, everyone has a reason to preserve snail darters that has nothing to do with respecting each other: their appreciation of the species provides them with a reason, unmediated by respect for persons. After all, they all value it, and cherishing and preserving are the appropriate responses to valuing something. Here their private reasoning converges. But in the latter case, in which Alf cannot bring others to appreciate the value of snail darters, Kantian liberalism can still provide others with a reason to protect them—as manifestation of their respect for Alf. The crucial difference between environmental ethics and Kantian liberalism thus concerns those cases of disagreement about environmental value. The Kantian liberal insists, first, that respect for persons precludes the environmentalist from imposing his private value judgments on others but, second, it also indicates that a publicly justified morality must take account of the environmentalist's value judgment, even when those values are not shared by others.

VI. CONCLUSION

H. J. McCloskey observes that "[p]ollution, vandalism of nature, and such like, must be of the greatest concern to anyone who believes that he ought to show respect for his fellow man."[84] My aim in this essay has been to show in what ways, and why, this is so. A dominant version of Kantian liberalism, I have argued, has little room for environmental values, except as resources for the projects of agents. But I have suggested that such a view is problematic, and have proposed an alternative formulation. This reformulated view can, I have tried to show, take environmental values seriously, and achieves some of the goals of an environmental ethic. But its commitment to value pluralism, and its insistence that respect for persons precludes the straightforward imposition of environmental values, assures that it will be rejected by the more monistically minded adherents of environmental ethics.

NOTES

I would like to thank Robert Elliot for his help with these matters during my stay as a Visiting Research Fellow in Philosophy at the University of New England, Armidale, NSW. I am also indebted to him and to Holmes Rolston III for their written comments on an earlier version of the paper.

1. This is not to say that contemporary Kantian liberals are always faithful followers of Kant. As John Rawls, the preeminent Kantian liberal, says, "the adjective 'Kantian' expresses analogy and not identity; it means roughly that a doctrine sufficiently resembles Kant's in enough fundamental respects so that it is far closer to his view than to other traditional moral conceptions that are appropriate for use as benchmarks of comparison." "Kantian Constructivism in Moral Theory," *Journal of Philosophy* 77 (September 1980): 517. Not too surprisingly, Kant scholars are often critical of this use of the adjective. See, e.g., Onora O'Neill, *Constructions of Reason* (Cambridge: Cambridge University Press, 1989): esp. chap. 11.

2. Michael Sandel, *Liberalism and the Limits of Justice* (Cambridge: Cambridge University Press, 1982): 1-7.

3. For some applications of Kantian liberalism, see Alan Gewirth, *Human Rights: Essays on Justification and Applications* (Chicago: University of Chicago Press, 1982), part II; Derek L. Phillips, *Toward a Just Social Order* (Princeton, N.J.: Princeton University Press, 1986).

4. Christina Hoff, "Kant's Invidious Humanism," *Environmental Ethics* 5 (Spring 1983): 63, 70. See also Holmes Rolston III, *Environmental Ethics: Duties to and Values in the Natural World* (Philadelphia: Temple University Press, 1988), 338–41.

5. Richard and Val Routley, "Human Chauvinism and Environmental Ethics," in *Environmental Philosophy*, ed. Don Mannison, Michael McRobbie and Richard Routley, Department of Philosophy Monograph Series number 2 (Canberra: Australian National University, Research School of Social Sciences, 1980), 96–97.

6. Bernard Williams, *Ethics and the Limits of Philosophy* (London: Fontana Press/Collins, 1985), 55–64. I follow the outlines of Williams's exposition. Williams's sketch summarizes the main elements of Alan Gewirth's argument in *Reason and Morality* (Chicago: University of Chicago Press, 1978). The sketch also has significant similarities to S. I. Benn's *A Theory of Freedom* (Cambridge: Cambridge University Press, 1988) and Jeffrey Reiman, *Justice and Modern Moral Philosophy* (New Haven, Conn.: Yale University Press, 1990).

7. Williams, *Ethics and the Limits of Philosophy*, 55.

8. This step in the argument—from the claim that one desires non-interference to the claim that one must demand it as a right—is obviously

problematic. See Martin Golding, "From Prudence to Rights: A Critique," in *NOMOS XXII: Human Rights*, ed. J. Roland Pennock and John W. Chapman (New York: New York University Press, 1981) 165–74; R. M. Hare, "Do Agents Have to Be Moralists?" in *Gewirth's Ethical Rationalism*, ed. Edward Regis (Chicago: University of Chicago Press, 1984), 52–58.

9. Stephen L. Darwall, "Two Kinds of Respect," *Ethics* 88 (October 1977): 8:38ff.

10. Benn, *A Theory of Freedom*, 107

11. Jeffrey Reiman, *Justice and Modern Moral Philosophy*, 141–42. Emphasis in original. "Sovereign interests" derive from the desire of an agent to lead the sort of life he wants to lead. Ibid., 49ff.

12. Robert Young, *Personal Autonomy: Beyond Negative and Positive Liberty* (London: Croom-Helm, 1986), 19.

13. Gerald Dworkin, *The Theory and Practice of Autonomy* (Cambridge: Cambridge University Press, 1988), 31. See also Benn, *A Theory of Freedom*, chap. 9.

14. "Autonomy is an excellence . . . to which people can approximate in varying degrees, and the perfection of which is a rarely realized ideal. Persons are admirable according to the degree of autonomy they attain." Benn, *A Theory of Freedom*, 176. Cf. Young: "Autonomy is a virtue which can and should be cultivated by the many, not just the few," *Personal Autonomy*, 19. On the status of autonomy as a value, see also Dworkin, *The Theory and Practice of Autonomy*, chap. 2; Joseph Raz, *The Morality of Freedom* (Oxford: Clarendon Press, 1986), 390–95.

15. This is related to what Darwall ("Two Kinds of Respect") calls "appraisal respect," being based on appreciation of a thing's value or merit. It is an interesting and problematic feature of contemporary liberalism that, starting out with the idea of respect for persons as a deontological constraint on how persons are to be treated, it tends to slide into a teleological doctrine about how to promote a certain sort of valuable personality. On "respect for autonomy" understood as a goal to be achieved, see Richard Lindley, Autonomy (London: Macmillan, 1986), chap. 6; Young, *Personal Autonomy*, chap. 3; Bruce A. Ackerman, *Social Justice in the Liberal State* (New Haven, Conn.: Yale University Press, 1980), 367–69. See also Richard Dagger, "Politics and the Pursuit of Autonomy," in *NOMOS XXVIII: Justification*, ed. J. Roland Pennock and John W. Chapman (New York: New York University Press, 1986), 270–90; Benn, *A Theory of Freedom*, chaps. 9–13.

16. John Passmore, *Man's Responsibility for Nature* (London: Duckworth, 1974), 65.

17. Thus understood, conservation becomes a case of intergenerational justice. Passmore considers the application of John Rawls' Kantian liberalism to this question in ibid., chap. 4.

18. Rolston, *Environmental Ethics*, 1. See also Tom Regan, "The Nature and Possibility of an Environmental Ethic," *Environmental Ethics* 3 (Spring 1981): 19–34.

19. Kant himself insists that nonhuman living beings can only possess instrumental value. See J. Baird Callicott, "Intrinsic Value of Nonhuman Species" in *The Preservation of Species*, ed. Bryan G. Norton (Princeton, N.J.: Princeton University Press, 1986), 138–72, esp. p. 152.

20. S. I. Benn, "Personal Freedom and Environmental Ethics: The Moral Inequality of the Species," in *Equality and Freedom: International Comparative Jurisprudence*, ed. Gray Dorsey (Dobbs Ferry, N.Y.: Oceana, 1977), 2:411.

21. Thomas Scanlon, "Contractualism and Utilitarianism," in *Utilitarianism and Beyond*, ed. Amartya Sen and Bernard Williams (Cambridge: Cambridge University Press, 1982), 113–15. I have criticized Scanlon's proposal in my *Value and Justification: The Foundations of Liberal Theory* (Cambridge: Cambridge University Press, 1990), 367–72.

22. Paul Taylor, *Respect for Nature: A Theory of Environmental Ethics* (Princeton, N.J.: Princeton University Press, 1986), 33–41.

23. Ibid., 121–22. Cf. G. E. Scott, *Moral Personhood* (Albany: State University of New York Press, 1990), 111–16.

24. Taylor, *Respect for Nature*, chap. 4. Taylor defends other duties in addition to those mentioned here.

25. Williams raises this question. *Ethics and the Limits of Philosophy*, 58–59.

26. See here Loren E. Lomasky, *Persons, Rights and the Moral Community* (New York: Oxford University Press, 1987), chap. 4.

27. Mary Midgley criticizes social contract theory on precisely this ground—that morality rests on reciprocity, and so seeks to exclude animals. *Animals and Why They Matter* (Harmondsworth, U.K.: Penguin, 1983), 83ff., 68ff.

28. See Darwall, "Two Kinds of Respect," 45–46.

29. This problem is carefully discussed by A. I. Melden, *Rights and Persons* (Oxford: Basil Blackwell, 1977), 189ff. Cf. Erol E. Harris, "Respect for Persons," in *Ethics and Society*, ed. Richard T. De George (London: Macmillan, 1968), 120–24.

30. For threshold arguments, see Gewirth, *Reason and Morality*, 120ff.; Dworkin, *Theory and Practice of Autonomy*, 31–32. Cf. my *Modern Liberal Theory of Man* (New York: St. Martin's Press, 1983), 187ff.

31. Taylor, *Respect for Nature*, 153. For criticisms and discussions, see Louis G. Lombardi, "Inherent Worth, Respect and Rights," *Environmental Ethics* 5 (Fall 1983): 257–70; Bryan G. Norton's review of *Respect for Nature* in *Environmental Ethics* 9 (Fall 1987): 261–67; Rolston, *Environmental Ethics*, 64ff.

32. Williams, *Ethics and the Limits of Philosophy*, 61–62. Citation in quotation deleted.

33. For an opposing view, see Charles Taylor, *The Explanation of Behaviour* (London: Routledge & Kegan Paul, 1964), chaps. I–II, esp. 27ff. Because most contemporary analytic philosophers embrace Hume's theory that all action involves the satisfaction of desire, they are led to this teleological view of action. I have criticized this Humean theory in S. I. Benn and G. F. Gaus,

"Practical Rationality and Commitment," *American Philosophical Quarterly* 23 (July 1986): 255–66; and my *Value and Justification*, 84–101, 253–61.

34. Geoffrey Brennan and Loren E. Lomasky, "Large Numbers, Small Costs: The Uneasy Foundations of Democratic Rule," in their edited collection, *Politics and Process: New Essays in Democratic Thought* (Cambridge: Cambridge University Press, 1989), 48.

35. See here G. E. M. Anscombe, Intention, 2nd ed. (Ithaca, N.Y.: Cornell University Press, 1976), 9ff.

36. This point is explored by Benn and Gaus, "Practical Rationality and Commitment."

37. This characterization cannot fully defended here, especially the claim that beliefs and reasons can be casual. I have argued for this thesis more fully elsewhere. See Gerald F. Gaus, *Justificatory Liberalism: An Essay on Epistemology and Political Theory* (New York: Oxford University Press, 1996), 17–29. See also Benn and Gaus, "Practical Reason and Commitment"; Gaus, "Practical Reason and Moral Persons," *Ethics* 100 (October 1989): 127–48. See also David A. J. Richards, *A Theory of Reasons for Action* (Oxford: Clarendon Press, 1971), 54–59.

38. Milton Friedman's explanation of the growth of leaves on trees notwithstanding. "The Methodology of Positive Economics," in *Philosophy and Economic Theory*, ed. Frank Hahn and Martin Hollis (Oxford: Oxford University Press, 1979), 30–31.

39. See Scott, *Moral Personhood*, 23ff.

40. This account, I think, can be made consistent with the view that persons are to be viewed as intentional systems; we explain and predict their actions by taking the "intentional stance" toward them. For a useful account, see ibid., esp. chap. 2.

41. To say that they are private reasoners is not to say that they are asocial. See Gaus, *Justificatory Liberalism*, part II.

42. Kant quoted in Onora O'Neill, "The Public Use of Reason," in her *Constructions of Reason*, 46.

43. For a survey, see Lawrence A. Kurdek, "Perspective Taking as the Cognitive Basis of Children's Moral Development: A Review of the Literature," *Merrill-Palmer Quarterly* 24 (January 1978): 3–28. See also Dennis Krebs and Janet Gillmore, "The Relationship among the First Stages of Cognitive Development, Role Taking Abilities, and Moral Development," *Child Development* 53 (1982): 877–86. Lawrence Kohlberg argues that only those at the highest stage of moral development fully assume the viewpoint of others. See his "Justice as Reversibility: The Claim to Moral Adequacy of a Highest Stage of Moral Development," in his edited collection, *Essays on Moral Development*, vol. 1: *The Philosophy of Moral Development* (New York: Harper & Row, 1981), chap. 5.

44. Public reasoners thus overcome what Jean Piaget calls "egocentrism." See, e.g. "The Growth of Logical Thinking from Childhood to Adolescence," in

The Essential Piaget, ed. Howard Gruber and J. Jacques Vonéche (London: Routledge & Kegan Paul, 1977), 405–44.

45. Lomasky, *Persons, Rights and the Moral Community*, 27ff.

46. I consider the essentially private view of the psychopath in some depth in my *Value and Justification*, 292–300.

47. Although much of what Kant says suggests this account, it is clearly not Kant's precise view. Kant maintains that a person occupying a civil post employs his private reason *when performing his duties*, as his considerations are not addressed to the world at large. "What Is Enlightenment?" in *Kant on History*, ed. Lewis White Beck (Indianapolis, Ind.: Bobbs-Merrill, 1963): 5-6. Presumably public servants do not act contrary to respect for persons; it would seem, then, that acting on public reason is not, for Kant, necessary for respecting others. In any case, Kant's characterization of public servants seems dubious: acting on private reason seems impermissible. See S. I. Benn and G. F. Gaus, "The Public and Private: Concepts and Action," in their edited collection, *Public and Private in Social Life* (New York: St. Martin's Press, 1983): 9–10. Underlying Kant's position here may be well be the conviction that submission to such authorities is ungrounded. See O'Neill, "Reason and Politics in the Kantian Enterprise," in *Constructions of Reason*, 16–17.

48. On such "reactive attitudes" and their presuppositions, see Thomas Nagel, *The Possibility of Altruism* (Princeton, N.J.: Princeton University Press, 1979), 84–85; Richards, *A Theory of Reasons for Action*, 250ff.; Charles Fried, *An Anatomy of Values* (Cambridge, Mass.: Harvard University Press, 1970), 56–57; P. F. Strawson, *Freedom and Resentment* (London: Methuen, 1974), chap. 1; Benn, *A Theory of Freedom*, 97ff.; Gaus, *Value and Justification*, 269ff.

49. "Private judgments differ; for them to have moral supremacy is the core of the Hobbesian state of nature." R. E. Ewin, *Liberty, Community and Justice* (Totowa, N.J.: Rowman and Littlefield, 1987), 2; see also his *Virtues and Rights: The Moral Philosophy of Thomas Hobbes* (Boulder, Colo.: Westview Press, 1991). Kant too traces the insecurity of the state of nature to the fact that each acts on his private judgment as to what is right and good. *Metaphysical Elements of Justice*, trans. John Ladd (Indianapolis, Ind.: Bobbs-Merrill, 1965), §44.

50. See O'Neill, "Reason and Politics in the Kantian Enterprise."

51. That much contemporary social theory only conceives of persons as capable of private reason helps explain the popularity of game theoretic approaches to moral relations.

52. Immanuel Kant, "On the Common Saying: 'This May Be True in Theory, But It Does Not Apply in Practice,'" in *Kant's Political Writings*, ed. Hans Reiss (Cambridge: Cambridge University Press, 1970), 79.

53. See John Rawls, *A Theory of Justice* (Cambridge, Mass.: Harvard University Press, 1971), 11.

54. Ibid., 454.

55. Ibid.

56. Rawls, *A Theory of Justice*, 221, 12. But cf. his rejection of the idea that the contract is a mere modus vivendi. "The Idea of an Overlapping Consensus."

57. I have developed this point more fully in "The Commitment to the Common Good," in *On Political Obligation*, ed. Paul Harris (London: Routledge, 1990), 26–64.

58. Immanuel Kant, *Foundations of the Metaphysics of Morals*, trans. Lewis White Beck (Indianapolis, Ind.: Bobbs-Merrill, 1950), section 2. This also suggests that Kant was correct to stress the intimate link between autonomy and the categorical imperative. Cf. Rüdiger Bittner, *What Reason Demands*, trans. Theodore Talbot (Cambridge: Cambridge University Press, 1989), 77ff. *Pace* Thomas Nagel, justified deontic demands do indeed express a person's autonomy. *The View from Nowhere* (New York: Oxford University Press, 1986), 181.

59. O'Neill. "Reason and Autonomy in *Grundlegung* III," in her *Constructions of Reason*, 57.

60. See O'Neill, "Action, Anthropology and Autonomy," in ibid., 66–77.

61. Kant, *Foundations of the Metaphysics of Morals*, 59.

62. Rawls stresses the place of shared methods of inquiry in "The Idea of an Overlapping Consensus." Ewin stress the place of shared concepts in the formation of judgments. *Liberty, Community and Justice*, e.g., chap. 4.

63. Williams, *Ethics and the Limits of Philosophy*, 118–19.

64. There are approximately 130 species of snail darters (a small fish); 45 of these species lived in the Tennessee River, which was to have been effected by the construction of the Tellico Dam. It was argued that the dam threatened the snail darter. See Stephen R. Kellert, "Social and Perceptual Factors in the Preservation of Animal Species," in *The Preservation of Species*, ed. Norton (Princeton, N.J.: Princeton University Press, 1986), 53–54.

65. See Rolston, *Environmental Ethics*, 12–13.

66. I have considered these matters in much more depth in my *Value and Justification*, part I.

67. In this regard Hoff's critique of contemporary Kantian ethics is on the mark: "Despite the prevailing theoretical focus on 'agency' in moral philosophy, the revolutions in morals are to be seen in the expansion of the domain of moral patients." "Kant's Invidious Humanism," 69.

68. It is difficult to read much environmental ethics without being struck by the awe of such writers at the environment; the value of environmental objects is so manifestly obvious to many of these philosophers that one (or, at least I) perceives more than a little exasperation with the need to *argue* for it all.

69. Rolston, *Environmental Ethics*, 41. Benn, I think, would agree. He supplements his principle of respect for persons with a theory of objective value (including environmental value) that provides everyone with reasons to act. See his "Personal Freedom and Environmental Ethics," and *A Theory of Freedom*, chap. 4.

70. This is a slight overstatement; I have argued that some value judgments provide agent-neutral reasons of a sort. *Value and Justification*, chap. 4. For a thoroughly agent- relative account of value and reasons, see Eric Mack, "Moral Individualism: Agent-Relativity and Deontic Restraints," *Social Philosophy & Policy* 7 (Autumn 1989), 81–111.

71. See here Ronald Dworkin, "Liberalism" in his *A Matter of Principle* (Cambridge, Mass.: Harvard University Press 1985), 181–204.

72. Thomas E. Hill Jr., *Autonomy and Self-respect* (Cambridge: Cambridge University Press, 1991), 110n.

73. Ibid., 115.

74. Ibid., 113.

75. The title of his chapter is "Ideals of human excellence and preserving the natural environment."

76. I consider this sort of reaction in some depth in *Value and Justification*, 190ff.

77. See Charles Larmore, "Pluralism and Reasonable Disagreement," *Social Philosophy & Policy* 11 (Winter 1993): 61–79.

78. Passmore considers such conflicts and trade-offs with great sensitivity. *Man's Responsibility for Nature*, esp. chap. 5.

79. Ibid., 110

80. Ibid., 111

81. See Rolston, *Environmental Ethics*, esp. chap. 6.

82. Ibid., 127.

83. Ibid., 137–38.

84. H. J. McCloskey, "Ecological Ethics and Its Justification: A Critical Appraisal," in *Environmental Ethics*, ed. Mannison, McRobbie, and Routley, 67.

13

Susan Feldman

From Occupied Bodies to Pregnant Persons

How Kantian Ethics Should Treat Pregnancy and Abortion

Philosophers have seldom worried much about pregnancy, and Kant is no exception. One likely explanation is that pregnancy is experienced only by women, and women are excluded from the range of the normal: the normal (hu)man is a man; women are at best an exception to the rule. "Man" does not get pregnant.

But, of course, women are a (or the) normal case of humanity, when "normal" is read as statistically frequent, and pregnancy is a normal event in the lives of normal human beings. I suggest we take as a requirement for any adequate moral theory that women be treated as a normal case of humanity, and I adopt this strategy in this paper. Applying this strategy to Kant's moral theory in connection to abortion, we achieve astonishing results: in many cases, abortion is morally defensible, and particularly in the "hard" cases of abortion, procured for reasons of the pregnant woman's life course and plans, that is, abortion for "convenience."

In what follows, treating women as the normal case, I will ask the Kantian question: under what conditions can persons develop their own life courses, regard themselves with respect, recognize their moral agency and autonomy and carry out their duties to themselves if they are likely, several times in their lives, to be pregnant? The answer will be: First, that pregnant women be regarded, not as containers for fetuses but as dignified, free persons engaged in the useful work of growing a baby. Second, the work itself must be voluntary, so that women can choose to terminate the pregnancy when this pregnancy is incompatible with the realization of their carefully chosen goals, connected with the duty of self-improvement. Sometimes, people have strong moral reasons for abortion. For Kantian reasons, it is morally wrong to prohibit abortions.

I will discuss some preliminaries concerning the treatment of bodily states and sexuality in Kant's work, in order to draw out the relevant implications concerning pregnancy. I will then discuss a typical "Kantian" treatment of abortion, focusing on the way it neglects the viewpoint of women as moral agents. Next, I develop a Kantian framework, which treats women as normal, to frame the significant moral issues about abortion. Finally, I will discuss the prohibition against homicide as it relates to the fetus.

I

A striking feature of the ethics literature about pregnancy and abortion is the mystified treatment of pregnancy. Is it a disease? A disability? A host-parasite relationship? A containment? Writers stretch to find examples that will illuminate the true nature of pregnancy. What categories does it best fit? What is pregnancy most like?

But this reasoning is perverse. An experience as common, as all pervasive, as "natural" as pregnancy can be seen as a hard-to-describe, peculiar condition only if the experiences of women are not taken to be stereotypical human experiences. But they are, and should be so taken. A commonplace experience like pregnancy must be understood in its own terms. We should try to liken a lesser-known phenomenon to a well-known one, not vice versa, and it is pregnancies, not host-parasite relationships, that are commonplace. Few human experiences are as widespread and well known as pregnancy. Other conditions may, indeed, be relevantly similar in some respects to pregnancy, and to the extent that they are, the analogy to pregnancy can help illuminate them. Thus, the consideration of pregnancy and all that follows it should be an unexceptional part of a social and moral account of human life, instead of being relegated to a footnote.

Thinking of pregnancy as a normal life experience changes the focus of the abortion issue. Instead of casting it as a competition between rights held by fetuses and "mothers," we should now think in terms of the way in which pregnancies can be parts of the lives of self-respecting, dignified moral agents. Here, Immanuel Kant's moral theory, specifically the theory of the dignity of persons and the respect owed them, the prohibition against treating persons as mere means, and the duty of self-perfection will provide surprising insights. This last will come as a shock to anyone familiar with the abortion literature. To use "Kant" and "abortion" in the same sentence nearly always yields the response: "not morally permissible." Probably this is explained by the assumption that abortion can only be justified by the sort of consequentialist reasoning ruled out by Kantian moral theory.

From at least one remark, we can guess that Kant would have automatically prohibited abortion.[1] My claim, however, is that even if Kant did not morally approve of abortion, he could have, and should have. I will use Kantian texts to show that had they been written as if women were the normal case of humanity, Kant would have found some abortions morally permissible. Further, a concern with the development of the moral agent as aware of her agency leads to the conclusion that prohibiting abortions is wrong.

Kant of course did not directly address these issues at all. But he did discuss other bodily processes: eating, drinking, and sex. Because of his apparent hostility to bodily functions in his repeated contrasts between the merely animal and the truly human, his treatment of the body might seem to be a problem for a woman-centered view that takes pregnancy seriously.[2] Two options are available to us. One approach is to reject this separation between the merely animal and bodily, and the truly human, and reembrace the animal and bodily. This tack is taken by numerous feminist philosophers, and its rationale involves the observation that the body is usually identified with the female (just as humanity with its characteristic rationality is male), and that the denial of the body is part of the rejection of the female, which is a requisite move in, as well as a product of, men's domination of women.

However, another move suggests itself. To stay true to Kant, the separation between "mere animality" and "humanity," a contrast he frequently draws, cannot be easily dismissed. And there is no obvious reason to assert that female bodies are more animal than male bodies, and that female persons are more embodied than male persons, or indeed, have a more problematic connection with their bodies than male persons. True, females have been identified more with the animal, but this is part of the history of degradation and subordination of women. To therefore reidentify the female person with the female body, and that with the animal, in fact repeats the misogynist identifications of the past. Instead, we can see that both the male and female human being pose the same problem to a Kantian, which is: How is a moral life of the embodied person possible?

A look at Kant's discussion of the bodily vices of lust, gluttony, drunkenness in the DV shows that it is not the bodily functions of eating, sexuality, and drinking as such that are morally problematic. Instead, it is the use of oneself, including one's body, as a thing or vehicle for pleasure, reducing oneself (for example, in the case of gluttony) to bovine stupor, which is objectionable. Bodily activities as such are morally neutral, and are permissible when they are consistent with one's status as human being, and impermissible when they change the functioning of a person to that of an animal (DV 427, pp. 222–23). In this context then, we can turn to his treatment of sex.

Kant's treatment of sex is, for the modern reader, strange. For Kant, sex involves the impermissible use of the body for pleasure, unless a lifelong right is established through marriage (DR 277–78, p. 96). Here Kant's reasoning is obscure if not confused. It seems that procreation, while a natural end of sexual activity, need not be the actual point of any given act. "It is not requisite for human beings who marry to make this (procreation) their end in order for their union to be compatible with rights, for otherwise marriage would be dissolved when procreation ceases" (DR 277, p. 96). Erotic pleasure involves treating oneself and the other as a thing. This objectification is permissible, but only when one's partner also objectifies and is objectified in turn, and when this mutual objectification is redeemed morally by marriage. Within marriage, the act of sex for the purpose of pleasure is per-missible, because the objectification it involves is mitigated by the institution of marriage, which confers upon each partner full rights to the other's person. So it is neither the sex nor the pleasure that is degrading in itself. As Barbara Herman notes, what troubles Kant is the objectification that he sees as inherent in sexual relations.[3]

Kant's discussion of sex seems to miss the mark concerning objectification. Surely, objectification of oneself and the other is not a necessary part of a sexual encounter. While I do not propose here to provide an account of sex, I suggest we take up Pamela Foa's proposal of "sex between friends" as a model of morally sound sex between mutually respecting and self-respecting moral agents.[4] If we do so, I see no reason why sex between friendly partners involves any violation of respect owed to self or other (any more than conversation, or a game of tennis does).

Thus, for Kant bodily activities are degrading and morally impermissible only when they treat one's self, or another, as a mere vehicle, for pleasure, or for pleasing or serving another—that is to say, only if they involve the morally impermissible objectification of a person, or reduce the person to an animal-like state. Pregnancy as a bodily state would be problematic if or when it objectifies or reduces to animal status the person who is pregnant. Can this be avoided? That is, is pregnancy compatible with the respect owed to persons? How do we think of, and treat, a moral agent who is growing an embryo into a baby?

II

Contrast these questions arising in the context of treating women as the normal case with the usual way of raising the abortion question in Kantian terms. For example, consider R. M. Hare's self described "Kantian" argument about abortion.[5] Kant's moral philosophy is reduced to a universalizability test, and it is assumed that (most) abortion fails this. Since each of us is a former, unaborted fetus, Hare argues, and since each of us (presumably) is glad our mothers had not aborted us, abortion fails the universalizability test, so that, as a general principle with some exceptions, abortions should not be performed.

There are problems this argument. First, there is the general danger of thinking backwards. It is true that each living person is a former fetus. But each of us is also the improbable product of a series of causal chains marked by happenstance, absurdities, and historical abominations. Many people are alive today because their parents survived Nazi death camps, having lost their families. These survivors married and started new families, but none of this ever would have happened if their first families were not murdered. Other people are alive today because slavery brought their ancestors to these shores, and slave masters raped and impregnated their great great grandmothers.[6]

Each of us probably has such tragedies in our ancestries. Most of us are glad to be alive. But our inability to will our own nonexistence, all things considered, is very different from an ability to will, as a universal law of nature, that a woman be enslaved and raped, in order that she have specific children and grandchildren (i.e., us). Applied to Hare's example, that we are happy to be alive is compatible with our willing that history had been different and that the tragedies and exploitations leading to our births had never happened, even though that would mean we would have never existed. Remember what Hare forgets: Not only are all of us former fetuses, we are also (presuming women to be the normal case) potentially unwillingly pregnant. These reflections make it even more difficult to imagine how such maxim of involuntary pregnancy could become a law for a kingdom of ends.

Second, we must also remember that when we are morally assessing actions, we are dealing with their maxims—the subjective principle of an act, which highlights the agent's reasons and desires

(DV 421). Thus, for example, Kant's famous prohibition of suicide is actually a prohibition of suicide based on self love (supposing of course that this would be the typical case) (DV 422). Abortions too, have different maxims, or reasons. Hare, unfortunately, but typically, fails to explore the reasons women have for aborting pregnancies.

In the Kantian context, the reasons women have for aborting a pregnancy are crucial. Being an agent involves making reasoned choices about one's actions. Yet it is understandable that Hare and others ignore this, given that we typically think of pregnancy as something a woman undergoes or suffers as patient, not agent. She is a passive object of the state of pregnancy (like a person with a cancerous tumor).[7] Or again, she is the vessel for the fetus, or the "flowerpot" in which the seed grows.[8] I conjecture that passive metaphors for pregnancy are pervasive because of the social views and treatment of women, and not because of the facts of reproductive biology. First, there is the assumption that women are not true moral agents—not the normal person. Second, historically, becoming pregnant and avoiding pregnancy have been hard for women to control, and not just for biological reasons, although these play a role as well. Many people try repeatedly to become pregnant and cannot. Many try to avoid pregnancy but fail. Birth control often does not work, even when it is available. Women's subordinate social position plays a role here. In order to raise the chances of contraceptive success, women's male sexual partners must cooperate, but often they refuse, and women have too often lacked the power to compel men to refrain from having sex with them. To compound matters, to the extent that passivity is incorporated into the norms of acting and the ways in which women frame their lives, pregnancy (along with unwanted sex) becomes that much harder to control.

Recognizing women's agency in pregnancy is both conceptually and morally appropriate. It avoids treating women merely as a "flowerpot" or occupied body during pregnancy and emphasizes women's activity and volition in pregnancy (and not just in becoming pregnant). Instead of thinking of women as the flowerpot in which new humans grow, pregnant women can justifiably be thought of as the gardener growing the new crop (if we must think of pregnancy as anything other than itself). Emphasizing activity and agency in pregnancy leads to consideration of women's will or choice, and her reasons for her choices. Moral agents choose which activities to perform and which to decline. To be an agent is to make choices, and to have reasons for these choices.

This last will strike some as unpersuasive concerning abortion. "A woman has a choice," they might say, "to engage in sex, but once she does, and a pregnancy results, she shouldn't be permitted to back out of the consequence of her chosen activity. Thus, having the choice whether or not to have sex is sufficient to make any pregnancy that results the result of that choice, hence voluntary."

This objection rests on the general principle: If S chooses to engage in A, and C is a possible consequence of A, then A has chosen C as well. (We could add clauses that S is aware (or should be) that C is a consequence of A, and that C is a likely, not merely possible, consequence of A.) In any version, it is not clear why this principle should be accepted. Only defenders of radical human free choice would accept a principle such as this. For instance, if I fly in a commuter plane, and I am aware that it is more likely that such a plane would crash than larger planes, it seems artificial to say, that if worse comes to worse, I have chosen the crash. Of course, it could be objected that plane crashes are statistically rare outcomes of flying, even on commuter planes. Pregnancy is a likely outcome of heterosexual relations.

But losing is a likely outcome at the race track. So, only if we are willing to say that a person who bets at the race track chooses to lose, a sexually active person chooses to have AIDS, and that a smoker chooses lung cancer (since these are all foreseeable, reasonably likely consequences), can we say that a woman who chooses sexual relations with a man chooses any pregnancy that may result.

However, this result is implausible and I do not see why any theory of human choice needs to take this position. Those who wish to hold on to a position defending radical freedom and responsibility bear a burden of developing a tenable account of human agency. Later, I will suggest that the conditions under which a person thinks of herself as an agent require bodily control and integrity, and this involves the possibility of controlling and ending pregnancy.

III

Earlier we saw the difficulties in considering the moral legitimacy of abortion without considering the reasons women have for aborting. It is true that much discussion in both popular and specialized literature makes some distinctions: abortions to save the life (or health) of a pregnant woman are usually condoned, as are abortions of pregnancies resulting from rape or incest. Abortions sought because of fetal defect are sometimes condoned; those for economic or family reasons perhaps less so. Yet these categories do not treat women's reasons as they understand their lives and their pregnancies so much as impose third-party classifications on them. They do not address the reason the moral agent has, from her point of view, for acting to end a pregnancy.

There is another category that lumps together abortions that do not fit into those listed above: abortions for "convenience." These are abortions for which the moral agent has self-regarding reasons. They have been hard for popular morality to countenance, possibly because of the passive view of women and pregnancy. On that view, women who seek actively to control or stop pregnancy (as imperfect as that control is) will be seen as the aberration.

"Convenience" is a pejorative term, dismissing the reasons for the abortion so categorized as trivial. What are these reasons? First, we can think of a pregnancy interfering with other plans. A woman might be a student, or involved in a project at work. She might be about to go around the world, or into Biosphere, or to Calcutta to work with Mother Theresa. She might be struggling to hold onto her farm, or nurse along an embryonic business. In other words, she is in the middle of living her life, one with no room at that time for pregnancy and a baby.

Second, "convenience" might involve family status. An unmarried woman might find herself pregnant, unable to support a pregnancy or child on her own, and unable or unwilling to turn to her family or friends, or a man for help. That is, she might not be willing to surrender her independence to others.

Whether these two sorts of reasons exhaust the category of "convenience abortions" is not important since the point is that at least two major kinds of "convenience" abortions are sought either for preservation of life plans or independence. Neither of these reasons are morally negligible. Indeed, they may represent the sort of projects Kant would think of as self-improvement and the kinds of lives required for self-respect. When we assume women are the normal case, we see that those concerns that were morally marginalized on a view of women as the passive objects of pregnancy now come to the forefront. I want to focus on abortions for "convenience" due to commitments to significant projects both because of the moral scorn usually heaped upon them, and because examination of the conditions for a pregnant person to see herself as an agent, having dignity and holding herself in esteem, relate directly to them. However, I do not mean to imply that abortions sought for some other reasons would not be permissible.

Our discussion will involve three interconnected Kantian themes: (1) the duty moral agents have to develop their talents; (2) the prohibition against treating rational beings as mere means or things, connected to the prohibition against servility, and (3) the recognition of one's rational agency and hence autonomy.

Let us first consider the duty we have to ourselves to develop our talents, an imperfect duty to oneself (Gr 423, 430; DV 444–46, pp. 239–40). An imperfect duty is a duty of virtue, whose fulfillment can be morally meritorious. Failure to fulfill this duty is not morally wrong, but involves a deficiency in moral worth. However, adopting as a principle not to fulfill such a duty is morally wrong (DV 390, p. 194). It is a moral requirement to adopt a pattern of life that includes projects of self-development, whatever they might be:

> When it is said that it is in itself a duty for a man to make his end the perfection belonging to man as such (properly speaking, to humanity), this perfection must be put in what can result from his deeds, not in mere gifts for which he must be indebted to nature; for otherwise it would not be a duty. This duty can therefore consist only in cultivating one's capacities (or natural predispositions), the highest of which is understanding, the capacity for concepts and so too for those concepts that have to do with duty. . . . Man has a duty to raise himself from the crude state of his nature, from his animality, more and more toward humanity. (DV 386–87, p. 191)

Pregnancy can sometimes disrupt the projects involved in self-development. While some people find that their ongoing projects are perfectly compatible with pregnancy, other people with different projects determine that they are not. We should not assume that being pregnant is a purely bodily, fairly automatic condition, like digestion, taking little or no effort—this is the picture of women as the passive objects of pregnancy. Besides the issues of moral agency discussed earlier, biology also tells us that pregnancy is a period of development and growth of a pre-embryo to embryo, to fetus, that the growth of the fetus is dependent upon environmental conditions (conditions directly encountered within the uterus, but usually involving physical and psychological states of the woman whose uterus it is), so that maternal health and well-being are causally linked to neonatal health and well-being. Pregnancy may be automatic (a comatose woman can "do" it), but the quality of its outcome is strongly affected by the effort that the pregnant woman puts into it. Knowing this, it is less plausible that anyone or nearly everyone can sustain a healthy pregnancy in combination with every sort of demanding project. Sometimes it is possible. Sometimes it is not. You can't always do two things at once.[9]

The prohibition against disrespectful and "thingifying" treatment enters into our reflections at this point (Gr 428–29). It is true that pregnancy is of limited duration. Childrearing, the usual next step after pregnancy, is also not always compatible with the life chosen by a moral agent. But a person could bring a pregnancy to term and then turn the infant over to others to rear; this is often urged as a moral choice. But if we think of pregnancy as an activity of a moral agent, we see that it has a purpose: to grow and have a baby. Why would a person do this? One reason could be to involve one's life in the most intimate fashion possible with another being who will grow into an intrinsically valuable person, and it would be hard to find grounds for moral objection to this. But another purpose might be to use one's body to provide a baby for another, or simply to provide life for another. This falls dangerously close to thinking of a oneself as valuable only as is the means to an end—the baby. One's own worth is overshadowed.

Here we can find Kant illuminating, if we rewrite him to treat women as the normal case. This is what he says about the morally objectionable trait of servility (with "woman" etc. substituted for "man" etc., throughout, emphasizing that women are the normal case):

> But woman regarded as a person, that is, as the subject of a morally practical reason, is exalted above any price; for as a person she is not to be valued merely as a means to the ends of others or even to her own ends, but as an end in herself, that is, she possesses a dignity by which she exacts respect for herself from all other rational beings in the world. She can measure herself with every other being of this kind and value herself on a footing of equality with them. . . . Since she must regard herself not only as a person generally but also as a woman, that is as a person who has duties her own reason lays upon her, her insignificance as a human animal may not infringe upon her consciousness of her dignity as a rational woman. (DV 434–35, p. 230)

For a woman to think of herself primarily in her reproductive role, of value directly to a fetus and indirectly to others, even for a few months, is for her to fall into servility, failing to confer on herself the self esteem morally appropriate to her. For others to think of her in this way violates the duty of respect owed to persons.[10]

One issue not addressed by Kant is how a person comes to be servile, to think of herself as a lesser being, valuable only as a vehicle to greater ends. This is an empirical question, but is important nonetheless, since moral agents develop over time, and our ability to carry out our duties, including our duties of self-respect, have a great deal to do with the empirical conditions of our development.

It seems likely that one way in which a person comes to think of herself as a lesser being or a mere thing is through treatment by others as such. The prohibition of abortion involves such a treatment. One effect of such a prohibition is to diminish the empirical moral life of the moral agent. In Kantian language, it will lessen the likelihood that a person will recognize her own status as autonomous rational being, and her own worth as such.

Readers of Kant do not need to be reminded that the concept of autonomy is both crucial and problematic in Kant's moral theory. Now, it is clearly wrong to interpret Kant's vision of autonomous moral agents as requiring control over the empirical circumstances of their lives, or the empirical outcomes of their choices. Nor is Kant's conception of autonomy that of the existentialist self-actualizer. To think of ourselves as autonomous is to think ourselves as free to decide which incentive we will incorporate into our maxim of action: to decide how we will act and why. This idea of autonomy as spontaneous freedom is fundamental to our idea of ourselves as rational agents in general (and as moral agents in particular). As Allison puts it: "I cannot conceive of myself as such a (rational) agent without regarding myself as pursuing ends that I frame for myself and that I regard as rational to pursue. Correlatively, I cannot conceive of myself as such an agent without assuming that I have a certain control over my inclinations, that I am capable of deciding which of them are to be acted upon (and how) and which are to be resisted." Thinking of oneself as a rational agent requires a thinking of oneself as making choices, and having choices to make.

Our empirical lives play a role in our ability to think of ourselves as making choices and having reasons for them. If half of one's life (especially the formative years) is spent knowing that one's body is subject to use by others, with one's refusal or assent irrelevant, the self-awareness required for thinking of oneself as a rational agent is less likely to emerge. If, on the empirical level, a person does not think of herself as possessing agency, she is unlikely to come to conceive of herself under the idea of freedom. While others may rightfully regard such a person as a moral agent, and make moral judgments about her accordingly, she will remain *morally immature*—not thinking of herself in terms of agency and moral freedom. Whatever moral beliefs this person has will be based on habit, social convention, religious belief, or fear: heteronomous sources all. Her sense of self-worth will be comparative, not absolute.

For a person to come to recognize her own agency, she must be in a position to exercise some control over her body, sexually and repro-ductively. Without this, the connections between what is chosen and what occurs will not be there to be learned. She will be unable to distinguish between choices and idle wishes, since both will lack effectiveness, in her experience. She will feel, and think of herself as a helpless patient—someone to whom things happen. To develop agency, a person must be able to either assent to, or refuse, sex and pregnancy, before or after the fact. Morally relevant grounds for refusal include (among others) commitments to seriously undertaken projects. Denial of this will reinforce a belief in her own inferiority, her lack of right to exercise her rights, so to speak. In other words, it will tend to make her servile. It will make her see herself as the object of the choices of others, and not the subject with reasoned choices of her own. Finally, it will tend to make her unable to carry out her duty of self-development: carrying out sustained projects and plans that involve the cultivation of talents and abilities. A person who can never know whether reproduction will call her away from a project is much less likely to commit herself seriously to one.

Historically, women have taken a fatalistic attitude toward unplanned and unwanted pregnancy: it is simply one more misfortune in a life beyond control. However, this attitude is rooted in a past in which few people, men or women, had much control over their lives, and had access to education or to circumstances that would allow them to engage in the projects of self-improvement that Kant holds to be required by duty. The Enlightenment changed the view of persons into, finally, Kantian self-governing, dignified agents, and historical circumstances allowed more people to think of themselves in this way. Women of course lagged behind. (Even today, those women who oppose abortion rights hold what are taken to be "traditional" views of women and their roles, views emphasizing acceptance rather than control.[11])

It is likely that if women had more actual control over their lives, including their sex lives, and felt entitled to this control, unwanted pregnancy would be less common. They would probably be more willing to plan out the most effective forms of contraception, if they choose to sleep with men. But one of the factors that leads to unwanted pregnancy is women feeling unable and unentitled to make choices about their lives.[12] They are moral patients, not agents—things "just happen" to them. Ironically, the very lack of control over reproduction represented by a ban on abortion probably reinforces unwanted pregnancy.

This suggests that moral agency is compatible with pregnancy only if we think of, and treat, a person who is pregnant as involved in the voluntary activity of growing a baby.[13] The person so engaged in this activity is the subject, not object. That this activity is chosen, or voluntary implies that women must choose whether to engage in this activity.[14] Having a choice of course requires the ability effectively to assent and to refuse. On these terms, it becomes more likely that a moral agent will come to see herself as such, to recognize her autonomy, dignity, and self-worth. If women are denied the ability to make this choice, they are condemned to the life of a less mature, less respected, and less self-respecting moral patient—a morally lesser being.[15]

IV

So far, we have seen that there are reasons women may have for abortion that relate directly to their moral duties to themselves. We have seen that the ability to decide whether to refuse or accept pregnancy is crucial to the development of self-respecting, mature moral agents, aware of themselves as such. It is hard to see why, reflecting on the relationship between the ability to make decisions in general about one's own body, and one's moral development, that abortion because of incompatibility of pregnancy and childrearing with life plans would be held to be morally impermissible. "All pregnancies incompatible with the projects of moral agents may be terminated" can certainly be willed as universal law (particularly if women are the rational willers).

The strongest response to this is that abortion involves the impermissible killing of another, no matter what the consequences are to a particular woman forced to continue a pregnancy, or women in general, who face a lifetime of possible unwanted pregnancy.

Notice how taking women as the normal moral agent has changed the framework in which the abortion discussion usually occurs. Typically, the issue of the fetus comes up first and the scenario involves a conflict of rights: maternal versus fetal, and since the maternal claim is a right to continue with her life without a pregnancy ("convenience") while the fetal claim is to life itself, the latter claim trumps the former. In Kantian language, it seems to pit a perfect duty not to kill the fetus against an imperfect duty of self-development, and in such a case, the perfect duty wins out.

But this analysis presupposes that women are not the normal case and that pregnancy is an unusual event, to be understood as a sort of conflict between two competing interest groups (like logging companies vs. the spotted owl). But Kantian ethics in which the lives of women are taken seriously, and pregnancy is construed on its own terms, as a normal event in the lives of moral agents, makes it implausible that the active moral agent growing a fetus could be seen as morally equivalent to the fetus she is growing. What makes a woman (or man) morally important for Kant is her rationality—being both source and subject of the moral law. This does not mean that we are morally valuable only when we are rational. It is instead our capacity to think, judge, act on reasons, and to choose which to act on, that makes us valuable. A woman, pregnant or not, is fully capable of thinking, judging, and choosing and acting on reasons, and in a world in which women were normal, would be a paradigm case of rational, hence morally valuable being. The fetus is an organism in the process of very rapid biological development. Should this process go well for it, it is likely to become a person. However, it still has biological obstacles before it (and in many cases, development will cease and fetal death will occur). The fetus, if valuable at all, is valuable as a potential rational being. That is, it has the potential to become valuable. But a potential value must in every case be less than that value fully realized. The life of a woman is priceless (Gr 435) and her projects, involving her duty of self-development, must be respected.

Even if fetuses were considered to be moral persons, it is not morally permissible to appropriate other persons' bodies to sustain them any more that it would be to force a person to donate a kidney to save the life of another.[16] The woman-centered view highlights the moral requirement that a woman not be treated disrespectfully, as a mere thing.

But there is an imperfect duty to others of beneficence: promoting "according to one's means the happiness of others in need, without hoping for something in return" (DV 453, p. 247). Sustaining the life of another person, whether by donating money, or a kidney, or continuing a pregnancy, if we did regard a fetus as a person, would fall under the duty of beneficence. It is a duty of wide scope, holding for maxims and not types of acts. But there are no mechanical rules for determining when such an act is appropriate, Kant explains. "How far it should extend depends in large part, on what each person's true needs are in view of his sensibilities, and *it must be left to each to decide this for himself* [sic]. For a maxim of promoting others' happiness at the sacrifice of one's own happiness, one's true needs, would conflict with itself if it were made a universal law" (DV 393, 197; emphasis mine).

This fits in with Kant's response to the casuistical question: How far should one go in using her resources to help another? He answers: Not so far as to require the beneficence of others (DV 454, p. 248). Casuistical questions for Kant involve not a systematic method but a practice seeking truth in ethics, a field that requires the exercise of *judgment* in determining maxims and principles to apply to particular cases (DV 411, p. 211). That he raises this casuistical question is further evidence that there cannot be a general determination *in advance* of the rights and wrongs in cases such as these; judgment weighing the conflicting duties of self-perfection and beneficence is required. Even if we did regard the fetus as a person, continuing to sustain it would be an act of beneficence, not morally required in all cases. It is the agent herself, as Kant says, who must weigh the relevant factors to determine whether her needs outweigh those of the developing life.

But, as I have already argued, we have no reason to regard the developing life as on par with the already developed life of a rational being. Still, it might be appropriate to think of continuing some pregnancies as acts of beneficence. To whom would the beneficence be directed?

Perhaps we could say that any duty of beneficence we might have in connection with pregnancy is not directly connected to the fetus but to the future world in general. In other words, carrying a pregnancy could be an instance of the sort of future-directed beneficent act of which building a museum, improving water quality, or planting trees are also exemplars—acts of benefiting indefinite future others in the future world.[17] If there is such a duty, it does not cancel out the imperfect duty of self-perfection, but must be balanced with it.

Thus, the moral legitimacy of aborting or continuing an unplanned or unwanted pregnancy has to be contingent on the course of life of the woman in question. To assume otherwise is to imply that women's projects are less worthy than "regular" people's projects, since the former, but not the latter, should be dropped at a moment's notice to accommodate pregnancy and childrearing. For pregnancy to be compatible with the embodied life of moral agents, and for women to develop a view of themselves as moral agents, women must be able to decide whether to continue a pregnancy, even if the decision is morally mistaken in a given case.

If this result seems odd, perhaps it is because men and women have become accustomed to the disrespectful objectification of women. Forcing reproduction on women, therefore, seems natural. But to require that a woman remain pregnant, when she wants otherwise, is morally wrong, in the same way that imposed sex is morally wrong. It treats her as a mere object. It undercuts her ability to recognize her own agency and autonomy, and it interferes with her duty of self-perfection. Attempts to exhort the woman to remain pregnant may involve appeal to sustaining the life of a potential other: the fetus. She is to give her body over for the use of someone else. I can think of no better illustration of "treating a person as a mere means" than this. Appeal to the woman's alleged "duty" to the species, nation, race, or infertile couples treats the woman as a vehicle. The woman as respected person drops out of the picture, and all that remains is her reproductive capacity.

The last type of appeal, to the good of the species, race, or nation, reveals why consequentialist defenses of the permissibility of abortion are inadequate. Such a justification would limit a woman's legitimate ability to consent or refuse to reproduce on contingent empirical factors, such as population pressures. We can imagine a scenario in which a population crash might lead to a consequentialist justification for mandatory childbirth for all fertile women. The old objection against utilitarianism based on its instrumental treatment of persons applies doubly to persons who are women.

The implications of this for pregnancy is that for pregnancy to be part of the life of a respected and self-respecting moral agent, it must be chosen. This is not to say that moral agents need to be able to control all aspects (or even most) of their lives. It is to say that this kind of choice is necessary in order that a person recognize her own agency, autonomy, and worth. Prohibiting abortions and forcing pregnancy on women treat women as things, making it less likely that women can achieve a recognition of their autonomy. Aborting a pregnancy not compatible with a person's seriously considered life plans is morally permissible.

We have seen the subversion of expectation that follows from taking women as the normal case in ethics. Pregnancy plays a normal role in these normal lives, and pre-analytic intuitions about what autonomy, self-respect, and duty require are overturned as we think through their implications in the lives of women. Our reflections here have shown that many abortions are morally permissible, and that the ability to abort a pregnancy is a precondition of any pregnancy being compatible with the dignity of persons and self-respect. It is probably true that Kant would have claimed abortion to be morally wrong. But Kant's sister might have known otherwise.

NOTES

1. In the "Doctrine of Virtue," (DV) in discussing suicide Kant says, "Willfully killing oneself can be called murdering oneself only if it can be proved that it is in general a crime committed either against one's own person or also, through one's killing oneself, against another (as when a pregnant woman takes her life)"(DV 422, from *Metaphysics of Morals*, trans. Mary Gregor [Cambridge: Cambridge University Press, 1991], 218). All subsequent references to the Doctrine of Right (DR) and the Doctrine of Virtue (DV) will be to the Gregor translation. The first numbers after DV, and DR, refer to pages in *Kants Gesammelte Schriften* (Berlin: Königlichen Preußischen Akademie der Wissenschaften, 1902).

2. For example, in discussing gluttony and drunkenness, Kant refers to a drunk as "like a mere animal not to be treated as a human being" (DV 427, p. 222); a man is debased, below the animal level when drunk, or stuffed with

food, or under the influence of opium (DV 427, p. 223). Unnatural vice debases a man "beneath the beasts" (DV 425, p. 221). Rather, we have a duty to raise ourselves above the crude animal level (DV 387, p. 191).

3. In her recent "Could It Be Worth Thinking about Kant on Sex and Marriage?" in *A Mind of One's Own: Feminist Essays in Reason and Objectivity*, ed. Louise Antony and Charlotte Witt (Boulder, Colo.: Westview Press, 1993), 49–67, Barbara Herman reaches similar conclusions. She is struck by the remarkable and unexpected similarity of views on sexuality between Kant and radical feminist theorists Catharine MacKinnon and Andrea Dworkin. Both Kant and these feminist theorists see sexuality as a moral problem. Its solution cannot be relegated to the private sphere. Kant and Dworkin, Herman notes, maintain that sexual regard is directed to the bodily parts, not to the person, thus involving morally disrespectful objectification (57). MacKinnon and Dworkin insist that the objectification through sexuality constitute the categories of gender itself, that to be "woman" or "man" is to be the passive or the active object in the sexual relationship (59). Both Kant and MacKinnon and Dworkin argue that merely private acts of consent cannot de-objectify this relationship. For Kant, only the very public act of marriage morally redeems sexuality, by creating public roles of rights and responsibilities for husband and wife, whose function is to "secure regard for one's partner as a person with a life, which is what the sexual appetite by itself causes one to disregard" (63). Dworkin and MacKinnon do not champion marriage, or Kant's conception of it, but argue that only through the very public, social transformation (or abolition) of gender, can sexuality be morally redeemed.

4. Pamela Foa, "What's Wrong with Rape?" in *Feminism and Philosophy*, ed. Mary Vetterling-Braggin, Frederick Elliston, and Jane English (Totowa, N.J.: Littlefield, Adams, 1977), 347–59.

5. R. M. Hare, "A Kantian Approach to Abortion," *Social Theory and Practice* 15.1 (Spring 1989). Reprinted in Luper-Foy and Brown, eds. *The Moral Life* (San Diego, Calif.: Harcourt, Brace, Jovanovich, 1992).

6. In support of a different point, Annette Baier raises similar considerations in her essay "For the Sake of Future Generations," in *Earthbound*, ed. Tom Regan (New York: Random House, 1984).

7. Emily Martin is particularly perceptive about the cultural constructions of menstruation, pregnancy, and birth. See her *Woman in the Body* (Boston: Beacon Press, 1987).

8. The "flowerpot" model of pregnancy was identified and named by Carolyn Whitbeck, in "Theories of Sex Difference," in Women and Values, ed. Marilyn Pearsall (Belmont, Calif.: Wadsworth, 1986), 35.

9. A friend of mine who plays the flute read a draft of this paper and recounted how one of her pregnancies prevented her from playing the flute, because of the pressure of the uterus on her diaphragm. I suspect that academics in general, and philosophers in particular, extrapolate too much from their own experience when thinking of pregnancy and its compatibility with one's ongoing work. Pregnancy does not interfere too much with reading,

writing, lecturing, and so on. It might however, be in conflict with the work of a research scientist, or an artist, working with mutagenic or teratogenic chemicals.

10. See Thomas Hill's "Servility and Self-Respect" and "Self-Respect Reconsidered" in his *Autonomy and Self-Respect* (Cambridge: Cambridge University Press, 1991), 4–24. The former essay remains the indispensable source concerning the significance of Kant's discussion of servility.

Why not be servile for a few months, and then become self-respecting? This supposes that a little bit of servility is justifiable for a good enough end. But avoiding servility and "thingification" are duties. Self-respect is a duty. A little bit of servility does not just go a long way; it goes too far.

11. See Kristin Luker's *Abortion and the Politics of Motherhood* (Berkeley: University of California Press, 1984).

12. See Catharine MacKinnon's *Toward a Feminist Theory of the State* (Cambridge, Mass.: Harvard University Press, 1989), especially chapter 10, in which MacKinnon emphasizes women's self-perceived lack of power over their own sex lives.

13. Notice, on the other hand, that we do not regard having a tumor as an activity. Rather, an afflicted person is regarded as the victim of cancer, a "patient" in both the medical and moral sense. To regard pregnancy, a positive experience of normal and healthy moral agents, as something to be suffered or borne in the way cancer is, is to regard women not as normal moral agents, but as potential sufferers of affliction—patients, not agents.

14. It is clear that Kant believes that goals and activities must be chosen by the agents who undertake them. Kant argues that it is self-contradictory to make another person's perfection my duty. Only the individual agent herself can perfect herself, since this process involves the agent herself setting "his end in accordance with his own concepts of duty" (DV 386, p. 191).

15. Some theorists (Freud, for example) accept this result as the natural outgrowth of physiological difference between the sexes. It would be hard, however, to imagine Kant accepting a moral distinction based on physiology.

16. Of course, this is a version of the point made by Judith Jarvis Thomson in her "A Defense of Abortion," *Philosophy and Public Affairs* (Fall 1971): 47–66.

17. See Baier, "For the Sake of Future Generations."

14

Holly L. Wilson

Kant's Evolutionary Theory of Marriage

It is well known that Kant believed that the human species is progressing toward the better in its institutions and constitutions, yet no application of this general principle has yet been made to the institution of marriage. One of the prominent passages in which Kant makes his argument for progress from the impulse of unsociable sociability can be found in the Characteristic of the *Anthropology from a Pragmatic Point of View*. The character of the species, according to Kant, is this:

> that, taken collectively (the human race as one whole), it is a multitude of persons, existing successively and side by side, who cannot do without associating peacefully and yet cannot avoid constantly offending one another. Hence they feel destined by nature to [form], through mutual compulsion under laws that proceed from themselves, a coalition in a cosmopolitan society (cosmopolitismus)— a coalition which, though constantly threatened by dissension, makes progress on the whole.[1]

Along with this account of unsociable sociability in the Characteristic, we also find an extended discussion of marriage under the heading of "The Character of the Sexes." In spite of the more general heading the discussion concerns primarily the domestic relationship between the sexes in marriage or in courtship leading to marriage. Kant makes some general remarks about the purposes of sexual differentiation in nature, but quickly concludes that monogamous marriage is what nature intends in sexual differentiation. The question under consideration here is whether Kant also believed that marriage as an institution is progressing toward betterment under the impulse of unsociable sociability even as he clearly maintained the progress of our legal and political institutions. I believe he did, and hence his account of the state of marriage in his time can only represent a stage in the evolution of marriage.

If we assess his comments on marriage in the context in which he intended them, that is, within the concrete pedagogical context of his lectures on anthropology, I think it will be clear that Kant is not advocating the current state of marriage (of the time), but is rather showing the agency occurring in marriage in order to undercut the spell of gallantry under which marriage was suffering at the time. If, in addition, we recognize the role of marriage in the overall teleological plan of nature that guides Kant's discussions throughout the *Anthropology*, we will also have to conclude that Kant believed that the institution of marriage was evolving toward the better, even if he was not prepared to assert this explicitly. I choose the term *evolution* instead of the term *progress* here, since the concept of unsociable sociability that characterizes the human species in general is meant to convey a natural dynamic of instability that impels human beings to use their reason to move beyond whatever state their institutions are currently in toward a more civilized state. In order to engage Kant's discussion on marriage then, we will have to deal with these three topics: (1) the intent of the lectures, (2) the use of teleological judgment in the *Anthropology*, and (3) the evolutionary impulse of unsociable sociability.

THE INTENT OF THE ANTHROPOLOGY LECTURES

Kant indicated his intent for his anthropology lectures in the article "On the Different Races of Human Beings," which appeared as the announcement of his lectures for physical geography in the summer semester, 1775. There he closely associated the two lectures, physical geography and anthropology, under the heading of *"pragmatische Weltkenntnis."* This *Weltkenntnis*

> is that which is helpful in bringing all sciences and skills otherwise achieved to a pragmatic usefulness, through which they would be

useful not only for the school [university], but also for life, and where the finished student would be introduced to the theater of his destiny, that is, the world.[2]

Knowledge of the world could be gained in a two-part lecture course in which the fields of nature and human beings were covered, first, by physical geography, and, then, by anthropology. The purpose of the two courses was not just to introduce the students to the scientific facts of outer and inner nature, but also to help them orient themselves in relationship to the world as physical and cultural. In other words, the intent was not only to make them scientifically competent, but also to prepare them for social, pragmatic, and practical realities.

It is clear from the intimate association of the two courses that Kant meant the anthropology lecture to have the same popular and pragmatic worth that he had accorded his physical geography lectures in the previous years. From the *Nachricht von der Einrichtung seiner Vorlesungen 1765–66*,[3] we gather more information about what he intended for these lectures in physical geography. Kant writes:

> When I recognized immediately at the beginning of my academic lecture [career] that a great negligence existed among the young students, that they learned early to reason, without possessing sufficient historical knowledge, which could take the place of [lack of] experience: I formed the resolution to make the history of the current condition of the earth or geography, in the broadest meaning, into a pleasant and easy summary, which could serve to prepare them for practical reason. . . . I called such a discipline . . . Physical Geography.[4]

At the time of the writing of the *Nachricht* (1865–66), Kant's interest in anthropology was still developing, but he already had a very strong interest in his students and in their acquisition of pragmatic knowledge of the world. He saw the failing of scholastic instruction in that it taught the students to be clever in the use of reasoning without setting limits to that knowledge or showing how it could be used for life. He referred sarcastically to the "loquaciousness of young thinkers, who are blinder than any other self-conceited person, and as incurable as ignorance."[5] Kant was very critical of the smug intellectual attitudes of his students since they were memorizing philosophy, but were not developing the judgment needed to apply their knowledge. In this same context, Kant alludes to the great impulse of the Enlightenment as he understood it, that his students should not learn philosophy, but rather learn how to philosophize. He saw his task as that of teaching

them to philosophize and to think through the problems for themselves: "In short, he [the student] should not learn thoughts, but to
think; no one should carry him, rather lead him, if we want that he
should, in the future, go skillfully for himself [into the world]."[6] In his
letter to his friend Marcus Herz (1773), Kant claims he is working on a
"doctrine of observation" for his students, which teaches them how to
exercise their skills in prudence and wisdom.[7] Finally, in the *Anthropology*, Kant lays out the enlightenment maxims of wisdom: think for
yourself, think yourself in the place of others, and think consistently
with yourself.[8]

Two intents for the anthropology lectures clearly emerge: (1)
students should overcome their egoism, and (2) students should think
for themselves and critically evaluate what they are being taught. Kant
is interested in developing their judgment and bringing them out of
their self-imposed tutelage (*Unmundigkeit*). Now the question arises
how a teacher can best accomplish these two ends. Kant's answer is to
introduce them to the stage of their destiny (knowledge of the world)
and teach methodical thinking (pragmatic) by example.

Pragmatic anthropology is about "what *man* as a free agent makes,
or can and should make of himself."[9] This means that Kant is talking
about actual human agency, not just about what one ought to do, but
also what one has in one's power to do with the capacities and predispositions the species has. "Pragmatic" in the second sense refers to a
predisposition toward social life. Kant seems to be guiding his students
in wisdom, discerning judgment (*iudicium discretivum*)[10] and practiced
judgment (*geubte Urteilskraft*).[11] Kant writes about the difficulty in
acquiring practiced judgment:

> instruction can enrich natural understanding with many concepts and
> equip it with rules. But the second intellectual power, *judgment*
> (*judicium*)—the power of deciding whether or not something is an
> instance of the rule—cannot be *instructed*; it can only be *exercised*. This
> is why we speak of growth in judgment as *maturity*, and call judgment
> the kind of understanding that comes only with years.[12]

Kant's lectures on anthropology were meant to help broaden his
students' experiences in order that they could then exercise their
judgment.

Kant's *Anthropology* was published only late in his life, but it
reflects fairly well the content and organization of his lecture notes.[13]
Kant begins with the distinction between egoism and pluralism in the
Didactic, and then develops the idea of the powers and vulnerabilities
of the mind. In the Characteristic, he continues with an account of

character, both freely chosen and that which arises out of physical or social groupings (sex, nationality, species). Kant, then, concludes the lectures with the ideal of the cosmopolitan society that emerges as the only desirable institution in light of the miserable conflict of egos. He is exposing his students to the basis for prudence that normally only extensive experience could make possible. Prudence is not morality, but it can lead one to the door of morality, certainly much better than memorizing philosophical systems can. Prudence is "using other men for his purposes."[14] The very word "use" that Kant has in mind here is reciprocal, uncoerced, and consensual use, not the kind of use that is associated with cunning.[15]

The very language of "use" draws the connection between prudence and judgment, specifically teleological judgment. Teleological judgment concerns final causes or a "causality of nature by analogy with the causality we have in the technical use of reason."[16] The technical use of reason is also what Kant calls "art" or "bringing about something we want to exist."[17] Like the technical use of reason, prudence is "skill in the choice of means to one's own greatest well-being."[18] Both prudence and the technical use of reason are exercised through teleological judgment that brings together means and ends.

The Teleological Methodology in the *Anthropology*

Throughout the *Anthropology*, Kant speaks of providence, nature's intent, or the end of some natural process. In the context of "the Character of the Sexes" these concepts play an exceedingly significant role. The principle of sexual differentiation cannot be "what we make our end, but what the end of nature was in the organization of femininity."[19] The two natural ends provisioned for femininity include (1) the preservation of the species, and (2) the cultivation and refinement of society through femininity. These two intents taken together tell us that femininity is not an essential feature of women, even though Kant generally associates women and femininity. Femininity achieves its end only in a long developmental process, and in the progress of society, femininity also evolves.[20] The character of femininity is both natural and socially constructed, and so it must be understood through teleological judgment.

In the Critique of Teleological Judgment, Kant maintains that teleology forms a "special part of the critique," which grounds the special principles, that can and must be applied to natural beings.[21] Kant uses the term in the traditional sense as related to natural products, or more precisely natural beings, not as related to products of human intention, since these are really arts or the products of arts. The distinction between teleology as an account of human intention, or purpose (*Zweckbegriff*), and as concerned with the types of judgments we make concerning natural beings (*Wesensbegriff*) is crucial.[22] Purposive intention, in contrast, is human rationality oriented towards ends which can be achieved by means. In other words,

> To say end [*Zweck*], is also to say means. To say telos is in no way to say means: the Greek concept is not as strictly coupled with the sphere of the will as the German concept [*Zweck*]. This is shown most clearly in the telos-thought of the entelechie which is an artificial concept derived from Aristotle . . . it designates a power of striving immanent in the being of every being.[23]

Certainly Kant's teleology shares more in common with Aristotle than with the contemporary debate concerning teleological intentions, yet his concept of natural being also differs considerably, as it was Kant's intention to make any talk of teleology critical insofar as it is grounded in the faculty of reflective teleological judgment.[24] Teleological judgment judges only in analogy to human intention, and finds the analogy inadequate when it comes to organic beings.[25] Organic beings have an organization quite unlike the outwardly directed goal orientation of human intention. First, there is no end outside of the organism as it is its own end. Yet neither does Kant want to say that the end of the organism is its perfection alone. The living organism is "an organized product of nature . . . in which everything is a purpose and reciprocally also a means."[26] This means that nothing is gratuitous or purposeless in the being, and Kant is indicating that he is appealing to the metaphysical principle of teleology that nature does nothing in vain.[27] A modern way of explicating Kant's teleological judgment is in terms of the organism's adaptation to the environment. The meaning of adaptation for Kant is that the organism in its own purposive organization points beyond itself to a larger system of purposes, it is organized to be adapted for an environment. Kant argues that what we find in the part we ought to expect in the whole, in other words, the part cannot be inconsistent with the whole since the part is a part of the whole.[28] Therefore, because we find purposiveness in organic beings, Kant argues that he is now entitled to consider the whole of nature as a system on analogy with the organization in the organism.[29] "Providence" is the name for the expectation of the purposive organization in the whole of nature.

Sexual differentiation cannot be understood, according to Kant, without an appeal to the larger organization of nature or providence.

Kant rejects attempts, such as Pope's, to define sexual differentiation according to human intentions.[30] Sexual differentiation must be understood as natural purposiveness, or in other words as an expression of purposes of nature that extend beyond all human willing. One way to establish the importance of such a perspective is simply to recognize that nature could have done otherwise. Sexual differentiation is not necessary for the propagation of the species. Hence, some other purpose must be assumed in order to account sufficiently for sexual differentiation. Kant proposes the idea that nature's purpose in sexual differentiation is to bring about sociable relations between separate beings. This sociable relation takes a specific form, and that is the form of sexual intercourse. The second purpose that nature has is already implicit in such a formulation. Since the propagation of the species does not occur spontaneously, it must be brought about. Bringing about means that human beings must engage in intentional action in order to propagate the species. This intentional action is hence more than just natural, but also implies art, or the use of means in order to bring about an end. In other words, nature purposes that humans use their reason to bring about the propagation between the sexes. Kant opens his discussion on the character of the sexes using the metaphor of a machine, which, for Kant, implies human art.[31]

Hence sexual differentiation already implies a task of sociability for human beings. The way in which human beings bring about the propagation of the human species is already a question for reason. For Kant, this means that nature "provided them, in this capacity of theirs (as rational animals), with social inclinations to stabilize their sexual union in a domestic union."[32] Sexual differentiation provides the task of securing some kind of domestic relation between the pair. What kind of domestic relation this should be, however, is unclear simply from the fact of sexual differentiation. Further indication is required from nature in order to determine the kind of domestic relation sufficient for rational beings.

Sexual differentiation in the human species reveals a third purposive feature, for Kant, and that is the inherent difference in function between the two sexually differentiated beings. Any machine, Kant writes,

> that is supposed to accomplish just as much as another machine, but with less force, implies *art*. So we can already presuppose that nature's foresight put more art into the make-up of the female than of the male; for it provided the man with greater strength than the woman in order to bring them together into the most intimate *physical* union, which, insofar as they are still rational beings, too, it orders to the end most important to it, the preservation of the species.[33]

Nature not only has the purpose of the propagation of the species, but also the purpose of the preservation of the species. The domestic union that natural sociable inclinations encourage must also be organized in such a way that it promotes the preservation of the species. Achieving the end of the propagation of the species, though it requires some sort of art, is still for all that, easily accomplished by nature in that she provided one of the sexually differentiated pairs, the male, with greater strength. In a context of separate beings physical strength is a dominant trait and is a standard and well-defined means for accomplishing ends, including sexual ends. However, achieving the end of the *preservation* of the human species sets a far more delicate and complicated task in that the end is not well defined since it is a continuous progress, and the means hence cannot be defined completely. The end is indeterminate because the species is constantly progressing.

One of nature's purposes in the female sex is "the preservation of the species."[34] For this reason, Kant claims that "the proper nature of the female sex is more a study for the philosopher than that of the male sex."[35] The proper nature of the female sex is civilization itself. The nature of femininity cannot be defined in a context in which physical strength is the rule. Femininity evolves as civilization evolves, since, as we will later see, femininity does not even arise until the transition from the state of nature to the civilized state. Brute force and domination rule in the state of nature, femininity can rule only in civilization. Kant maintains that a "woman's art of using men for her purposes by the love she inspires in them" involves no force, because "instead of superior strength (which is what the word dominate means here), they use charm, which implies a desire on man's part to be dominated."[36] Hence it is more instructive to watch the transition of civilization in woman.

As civilization progresses, femininity reveals its strengths: "we call feminine ways weaknesses, and joke about them. Fools jeer at them, but reasonable men know very well that they are precisely the rudders women use to steer men and use them for their own purposes."[37] This strength of the feminine character, however, is not revealed until some sort of civil society has been accomplished: "in a still uncivilized state, on the contrary, all superiority is on the man's side."[38] In the civilized state feminine qualities develop "and, under favoring conditions, become discernible."[39]

Sexual physiological difference gives rise to the tendency to different gender traits in this way: as civilization progresses, feminine traits emerge. One of the clear feminine tendencies evident in the institution of marriage as Kant saw it in his time was the verbal and rhetorical capacity of women. Women, according to Kant, are more fearful about the preservation of the species and physical harm and this causes her to be more timid. In civil society, this reticence translates into modesty, but not at the cost of her agency, which she expresses in "her eloquence in speech and expression."[40] Because women cannot dominate physically, they develop the verbal skills that would allow them to dominate men or express equality of agency. As Kant puts it, "woman wants to dominate, man to be dominated (especially before marriage)."[41]

According to Kant, "the gallantry of ancient chivalry has its source in this."[42] Kant describes a kind of courtship in which women are better versed in pleasing and charming sociability, and men are sometimes self-conscious, sometimes ardent, and sometimes jealous.[43] Men are ruled by emotions and unsociable impulses that women know well to elicit and direct toward their advantage. She guides him into a marriage, because "it is by marriage that woman becomes free: man loses his freedom by it."[44] A woman gains freedom from being "degraded to a mere means for satisfying man's desire,"[45] or, in other words, in a society where women do not have the right to property, she gains protection through the institution of marriage and the financial security associated with it. At least in this one sense, however, women have a civil right in Kant's time, and that is the civil right to marriage, and the rights of married life.

Kant claims that the man loses freedom when he marries and this cannot, of course, refer to practical freedom, but rather to the freedom of being able to give his "inclinations wider scope and freer play."[46] The man enters into a reciprocal relationship with the woman. In the domestic situation, the woman and her inclinations now "reign" and the man's understanding concerning his own business affairs "governs."[47] The man must persuade his wife that he is not motivated by his own inclinations, but rather that "his wife's welfare is the thing closest to his heart."[48] In the type of marriage that Kant describes, the man may no longer allow feelings and inclinations of jealousy to rule him, since "with the matrimonial alliance, man puts aside any such claim.—So it is unjust of him to be jealous because of this coquetry of women."[49] The husband may lose the credibility of his authority if he becomes too jealous or if he is not jealous enough because "conjugal love is by its nature intolerant."[50] He must govern with his understanding and judgment, not with his inclinations. His inclinations are now no longer a sure guide. If he has developed the habit of only being moved by his inclinations as he "lewdly squandered his sexual power"[51] before marriage, he may now lose his credibility in marriage if he fails to "fulfill any reasonable claims made on him."[52]

With this account Kant does not want to perpetuate the myth of gallantry, and he is not giving a stamp of approval to the status quo, because what he is describing is a stage of marriage and each stage has its own weakness. Gallantry, for Kant, allows women the "degree of feminine freedom" in which "she lays claim to freedom over against the man."[53] Kant recognizes women's agency in that he argues that women have the same inclination to dominate as do men and they have the same capacity for dissemblance, when he claims that the "inclination to dominate is woman's real aim, while pleasing in public, insofar as it widens the field for her charm, is only the means for giving effect to that inclination."[54] Women are just as capable of desiring domination as men and just as capable if not more so of concealing that fact behind a veil of pleasing action. Gender difference that arises then expresses itself in women's tendencies to verbal *domination* ("she does not shrink from domestic warfare, which she wages with her tongue"),[55] the *capacity for reproach* ("she reproaches him with his lack of generosity"),[56] the *capacity for inspiring respect* ("and the right to demand respect for herself even if she does not deserve it"),[57] and the *power of refusal* ("the woman refuses, the man courts her").[58]

On the other hand, equality of agency in the domestic relation is problematic, according to Kant. Harmony in the marriage is not insured by equality, but is rather threatened by it. Kant raises this point in two places, in one place in reference to equality of age and in the other place in reference to equality of claims. With respect to age, Kant claims "we cannot count positively on the harmony that is based on equality" because "as the years pass, the woman ages earlier than the man."[59] If a woman matures at a faster rate than a man, then he will lose the credibility of his authority and hence her confidence that he can protect her. In a relation in which there is physiological superiority on the part of the man, "the party who is subject to the other in the sexual relation is apprehensive that the other will violate her right, and so feels compelled to comply with his wishes, to be obliging and attentive in her treatment of him."[60] Women, in this type of marriage, fear being violated by the man, and hence respect his authority and rule. Nonetheless, the weakness in this stage of marriage is that the woman develops more quickly than the man, and may not want to be attentive out of fear, but rather out of inclination. Once a woman gives free reign to her inclinations the marriage moves to gallantry, where the man must give up his jealousy.

This natural developmental inequality, like the physiological inequality we encountered earlier, creates a dynamic tension in the relationship. Physiological inequality gives males the advantage; developmental inequality gives females the advantage. Any advantage is going to make the other party insecure and arouse their sense of injustice and unfairness. Feelings of insecurity and unfairness may lead to disharmony in the relationship. Disharmony in domestic life furthers unsociability rather than the sociable end that marriage is intended to achieve.

Kant's solution to the inevitable inequality that threatens the sociable end of marriage is a compromise that acknowledges inequality while dissolving its divisive tendency. He suggests that

> if a union is to be harmonious and indissoluble, it is not enough for two people to associate as they please; one party must be *subject* to the other and, reciprocally, one must be the *superior* of the other in some way, in order to be able to rule and govern him. For if two people who cannot dispense with each other make *equal* claims, self-love produces nothing but wrangling. As *culture* advances, each party must be superior in his own particular way: the man must be superior to the woman by his physical strength and courage; the woman to the man, however, by her natural talent for gaining mastery over his desire for her.[61]

Kant's response to natural and developmental inequality in gender relations is that each person must subject themselves to the other, but in different ways. Each must acknowledge the superiority of the other in their respective governance. A man is "superior to the woman by his physical strength and courage; the woman to the man, however, by her natural talent for gaining mastery over his desire for her."[62] Women must acknowledge the superiority of physical strength and courage and the man's obligation to "defend [the home] against enemies from without."[63] She "depends on the right of the weaker to have the male's protection against men,"[64] whereas a man must acknowledge the superiority of a "woman's ways."[65] The point that Kant does not make in this context is that each governance is not based on arbitrary rule, although from this description one ought to draw that conclusion. The nonarbitrariness of the rule traces back to the sociable ends that are to be achieved in marriage, propagation and preservation. Propagation and preservation require some sort of art and organization. Such art and organization require skill and the coordination of skill. Coordination of activities requires some rule-governing in order for the two people to anticipate and coordinate with each other's actions.

As sexist as some of Kant's descriptions sound to our contemporary ears, there is a kernel of wisdom in Kant's overall point of view on the harmony of a unity of two people in a domestic relation. His suggestion is that if the two domestic parties are equal and hence make equal claims based on self-love, there will be constant disagreement and no possibility of mediation. On the other hand, if there is a recognition of the legitimate authority of one another then there is a possibility of harmony. If we acknowledge the different ends that males and females tend toward, there is a possibility of mediation and compromise. When we assume that both partners want the same things (each their own self-love), then there is only wrangling, but if we assume that both partners want different things then there is the possibility of compromise. As Kant puts it, "feminine and masculine virtue or lack of virtue are very different from each other, more as regards their incentive than their kind."[66] If both partners recognize each other's superiority in their own realm of skill and interest, then there is the possibility of respect for the other's authority.

For example, a man's skill in protection can be and is evaluated by the woman as she reproaches him; while a woman's skill in attracting and holding a man is evaluated by the man in his jealousy if she is attracting other men at his expense. The marital claim on the man is that he defend his house from enemies, but if he fails in that duty, she has the right to reproach him.[67] If he misdirects that authority in her direction, she may disarm him with tears and emotional eloquence. The claim that a man has on a woman is that she not yield immediately to his ardent love, but when she does that she yield only to him and reassure him of that attention.[68] If she does not reassure him, but seeks out the attention of other men, then he has to be tolerant, at least in the stage of gallantry.[69] Kant justifies this duty to tolerance by explaining that "even a married woman must try to please men generally, so that in case she is widowed young, she will find suitors."[70] A woman's natural end and tendency toward preservation may also extend legitimately to her own preservation. A man's natural end and tendency toward propagation may extend legitimately toward his own forbearance. In the stage of gallantry, men learn to tolerate and bear; women learn to propagate their charms. Women and men are different physiologically and developmentally, and as a result they tend toward different natural ends, one preservation, the other propagation, but in the institution of marriage these ends may well be pursued by the other sex as well.

UNSOCIABLE SOCIABILITY AND THE INSTITUTION OF MARRIAGE

In the Characteristic of the *Anthropology*, Kant employs his principle of unsociable sociability in the analysis of human action on a larger scale, namely, in the human species. Kant defines the mechanism of unsociable sociability in the human species in the description that human persons, taken collectively, are those "who cannot *do without* associating peacefully and yet cannot *avoid* constantly offending one another."[71] This tension leads people to submit themselves to laws that allow for mutual compulsion. This theory of the development of reason in the human species is consistent with Kant's account in the individual because it is viewed as an educational process.

Nature is the teacher; the human species is the student. "It is *only from Providence* that man anticipates the education of the human race, taking the species a whole. . . . Only from Providence does he expect his species to tend toward the civil constitution it envisages."[72] Providence has organized human nature in such a way that their sociable tendencies combat their unsociable tendencies. Individuals eventually give up their schemes of manipulation when they learn that they really do not bring lasting happiness. Human beings pursue happiness naturally because they have a pragmatic predisposition or a predisposition to humanity.[73] The human species will develop legitimate constitutions based on the principles of freedom and legitimate constraint when they "feel ever more keenly the injuries their egoism inflicts on one another."[74] When human beings feel the pain they are causing, they will feel impelled to submit to law that will restrain their egoism. Unlike the accounts of unsociable sociability in his other writings, Kant takes the position here that human beings will subject themselves to universally valid laws because they "feel" the injury they cause.

This mechanism impelling submission to law differs quite remarkably from the formulations in Kant's other works. In the Critique of Teleological Judgment, it is the "impairment of freedom which results from the mutually conflicting freedom [of the individuals]" that is countered by the "lawful authority within a whole called civil society."[75] Kant refers to the progress of culture within a class society, and the misery that results from class divisions. The higher classes oppress the lower classes and achieve luxury only to find themselves oppressed by insatiability. Freedom is impaired by oppression and insatiable inclinations. It is out of a negative experience of impaired freedom that people willingly submit to lawful authority. The mechanism appears similar in the "Idea for a Universal History with a Cosmopolitan Intent," where it is "necessity" that "compels men, who are otherwise so deeply enamored with unrestricted freedom, to enter into this state of coercion; and indeed, they are forced to do so by the greatest need of all, namely, the one that men themselves bring about, for the propensities do not allow them to coexist for very long in wild freedom."[76] The discomfort of antagonism between free people impels them to submit to a "law-governed order in society."[77] Though the formulations differ, the mechanism functions similarly in that it is the negative experiences of impaired freedom and antagonism in individuals that bring them to submit to societal order. In the *Anthropology*, on the contrary, it is fellow feeling that brings about the willingness to submit to lawful freedom. It is in recognizing the injury to *others* that results from egoism and the feeling of already belonging to a common collective (*Gemeinsinn*) that brings people to submit their private interest to public interest and the discipline of civil constraint. It is the feeling of empathy with others and not just with oneself that functions as the mechanism of unsociable sociability in the *Anthropology*.

That empathy or common sense rather than necessity should be the mechanism of unsociable sociability in the *Anthropology*, makes sense, given Kant's previous discussion of marriage, his account of the pragmatic predisposition, and also in light of the overall intent of an anthropology from a pragmatic, rather than physiological, point of view. Marriage serves the sociable ends of human beings and Kant gives an account of those ends not only as natural inclinations (propagation and preservation), but also in terms of the pragmatic predisposition or predisposition to humanity. Kant defines the pragmatic predisposition in the *Anthropology* as "man's predisposition to become civilized by culture, especially the cultivation of social qualities, and his natural tendency in social relations to leave the crude state of mere private force and to become a well-bred (if not yet moral) being destined for concord."[78] The pragmatic predisposition is our predisposition to happiness and self-love through harmonious sociable relations. It is the tendency we have to leave private force and submit ourselves to civilized public norms and laws. The mechanism of unsociable sociability would not work if human beings did not also have a predisposition to sociability.

Kant tells us more about the pragmatic predisposition in his *Religion within the Limits of Reason Alone*, but there he calls it the predisposition to humanity. The connection between the sociable end of this predisposition and the end of individual happiness becomes clear when Kant subordinates the predisposition to humanity to self-love that is both physical and social. Social self-love compares: "we judge ourselves happy or unhappy only by making comparison with others. Out of this self-love springs the inclination to acquire worth in the opinion of others."[79] Social self-love raises us from the use of mere private force if the use of force is censored in the eyes of others. Love of honor and the desire for equality can motivate one to give up unsociable qualities.

The dark side of the predisposition to humanity is already inherent in the act of comparison. Since the original desire of this predisposition is equality of worth with other human beings, it also entails allowing "no one superiority above oneself" and it is "bound up with a constant care lest others strive to attain such superiority; but from this arises gradually the unjustifiable craving to win it for oneself over others."[80] When we compare ourselves to others we immediately notice inequalities, whether natural or earned, and we notice "the anxious endeavors of others to attain a hated superiority over us."[81] The jealousy and rivalry that then are aroused in comparing oneself to others, according to Kant, may breed all kinds of vices of envy, ingratitude, and spitefulness, or they may simply breed inclinations to gain superiority over others "as a measure of precaution and for the sake of safety."[82] In other words, the predisposition to humanity predisposes us to compare ourselves with others and constantly evaluate our equality with others. Feelings of jealousy and rivalry incline us to seek superiority over others in order to dominate them or at least to ensure that we are not dominated.

These considerations are precisely what are at stake in Kant's discussion of courtship and marriage. Domestic relations between women and men create a situation in which two people are possibly unequal physiologically as well as developmentally. Comparison of equality arouses feelings of jealousy and rivalry, and the resultant inclination to dominate lest one be dominated. Wives may feel at a disadvantage in the face of the physical superiority of their husbands; husbands may feel at a disadvantage in the face of the verbal superiority of their wives. The struggle for domination that can ensue from the inclination to physical self-love may then create a thoroughly disharmonious marriage. Kant's suggestion that the couple subject themselves to the legitimate rule of one another will work as a solution only if the rule is legitimate and nonarbitrary, in other words, if it is not based on self-love, but rather on common sense (*Gemeinsinn*) and concern for the injury that egoism inflicts.

Finally, we come to the question of whether under unsociable sociability the institution of marriage is evolving toward the better. In general, Kant believes that "one can regard the history of the human species, in the large, as the realization of a hidden plan of nature to bring about an internally, and for this purpose, also an externally perfect national constitution, as the sole state in which all of humanity's natural capacities can be developed."[83] Unsociable sociability is the mechanism impelling the plan for the species that it improve its institutions through universally valid law. Over time, we can expect the constitution and laws to improve given the mechanism of unsociable sociability. However, in the short term, it can be that the state takes a dark path of preference for unsociability and domination that "hinders the citizen from pursuing his well-being in whatever ways consistent with the freedom of others he chooses."[84] If this happens the liveliness and power of the state are defeated. Is it possible that Kant believes that the institution of marriage is likewise progressing toward a more perfect form, and that sometimes in the short term it may take a dark path of domination?

We have some indication that Kant also thought of the institution of marriage as evolving over time and we can infer from some of his points that the dynamic of unsociable sociability was the mechanism of that evolution. Kant writes:

> In the crude state of nature it is quite different. There the woman is a domestic animal. The man leads the way with weapons in his hand, and the woman follows him, loaded down with his household belongings. But even where a barbaric civil constitution legalizes polygamy, the favorite woman in the man's prison (called a harem) knows how to gain control over him, and he had no end of trouble to make his life tolerably peaceful, with many women wrangling to be the one (who is to rule over him).
>
> In civil society woman does not give herself up to man's pleasure outside of marriage, and indeed *monogamous* marriage. Where civilization has not yet reached the degree of feminine freedom called *gallantry* (where a woman makes no secret of having lovers other than her husband), a man punishes his wife if she threatens him with a rival. But when gallantry has become the fashion and jealousy ridiculous (as never fails to happen in a period of luxury), the feminine character reveals itself; by man's leave, woman lays claim to freedom over against man and, at the same time, to the conquest of the whole male sex.—This inclination, though it indeed stands in ill repute under the name of coquetry, has some real basis of justification. For a young wife is always in danger of becoming a widow, and because of this she scatters her charms over all the men whom circumstances might make potential husbands for her, so that, should this situation occur, she would not be wanting for suitors.[85]

Kant describes several different stages of domestic relations between men and women in this paragraph. The first stage, is the "crude state of nature." In this state, women have no legal standing and are treated as animals. In the second stage, that Kant describes, there is indeed a civil constitution and women have legal standing within polygamy. The third stage described is the state of civil society where a woman has legal standing within monogamy, but is subject to her husband's rule and punishment. The fourth possible stage is that of gallantry where women have legal standing in monogamy, but also may have the freedom to express their independence of their husband's rule, since she "lays claim to freedom over against man."

We are not given an account of the transition from the "mere state of nature" to a civil constitution where domestic relations receive legal standing, but we do have indication of the mechanism of unsociable sociability at play once a civil constitution is in place.[86] In a "barbaric civil constitution" that legalizes polygamy, one woman gains control over a man, and other women create dissension trying to be the one woman controlling him. This disharmonious situation creates discomfort for the man. Possibly, the mechanism of antagonism and necessity is functioning to move the civil constitution toward monogamy.

In the civil monogamous marriage, a woman lays claim to more rights, since she "does not give herself up to man's pleasure outside of marriage."[87] The civil monogamous marriage, however, is not without tension: the man "loves domestic peace" but the woman "does not shrink from domestic warfare."[88] Where conjugal love is intolerant, the husband punishes his wife when she "threatens him with a rival."[89] However, rivalry does not cease to exist, but is rather transferred to the children, when the husband spoils the daughter and the wife spoils her son. The parents rival one another for the love of their children "in case the other should die," since in that case the remaining spouse would have someone to care for him/her. Although, Kant views this rivalry as having a justification, he does not view rivalry as virtuous since rivalry does not preserve freedom, but rather impairs it.

The monogamous relationship is not without envy as "a wife shows herself virtuous only under constraint and makes no secret of her wish that she were a man, so that she could give her inclinations wider scope and freer play. But no man would want to be a woman."[90] A woman could be envious of the freedom of men and could show her virtue only in constraining her envy. However, men recognized that to be a woman in Kant's time meant less freedom, and "no man would want to be a woman."[91] Her envy is thus legitimate, and indicates a gender disadvantage. Such a disadvantage can lead only to increasing tension since freedom is necessary for equality of agency.

The transition to gallantry may be occasioned by impaired freedom due to rivalry and a perceived disadvantage. In gallantry, the woman gains more freedom, but rivalry is only displaced not dispossessed. According to Kant, a woman is justifiably concerned about being widowed, and may lay claim to her freedom from her husband and her freedom to "play with her charms on every well-bred man" (coquetry).[92] Likewise, the man lays claim to "appearing to be in love with all women (gallantry)."[93] At this stage, like the stage of polygamy, the woman rivals other women, but unlike the stage of polygamy, where she rivals other women for the desire of one man, she now rivals other women for the desire of "all men."[94] While women judge one another strictly, men become tolerant and lenient toward women as they court "all women."

The transition to this stage of rivalry requires that a level of refined luxury be achieved, and this tells us that the transition to gallantry occurs only when the two partners no longer perceive an immediate concern for their preservation through their relation to each other or through their children. Luxury breeds insatiable inclinations and hence both women and men are vulnerable in this stage to wanting to be pleasing to all members of the opposite sex.

If we were to speculate how in the next stage of development we might apply the principle of unsociable sociability, we might want to see the weaknesses of gallantry. Kant claims that in gallantry the husband ought to be tolerant of coquetry. The weakness in this stage might be seen in the husband's discomfort with rivals and the impaired freedom resulting from intense jealousy, in this stage of gallantry, may well have been the mechanism effective in the transformation of the institution of marriage to the degree of freedom women currently enjoy in owning their own property.[95] Kant's suggestion that wives and husbands recognize one another's authority may well be the right course of action, but authority alone, without the power and freedom to carry through that authority, is not sufficient insurance against egoism. Even as the cosmopolitan society is established only through submission to legitimate law, the ideal institution of marriage can only be established through a reformation of the civil law governing marriage.

It appears then that Kant viewed the institution of marriage to be under the impulse of unsociable sociability. Not only is rivalry, antagonism, and impaired freedom evident in domestic relations, but the domestic relation is also evolving as it comes under increasingly refined civil legislation. We may want to take Kant's principles and extend them beyond his own considerations. What might we expect next? So far in Kant's account, I have referred only to the mechanisms of necessity (antagonism) and impaired freedom, and it may well be that the state of civil marriage has not yet reached the stage where the mechanism of empathy, common sense (*Gemeinsinn*), and concern over injury caused by egoism will impel the further evolution of marriage toward its greater perfection. I take it that marriage is about intimacy and basic human connectedness between two people and is an organization that promotes the disposition to care for others. It provides safety and security to people and their children. It provides opportunities that would not otherwise be possible. It almost inevitably allows for differentiation, but also maturation. According to Kant, we have to realistically view marriage as a challenge to egoism, but that challenge needs help from the civil constitution. Women, in Kant's account, have rights only in a civil marriage. The feminine character exercises that right through verbal discourse that can have effective power only because of the universal validity of the law.

The feminine character, according to Kant, furthers "the cultivation of society and its refinement" because of its connection with greater verbal eloquence. Yet it has not been the case so far that the institution of marriage has been improved because of empathy, common sense, and concern for injury, but rather because of necessity and impaired freedom.[96] Empathy, common sense, and concern for injury may well be the next mechanisms impelling the improvement of the institution of marriage.

In conclusion, the intent of Kant's anthropology lectures is to teach students to think for themselves and to compare their own experience with examples that he provided. Kant is not prescribing a certain set of gender roles for women and men, even though he seems to suggest that gender differentiation is inevitable. Prescription would undercut the intent that students learn to judge and think for themselves. Further, we see that Kant believes that inevitable gender differentiation does not always work to women's disadvantage. Gender differentiation works to women's and men's advantage in the long run when it leads to the further refinement of civilization and to the improvement of the institution of marriage. This point does not entail that all characteristics of gender differentiation are equally good. Kant still maintains the distinction between virtue and vice and the position that all human institutions have the purpose of combining the greatest freedom under laws that have irresistible power.[97] A perfect institution of marriage would allow the greatest freedom for both partners while allowing both people to feel uncoerced within the legal constraints of the civil institution. Such an ideal may be unrealizable in principle, but it may well still function as an ideal for the improvement of the legal institution of marriage and for an individual marriage.[98]

NOTES

1. Immanuel Kant, *Anthropologie im pragmatischer Hinsicht*, in *Kants Gesammelte Schriften*, edited by the Königlich Preußische [now Deutsche] Akademie der Wissenschaft, vols. 1–29 (Berlin: G. Reimer [now de Gruyter], 1902–), 7:331; *Anthropology from a Pragmatic Point of View*, trans. Mary J. Gregor

(The Hague: Martinus Nijhoff, 1974), 191 (now *Anthropology*, KGS, VII:331; p. 191, I will give the KGS pagination first and then the pagination of the translation when available).

2. Immanuel Kant, *Von den Vershiedenen Racen der Menschen*, in KGS 2:443.

3. Immanuel Kant, *Nachricht von der Einrichtung seiner Vorlesungen*, in KGS 2:312 [Now *Nachricht*, KGS 2:312].

4. *Nachricht*, KGS 2:312.

5. *Nachricht*, KGS 2:305.

6. *Nachricht*, KGS 2:305–6.

7. *Briefe*, KGS 10:145f.

8. *Anthropology*, KGS 7:200, 228; pp. 72, 96–97. Kant also calls these the maxims of the *sensus communis* or common sense in the *Critique of Judgment*. See Kant, *Kritik der Urteilskraft*, in KGS 5:194; translation, *Immanuel Kant's Critique of Judgment*, trans. Werner S. Pluhar, with foreword by Mary J. Gregor (Indianapolis, Ind.: Hackett, 1987) (now CJ, KGS 5:194; p. 34, when Pluhar's translation is used).

9. *Anthropology*, KGS 7:119; p. 3.

10. *Anthropology*, KGS 7:228; p. 96.

11. *Anthropology*, KGS 7:198; p. 70.

12. *Anthropology*, KGS 7:199; p. 71.

13. Compare the notes from the 70s and 80s in volume 15 of *Kants Gesammelte Schriften*.

14. *Anthropology*, KGS 7:201; p. 72.

15. Kant carefully distinguishes between cunning and prudence. *Anthropology*, KGS 7:198; p. 70.

16. KGS 5:383; p. 264.

17. Immanuel Kant, "Erste Einleitung zur Kritik der Urteilskraft," in KGS 20:199–200; trans. in Pluhar, p. 390 (now KGS, EE). See also KU, KGS 5:374; p. 254.

18. Kant, *Grundlegung zur Metaphysik der Sitten*, in KGS, IV, 416; *Grounding for the Metaphysics of Morals*, trans. by James W. Ellington, (Indianapolis, Ind.: Hackett, 1981), p. 26.

19. *Anthropology*, KGS 7:305–6. Translation is mine.

20. I have argued that the *Anthropology* requires teleological judgment as its presupposition. See Holly L. Wilson, "A Gap in American Kant Scholarship: Pragmatic Anthropology as the Application of Kantian Moral Theory," in *Akten des Siebten Internationalen Kant-Kongresses: Kurfürsliches Schloß zu Mainz, 1990*, ed. von G. Funke (Bonn: Bouvier, 1991), 403–19.

21. CJ, KGS 5:194; p. 34.

22. See Hegel's discussion in *Enzyklopädie der philosophischen Wissenschaften 1830* (Hamburg: Felix Meiner, 1969), 177–78.

23. See article "Zweck" in *Handbuch Philosophischer Grundbegriffe*, ed. von Krings, Baumgartner, and Wild (Munich: Kösel, 1974), 1823.

24. EE, KGS 5:216; pp. 403–4. Kant argues that reflective judgment has its own transcendental principle that *"Nature, for the sake of the power of judgment, makes its universal laws specific [and] into empirical ones, according to the form of a logical system.* This is where the concept of a purposiveness of nature arises. This concept belongs to reflective judgment."

25. CJ, KGS 5:374; pp. 253–54. Kant writes, "In considering nature and the ability it displays in organized products, we say far too little if we call this an *analogue of art."*

26. CJ, KGS 5:376; p. 255.

27. Ibid.

28. "Idea for a Universal History with a C osmopolitan Intent" KGS 8:25; p. 35. See also CJ, KGS 5:380–81; pp. 260–61.

29. CJ, KGS 5:381; p. 261.

30. Another way of putting this, is that sexual differentiation is not merely socially constructed.

31. *Anthropology*, KGS 7:303; pp. 166–67.

32. *Anthropology*, KGS 7:303; p. 167.

33. Ibid., 7:303; pp. 166–67

34. Ibid., 7:306; p. 169.

35. Ibid., 7:303; p. 167.

36. Ibid., 7:273; p. 140.

37. Ibid., 7:303–4; p. 167.

38. Ibid.

39. Ibid.

40. Ibid., 7:306; p. 169.

41. Ibid., 7:306; p. 169.

42. Ibid.

43. Ibid., 7:306; p. 170.

44. Ibid., 7:309; p. 172.

45. Ibid.

46. Ibid., 7:307; p. 170.

47. Ibid., 7:309; p. 172.

48. Ibid., 7:310; pp. 172–73.

49. Ibid., 7:310; p. 173.

50. Ibid.

51. Ibid., 7:309; p. 172.

52. Ibid.

53. Ibid., 7:304; p. 168.

54. Ibid., 7:305; p. 169.

55. Ibid., 7:304; p. 167.

56. Ibid.

57. Ibid., 7:306; p. 170.

58. Ibid.

59. Ibid., 7:308; p. 172.

60. Ibid., 7:308; p. 171.

61. Ibid., 7:303; p. 167.

62. Ibid.

63. Ibid., 7:304; p. 167.

64. Ibid.

65. Ibid., 7:303; p. 167.

66. Ibid., 7:307; p. 171.

67. Ibid., 7:304; p. 167.

68. Ibid., 7:308; p. 171.

69. Ibid., 7:304; p. 168.

70. Ibid., 7:310; p. 173.

71. Ibid., 7:331; p. 191.

72. Ibid., 7:328; p. 188.

73. In ibid., 7:322ff.; pp. 183ff., Kant lists the predispositions as the technical, the pragmatic, and the moral. In *Die Religion innerhalb der Grenzen der bloßen Vernunft*, KGS, 6:26; *Religion within the Limits of Reason Alone*, trans. Theodore M. Greene and Hoyte H. Hudson (New York: Harper & Row, 1960), 21 (now *Religion*, KGS, 6:26; 21), the three predispositions discussed are the predispositions to animality, humanity, and personality. The account of the predisposition to animality is missing in the *Anthropology*. In the *Religion*, the account of the technical predisposition is missing. This does not necessarily represent a conflicting account of the four original predispositions, since the descriptions are given with respect to different purposes. The *Anthropology* is contrasting human beings and animals, and discussing the specific differences between human beings and animals, not the commonalties between them. The *Religion* is attempting to determine the root of evil, and Kant investigates whether it can be rooted in animality, humanity, or personality. He does not seem to think that the technical predisposition is relevant to evil.

74. *Anthropology*, KGS 7:329; p. 190.

75. CJ, KGS 5:432; p. 320.

76. Immanuel Kant, *Idee zu einer allgemeinen Geschichte in weltbürgerlicher Absicht*, in KGS 8:22; translation, "Idea for a Universal History with a Cosmopolitan Intent," in *Perpetual Peace and Other Essays*, trans. Ted Humphrey (Indianapolis, Ind.: Hackett, 1983), 33 (now "Idea," KGS 8:22; p. 33).

77. "Idea," KGS 8:20; p. 31.

78. *Anthropology*, KGS 8:323; 185.

79. *Religion*, KGS 8:27; p. 22.

80. Ibid.

81. Ibid.

82. Ibid.

83. "Idea," KGS 8:27; p. 36.

84. Ibid., 8:28; p. 37.

85. *Anthropology*, KGS 7:304–5; p. 168.

86. It may well be argued that the antagonism of rivalry among men for women may well have impelled men initially to institutionalize marriage.

87. *Anthropology*, KGS 7:304; p. 168.

88. Ibid., 7:304; p. 167.

89. Ibid., 7:304; p. 168.

90. Ibid., 7:307; p. 170.

91. Ibid.

92. Ibid.

93. Ibid.

94. Ibid.

95. Kant does not speak of property rights in this context, even though he views sexual relations as morally permissible only on the basis of legitimate property rights, that is, a legitimate right of disposal over the other person. Barbara Herman has an interesting exposition of Kant's views on sexuality and the legal institution of marriage in his *Theory of Right*. See Barbara Herman, "Could It Be Worth Thinking about Kant on Sex and Marriage?" in *A Mind of One's Own: Feminist Essays on Reason and Objectivity*, ed. Louise M. Antony and Charlotte Witt (Boulder, Colo.: Westview Press, 1993), 49–67. Although she is skeptical about Kant's contentions, she does characterize Kant's point well when she writes that "Kant's argument has to be (and is) that there is something about the nature of persons and about the nature of the sexual relationship that makes a will to love insufficient to guarantee the autonomy and equality of sexually involved persons" (p. 55). The only sufficient guarantee of equality of agency is equality that comes through the juridically regulated institution of marriage, in which the domestic partners receive juridical standing. Such an account of the moral justification of the legal institution of marriage is not in conflict with what Kant suggests in the *Anthropology*. He is not attempting to justify equality in the *Anthropology*, but rather to give a theoretical account of the natural and developmental inequality in the domestic relation, and the resultant impulses that motivate human beings from the natural side to move from animal egoistical behavior to submit themselves to civil law and common sense. Kant is doing theoretical philosophy in the *Anthropology*, not practical philosophy. Theoretical philosophy is about nature

and human nature; practical philosophy is about human freedom. The moral law in practical philosophy provides sufficient incentive for action, but that does not preclude the possibility of examining the same action from a theoretical point of view.

96. *Anthropology*, KGS 8:306; p. 169.

97. "Idea," KGS 8:22; p. 33.

98. Ibid., 8:23; p. 33. Kant argues that the perfect civil constitution cannot be achieved without the education of the human species, because we all begin as animals with selfish propensities and we need necessity and coercive power to break "self-will" and force us "to obey a universally valid will."

BIBLIOGRAPHY

Ackerman, Bruce A. *Social Justice in the Liberal State*. New Haven, Conn.: Yale University Press, 1980.

Adkins, Arthur W. H. *Merit and Responsibility: A Study in Greek Values*. Oxford: Oxford University Press, 1960.

Allen, Theodore. *The Invention of the White Race*. Vol. 1: Racial Oppression and Social Control. London and New York: Verso, 1994.

Allison, Henry. *Kant's Theory of Freedom*. Cambridge: Cambridge University Press, 1990.

Arendt, Hannah. *Lectures on Kant's Political Philosophy*, edited by Ronald Beiner. Chicago: University of Chicago Press, 1982

Auxter, Thomas. "Kant's Conception of the Private Sphere." *The Philosophical Forum* (Summer 1982): 295–310.

———. *Kant's Moral Teleology*. Macon, Ga.: Mercer University Press, 1982.

———. "The Process of Morality." In *Hegel and Whitehead: Contemporary Perspectives on Systematic Philosophy*, edited by George R. Lucas Jr., 219–38. Albany: State University of New York Press, 1986.

———. "The Unimportance of Kant's Highest Good." *Journal of the History of Philosophy* (April 1979): 121–34.

Axelrod, Robert. *The Evolution of Cooperation*, New York: Basic Books, 1984.

Axinn, Sidney. "Kant, Authority, and the French Revolution." *Journal of the History of Ideas* (July 1971): 423–32.

Baier, Annette. "For the Sake of Future Generations." In *Earthbound*, edited by Tom Regan. New York: Random House, 1984.

Baldwin, James. "Negroes Are Anti-Semitic Because They're Anti-White." In Berman, *Blacks and Jews*, 31–41. First published in *New York Times Magazine*, 9 April 1967.

Baron, Marcia. "Kantian Ethics and Claims of Detachment." In *Feminist Interpretations of Kant*, edited by Robin May Schott. University Park: Pennsylvania State University Press, 1997.

Beck, Lewis White. *Commentary on Kant's Critique of Practical Reason.* Chicago: University of Chicago Press, 1961.

———. "Kant and the Right of Revolution." *Journal of the History of Ideas* (July 1971): 411–22.

Behrens, C. B. A. *Society, Government and the Enlightenment: The Experiences of Eighteenth-Century France and Prussia.* London: Thames and Hudson: 1985.

Benhabib, Seyla. *Critique, Norm, and Utopia.* New York: Columbia University Press, 1986.

———. *Situating the Self: Gender, Community and Postmodernism in Contemporary Ethics.* New York.: Routledge, 1992.

Benn, S. I. "Personal Freedom and Environmental Ethics: The Moral Inequality of the Species." In *Equality and Freedom: International Comparative Jurisprudence,* edited by Gray Dorsey. Dobbs Ferry, N.Y.: Oceana, 1977), 2:401–24.

———. *A Theory of Freedom.* Cambridge: Cambridge University Press, 1988.

Benn, S. I., and Gerald F. Gaus. "Practical Rationality and Commitment." *American Philosophical Quarterly* 23 (July 1986): 255–66.

———. "The Public and Private: Concepts and Action." In their edited collection, *Public and Private in Social Life.* New York: St. Martin's Press, 1983.

Berman, Paul, ed. *Blacks and Jews: Alliances and Arguments.* New York: Delacorte Press, 1994.

Bernal, Martin. *Black Athena: The Afroasiatic Roots of Classical Civilization.* Vol. 1: *The Fabrication of Ancient Greece 1785–1985.* New Brunswick, N.J.: Rutgers University Press, 1987.

Bittner, Rüdiger. *What Reason Demands,* translated by Theodore Talbot. Cambridge: Cambridge University Press, 1989.

Bogle, Donald. *Toms, Coons, Mulattoes, Mammies & Bucks: An Interpretive History of Blacks in American Films.* 1973; rev. ed. New York: Continuum, 1989.

Bowles, Samuel, and Herbert Gintis. "A Political and Economic Case for the Democratic Enterprise." In *The Idea of Democracy,* edited by David Copp, Jean Hampton, and John E. Roemer. Cambridge: Cambridge University Press, 1993.

Boxill, Bernard. "Self-Respect and Protest." In *Philosophy Born of Struggle: Anthropology of Afro-American Philosophy from 1917,* edited by Leonard Harris, 190–98. Dubuque, Iowa: Kandall/Hunt, 1983.

Brennan, William. Opinion in Supreme Court decision, Furman v. Georgia, 1972 (408 U.S. 238).

Brown, Wendy. "'Supposing Truth Were a Woman . . .': Plato's Subversion of Masculine Discourse." In *Feminist Interpretations of Plato,* edited by Nancy Tuana. Albany: State University of New York Press, 1994.

Burke, Edmund. "Reflections on the Revolution in France." In *The Works of Edmund Burke*, vol. 3. Boston: Little, Brown, 1884.

Burkert, Walter. *Greek Religion*. Cambridge, Mass.: Harvard University Press, 1985.

Byrd, Sharon. "Kant's Theory of Punishment: Deterrence in Its Threat, Retribution in Its Execution." *Law and Philosophy* 1 (1989): 151–200.

Callicott, J. Baird. "Intrinsic Value of Nonhuman Species." In *The Preservation of Species*, edited by Bryan G. Norton, 138–72. Princeton, N.J.: Princeton University Press, 1986.

Camus, Albert. "Reflections on the Guillotine." In *Resistance, Rebellion, and Death*, translated by Justin O'Brien. New York: Random House, 1960.

Card, Claudia.: "Women's Voices and Ethical Ideals: Must We Mean What We Say?" *Ethics* (October 1988): 99:1, 125–35.

Cassirer, Ernst. *Kant's Life and Thought*, translated by James Haden. New Haven, Conn.: Yale University Press, 1981.

———.*The Myth of the State*. Garden City, N.Y.: Doubleday, 1946.

———. *The Philosophy of the Enlightenment* (1932). Boston: Beacon Press, 1951.

Clark, Kenneth B. "Candor about Negro-Jewish Relations." In *Bridges and Boundaries*, edited by Jack Salzman, Adina Back, and Gretchen Sullivan Sovin, 91–98. New York: George Braziller and the Jewish Museum, 1992.

Clarke, John Henrik, ed. *Marcus Garvey and the Vision of Africa*. New York: Vintage Books, 1974.

Clymer, Adam. "Voter Bill Passes in G.O.P. Defeat." *The New York Times*, 11 May 1993.

Cohen, G. A. *Karl Marx's Theory of History: A Defence*. Princeton, N.J.: Princeton University Press, 1978.

Cole, Eve Browning. "Women, Slaves, and 'Love of Toil' in Aristotle's Moral Philosophy." In *Engendering Origins: Critical Feminist Readings in Plato and Aristotle*, edited by Bat-Ami Bar On. Albany: State University of New York Press, 1994.

Count, Earl W., ed. *This Is Race: An Anthology Selected from the International Literature on the Races of Man*. New York: Henry Schuman, 1950.

Cox, Oliver. *Caste, Class and Race*. New York: Modern Reader, 1948.

Cronon, E. David. *Black Moses: The Story of Marcus Garvey and the Universal Negro Improvement Association*. 1955; 2nd ed. Madison: University of Wisconsin Press, 1969.

Curtin, Philip, ed. *Imperialism*. New York: Walker, 1971.

Dagger, Richard. "Politics and the Pursuit of Autonomy." In *NOMOS XXVIII: Justification*, edited by J. Roland Pennock and John W. Chapman, 270–90. New York: New York University Press, 1986.

Dahl, Robert A. *A Preface to Economic Democracy*. Berkeley: University of California Press, 1985.

Darwall, Stephen L. "Two Kinds of Respect." *Ethics* 88 (October 1977): 36–49.

Davis, Michael. *Make the Punishment Fit the Crime*. Boulder, Colo.: Westview Press, 1992.

Di Stefano, Christine. "Dilemmas of Difference: Feminism, Modernity, and Postmodernism." In *Feminism/Postmodernism*, edited by Linda Nicholson, 63–82. New York: Routledge, 1990.

Douglas, R. Bruce, Gerald M. Mara, and Henry S. Richardson, eds. *Liberalism and the Good*. New York and London: Routledge, 1990.

Dworkin, Ronald. "Liberalism." In *A Matter of Principle*. Cambridge, Mass.: Harvard University Press, 1985.

Dworkin, Gerald. *The Theory and Practice of Autonomy*. Cambridge: Cambridge University Press, 1988.

Elster, Jon. "From Here to There; or, If Cooperative Ownership Is So Desirable, Why Are There So Few Cooperatives?" *Social Philosophy & Policy* 6 (Spring 1989): 93–111.

Elster, Jon, and Karl Ove Moene, eds. *Alternatives to Capitalism*. Cambridge: Cambridge University Press, 1989.

Engels, Friedrich. *Anti-Dühring*. Moscow: Progress, 1962.

Estrin, Saul. "Workers' Co-operatives: Their Merits and Their Limitations." In *Market Socialism*, edited by Julian Le Grand and Saul Estrin. Oxford: Clarendon, 1989.

Eze, Emmanuel. "The Color of Reason: The Idea of 'Race' in Kant's Anthropology." In *Anthropology and the German Enlightenment: Perspectives on Humanity*, edited by K. M. Faull, 196–237. Lewisberg, Pa.: Bucknell University Press, 1995.

Fackenheim, Emil. "Kant's Concept of History." *Kant-Studien* 48 (1956–57).

Fanon, Frantz. *The Wretched of the Earth*, translated by Constance Farrington. New York: Grove Press, 1968.

Feinberg, Joel, "The Expressive Function of Punishment." In *Doing and Deserving*. Princeton, N.J.: Princeton University Press, 1970.

Flax, Jane. "Postmodernism and Gender Relations." In *Feminism/Postmodernism*, edited by Linda Nicholson, 39–62. New York: Routledge, 1990.

Foa, Pamela. "What's Wrong with Rape?" In *Feminism and Philosophy* edited by Mary Vetterling-Braggin, Frederick Elliston, and Jane English, 347–59. Totowa, N.J.: Littlefield, Adams, 1977.

Foucault, Michel. "Un cours inédit." *Magazine littéraire* (Paris, May 1984).

Fredrickson, George. *White Supremacy: A Comparative Study in American and South African History*. New York: Oxford University Press, 1981.

Friedman, Michael. *Kant and the Exact Sciences*. Cambridge, Mass.: Harvard University Press, 1992.

Galston, William A. *Liberal Purposes: Good, Virtues, and Diversity in the Liberal State*. Cambridge, Mass.: Cambridge University Press, 1991.

———. "What Is Living and What Is Dead in Kant's Practical Philosophy?" In *Kant and Political Philosophy*, edited by Ronald Beiner and William James Booth. New Haven, Conn.: Yale University Press, 1993.

Gaus, Gerald F. "The Commitment to the Common Good." In *On Political Obligation*, edited by Paul Harris, 26–64. London: Routledge, 1990.

———. *Justificatory Liberalism: An Essay on Epistemology and Political Theory*. New York: Oxford University Press, 1996.

———. *Modern Liberal Theory of Man*. New York: St. Martin's Press, 1983, 187ff.

———. "Practical Reason and Moral Persons." *Ethics* 100 (October 1989).

———. *Value and Justification: The Foundations of Liberal Theory*. Cambridge: Cambridge University Press, 1990.

Gewirth, Alan. *Human Rights: Essays on Justification and Applications*. Chicago: University of Chicago Press, 1982.

———. *Reason and Morality*. Chicago: University of Chicago Press, 1978.

Giddens, Anthony. *Profiles and Critiques in Social Theory*. Berkeley: University of California Press, 1982.

Gilligan, Carol. *In a Different Voice: Psychological Theory and Women's Development*. Cambridge, Mass.: Harvard University Press, 1992.

Glazer, Nathan, and Daniel Patrick Moynihan. *Beyond the Melting Pot*. 1963; 2nd ed. Cambridge, Mass.: MIT Press, 1970.

Goldberg, David Theo. *Racist Culture: Philosophy and the Politics of Meaning*. Oxford: Blackwell, 1993.

Goldman, Alvin. "Ethics and Cognitive Science." *Ethics* 103 (1993): 337–60.

Gossett, Thomas. *Race: The History of an Idea in America*. 1963; reprinted New York: Schocken, 1965.

Gould, Carol C. *Rethinking Democracy*. Cambridge: Cambridge University Press, 1988.

Gould, Stephen Jay. *The Mismeasure of Man*. New York and London: W. W. Norton, 1981.

Gray, John. "Does Democracy Have a Future?" *The New York Times Book Review*, 22 January 1995.

Gross, Hyman. "Culpability and Desert." *Archiv für Rechts und Sozialphilosophie* 19 (1983). This essay is also reprinted in most editions of *Philosophy of Law*, edited by Joel Feinberg and Hyman Gross. Belmont, Calif.: Wadsworth, 1975, and later years.

Grosz, Elizabeth. "Contemporary Theories of Power and Objectivity." In *Feminist Knowledge; Critique and Construct*, edited by Sneja Gunew, 59–120. London: Routledge, 1990.

Guyer, Paul. *Kant and the Experience of Freedom*. Cambridge: Cambridge University Press, 1993.

Hall, Kim. "*Sensus Communis* and Violence: A Feminist Reading of Kant's *Critique of Judgment*." In *Feminist Interpretations of Kant*, edited by Robin May Schott. University Park: Pennsylvania State University Press, 1997.

Hampton, Jean. "The Moral Education Theory of Punishment." *Philosophy and Public Affairs* 13.3 (1984): 208–38.

Harding, Sandra, ed. *The "Racial" Economy of Science: Toward a Democratic Future*. Bloomington and Indianapolis: Indiana University Press, 1993.

Hare, R. M. "A Kantian Approach to Abortion." *Social Theory and Practice* 15.1 (Spring 1989). Reprinted in *The Moral Life*, edited by Steven Luper-Foy and Curtis Brown. San Diego: Harcourt, Brace, Jovanovich, 1992.

Harris, Erol E. "Respect for Persons." In *Ethics and Society*, edited by Richard T. De George, 111–32. London: Macmillan, 1968.

Harris, Leonard, ed. *Philosophy Born of Struggle: Anthology of Afro-American Philosophy from 1917*. Dubuque, Iowa: Kendall/Hunt, 1983.

Hegel, G. W. F. *Elements of the Philosophy of Right*, edited by A. Wood, translated by H. B. Nisbet. Cambridge: Cambridge University Press, 1991.

———. *Enzyklopädie der philosophischen Wissenschaften 1830*. Hamburg: Felix Meiner, 1969.

———. *The Philosophy of History*. New York: Dover, 1956.

Hentoff, Nat, ed. *Black Anti-Semitism and Jewish Racism*. New York: Richard W. Baron, 1969.

Herman, Barbara. *The Practice of Moral Judgment*. Cambridge, Mass: Harvard University Press, 1993.

Herrnstein, Richard, and Charles Murray. *The Bell Curve: Intelligence and Class Structure in American Life*. New York: The Free Press, 1994.

Hill, Thomas E., Jr. *Autonomy and Self-Respect*. Cambridge: Cambridge University Press, 1991.

———. *Dignity and Practical Reason in Kant's Moral Theory*. Ithaca, N.Y.: Cornell University Press, 1992.

Hoff, Christina. "Kant's Invidious Humanism." *Environmental Ethics* 5 (Spring 1983): 63–70.

Ignatiev, Noel. *How the Irish Became White*. New York and London: Routledge, 1995.

Isaacs, Harold. "Color in World Affairs." In *White Racism*, edited by Barry Schwartz and Robert Disch, 474–90. New York: Dell, 1970.

Jacoby, Russell, and Naomi Glauberman, eds. *The Bell Curve Debate: History, Documents, Opinions.* New York: Random House, 1995.

Jacques-Garvey, Amy, ed. *The Philosophy and Opinions of Marcus Garvey.* 2 vols. 1923, 1925; reprinted New York: Atheneum, 1992.

Jameson, Fredric. *Postmodernism, or, The Cultural Logic of Late Capitalism.* Durham, N.C.: Duke University Press, 1991.

Jencks, Christopher. *Rethinking Social Policy: Race, Poverty, and the Underclass,* Cambridge, Mass.: Harvard University Press, 1992.

Johnston, Otto W. "Erzählte Kriminalität in Grillparzers *Ahnfrau.*" In *Ethik und Ästhetik. Werke und Werte in der Literatur vom 18. bis zum 20. Jahrhundert,* edited by Richard Fisher. Bern: Peter Lang, 1995.

————."Schiller: das bourgeois-liberale Programm der Französischen Revolution." In *Verlorene Klassik?* edited by Wolfgang Wittkowski. Tübingen: Max Niemeyer, 1986.

Jordan, Winthrop. *White over Black: American Attitudes Toward the Negro, 1550–1812.* 1968; reprinted New York and London: W. W. Norton, 1977.

Kant, Immanuel. *Kants Gesammelte Schriften.* Berlin: Ausgabe der Königlichen Preußischen Akademie der Wissenschaften, 1902–.

Translations:

————. *Anthropology from a Pragmatic Point of View,* translated by Mary J. Gregor. The Hague: Martinus Nijhoff, 1974.

————. *Anthropology from a Pragmatic Point of View,* translated by Victor Lyle Dowdell. Carbondale and Edwardsville: Southern Illinois University Press, 1978.

————. *The Conflict of the Faculties,* translated by Mary J. Gregor. New York: Abaris Books, 1979.

————. *Critique of Judgment,* translated by Werner S. Pluhar. Indianapolis, Ind.: Hackett, 1987.

————. *Critique of Practical Reason,* translated by Lewis White Beck. Indianapolis, Ind.: Bobbs-Merrill, 1956.

————. *Critique of Pure Reason,* translated by Norman Kemp Smith. New York: St. Martin's Press, 1963.

————. *The Critique of Pure Reason,* edited and translated by Paul Guyer and Allen W. Wood. New York: Cambridge University Press, 1997.

————. *Dreams of a Spirit-Seer,* translated by John Manolesco. New York: Vantage, 1960.

————. *Foundations of the Metaphysics of Morals,* translated by Lewis White Beck. Indianapolis, Ind.: Bobbs-Merrill, 1959.

————. *Groundwork of the Metaphysic of Morals,* translated by H. J. Paton. 1948; reprinted New York: Harper & Row, 1964.

————. *Kant on History*, edited by Lewis White Beck. New York: Macmillan, 1985.

————. *Kant: Selections*, edited by Lewis White Beck. New York: Macmillan, 1988.

————. *Lectures on Ethics*, translated by Louis Infield. New York: Harper & Row, 1963.

————. *Lectures on Logic*, translated by Michael Young. Cambridge: Cambridge University Press, 1994.

————. *The Metaphysical Elements of Justice*, translated by John Ladd. Indianapolis, Ind.: Bobbs-Merrill, 1965.

————. *The Metaphysics of Morals*, translated by Mary J. Gregor. Cambridge: Cambridge University Press, 1991.

————. *Observations on the Feeling of the Beautiful and the Sublime*, translated by John T. Goldthwait. Berkeley: University of California Press, 1960.

————. *On the Old Saw: That Might Be Right in Theory but It Won't Work in Practice*, translated by E. B. Aston. Philadelphia: University of Pennsylvania Press, 1974.

————. *Perpetual Peace and Other Essays*, translated by Ted Humphrey. Indianapolis, Ind.: Hackett, 1983.

————. *Political Writings*, edited by H. Reiss. 2nd enlarged ed. Cambridge: Cambridge University Press, 1991.

————. *Religion within the Limits of Reason Alone*, translated by Theodore M. Greene and Hoyt H. Hudson. New York: Harper & Row, 1960.

————. *Writings on Anthropology, History and Education*, edited by Günter Zöller. New York: Cambridge University Press, forthcoming.

————. *Writings on Practical Philosophy*, edited and translated by Mary J. Gregor. New York: Cambridge University Press, 1996.

————. *Writings on Religion and Rational Theology*, edited and translated by Allen W. Wood and George diGiovanni. New York: Cambridge University Press, 1996.

Kellert, Stephen R. "Social and Perceptual Factors in the Preservation of Animal Species." In *The Preservation of Species*, edited by B. G. Norton, 50–73. Princeton, N.J.: Princeton University Press, 1986.

Kerenyi, C. *Eleusis: Archetypal Image of Mother and Daughter*. Princeton, N.J.: Princeton University Press, 1967.

Kiernan, V. G. *The Lords of Human Kind: Black Man, Yellow Man, and White Man in an Age of Empire*. 1969; reprinted New York: Columbia University Press, 1986.

Kneller, Jane. "The Aesthetic Dimension of Kantian Autonomy." In *Feminist Interpretations of Kant*, edited by Robin May Schott. University Park: Pennsylvania State University Press, 1997.

Koestler, Arthur. *Reflections on Hanging*. New York: Macmillan, 1957.

Kofman, Sarah. "The Economy of Respect: Kant and Respect for Women." In *Le Respect des femmes*. Paris: Galilee, 1982; reprinted in *Feminist Interpretations of Kant*, edited by Robin May Schott. University Park: Pennsylvania State University Press, 1997.

Korsgaard, Christine M. "The Right to Lie: Kant on Dealing with Evil." *Philosophy & Public Affairs* 15 (1986): 325–49.

Kovel, Joel. *White Racism: A Psychohistory*. 1970; reprinted New York: Columbia University Press, 1984.

Larmore, Charles. "Pluralism and Reasonable Disagreement." *Social Philosophy & Policy* 11 (Winter 1993): 61–79.

Lewis, Rupert, and Patrick Bryan, eds. *Garvey: His Work and Impact*. Mona, Jamaica: Institute of Social & Economic Research, University of the West Indies, 1988.

Lindley, Richard. *Autonomy*. London: Macmillan, 1986.

Livingstone, Frank. "On the Nonexistence of Human Races." In *The "Racial" Economy of Science*, 133–41. Bloomington: Indiana University Press, 1993.

Lomasky, Loren E. *Persons, Rights and the Moral Community*. New York: Oxford University Press, 1987.

Lombardi, Louis G. "Inherent Worth, Respect and Rights." *Environmental Ethics* 5 (Fall 1983): 257–70.

Luker, Kristin. *Abortion and the Politics of Motherhood*. Berkeley: University of California Press, 1984.

Lyotard, Jean-François. *The Postmodern Condition*, translated by G. Bennington and B. Massouri. Minneapolis: University of Minnesota Press, 1984.

McCall, John J. "Participation in Employment." In *Contemporary Issues in Business Ethics*, edited by Joseph R. DesJardins and John J. McCall. Belmont, Calif.: Wadsworth, 1985, 1990.

McCarthy, Sharon. "The Dilemma of Non-participation." In *Organizational Democracy: Taking Stock*, Vol. 1 of the *International Handbook of Participation in Organizations*, edited by Cornelius J. Lammers and György Széll. Oxford: Oxford University Press, 1989.

McCloskey, H. J. "Ecological Ethics and Its Justification: A Critical Appraisal." In *Environmental Ethics*, edited by Don Mannison, Michael McRobbie, and Richard Routley, 65–87. Canberra: Research School of Social Sciences, Australian National Iniversity, 1980.

MacIntyre, Alasdair. *After Virtue*. 2nd ed. Notre Dame, Ind.: University of Notre Dame Press, 1984.

———. *Whose Justice? Which Rationality?* Notre Dame, Ind.: University of Notre Dame Press, 1988.

MacKinnon, Catharine. *Toward a Feminist Theory of the State.* Cambridge, Mass.: Harvard University Press, 1989.

Maltby, Lewis L. *A State of Emergency in the American Workplace.* New York: American Civil Liberties Union, 1990.

Mannison, Don, Micahel McRobbie, and Richard Routley, eds. *Environmental Philosophy.* Department of Philosophy Monograph Series no. 2. Canberra: Research School of Social Sciences, Australian National University, 1980

Massey, Douglas, and Nancy A. Denton. *American Apartheid: Segregation and the Making of the Underclass.* Cambridge, Mass.: Harvard University Press, 1993.

Martin, Emily. *Woman in the Body.* Boston: Beacon Press, 1987.

Marx, Karl, and Friedrich Engels. *Collected Works.* New York: International Publishers, 1975–.

Melden, A. I. *Rights and Persons.* Oxford: Basil Blackwell, 1977.

Mendus, Susan. "Kant: 'An Honest but Narrow-Minded Bourgeois'?" In *Essays on Kant's Political Philosophy,* edited by Howard Williams. Cardiff: University of Wales Press, 1992.

Midgley, Mary. *Animals and Why They Matter.* Harmondsworth, U.K.: Penguin, 1983.

Miller, Alan. "Black Anti-Semitism—Jewish Racism." In *Black Anti-Semitism,* edited by Nat Hentoff, 79–114. New York: Richard W. Baron, 1969.

Miller, David. *Market, State and Community: Theoretical Foundations of Market Socialism.* Oxford: Oxford University Press, 1990.

———. "A Vision of Market Socialism." *Dissent* (Summer 1991): 406–14.

Mills, Charles. "Non-Cartesian *Sums*: Philosophy and the African-American Experience." *Teaching Philosophy* 17 (1994): 223–43.

———. "Revisionist Ontologies: Theorizing White Supremacy." *Social and Economic Studies* 43.3 (1994): 105–34.

Milne, A. J. M. *Human Rights and Human Diversity.* Albany: State University of New York Press, 1986.

Moen, Marcia. "Feminist Themes in Unlikely Places: Rereading Kant's *Critique of Judgement.*" In *Feminist Interpretations of Kant,* edited by Robin May Schott. University Park: Pennsylvania State University Press, 1997.

Moore, Michael S. "The Moral Worth of Retribution." In *Responsibility, Character and the Emotions: New Essays in Moral Psychology,* edited by Ferdinand Schoeman. Cambridge: Cambridge University Press, 1987.

Morris, Herbert. *On Guilt and Innocence.* Berkeley: University of California Press, 1976.

———. "A Paternalistic Theory of Punishment." *American Philosophical Quarterly* 18.4 (October 1981).

Mosse, George. *Toward the Final Solution: A History of European Racism.* 1978; reprinted Madison: University of Wisconsin Press, 1985.

Mulholland, Leslie A. *Kant's System of Rights.* New York: Columbia University Press, 1990.

Murphy, Jeffrie G. "Getting Even: The Role of the Victim." In *Punishment and Rehabilitation,* edited by Jeffrie G. Murphy. Belmont, Calif.: Wadsworth, 1994.

———. "The Highest Good as Content for Kant's Ethical Formalism." *Kant-Studien* (1965–66): 102–10.

———. *Kant: The Philosophy of Right.* London: Macmillan, 1970.

———. *Retribution, Justice and Therapy.* Dordrecht: Reidel, 1979.

———. *Retribution Reconsidered.* Dordrecht: Kluwer, 1992.

Nagl-Docekal, Herta. "Feminist Ethics: How It Could Benefit from Kant's Moral Philosophy." In *Feminist Interpretations of Kant,* edited by Robin May Schott. University Park: Pennsylvania State University Press, 1997.

Nash, Gary, and Richard Weiss, eds. *The Great Fear: Race in the Mind of America.* New York: Holt, Rineheart and Winston, 1970.

Nell, Onora. *Acting on Principle: An Essay on Kantian Ethics.* New York: Columbia University Press, 1975.

Nettleford, Rex. "Garvey's Legacy: Some Perspectives." In *Garvey: His Work and Impact,* edited by Rupert Lewis and Patrick Bryan, 309–21. Mona, Jamaica: University of the West Indies, 1988.

Neugebauer, Christian M. "The Racism of Kant and Hegel." In *Sage Philosophy: Indigenous Thinkers and Modern Debate on African Philosophy,* by H. Odena Oruka, 259–72. Leiden: E. J. Brill, 1990.

Nisbett, Richard, and Lee Ross. *Human Inference: Strategies and Shortcomings of Social Judgment.* Englewood Cliffs, N.J.: Prentice Hall, 1980.

Norton, Bryan G., ed. *The Preservation of Species.* Princeton, N.J.: Princeton University Press, 1986.

———. Review of *Respect for Nature. Environmental Ethics* 9 (Fall 1987): 261– 67.

Nove, Alec. *The Economics of Feasible Socialism Revisited.* London: HarperCollins, 1983, 1991.

Nussbaum, Martha, and Amartya Sen, eds. *The Quality of Life.* Oxford: Clarendon Press, 1993.

Nye, Andrea. "Irigaray and Diotima at Plato's Symposium." In *Interpretations of Plato,* edited by Nancy Tuana. University Park: Pennsylvania State University Press, 1994.

Okihiro, Gary. *Margins and Mainstreams: Asians in American History and Culture.* Seattle and London: University of Washington Press, 1994.

Okin, Susan Moller. *Justice, Gender, and the Family.* New York: Basic Books, 1989.

O'Neill, Onora. *Constructions of Reason: Explorations of Kant's Practical Philosophy.* Cambridge: Cambridge University Press, 1989.

――――. "Justice, Gender, and International Boundaries." In *Quality of Life* edited by Martha Nussbaum and Amartya Son, 303–23. Oxford: Clarendon Press, 1993.

Oruka, H. Odera. *Sage Philosophy: Indigenous Thinkers and Modern Debate on African Philosophy.* Leiden: E. J. Brill, 1990.

Passmore, John. *Man's Responsibility for Nature.* London: Duckworth, 1974.

Paton, H. J. *The Categorical Imperative.* New York: Harper & Row, 1967.

Perry, Michael J. *Love and Power: The Role of Religion and Morality in American Politics.* Oxford: Oxford University Press, 1991.

Phillips, Derek L. *Toward a Just Social Order.* Princeton, N.J.: Princeton University Press, 1986.

Pieterse, Jan Nederveen. *White on Black: Images of Africa and Blacks in Western Popular Culture.* 1990; reprinted New Haven and London: Yale University Press, 1992.

Pinkard, Terry. *Democratic Liberalism and Social Union.* Philadelphia: Temple University Press, 1987.

Piper, Adrian M. S. "Xenophobia and Kantian Rationalism." *Philosophical Forum* 26.1–3 (1992–93); reprinted in *Feminist Interpretations of Kant,* edited by Robin May Schott. University Park: Pennsylvania State University Press, 1997.

Pippin, Robert B. "On the Moral Foundations of Kant's *Rechtslehre*." In *The Philosophy of Immanuel Kant,* edited by Richard Kennington. Studies in Philosophy and the History of Philosophy, vol. 12. Washington, D.C.: Catholic University Press of America, 1985.

Poliakov, Leon. *The Aryan Myth: A History of Racist and Nationalist Ideas in Europe,* translated by Edmund Howard. New York: Basic Books, 1971.

――――. "Racism from the Enlightenment to the Age of Imperialism." In *Racism and Colonialism* edited by Robert Ross, 55–64. The Hague: Martinus Nijhoff, 1982.

Potter, Nelson. "Kant on Obligation and Motivation in Law and Ethics." *Jahrbuch für Recht und Ethik* 2 (1994): 95–112.

――――. "Maxims in Kant's Moral Philosophy." *Philosophia* 23.1 (July 1994): 59–90.

Putterman, Louis. "After the Employment Relation: Problems on the Road to Enterprise Democracy." In *Markets and Democracy: Participation, Accountability and Efficiency,* edited by Samuel Bowles, Herbert Gintis, and Bo Gustafsson. Cambridge: Cambridge University Press, 1993.

Rawls, John. "Kantian Constructivism in Moral Theory." *Journal of Philosophy* 77 (September 1980): 515–72.

———. *Political Liberalism.* New York: Columbia University Press, 1993.

———. *A Theory of Justice.* Cambridge, Mass.: Harvard University Press, 1971.

Raz, Joseph. *The Morality of Freedom.* Oxford: Clarendon Press, 1986.

Regan, Tom. "The Nature and Possibility of an Environmental Ethic." *Environmental Ethics* 3 (Spring 1981): 19–34.

Reiman, Jeffrey. *Justice and Modern Moral Philosophy.* New Haven, Conn.: Yale University Press, 1990.

Reiss, Hans, ed. *Kant: Political Writings.* 1970; 2nd ed. Cambridge: Cambridge University Press, 1991.

Riley, Patrick. *Kant's Political Philosophy.* Totowa, N.J.: Rowman and Littlefield, 1983.

———. "The 'Place' of Politics in Kant's Practical Philosophy." In *Proceedings of the Sixth International Kant Congress,* vol. 2, edited by Gerhard Funke and Thomas M. Seebohm. Lanham, Md.: Center for Advanced Research in Phenomenology and University Press of America, 1989.

Roberts, J. W. *City of Sokrates.* London: Routledge and Kegan Paul, 1984.

Robinson, Cedric. *Black Marxism: The Making of the Black Radical Tradition.* London: Zed Press, 1983.

Roediger, David. *The Wages of Whiteness: Race and the Making of the American Working Class.* London and New York: Verso, 1991.

Roemer, John E. *A Future for Socialism.* Cambridge, Mass.: Harvard University Press, 1994.

Rolston, Holmes, III. *Environmental Ethics: Duties to and Values in the Natural World.* Philadelphia: Temple University Press, 1988.

Ross, Robert, ed. *Racism and Colonialism.* The Hague: Martinus Nijhoff, 1982.

Rossi, Philip. "The Social Authority of Reason: The 'True Church' as the Locus for Moral Progress." In *Proceedings of the Eighth International Kant Congress,* vol. 2, edited by Hoke Robinson. Milwaukee, Wis.: Marquette University Press, 1995.

Rousseau, Jean-Jacques. *Social Contract and Discourses,* translated by G. D. H. Cole. New York: Dutton, 1950.

———. *On The Social Contract and Discourses,* translated by Donald A. Cress. Indianapolis, Ind.: Hackett, 1983.

Routley, Richard, and Val Routley. "Human Chauvinism and Environmental Ethics." In *Environmental Philosophy,* edited by Don Mannison, Michael McRobbie, and Richard Routley, 96–189. Canberra: Research School of Social Sciences, Australian National University, 1980.

Rumsey, Jean. "Re-Vision of Agency in Kant's Moral Theory." In *Feminist Interpretations of Kant*, edited by Robin May Schott. University Park: Pennsylvania State University Press, 1997.

Said, Edward. *Culture and Imperialism*. New York: Knopf, 1993.

Sale, Kirkpatrick. *The Conquest of Paradise: Christopher Columbus and the Columbian Legacy*. New York: Knopf, 1990.

Sandel, Michael J. *Liberalism and the Limits of Justice*. Cambridge: Cambridge University Press, 1982.

Salzman, Jack, Adina Back, and Gretchen Sullivan Sorin, eds. *Bridges and Boundaries: African Americans and American Jews*. New York: George Braziller in association with the Jewish Museum, 1992.

Scanlon, Thomas. "Contractualism and Utilitarianism." In *Utilitarianism and Beyond*, edited by Amartya Sen and Bernard Williams. Cambridge: Cambridge University Press, 1982.

Scheid, Don, "Kant's Retributivism." *Ethics* 93 (1983): 262–82.

Schor, Juliet B. *The Overworked American: The Unexpected Decline of Leisure*. New York: Basic Books, 1991

Schott, Robin May. *Cognition and Eros: A Critique of the Kantian Paradigm*. Boston: Beacon Press, 1988; paperback University Park: Pennsylvania State University Press, 1993.

———. "Feminist Perspectives on the Western Canonical Tradition: Kant." In *Companion to Feminist Philosophy*, edited by Alison Jaggar and Iris Young. Oxford: Blackwell, 1997.

———. "The Gender of Enlightenment." In *What Is Enlightenment? Eighteenth-Century Answers and Twentieth-Century Questions*, edited by James Schmidt. Berkeley: University of California Press, 1996; reprinted in *Feminist Interpretations of Kant*, edited by Robin May Schott. University Park: Pennsylvania State University Press, 1997.

———, ed. *Feminist Interpretations of Kant*. University Park: Pennsylvania State University Press, 1997.

Schroder, Hannelore. "Kant's Patriarchal Order." In *Feminist Interpretations of Kant*, edited by Robin May Schott. University Park: Pennsylvania State University Press, 1997.

Schwartz, Barry, and Robert Disch, eds. *White Racism: Its History, Pathology and Practice*. New York: Dell, 1970.

Schweickart, David. *Against Capitalism*. Cambridge: Cambridge University Press, 1993.

Scott, G. E. *Moral Personhood*. Albany: State University of New York Press, 1990.

Sedgwick, Sally. "Can Kant's Ethics Survive the Feminist Critique?" *Pacific Philosophical Quarterly* 71 (1990): 60–79; reprinted in *Feminist Interpretations of Kant*, edited by Robin May Schott. University Park: Pennsylvania State University Press, 1997.

Shell, Susan Meld. *The Rights of Reason: A Study of Kant's Philosophy and Politics.* Toronto: University of Toronto Press, 1980.

Silber, John. "The Copernican Revolution in Kant's Ethics: The Good Re-examined." *Kant-Studien* 51 (1959–60): 85–101.

———. "The Importance of the Highest Good in Kant's Ethics." *Ethics* 73 (1962–63): 179–97.

———. "Kant's Conception of the Highest Good as Immanent and Transcendent." *Philosophical Review* 68 (1959): 469–92.

Smith, Steven B. "Defending Hegel from Kant." In *Essays on Kant's Political Philosophy*, edited by Howard Williams. Cardiff: University of Wales Press, 1992.

Spelman, Elizabeth V. *Inessential Woman: Problems of Exclusion in Feminist Thought*. Boston: Beacon Press, 1988.

Stannard, David. *American Holocaust: The Conquest of the New World*. New York and Oxford: Oxford University Press, 1992.

Steinberg, Stephen. *The Ethnic Myth: Race, Ethnicity, and Class in America.* 1981; rev. ed. Boston: Beacon Press, 1989.

———. *Turning Back: The Retreat from Racial Justice in American Thought and Policy*. Boston: Beacon Press, 1995.

Stevens, Rex. *Kant on Moral Practice*. Macon, Ga.: Mercer University Press, 1981.

Stoddard, Lothrop. *The Revolt against Civilization: The Menace of the Under Man.* New York: Charles Scribner's Sons, 1923.

———. *The Rising Tide of Color against White World-Supremacy*. New York: Charles Scribner's Sons, 1920.

Strauss, George. "Workers' Participation and U.S. Collective Bargaining." In *Organizational Democracy: Taking Stock*, edited by C. J. Lammers and G. Szeil. New York: Oxford University Press, 1989.

Sullivan, Roger. *Immanuel Kant's Moral Theory*. Cambridge: Cambridge University Press, 1989.

Sullivan, William M. *Reconstructing Public Philosophy*. Berkeley and Los Angeles: University of California Press, 1982.

Taylor, Charles. *The Explanation of Behaviour.* London: Routledge & Kegan Paul, 1964.

Taylor, Paul. *Respect for Nature: A Theory of Environmental Ethics*. Princeton, N.J.: Princeton University Press, 1986.

Thagard, Paul. *Conceptual Revolutions*. Princeton, N.J.: Princeton University Press, 1992.

Thomas, Laurence. "Group Autonomy and Narrative Identity: Blacks and Jews." In *Blacks and Jews* edited by Paul Berman, 286–303. New York: Delacorte Press, 1994.

———. "Self-Respect: Theory and Practice." In *Philosophy Born of Struggle: Anthology of Afro-American Philosophy from 1917*, edited by Leonard Harris, 174–89. Dubuque, Iowa: Kandall/Hunt, 1983.

———. *Vessels of Evil: American Slavery and the Holocaust.* Philadelphia: Temple University Press, 1993.

Thomson, Judith Jarvis. "A Defense of Abortion." *Philosophy and Public Affairs* (Fall 1971): 47–66.

Toner, Robin. "Bitter Tone of the '94 Campaign Elicits Worry on Public Debate." *New York Times,* 13 November 1994.

Turner, Patricia. *I Heard It through the Grapevine: Rumor in African-American Culture.* Berkeley and Los Angeles: University of California Press, 1993.

Van de Pitte, Frederick P. *Kant as Philosophical Anthropologist.* The Hague: Martinus Nijhoff, 1971.

Van den Berghe, Pierre. *Race and Racism: A Comparative Perspective.* New York: Wiley, 1967.

Van der Linden, Harry. "Cohen, Collective Responsibility, and Economic Democracy." *Il Cannocchiale: Rivista di Studi Filosofici* (1991): 345–60. Naples: Edizioni Scientifiche Italiane.

———. "Cohens sozialistische Rekonstruktion der Ethik Kants." In *Ethischer Sozialismus: Zur politischen Philosophie des Neukantianismus*, edited by Helmut Holzhey. Frankfurt am Main: Suhrkamp, 1994.

———. "Kant, the Duty to Promote International Peace, and Political Intervention." In *Proceedings of the Eighth International Kant Congress*, vol. 2, edited by Hoke Robinson. Milwaukee, Wis.: Marquette University Press, 1995.

———. *Kantian Ethics and Socialism.* Indianapolis, Ind.: Hackett, 1988.

Velkley, Richard. *Freedom and the End of Reason: On the Moral Foundations of Kant's Critical Philosophy.* Chicago: University of Chicago Press, 1989.

von Krings, Baumgartner, and Wild, ed. "Zweck." In *Handbuch Philosophischer Grundbegriffe*, 1817–27. Munich: Kösel, 1974.

Waldron, Jeremy. "Lex Talionis." *Arizona Law Review* 34 (1992): 25–51.

Walzer, Michael. *Spheres of Justice.* New York: Basic Books 1983.

Weisskopf, Thomas E. "Challenges to Market Socialism: A Response to Critics." *Dissent* (Spring 1992): 250–61.

———. "A Democratic Enterprise-Based Market Socialism." In *Market Socialism: The Current Debate*, edited by Pranab Bardhan and John Roemer. Oxford: Oxford University Press, 1993.

West, Cornel. *Prophesy Deliverance! An Afro-American Revolutionary Christianity.* Philadelphia: Westminster Press, 1982.

———. *Race Matters.* Boston: Beacon Press, 1993.

Weyand, Klaus. *Kants Geschichtsphilosophie: Ihre Entwicklung und ihr Verhältnis zur Aufklärung.* Kant-Studien Ergänzungsheft 85. Cologne: Kölner-Universitäts, 1963.

Whitbeck, Carolyn. "Theories of Sex Difference." In *Women and Values,* edited by Marilyn Pearsall. Belmont, Calif.: Wadsworth, 1986.

Wilkins, B. T. "Teleology in Kant's Philosophy of History." *History and Theory* 5 (1966).

Williams, Bernard. *Ethics and the Limits of Philosophy.* London: Fontana Press/ Collins, 1985.

Williams, Howard. *Kant's Political Philosophy.* Oxford: Basil Blackwell, 1983.

———, ed. *Essays on Kant's Political Philosophy.* Chicago: University of Chicago Press, 1992.

Wilson, Holly L. "A Gap in American Kant Scholarship: Pragmatic Anthropology as the Application of Kantian Moral Theory." In *Akten des Siebten Internationalen Kant-Kongresses: Kurfürstliches Schloß zu Mainz, 1990,* edited by G. Funke. Bonn: Bouvier, 1991.

Wood, Allen W. "Unsociable Sociability: The Anthropological Basis of Kantian Ethics." *Philosophical Topics* 19.1 (1991).

Woodward, C. Vann. *The Strange Career of Jim Crow.* 1955. 3rd ed. New York: Oxford University Press, 1974.

Wright, Bruce. *Black Robes, White Justice.* New York: Lyle Stuart, 1987.

Wright, Robert. "Hyperdemocracy." *Time,* 13 January 1995, 15–21.

Yovel, Yirmiyahu. *Kant and the Philosophy of History.* Princeton, N.J.: Princeton University Press, 1980.

Young, Iris. *Throwing Like a Girl and Other Essays in Feminist Philosophy and Social Theory.* Bloomington: Indiana University Press, 1990.

Young, Robert. *Personal Autonomy: Beyond Negative and Positive Liberty.* London: Croom-Helm, 1986

CONTRIBUTORS

Sharon Anderson-Gold is associate professor of philosophy at Rensselaer Polytechnic Institute in Troy, New York. She has published articles on Kant's religion, ethics, and political philosophy.

Thomas Auxter is associate professor of philosophy at the University of Florida. He is the author of *Kant's Moral Teleology* (1982) and *Choosing Fates* (forthcoming). He has published journal articles on topics in ethics, history of philosophy, and philosophy of culture.

Sidney Axinn is emeritus professor of philosophy at Temple University, Philadelphia. A board member of the *Journal of the History of Ideas*, his publications include *A Moral Military* (1989) and *The Logic of Hope: Extensions of Kant's View of Religion* (1994), and more than 35 journal articles in applied ethics, logic, and on Kant.

Susan Feldman is associate professor of philosophy at Dickinson College in Pennsylvania. She has published papers on Kant, external world skepticism, MacIntyre's virtue ethics, and "high-tech" reproduction.

Gerald F. Gaus is professor of philosophy and political science at the University of Minnesota, Duluth. He is the author of *The Modern Liberal Theory of Man* (1983), *Value and Justification* (1990), and *Justificatory Liberalism* (1996). With Stanley Benn, he edited *Public and Private in Social Life* (1983).

Jane Kneller is assistant professor of philosophy at Colorado State University. She also teaches women's studies and serves on the advisory board for the Women's Studies Program at Colorado State. She has published numerous articles on Kant's aesthetic theory and on Kantian aesthetics and feminist theory, and is currently vice president of the North American Kant Society.

Charles W. Mills is associate professor of philosophy at the University of Illinois, Chicago. His main area of research interest is radical political theory, particularly around issues of class, race, and gender. Recently he has begun to work systematically on race, examining how these concerns can be brought into mainstream philosophy.

Nelson Thomas Potter Jr., has taught for many years at the University of Nebraska, Lincoln. His research interests center on Immanuel Kant's practical philosophy and he has published widely in this area.

Philip J. Rossi, S.J., is professor of theology at Marquette University in Milwaukee, Wisconsin, and editor of *Philosophy and Theology: Marquette University Quarterly*. He is the author of *Together Toward Hope: A Journey to Moral Theology* (1983), and co-editor of *Kant's Philosophy of Religion Reconsidered* (1991) and *Mass Media and the Moral Imagination* (1994). He has published articles on Kant's ethics and philosophy of religion, on the role of imagination in moral life, and on community as the context for moral discourse.

Robin May Schott is associate professor of philosophy at the University of Copenhagen. She is the author of *Cognition and Eros: A Critique of the Kantian Paradigm* (1993) and co-editor, with Bente Rosenbeck, of *Reproduction, Gender and Technology* (1996). Her work focuses on developing feminist critiques and revisions of rationality, and contributing to feminist materialist theory by analyzing the political frameworks of motherhood.

Harry van der Linden is associate professor of philosophy at Butler University, Indianapolis. His publications include *Kantian Ethics and Socialism* (1988) and articles on Marburg Neo-Kantianism.

Holly L. Wilson teaches philosophy at Marquette University. She has published articles on Kant, hermeneutics, and ecofeminism and has translated Kant's essays on race for Cambridge University Press. She has written on Kant's anthropology and theory of teleology, and on Enlightenment pedagogy.

Robert Paul Wolff taught philosophy at Harvard, Chicago, Columbia, and the University of Massachusetts for thirty-four years before joining the W. E. B. DuBois Department of Afro-American Studies at the University of Massachusetts in 1992. He is the author or editor of twenty books, four of which have dealt with the philosophy of Immanuel Kant, including *The Autonomy of Reason: A Commentary on Kant's Groundwork of the Metaphysic of Morals* and *Kant's Theory of Mental Activity: A Commentary on the Transcendental Analytic of the Critique of Pure Reason.*

Allen W. Wood is professor of philosophy at Yale University. He is author of books and articles on Kant, Fichte, Hegel, Marx, and on topics in moral and political philosophy, including *Kant's Rational Theology* and *Nature in Kant's Philosophy*, and is a general editor of the *Cambridge Edition of the Writings of Immanuel Kant*.

INDEX